The College of Law
Braboeuf Manor
Portsmouth Road, Guildford
Surrey GU3 1HA

The College of Law
of England and Wales

LIBRARY SERVICES

The History of the
Law of Landlord and Tenant
in England and Wales

The History of the
Law of Landlord and Tenant
in England and Wales

Mark Wonnacott

Barrister, Lincoln's Inn, London

THE LAWBOOK EXCHANGE, LTD.
Clark, NJ

© 2011 Mark Wonnacott

ISBN 9781616192235 (hardcover)
ISBN 9781616192242 (paperback)

Lawbook Exchange edition 2012

THE LAWBOOK EXCHANGE, LTD.
33 Terminal Avenue
Clark, New Jersey 07066-1321

*Please see our website for a selection of our other publications
and fine facsimile reprints of classic works of legal history:*
www.lawbookexchange.com

Library of Congress Cataloging-in-Publication Data

Wonnacott, Mark.
  The history of the law of landlord and tenant in England and Wales /
by Mark Wonnacott.
      p. cm.
  Includes bibliographical references and index.
  ISBN 978-1-61619-223-5 (hardcover : alk. paper) –
ISBN 978-1-61619-224-2 (pbk. : alk. paper)
  1. Landlord and tenant--England--History. 2. Leases--England--History.
3. Landlord and tenant--Wales--History. 4. Leases--Wales--History. I.
Title.
  KD899.W656 2011
  346.4204'3409--dc23   2011041170

Printed in the United States of America on acid-free paper

Contents

The College of Law
Braboeuf Manor
Portsmouth Road, Guildford
Surrey GU3 1HA

Preface and Acknowledgments

Does the history of the law of landlord and tenant really matter? Will a 'rumble in the dust of antiquity' do more than 'cast a mist before our eyes'?[1] Would it not be 'best' to return the old cases 'to the historical scrapheap'?[2]

I believe the history is important. The House of Lords would not have decided that any lease granted for an uncertain term was void[3]—a 'bizarre' and 'absurd' result[4]—and the Law Commission could not have thought that chapter 23 of the Statute of Marlborough 1267 was an 'obsolete' provision imposing criminal penalties for bad farming,[5] if the true history of either point had been known. In property law, more than anything else, getting to the right result requires a thorough understanding of the history, and we have nearly a thousand years of it.

Sir William Holdsworth and Brian Simpson both wrote excellent guides to the history of real property, and there is a flourishing industry trying to make old quasi-contract cases fit new restitution theories. But almost nothing has been written about the law of the landlord and tenant, except as social history. That is not for lack of material or because the relationship is unimportant. Rather, it is because the law of landlord and tenant has always been real property's poor and embarrassing relation; 'the mad Victorian aunt locked in the attic of the great house.'[6]

This book is an attempt to fill the gap, providing a framework which puts the available material into rational order. The outlook is unashamedly broad-brush and positivist. It is a practising lawyer's

---

[1] Per Sir Francis Bacon in argument in *The Claim to the Barony of Roos* (1616). See A. Collins, *Claims and Controversies concerning Baronies* (London, Wotton, 1734) 162, 170.

[2] Per Briggs J. in *John Smith & Son* v. *Hill* [2010] 2 BCLC 556 ¶.23.

[3] *Prudential Assurance* v. *London Residuary Body* [1992] 2 AC 386.

[4] Per Lord Brown-Wilkinson, with whom the majority agreed, ibid, 396H-397A.

[5] Statute Law Reform Consultation Paper 2010, SLR/310 14-5.

[6] M. Dixon, Editorial, [2010] 74 Conv. 423.

chronological account of what the law on each point of importance was in the past, and how, when and why it changed; and it has been written in the hope that examining the past might prove useful to those who wish to see this part of the common law develop in more ordered and principled way than of late, 'for out of old fields must come the new corn'.[7] If it also provides a useful structure for any legal historian interested in further research on the subject, so much the better.

Except where they are more commonly known by some other name, statutes in the text are referred to by their short titles, or the short titles which were given to them by the now repealed Short Titles Act 1896 and Statute Law Revision Act 1948, where they were given one. The regnal years and chapter numbers for those Acts can be found in the table at the front. Where possible, years in figures have otherwise been given as calendar years throughout.

Thanks are due to Juanita Roche of Keele University, who made many useful comments on an early draft of the manuscript, and to Simon Pulleyn, of the Guildford College of Law, for the encouragement and the Latin. Philomena Harrison of Maitland Chambers, Martin Hutchings QC of Wilberforce Chambers, and Nicholas Isaac of Tanfield Chambers, all looked over the manuscript too. I am fortunate that my Chambers are within a minute's walk of Lincoln's Inn library, one of the largest and best managed resources for English legal history in the world, and to have found a publisher which has done so much to make legal history more accessible. I am also grateful to Gabrielle Higgins, of Maitland Chambers, for removing some of the more annoying footnotes, and to the Croquet Association, for inadvertently providing me with the time needed to write this book.

All law books contain some errors. Bracton (if indeed he was the author of the work that bears his name) asked the reader to pass over anything superfluous or erroneous with eyes half closed, and to keep in mind that to err in nothing is divine rather than human. It would be hard to beat George Townesend's excuse. He explained that he had finished his book of pleadings in the country, far away from his London library, on account of the 'great visitation of the plague'. Only the pressures of practice and the unreliability of the

---

[7] Coke, *Fourth Institute* 109.

Northern Line have kept me away from mine. So I offer none. I can only suggest, like one of the Year Book printers, that the 'faults are such that they may be easily amended with a penne'.

Lincoln's Inn
2nd November 2011

Table of Cases

Chronological List of References to the Year Books and Brook's New Cases

Alphabetical List of Cases in the Law Reports

Chronological Table of Statutes

Table of Works Referred to Frequently

In citing works in the footnotes, short titles have generally been used. Works frequently cited have been identified by the following abbreviations:

Ashburner, Equity: W. Ashburner, *Principles of Equity*, London, Butterworths, 1902

Bl.Comm: Sir William Blackstone, *Commentaries on the Laws of England*, 11th edn., London, Strahan & Woodfall, 1791

Bracton: Bracton, *De Legibus Angliæ*, trans S. Thorne, Cambridge, Mass, Belknap Press, 1969

Challis, Real Property: H. Challis, *The Law of Real Property*, 3rd edn., ed. C. Sweet, London, Butterworths, 1911

Chambers, Leases: C. Chambers, *A Treatise on Leases and Terms of Years*, London, A. Strahan, 1819

Coke, 2ⁿᵈ Inst: *Sir Edward Coke's Second Institute*, London, Clarke & Sons, 1817

Co.Litt: *Sir Edward Coke's First Institute, or Commentary on Littleton*, 19th edn., London, Clarke & ors, 1832

Coote, Leases: R. Coote, *The Law of Landlord and Tenant*, London, Saunders and Benning, 1840

D'Anvers' Abridgment: K. D'Anvers, *A General Abridgment of the Common Law*, London, Gosling, 1832

Doctor and Student: C. St.Germain, *Doctor and Student*, Cincinnati, Robert Clarke, 1874

Gilbert, Rents: G. Gilbert, *A Treatise on Rents*, Philadelphia, Littell, 1838

Halsbury's Laws, Real Property: E.Nugee & C.Furze, Halsbury's *Law of England, Real Property*, 4th edn., vol.39(2), London, Butterworths, 1998

Holdsworth, HEL: W. Holdsworth, *A History of English Law*, 7th edn., London, Methuen, 1956

Kaye, Medieval English Conveyances: J. Kaye, *Medieval English Conveyances*, Cambridge University Press, 2009

Littleton, Tenures: T. Littleton, *Treatise on Tenures, in Co.Litt.*

Maitland, Equity: F. Maitland, *Equity*, Cambridge, Cambridge University Press, 1909

Norton on Deeds: R. Norton, *A Treatise on Deeds*, 2nd edn., London, Sweet and Maxwell, London, 1928

Oxford History of the Laws of England: *The Oxford History of the Laws of England*, general editor Sir John Baker, Oxford, Oxford University Press, vol.6 2003, vol.12 2010

Perks: J. Perkins, *A Profitable Book treating of the Laws of England*, 15th edn., London, Davies, 1827

Platt, Covenants: T. Platt, *The Law of Covenants*, London, Saunders & Benning, 1829

Platt, Leases: T. Platt, *Law of Leases*, London, Maxwell, 1837

Pollock and Maitland: F. Pollock & F. Maitland, *A History of English Law*, 2nd edn., Cambridge University Press, 1923

Pollock, The Land Laws: F. Pollock, *The Land Laws*, 3rd edn., London, MacMillan, 1896

Preston, Conveyancing: R. Preston, *A Treatise on Conveyancing*, 3rd edn., London, W. Clarke & Sons, 1819

Plucknett, Concise History: T. Plucknett, *A Concise History of the Common Law*, 5th edn., Boston, Little Brown and Co, 1956

Simpson, History of Land Law: B. Simpson, *Introduction to the History of Land Law*, 2nd edn., Oxford, Oxford University Press, 1961

Simpson, History of the Common Law of Contract: B. Simpson, *A History of the Common Law of Contract*, Oxford, Clarendon Press, 1975

Shep.Touch: W. Sheppard, *Touchstone of Common Assurances*, 7th edn., London, Clarke, 1820

Statham's Abridgment: *Statham's Abridgment of the Law*, trans. M. Klingelsmith, Reprint, Clark, NJ, Lawbook Exchange, 2007

Stewart, Practice of Conveyancing: J. Stewart, *Practice of Conveyancing*, London, Butterworths, 1827

Viner's Abridgment: C. Viner, *A General Abridgment of Law and Equity*, 2nd edn., London, Robinson & ors, 1792

Woodfall, Landlord and Tenant: W. Woodfall, *The Law of Landlord and Tenant*, 2nd edn., London, Butterworths, 1804

Chapter 1
Grant and Conveyance

---

1. Formalities

2. Capacity

3. Lease or licence

4. Entry and interesse termini

5. Registration

6. Equitable leases

7. Leases of incorporeal hereditaments

8. Prescriptive rights

A leasehold tenancy[1] is a curious mix. One part a personal promise, enforceable between the parties, and the other part an estate in land, enforceable against the world; the tension[2] is

---

[1] 'Tenant' is from 'tenaun', 'borrowed from Anglo-French *tenaunt* and Old French *tenant*', noun use of the present participle of *tenir* to hold: Barnhard, *Chambers Dictionary of Etymology* (New York, Chambers, 2000). 'Tenant' is a wider term than 'lessee'. All private persons who own land technically 'hold' it of some superior lord, and ultimately the Crown. So 'tenant' is an accurate description of someone who holds freehold as well as leasehold land: *Bl. Comm.* Bk.II 51, 59. But it became much less usual to think of a freeholder as a 'tenant' after the enactment of the Tenures Abolition Act 1660 which stripped superior lords of most of the benefits of tenure. 'Lease' is 'borrowed through Anglo-French *les*, from *lesser* to let or let go, from Old French, *laissier, lessier*' (Barnhard, supra). For Coke's etymology, see *Co.Litt.* 43b.
[2] Charles Butler, in his *Reminiscences*, 3rd edn. (London, John Murray, 1822) 59 called this: 'The perpetual conflict between the law of tenure and the law of contract'. The same point is made in K. Low, *Leases and the Fixed Maximum Duration Rule Yet Again, but with a Twist* (2011) 127 LQR 31, 34: 'Borne of contract but bred in property, the lease does not appear to have completely

inherent in the medieval term for it, a chattel real'.[3]

This chapter is about the estate part of the mix: the ingredients needed in order to turn what would otherwise be purely personal rights into an estate in land.

1. Formalities

At common law, the formal requirements for making or assigning a lease differed, depending on what exactly was being let.

A lease of an incorporeal hereditament could only ever be made or assigned by deed. The difference between corporeal and incorporeal hereditaments is considered in more detail below,[4] but the broad distinction is between a claim to the enjoyment of physical land itself ('corporeal') and one to enjoyment of an intangible right ('incorporeal').[5] At common law, incorporeal hereditaments lay only in grant, meaning that the right itself could only be granted by deed.[6] Since a deed was always

---

jumped the barrier between rights in personam and rights in rem. Instead, the splicing of the privity of contract with privity of estate appears to have produced mutant offspring, partaking of incidents of both yet resembling neither.'

[3] *Abbot of Bermondsey's Case* (1401) YB 2 Hen.4 f.19 pl.14. A term of years is chattel because, at common law, it passed on death to the tenant's personal representatives, unlike the fee which vested directly in the legatee or heir (see ch.8 heading 'Devolution on death'), but it is 'real' because it derives out of the real estate: Halsbury's Laws, *Real Property*, 4th edn., vol. 39(2). ¶3. Challis objected to the expression 'leasehold tenure', as a description of the relationship between a landlord and tenant for a term of years, on the grounds that 'tenure' could only properly refer 'to those relations which were comprised within the feudal organisation of the realm', and, in particular, the duties owed to a superior lord: Challis, *Real Property*, 7. But the expression is as old as Littleton, ibid 65. See also H. Challis, *Are Leaseholds Tenements?* (1890) 6 LQR 69, and *Attorney-General* v. *Parsons* [1956] AC 421, 450. But 'it would be hard to discover a more inappropriate name for this kind of property, for it was not a chattel (or moveable) and was not real (or specifically recoverable)': *Topham's Real Property*, 11th edn. (London, Butterworths, 1969) 8. In truth, the 'idea that the termor had a *tenementum* is indeed an afterthought of the common law, whose implications were never really worked out with any consistency': Simpson, *History of Land Law*, 70.

[4] Heading 'Leases of incorporeal hereditaments'.

[5] Bracton, vol. 2 39 (f.7).

[6] L. Pike, *Feoffment and Livery of Incorporeal Hereditaments* (1889) 5 LQR 29.

necessary to grant the right, the rule was that leases of that right could only be granted or assigned by deed too.

Much less formality was necessary to grant or assign a lease of a corporeal hereditament. Here, the crucial distinction was between a lease for life and a lease for any other term.

A lease for life was a freehold 'tenement', meaning that it was a form of tenure which had a recognised place within the feudal system.[7] Indeed, immediately after the Norman Conquest, it was probably the most common form of aristocratic land-holding.[8]

Accordingly, a lease for life could be granted or assigned in any of the ways in which a fee simple could be granted or conveyed.[9] For corporeal land, that included an oral grant[10] if accompanied by a physical delivery of the land to the tenant.[11] This was 'livery of seisin'.[12] In practice it was rare after the

---

[7] In Scotland, the equivalent was a 'liferent'.

[8] Grants of land were typically made for life in return for knight service. See S. Milsom, *English Feudalism and Estates in Land*, [1959] CLJ 193.

[9] Holdsworth, *HEL* vol. 7 245, *Sharp's Case* (1599) 6 Rep 26a.

[10] The words 'I hereby demise unto you', said on the land, were held not to be sufficient to amount to a livery of seisin in that case. In *Roe d. Heale* v. *Rashleigh* (1819) 3 Barn & Ald 156 a power to deliver seisin which was given to an attorney by deed, was held not to be limited to doing so on the day that the lease was granted, but also to encompass retrospective validation by delivering seisin afterwards. See also *Bl.Comm.* Bk.II 314–316 and O. Bridgman, *Precedents of Conveyances* (London, Atkins, 1702) vol. 2 23, 54–55.

[11] (1440) 18 Hen.6 f.16b pl.6. 'Livery in deed was carried out by the owner going with the proposed tenant or purchaser onto the land, and there by formal and proper words giving him the vacant possession of the land . . . This was sufficient to convey all the land intended to be conveyed in the county in which the delivery was performed, but not in other counties; and, where land was situate in several counties, it was necessary for the livery of seisin to be performed in each county. Livery in law was done in sight of the land without going on to it, by the feoffor telling the feoffee to enter and take possession; but the transfer of the property was not completed until he had actually entered and taken possession. This form of livery was sufficient to convey land although it lay in another county': B. Adkin, *Copyhold and Other Land Tenures* (London, Estates Gazette, 1907) 36.

[12] *Jones* v. *Weaver* (1556) Dyer 117b. 'Note there is a diversity between livery of seisin of the land, and the delivery of a deed; if a man delivers a deed without saying anything, it is a good delivery, but to a livery of seisin of land words are necessary, as taking in his hand the deed and the ring of the door (if

medieval period for a lease for life to be created without some form of writing. Even where the grant was by livery of seisin,[13] there was usually[14] a preliminary charter of feoffment, which would be necessary, in any event, if the grant was to contain any covenants[15] or conditions;[16] and a charter of feoffment became compulsory after the Statute of Frauds (1677) as appears below.

Even less formality was required, at common law, to make a lease for a term of years of corporeal land, or to assign it.[17] A 'term of years', for this purpose, included a fixed term of less than a year[18] and a periodic tenancy, although, as we shall see, periodic tenancies were not recognised as valid until the eighteenth century.[19]

In feudal theory, a lease for a term of years, no matter how long the term, was an insignificant chattel interest, more like a contract than real property, and there was some justification for treating leases for years in this way before the sixteenth century, when the law did little to protect them.[20] So pure words were sufficient to grant a right to a term of years, which would take effect as a lease, when the tenant entered on the land, or as an assignment of the lease, when the assignee entered on the land, afterwards.[21]

The Statute of Frauds, which came into force on 24th June 1677, change that by requiring a deed or signed writing for all

---

it be a house) or turf or twig (if it be land) and the feoffee laying his hand on it, the feoffor say to the feoffee, here I deliver to you seisin of this land . . . to have and to hold for you for life, or to you and the heirs of your body, or to you and heirs for ever, as the case shall require': Co.Litt. 49b, Perks, ¶.209–213. For an amusing account of the equivalent process in Scotland, see K. Reid with ors., *The Law of Property in Scotland* (Edinburgh, LexisNexis UK, 1996) ¶.89.

[13] For the other methods of creating a lease for life, see ch.4 heading 'For life'.

[14] Co.Litt. 271b.fn (1).

[15] See ch.5 heading 'Express, implied and usual'.

[16] Littleton, *Tenures*, s.365. *Doctor and Student*, 27, *The Grounds and Rudiments of Law and Equity*, 2nd. edn. (London, Osborne, 1751) 35. A feoffment could not take effect without livery of seisin: *Perks*, ¶.182. For the differences between a covenant and a condition, see ch.6 heading 'Conditions.'

[17] *Wilston* v. *Pilkney* (1673) 1 Vent 242.

[18] That is 'years, months, weeks or days': F.Bacon, *The Use of the Law* (London, Moore, 1630) 50.

[19] See ch.4 heading 'Periodic'.

[20] See ch.4 heading 'Fixed terms' and ch.9 heading 'Ejectment'.

[21] Littleton, *Tenures*, s.59. Heading 'Entry and interesse termini' below.

significant dispositions of land,[22] in addition to any formal requirement which already applied, either because of nature of disposition[23] or the status of the person making the grant,[24] and its application specifically to leases is explained below.

The recital to the Act stated that its purpose was 'the prevention of many fraudulent practices, which are commonly endeavoured to be upheld by perjury and subornation of perjury'.[25] The root of the problem was a rule of evidence. The parties to litigation were not allowed to give oral evidence at the trial.[26] In those circumstances, the evidence of a helpful 'friend', who might claim to have overheard the relevant conversation, could prove conclusive;[27] for, by 1677, the time when juries[28] could be expected to decide facts based on their own local knowledge was long past.[29]

---

[22] For Ireland, the corresponding Act was 7 Wm.3 c.12 (Ir) (1695).

[23] Supra.

[24] See heading 'Capacity' below.

[25] Recital, Statute of Frauds (1677). For the origin of the expression, see 43 Eliz.1 c.5, Reeves, ed. W. Finlason, *History of English Law* (London, Reeves and Turner, 1869) vol. 3 669. See also P. Hamburger, *The Conveyancing Purposes of the Statute of Frauds* (1983) 27 Am.J.Legal.Hist. 354.

[26] The rule that a party could not be a witness in a civil action was, eventually, reversed by s.2 Evidence Act 1851. See also Holdsworth, *HEL* vol. 9 193–198. In courts of equity, the evidence of the parties could be given by deposition, but it was the practice of courts of equity to require any dispute of fact to be resolved by a trial at common law (*Bl.Comm.* Bk.III 452) until the enactment of the Chancery Regulation Act 1862. See also ch.9 heading 'Equitable relief '.

[27] Accordingly Thomas Egerton (Lord Ellesmere) said in 1597/8 'for avoiding perjuries and other abuses', he would not give equitable relief to a tenant claiming by parol only: *Anon* (1597/8) Cary 7. See also *Anon* (1603) Cary 27. In the same year (and perhaps in the same case) he said that he would not help anyone claiming a lease for a thousand years, because these leases were made to defraud the Crown of its customary revenues: *Risden v. Tuffin* (1597) Tothill 122. See also *Rothwel v. Hussey* (1674) 2 Ch.Cas 202.

[28] s.1 Common Law Procedure Act 1854 first allowed the parties to a common law civil claim to dispense with the jury, and ask the judge to find the facts instead. The right to demand jury trial was removed, for most civil actions, by s.1 Juries Act 1918.

[29] Less than 100 years later, Mansfield CJ could say, in *Mylock v. Saladene* (1764) 1 Wm. Black 480, 481: 'A juror should be as white as paper, and know neither plaintiff nor defendant, but judge the issue merely as an abstract proposition upon the evidence produced before him'. See also *Pollock &*

To the modern mind, the obvious solution[30] would have been to allow the parties to give oral evidence, and then be cross-examined on what had happened.[31] Instead, the Statute of Frauds[32] solved the problem by requiring written corroboration for all significant property transactions made out of court. So, afterwards, there were three new rules for leases, including leases for lives, which applied generally and in addition to any common law requirement for that particular type of disposition.

First, a contract to grant or assign a lease had to be made or evidenced by signed writing.[33]

Secondly, an assignment of a lease required the assignor's deed[34] or signed writing.[35]

Thirdly, subject to one exception, the grantor's deed or signed writing[36] was also necessary in order to make the

---

Maitland vol. 2 622–624, Platt, *Leases*, vol. 2, 2.

[30] Modern solutions are not necessarily better solutions. Today, in civil trials, evidence in chief consists of written witness statements, prepared by the parties' lawyers. This is generally a test of the care and skill of the lawyer who prepared the statement, rather than of the truthfulness of the witness, and a dishonest witness, who has read the bundles and understood the chronology, often performs better in cross-examination than an honest one who has not.

[31] Cf. T. Plucknett, *Concise History*, 55–56 and E. Rabel, *The Statute of Frauds and Comparative Legal History* (1947) 63 LQR 174.

[32] There is a long tradition that Sir Matthew Hale was responsible for the drafting of this Act. The change certainly reflected his views: see J. Baker and S. Milsom, *Sources of English Legal History*, 2nd edn. (Oxford, Oxford University Press, 2009) 481–482. But Sir Heneage Finch (afterwards, Lord Nottingham) produced the first draft: Simpson, *History of the Common Law of Contract*, 601–605. Hale, by tradition, is also unfairly blamed for the drafting of the Tenures Abolition Act 1660: Challis, *Real Property*, 23. But at least nobody appropriated his name to a bad set of someone else's reports, which is what happened to Finch: J. Wallace, *The Reporters*, 3rd edn. (Philadelphia, Johnson, 1855) 304.

[33] s.4. So a contract made by deed had to be signed, as well as sealed and delivered: fn.A1 by Mr Thomas to *Pelham's Case* (1588) 1 Co.Rep 3a, 7a (1826) edn. (76 ER 17) cf. *Cooch* v. *Goodman* (1842) 2 QB 580. For the circumstances in which a deed would be valid as such without any signature, see ch.5 heading 'Express, implied and usual'.

[34] s.3.

[35] *Beck d. Fry* v. *Philips* (1772) 5 Bur 2827.

[36] s.1. In *Browne* v. *Warner* (1807) 14 Ves 156, 158, Lord Eldon is reported as having said that a deed was necessary for a lease for life, and Lawrence J had said something similar when the same case had been tried at common law: *Warner* v. *Brown* (1807) 8 East 165. But Ellenborough CJ's description of 'not

lease itself.[37]

The exception was that a lease for a term of three years or less could still be made orally, if the rent reserved was at least two thirds of the market rent.[38] The reason for the exception was that there was unlikely to be any fraud in a case where the tenant had actually entered, was paying something close to the market rent, and was not claiming any right to remain for longer than three years. Otherwise mere spoken words could no longer be sufficient for a grant or assignment of a lease,[39] or a contract[40] to grant or assign a lease.

The Act was clear about the sanction for non-compliance. The tenant would acquire an interest 'at will' only which would be terminable by either party at any time without notice, and the tenancy would not 'either in law or in equity be deemed or taken to have any other or greater force or effect'.[41]

Firm rules, however, frequently produce hardship in individual cases, and judges have always felt the tension between the need to ensure that the law is clear and consistent on a general level, and the wish to produce a just result in accordance with the perceived underlying merits of individual cases.[42]

---

by parol' is more accurate. Although, at this time, a lease for life would normally have been made by a conveyance to uses under the Statute of Uses (1536) which, by virtue of the Statute of Enrolments, would have required a deed (see ch.7 heading 'Enlargement'), in theory it could still have been made by livery of seisin accompanied by signed writing as required by the Statute of Frauds: *Shep. Touch.* 267. Indeed, even after 1845, an infant who had attained the age of 15, and who was seised of gavelkind land, could still make a lease for life by personal livery of seisin accompanied by signed writing: Challis, *Real Property*, 402. That was finally prohibited by s.1(6) and s.51(1) Law of Property Act 1925.

[37] Ibid.

[38] s.2. In *Legg* v. *Strudwick* (1709) 2 Salk 414 it was said that a tenancy from year to year was within the exception on the grounds that there could never be more than two years of the term in existence at any one time; i.e. the current year and (if no notice to quit had been served during the current year) the next year.

[39] s.3. *Botting* v. *Martin* (1818) 1 Camp 317.

[40] s.4. The prohibition included an executory contract to grant a short lease, which, if it had been granted, would have fallen within the exemption for leases of three years or less: *Edge* v. *Strafford* (1831) 1 Compt & Jerv 391.

[41] s.1.

[42] *Poultney* v. *Holmes* (1720) 1 Strange 405, discussed in ch.2 heading

Enough hard cases can quickly subvert the original legislative intent, and that is what happened to the Statute of Frauds.[43]

The common law courts subverted the statute, from the middle of the eighteenth century, by implying a collateral parol agreement to create a tenancy from year to year, which would fall within the exception for short leases, if the tenant entered and paid rent,[44] subject to automatic termination at the end of the agreed term.[45]

Equity subverted the statute too. As early as 1683 it was being used to enforce parol leases where the tenant had spent money on the premises,[46] and by the eighteenth century, if the tenant had entered at all, equity could enforce all the terms of the otherwise invalid lease.[47] So by then, the statute was really only still biting on purely executory agreements.[48] In Maitland's

---

'Underletting', is a good example. In that case, there was an oral assignment of a short lease, reserving a rent to the assignor. As an oral assignment, it was void: had it been an underletting, it would have been valid. So the court stretched the point, and held it was an underlease.

[43] *Simon* v. *Metivier* (1766) 1 Wm. Black 599 per Mansfield CJ, 600: 'The key to the construction of the Act is the intent of the Legislature; and therefore many cases, though seemingly within the letter, have been let out of it; more instances have indeed occurred in Courts of Equity than of Law, but the rule is in both the same'. Per Wilmot J (ibid): 'Had the Statute of Frauds been always carried into execution according to the letter, it would have done ten times more mischief than it has done good, by protecting, rather than preventing, frauds'. 'Statutes against frauds are to be liberally construed and beneficially expounded': *Bl.Comm.* Bk.I 88.

[44] See ch.4 heading 'Periodic'.

[45] *Doe d. Tilt* v. *Stratton* (1828) 4 Bing 444.

[46] *Hollis* v. *Edwards* (1683) 1 Vern 159.

[47] *Earl of Aylesford's Case* (1727) 2 Strange 783, *Morphett* v. *Jones* (1818) 1 Swan 172. Equity could ignore the statute in the case of fraud too: see *Pym* v. *Blackburn* (1796) 3 Ves Jun 34, 38.fn (25), *Anon* (1684) Skin 159.

[48] The distinction between executory and executed contracts was taken as early as 1722 in *Savage* v. *Foster* (1722) 9 Mod. 35, 37. The advice of Edward Sugden (afterwards, Lord St Leonards LC) at the beginning of the nineteenth century was: 'There are, indeed, cases where equity on the ground of the party admitting the agreement, or of fraud, as where the purchaser has been let into possession, and in performance of the agreement, has laid out money in repairs, will compel the fulfilment of an agreement, although merely verbal, and not reduced to writing, and signed by the parties . . . To this, however, a party should not trust'. E.Sugden, *Letters to a Man of Property* (Philadelphia,

words: 'A bold step certainly was made here, but yet perhaps a necessary one'.[49]

Under the Statute of Frauds signed writing was as good as a deed for the purpose of making or assigning a lease.[50] Both had the same force and effect.

That was changed by s.3 Real Property Act 1845,[51] which required the actual grant or assignment of a lease to be made by deed in all cases, preserving only the exception which allowed leases for a term of three years or less to be made, but not assigned, informally.[52] But executory contracts to grant or assign a lease continued to be regulated by the Statute of Frauds afterwards, so signed writing was still sufficient to make or evidence a contract[53] to grant or assign a lease, although it was no longer sufficient for the actual grant or assignment itself.

The consequence of that change was that, whenever there was signed writing, but no deed, the courts would strive to construe that instrument as being an executory contract to grant or assign the lease, rather than as the lease or assignment itself, so that it could be enforced as a contract in equity by specific performance in the usual way.[54]

Farrand & Nicholas, 1811) 59–60, 71.

[49] Maitland, *Equity*, 241.

[50] For a precedent for an assignment by a note in writing under hand, see Woodfall, *Landlord and Tenant*, 681.

[51] The 1845 Act repealed the beguilingly entitled, but badly botched, 'Act to Simplify the Transfer of Property' (1844), which had been enacted in the previous session, which contained a similar provision (s.4), and which was in force from 31st December 1844 until 1st October 1845. See J. Stuart Anderson, *Lawyers and Makings of English Land Law 1832–1940* (Oxford, Oxford University Press, 1992) 17.

[52] There was one other exception, which was more theoretical than actual: customary leases for life of gavelkind land granted by infants continued to be regulated by the Statute of Frauds until 1926.

[53] *Rollason* v. *Leon* (1861) 7 H&N 73.

[54] *Bond* v. *Rosling* (1861) 1 B & S 371, *Tidey* v. *Mollett* (1864) 16 CB (NS) 298, *Hayne* v. *Cummings* (1864) 16 CB (NS) 421. Before there was any difference, the struggle was often to construe an agreement for lease as the lease itself, in order to avoid putting the tenant to the trouble and expense of obtaining an order for specific performance in equity before enforcing the lease at common law; see Coote, *Leases*, 87–103, *Baxter d. Abrahall* v. *Brown* (1775) 2 Wm. Black 973, *Weakly d. Yea* v. *Bucknell* (1776) 2 Cowp 473, and Edward Sugden's warning about the risks of an informal agreement for lease

Before the middle of the nineteenth century,[55] equitable rights could generally only be enforced in courts of equity. The common law courts administered justice according to the common law as if equity did not exist. So, for example, if a landlord served a notice to quit on a person who was, at common law, a periodic tenant, a common law court would have been obliged to make a possession order in favour of the landlord when the notice to quit expired, notwithstanding that, in equity, the defendant might have had a right to an unexpired term of ten years. The tenant needed to file a bill in a court of equity, in order to obtain a 'common injunction', to prevent the landlord enforcing the common law right[56] and remain for the full term of ten years.

But, afterwards, there was only one High Court, split into five[57] different divisions, and equitable rights could be enforced, and would trump common law rights, in each of them.[58] Once both systems were administered by the same courts, a valid

---

being construed as being the lease itself in *Letters to a Man of Property* (Philadelphia, Farrand & Nicholas, 1811) 72. There is a persistent myth that every failed lease would be construed as a contract for a lease: see eg. *Progressive Mailing House Pty Ltd* v. *Tabali Pty Ltd* [1985] HCA 14; (1985) 157 CLR 17, per Mason J: 'In Equity, however, a written lease not under seal was regarded as evidencing an agreement for lease'. The true principle was stated by Richard Preston as: 'The result of these cases appears to be, that the instrument will operate either as an actual lease or as an agreement for lease, according to the intention of the parties, as that intention can be collected from the entire instrument'; Preston, *Conveyancing*, vol. 2 177. That is not to say that an instrument which was intended to be a final lease, and which fails as such, cannot be saved in equity by an order analogous to specific performance: *Australian Hardwoods* v. *Commissioner for Rlys* [1961] 1 WLR 425. But the considerations for granting it are not necessarily the same: *Packenham Upper Fruit Co* v. *Crosby* (1924) 35 CLR 386, 394. For registered land, see now s.7(2) Land Registration Act 2002.

[55] For the detail, see ch.9 heading 'Equitable relief'.

[56] Ibid.

[57] Since 1880, there have been only three Divisions: the Chancery Division; Probate, Divorce and Admiralty (now just 'Family', wills having gone to Chancery and wrecks to Queen's Bench); and King's or Queen's Bench, depending on the sex of the current monarch. The Technology and Construction Court (formerly, the Official Referees), and the Commercial Court are branches of the Queen's Bench Division.

[58] The County Court continued to have only limited equity jurisdiction, and the old rules continue to apply outside the limits of the County Court jurisdiction: *Foster* v. *Reeves* [1892] 2 QB 255.

contract to grant or assign a lease was, for most practical purposes, as good as an actual lease or assignment itself; for equity would treat anything which it would have ordered a party to do, as having been done already.[59]

So, by the end of the nineteenth century, there were two ways in which formal defects in leases might be cured in the same court. At common law, the statutory 'tenancy at will' would be turned into a periodic tenancy as soon as the tenant entered and paid rent; and, in equity, the full terms of the lease would be enforced in the same action, if there was an agreement to grant the lease, which was evidenced by the other party's signed writing or which had been partly performed by a transmission of possession.

The provisions of the Statute of Frauds 1677 and of the Real Property Act 1845 were substantially re-enacted in the Law of Property Act 1925.[60]

Statutory force was given to the judge-made equitable exception for part performance by s.40(2), and s.54(2) made the exception when granting short parol leases slightly stricter, by imposing a requirement that the lease be at a full market rent, rather than merely two-thirds. The Act also made it necessary for an individual to sign an instrument before it could take effect as his or her deed.[61] Before then, sealing alone was sufficient, though it had been the practice for an individual to sign[62] too since the sixteenth century, and deeds were usually witnessed.[63]

The provisions of the Law of Property Act 1925 dealing with the formalities necessary for the grant or assignment of a lease remain in force. A deed remains necessary in all cases, except for the grant of a lease in possession[64] for a term of three years or less at the best rent that can be obtained without taking a fine.[65]

---

[59] *Walsh* v. *Lonsdale* (1881) 21 Ch.D 9.
[60] ss.40, 52, 54.
[61] s.73.
[62] Illiterate individuals customarily made their mark with a cross instead, which had its roots in the Anglo-Saxon period: Holdsworth, *HEL* vol. 3 231.
[63] See ch.5 heading 'Express, implied and usual'.
[64] For the meaning of this, see ch.2 heading 'Concurrent leases'.
[65] s.52, 54(2). The 'best' rent is not necessarily the highest offered. The status and ability of the tenant offering the rent are relevant too: *Doe d. Lawton* v.

But the rules about what counts as a deed have changed. For individuals, an instrument which is signed and attested by a witness will now normally be treated as a deed, even if it is not sealed.[66] A corporation can still make a deed simply by application of its corporate seal, albeit that in the case of companies, there is a more convenient alternative of execution by two officers, or one officer whose signature is witnessed, which provides additional protection for a purchaser.[67]

The formalities necessary to make an executory contract to grant or assign a lease have been changed too. The rules are now found in s.2 Law of Property (Miscellaneous Provisions) Act 1989. If a lease is a short lease, which can be granted orally, then a contract to grant it can now be made orally too.[68] A contract to grant or assign any lease can also now be made orally at a public auction.[69] But otherwise, the rules for contracts have become much stricter than before. It is no longer sufficient that the contract is merely evidenced by the signed writing of the other party. Now the whole contract has to be in writing, and be signed by or on behalf of both parties.[70] Nor can unsigned contracts be saved by part performance any more.[71]

Yet nothing really changes. The pressure to save invalid agreements in meritorious cases is still the same. Only the escape route is different. There is plenty of scope for that in the express saving for resulting, implied and constructive trusts,[72] and their close cousin, proprietary estoppel,[73] is already being used for that

---

Radcliffe (1808) 10 East 278. A 'rack rent' is only a rent of the full value of the tenement, or near it': *Bl.Comm.* Bk.II 43. But see also Halsbury's Laws, *Real Property*, vol. 39(2), 4th edn., ¶.85 fn(8).

[66] s.1(3) Law of Property (Miscellaneous Provisions) Act 1989.

[67] s.44 Companies Act 2006.

[68] s.2(5)(a).

[69] s.2(5)(b). Auction contracts were within the Statute of Frauds (1677). The necessary memorandum was normally created by the auctioneer, who had authority to sign as agent for both parties: *Simon* v. *Metivier* (1766) 1 Wm.Black 599.

[70] s.2(1).

[71] s.2(8).

[72] s.2(5).

[73] 'In such a situation, the word that comes instinctively to the mind of any judge is, of course "estoppel"—which is simply a way of saying that, for reasons which the court does not care to discuss, there must be judgment for the

purpose.[74] Nor, perhaps, does s.2 affect the law of part performance, where what is alleged is an informal conveyance, rather than an informal contract to convey.[75]

2. Capacity

This section is about the limits on the power of different types of landowners to grant leases, and the consequences if the power was exceeded.

The church: Monks, before the reformation, were 'civilly dead' in law.[76]

They could not hold or let property, nor sue or be sued in the temporal courts. By way of exception, an abbot, though a monk, could deal with the property of the institution of which he was abbot, and sue and be sued in that capacity. Those who survived the Reformation (and many of them did not) had no special status afterwards.

Archbishops and bishops originally had all the powers of disposition of their ecclesiastical possessions of an absolute owner. That rule was reversed by the Second Council of Nicaea in 787,[77] which prevented them from making any disposition for a period longer than their own lives, unless the disposition was confirmed by the Dean and Chapter.[78] The Enabling Act 1540[79] removed the need for that confirmation for certain leases. The lease had to be of a corporeal hereditament[80] made by

---

plaintiff': G. Gilmore, *Death of Contract* (Columbus, Ohio State University Press, 1974) 64.

[74] *Yaxley* v. *Gotts* [2000] Ch 162, *Kinane* v. *Mackie-Conteh* [2005] EWCA Civ 45.

[75] s.55(d) Law of Property Act 1925.

[76] Littleton, *Tenures*, s.655, *Co.Litt.* 347a, (1523) YB 14 Hen.8 f.16 pl.4.

[77] Canon No.12. See J. Mendham, *The Seventh General Council the Second of Nicaea* (London, Painter, 1852) 458.

[78] *Co.Litt.* 44a, R. Hunter, *The Law of Landlord and Tenant*, 4th edn. (Edinburgh, Bell & Bradfute, 1896) 69–70.

[79] s.1.

[80] *Jewel's Case* (1588) 5 Co.Rep 3a, *Talentine* v. *Denton* (1606) Cro Jac 111.

indenture;[81] it could only be granted for a term of up to 21 years or the longest of up to three lives[82] in being;[83] and it had to reserve at least the ancient rent, being the rent which had been charged during the previous 20 years.[84]

The power of a dean and chapter to confirm longer leases[85] granted by their bishop was removed by the Restraining Act 1558,[86] which also made any lease which did not reserve 'the old accustomed yearly rent or more' 'utterly void'[87] In practice, that

---

[81] For the meaning of 'indenture' see ch.5 heading 'Express, implied and usual'.

[82] But not both: *Elmer's Case* (1588) 5 Co.Rep 2a.

[83] *Doe d. Pemberton* v. *Edwards* (1836) 1 M&W 553, *Owen* v. *Ap-Rees* (1627) Cro Car 94. See the precedent in Stewart, *Practice of Conveyancing*, 331. It was the practice of the Bishop of Worcester to let land for three lives in the tenth century: F. Pollock, *The Land Laws*, 141.

[84] So once the rent had been increased, it could not be decreased again: *Orby* v. *Mahun* (1706) 2 Vern 531, *Viner's Abridgment*, 'Estates' R.a.6, *The Grounds and Rudiments of Law and Equity*, 2nd edn. (London, Osborne, 1751) 32–34.

[85] The Restraining Act 1558 did not apply to leases granted to the Crown prior to 1604 (1 Jac.1 c.3). Nor did it prevent the confirmation of shorter concurrent or other leases, not authorised by the Enabling Act: *Dean of Westminster's case* (1664) Cart 9, 12, cf. *Bayly* v. *Murin* (1673) 1 Vent 244, *Fox* v. *Colliers* (1589) 1 Leon 148.

[86] s.5. Moore 107, D'Anvers, *Abridgment*, vol. 3, 246. Catholic clergy, at the end of Mary's reign, saw which way the wind was blowing, and granted long leases to deprive their successors of the benefit of church land. 'Bishop Gardiner made no scruple of boasting of this practice, and used to say, in allusion to the length of his leases, that he should be a bishop a hundred years after he was dead': Reeves, ed. W. Finlason, *History of English Law* (London, Reeves and Turner, 1869) vol. 3 620.

[87] If the rent would have gone to the grantor personally during his lifetime, then it was only 'utterly void' against his successors: *Magdalene Hospital* v. *Knotts* (1879) 4 App.Cas. 324. In ecclesiastical leases, the description of the demised premises was often archaic, referring to features which no longer existed, and to buildings which had long since been pulled down, in order to demonstrate that the letting was of property which had previously been let and was at the old accustomed rent. For the problem this caused with repairing covenants, see Woodfall, *Landlord and Tenant*, 27, Platt, *Leases*, vol. 2 26. Coke's advice in *Lord Mountjoy's Case* (1589) 5 Co.Rep 3b, 6b was: 'And take great care (good reader) if you contract for any lease, under any of the said, or any other statutes, or with any person who hath power to make leases, by counsel on the sight and good consideration of them in making of your lease; and my hope is that the report of these cases concerning leases will bring to their memory some things tending to the repose and quiet of poor farmers'.

proved inconvenient, and on particular estates private Acts of Parliament sometimes authorised bishops to let for 99 years.[88]

But bishops had a personal financial interest in letting for lives[89] rather than for fixed terms of years. So their lettings were often still for lives right the way down to 1835, when control of their estates passed to the Church Estates Commissioners, who became the Ecclesiastical Commissioners, and who had extensive leasing powers and a rather more commercial outlook.[90]

Vicars and parsons originally had no power to make a lease binding on their successors at all, although a lease confirmed by the bishop, the patron and archdeacons or prebends would be binding.[91] The Enabling Act 1540 did not apply to them,[92] and a series of Restraining Acts made during the Elizabethan period[93] confined the power of confirmation to leases for up to 21 years or three lives in being, or 40 years in the case of town houses. The Ecclesiastical Leasing Act 1842 further restrained the power of confirmation to, in general, leases of not more than 14 years.

---

[88] Eg. (1702) 1 Anne c.xxvii.

[89] The whole of the customary fine payable on renewal went to the bishop personally, because it was treated as capitalised income falling due in that year. If the bishop let for years at an annual rack rent, then some of the rent might fall due after he had ceased to be the bishop, and go to his successor instead: F. Pollock, *The Land Laws*, 143. The deans of various cathedrals, who held land, were guilty of the same abuse until it was prohibited by s.9 Ecclesiastical Commissioners Act 1868, the only difference being that the dean had to share the spoils with the members of the chapter too.

[90] Ecclesiastical Leasing Acts 1842, 1858 & 1862, *Oxford History of the Laws of England*, vol. 12 113.

[91] *Clark's Case* (1584) 4 Leon 11, *Co.Litt.* 44a, Woodfall, *Landlord and Tenant*, 87. There is a precedent in W.West, *Simboleograph* (London, Stationers Company, 1610) pt.1 s.447 for a lease of parsonage, confirmed by the dean and bishop, but with a right for the parson to use the hall, buttery and kitchen, on two months' notice, should he be 'disposed hereafter to keep hospitalitie'.

[92] s.3 The Leases by Corporations Act 1541.

[93] The Ecclesiastical Leases Acts 1571, 1572 and 1575, The Hospitals for the Poor Act 1572, 43 Eliz.1 c.29, *Bl.Comm.* Bk.I 87, Reeves, ed. W.Finlason, *History of English Law* (London, Reeves and Turner, 1869) vol. 3 620 *et seq.* Those Acts bound the Crown: *The Grounds and Rudiments of Law and Equity*, 2nd edn. (London, Osborne, 1751) 32.

The Restraining Acts also applied to the property of ecclesiastical corporations aggregate, such as any land which was vested in a dean and chapter of a cathedral, which had unlimited leasing powers at common law.

The grantor and grantee on a disposition of property cannot be the same person, since people cannot contract with or make grants to themselves alone.[94] That rule applies even to someone who is acting in two different capacities.[95] So individuals who held property as a corporation sole (such as vicars and parsons) were never able to lease it to themselves alone in their natural capacity; and the same reasoning was applied to prevent a corporation aggregate making a lease to one of the members of the corporation too, except where the constitution of the corporation allowed the lease to be granted without the concurrence of that member.[96]

Companies and corporations generally: At common law a corporation could only take and dispose of land by deed.[97] Without a deed, there could only be a tenancy at will. But when, in the eighteenth century, the courts started treating leases made void for lack of formality by the Statute of Frauds (1677) as periodic tenancies,[98] they extended that concept to cases where the lease was void because one party had no power to grant or take a parol lease at all, so that if the tenant had entered and paid rent, that would be treated as a tenancy from year to year implied by law too.[99] Companies incorporated under a special Act of Parliament acquired the same power to grant parol leases as

---

[94] *Co.Litt.* 280a, *Rye* v. *Rye* [1962] AC 496.

[95] Even assents by personal representatives in favour of themselves are not a grant: they are simply a declaration that the property is now held in a different capacity.

[96] *Salter* v. *Grosvenor* (1724) 8 Mod. 303.

[97] *Perks*, ¶.64. There are numerous cases where common law claims on leases against corporations failed because of misnomer of the corporation in the lease. But relief was always available in equity: *Anon* (1603) Cary 31, Nottingham, *Prolegomena of Chancery and Equity* (Cambridge, Cambridge University Press, 1965) 203–204.

[98] See ch.4 heading 'Periodic'.

[99] *Wood* v. *Tate* (1806) 2 B & P (NR) 247, *Magdalene Hospital* v. *Knotts* (1879) 4 App.Cas. 324, 335.

individuals in 1845,[100] and companies incorporated under the Companies Acts acquired that power too in 1948.[101]

The extent to which the law of mortmain prevented the grant of leases to corporations is discussed in chapter 8.

Coparceners: Until 1926, when a fee simple owner died, and did not or could not dispose of the land by will,[102] the freehold passed to the heir at law.[103]

Normally, the heir was the eldest male descendant following the eldest male line,[104] but in the absence of any male heir by descent, the land went to all the closest female descendants together as coparceners.[105] Land held in fee tail general, rather than fee tail male, could also pass to them on the same basis. Coparceners technically held by one title. But, for all practical purposes, they were tenants in common. So even if they all joined in making a lease, it would still be treated as a number of leases of their separate shares,[106] and if one of them alone made a lease, then on a subsequent partition of the land, the lease would continue as a lease of the land allotted to that owner alone.[107]

Copyholders: Copyhold was originally 'unfree' or 'villein' tenure, meaning that the services to be performed in return for the land were uncertain and servile, as opposed to freehold tenure where the rent and services (if any) were fixed and

---

[100] s.97 Companies Clauses Consolidation Act 1845.

[101] s.32 Companies Act 1948.

[102] s.45(1) Administration of Estates Act 1925. See ch.8 heading 'Devolution on death'.

[103] See ch.8 heading 'Devolution on death'.

[104] There were various customary exceptions to this rule of primogeniture, most notably in Kent, where land passed to all surviving male children equally (gavelkind). They took as coparceners too.

[105] See, generally, Simpson, *History of Land Law*, 54–57 and Halsbury's Laws, *Real Property*, vol. 39(2), 4th edn., ¶.224. For the underlying reasons for the rule, see W. Holdsworth & C. Vickers, *The Law of Succession* (London, Stevens & Son, 1899) 107–108.

[106] *Milliner* v. *Robinson* (1600) Moor 682.

[107] *Anon* (1542) Dyer 52a.

honourable.[108] It was called 'copyhold' because, in order to transfer the land, it was technically necessary to surrender the land to the lord, who would then admit the new tenant. The surrender and admittance were recorded on the court roll of the lord's court, and a 'copy' of the entry would be provided to the tenant. At first, a copyhold was no more than a tenancy at will, and any claims concerning it could only be brought in the immediate lord's court.[109] Over time,[110] however, the services became fixed according to the custom of the particular manor,[111] and the terms on which a copyholder could retain and transfer the land to a third party became fixed by custom too. Danby CJ, in 1467, and Bryan CJ who followed him, both thought that a copyholder could bring trespass for damages against the lord, if evicted contrary to those customs, and that was settled by 1566.[112]

In 1588 a copyholder could recover possession by bringing ejectment too.[113] Since an action in ejectment was technically an action brought to recover possession of a leasehold term granted by the real claimant (i.e. a lease granted by the copyholder)[114] that brought to the fore the question of what leasing powers a copyholder actually possessed. The answer, given in 1629, was

---

[108] 'Free services [were] such as were not unbecoming to the character of a soldier or a freeman to perform; as to serve under his lord in wars, to pay a sum of money, and the like. Base services were such as were fit only for peasants, or persons of servile rank; as to plough the lord's land, to make hedges, or to carry his dung, or other means of employment': *Bl.Comm.* Bk.II 60–61, Holdsworth, *HEL* vol. 3 31.

[109] Copyhold tenure in ancient demesne (customary freehold) was an exception. The tenant held by copy of the court roll, but as a freeholder. It appears to have been confined to manors held by the Crown at the time of the conquest.

[110] In 1523 a villein could still be granted for life, like a piece of property: *Doctor and Student*, 153.

[111] *Bl.Comm.* Bk.II 147.

[112] Littleton, *Tenures*, s.77. For a detailed analysis of those remarks, see C. Gray, *Copyhold Equity and the Common Law* (Cambridge Mass, Harvard University Press, 1963) 54–58.

[113] *Rumnay & Eves's Case* (1588) 1 Leon 100, *Sparks' Case* (1599) Cro Eliz 676, C. Gray, *Copyhold, Equity and the Common Law,* 65–66. The Court of Common Pleas was a little slower to accept this than King's Bench: see Simpson, *History of Land Law,* 154–155, and *Stephens* v. *Elliot* (1596) Cro Eliz 484.

[114] See ch.9 heading 'Ejectment'.

that a copyholder had a general customary right to grant leases for up to one year, but risked forfeiture of the copyhold by granting a lease for any longer period without the lord's licence,[115] absent any special custom of the particular manor to the contrary.

By the beginning of the nineteenth century, the whole system was breaking down. The lord had to employ a steward, to hold the court, and to keep the court rolls, and although the lord was entitled to charge a customary 'fine' for each new admittance, often the expenses of running the system would exceed the income. From the copyhold tenant's point of view, the system was unsatisfactory too, not simply because of the fine payable to the lord on each change in ownership, but also because of the rag-bag of outdated and sometimes bizarre customs that applied in particular manors.[116] Voluntary enfranchisement (conversion to a fee simple) was common throughout the eighteenth and nineteenth centuries, and compulsory enfranchisement, which had first been suggested as a tax-raising measure as far back as the sixteenth century, became possible under the Copyhold Act 1852.[117] By s.191 Law of Property Act 1922 all remaining copyholds

---

[115] *Cramporn* v. *Freshwater* (1610) 1 Brownlow 133, *Viner's Abridgment*, 'Estates' S.a, *Turner* v. *Hodges* (1629) Het 127. One lease for discontinuous periods, amounting in total to more than a year, caused a forfeiture too: *Lutterell* v. *Weston* (1610) Cro Jac 308. In practice, the problem could be avoided by granting a lease for a year with covenants to renew: *Lady Montague's Case* (1612) Cro Jac 301, Coote, *Leases*, 33–35. There is a precedent for a lease of 15 years, made with the lord's licence, in *The Compleat Clerk*, 3rd edn. (London, Place, 1671) 700. A letting of copyhold land by an infant did not a cause a forfeiture, because no act of an infant was allowed to act to his or her prejudice: *Ashfield* v. *Ashfield* (1626) Noy 92, Godbolt 363, W Jones 157.

[116] In 1679, Thomas Blount attempted to record some of these for posterity, in his entertaining book, *Fragmenta Antiquitatis*, generally known as 'Blount's Jocular Tenures' or 'Tenures of Land and Customs of Manors'. For the custom of keeping a bull for the use of the parish, which features in Tristram Shandy, see *Yealding* v. *Fay* (1597) Cro Eliz 569.

[117] Holdsworth, *HEL* vol. 7 310–312. The Act did not apply to manors held by the Crown.

(other than copyholds for life or years)[118] were automatically turned into freeholds immediately before the Law of Property Act 1925 was brought into force on 1st January 1926.

The Crown: Crown lands are all those lands which form part of the residual royal demesne,[119] or are held as an augmentation[120] to it.[121] At common law, they were vested in the sovereign, and there was no distinction between the sovereign's personal property and state property. The sovereign was the state. Ordinary forms of conveyance were below the dignity of the sovereign, with the result that any voluntary[122] acquisition or disposition of crown lands required some suitable memorial of it to be made in a court of record. The practical effect was that the

---

[118] A copyhold for years was converted into a lease for years. A copyhold for life was converted into a lease for 90 years determinable on the relevant death; ss.133, 135 Law of Property Act 1922.

[119] There is a legal fiction that William I acquired the whole kingdom by conquest, extinguishing all previous grants of land, and making new grants in their place. The residual demesne consists of whatever remains, never having been granted out, and that which has fallen back into the Crown demesne by reason of an escheat, on a failure of heirs of a tenant in chief before 1926 (s.45 Administration of Estates Act 1925) or on an attainder before 1870 (s.1 Forfeiture Act 1870) and still on the dissolution of a corporation holding a fee simple.

[120] Between 1536 and 1554 additions to the royal demesne (mostly the spoils of the dissolution of the monasteries) were managed by the Court of Augmentations.

[121] Consequently, both the Duchy of Lancaster and the Duchy of Cornwall are excluded. The Duchy of Lancaster is held by the sovereign as a separate possession under a charter made by Hen.4 on acquiring the throne, in 1399. The Chancellor and Council were granted powers of leasing by the Duchy of Lancaster Acts 1812 and 1920. See now the Duchy of Lancaster Act 1988. The Duchy of Cornwall is held by the Prince of Wales, not the Crown (*The Prince's Case* (1605) 8 Co.Rep 1a) and leasing powers are contained in the Duchy of Cornwall Management Acts 1863–1893. See also J. Bray, *Feudal Law, the Case for Reform*, in *Modern Studies in Property Law* ed. M. Dixon, vol. 5 (Oxford, Hart, 2009) 115–120.

[122] *The Grounds and Rudiments of Law and Equity*, 2nd edn. (London, Osborne, 1751) 171–172. Where land devolved upon the Crown by operation of law, then an Inquest of Office was necessary in order to create the record; *Grosse* v. *Gayer* (1629) Cro Car 172, *Bl.Comm.* Bk.III 258–259, K. McNeil, *Common Law Aboriginal Title* (Oxford, Clarendon Press, 1989) 95–98.

Crown could only grant and accept leases by letters patent,[123] or under the seal of the Exchequer.[124] The Crown could not create or hold under a parol lease[125] nor be a tenant at will.[126]

The sovereign's leasing powers were curbed, in order to prevent a recurrence of William's III's habit of making extravagant gifts to his friends, by s.5 Crown Lands Act 1702, which prevented[127] the grant of any lease for a term longer three lives in being or 31 years, or 50 years in the case of a repairing or building lease.[128] George III surrendered his personal interest in crown lands, which were then placed under the management of the Commissioners of Woods and Forests, by the Crown Lands Act 1829.

With the exception of the sovereign's private estate, crown lands which are not actively required for the purpose of government,[129] are now generally vested in their successors, the Crown Estate Commissioners.[130] Those that are required for that purpose are held by the Secretary of State of some government department or some other government official, such as the Attorney-General. Although in constitutional theory these institutions are simply emanations of the Crown,[131] they have

---

[123] A misrecital in a grant by letters patent made the grant void; *Swift* v. *Heirs* (1639) March 31, *Wing* v. *Harris* (1591) Cro Eliz 231.

[124] *Predyman* v. *Wodry* (1606) Cro Jac 109, *Kemp* v. *Barnard* (1638) Cro Car 513. Prior to the enactment of s.5 Crown Lands Act 1906, it was necessary to enrol an assignment of a crown lease: *Stillingfleet* v. *Sir Harry Parker* (1704) 6 Mod. 248. Grants made by indenture to and by Hen.8 were retrospectively validated by 34 Hen.8 c.21 and 35 Eliz.1 c.3: *Atkins* v. *Longville* (1604) Cro Jac 50.

[125] *Lane's Case,* (1607) 2 Co.Rep 17.

[126] *Anon* (1704) 6 Mod. 248.

[127] It still regulates the disposition of royal palaces: see J. Bray, *Feudal Law, the Case for Reform,* in *Modern Studies in Property Law* ed. M. Dixon, vol. 5 (Oxford, Hart, 2009) 113–114.

[128] There was an exception for leases of advowsons.

[129] Parliament Square is an odd exception: s.38 Greater London Authority Act 1999.

[130] Crown Estate Act 1961. The Commissioners of Woods became the Commissioners of Crown Lands in 1924 (SR&O 1924 No.1370) and acquired legal personality in 1927 (s.1 Crown Lands Act 1927).

[131] *Town Investments* v. *Dept of Environment* [1978] AC 359.

their own legal personality,[132] and consequently the rules about lettings by and to the sovereign do not apply to them.[133]

Fee simple owners: The Law of Property Act 1925 reduced the number of legal estates in land to two: the fee simple absolute in possession and a term of years absolute.[134] Fee simple ownership is the second[135] nearest thing to absolute ownership in English land law.[136] Since the thirteenth century, a fee simple owner has been able to deal with it as he or she wishes, even if the grant was expressly made to that individual's 'heirs' as well.[137] Consequently, since then, a fee simple owner, not under any personal disability, has always had full power to grant any lease he or she wishes,[138] which is not otherwise contrary to law.

Fee tail owners: In 1285 the Statute of Westminster II[139] created a new form of common law estate, the fee tail. It was a grant to the grantee and the grantee's heirs (normally, following the male line only)[140] but on condition that, if the line died out, the land would revert to the grantor or the grantor's heirs.[141]

Now conditional fees, under which the land would revert if

---

[132] For a list of government officials who had separate legal personality at the end of 1947, see J. Bickford-Smith, *The Crown Proceedings Act 1947* (London, Butterworths, 1948) 23–24.

[133] Platt, *Leases*, vol. 1 543.

[134] s.1(1) Law of Property Act 1925. The expression 'term of years absolute' includes a periodic tenancy and a tenancy for a fixed term of less than a year: s.205(xxvii) Law of Property Act 1925. See also *Bl.Comm.* Bk.II 140.

[135] The nearest thing is land held by the Crown absolutely, as part of the residual royal demesne. See the previous sub-section.

[136] 'It is the highest form of tenure known to the English law, and the tenant of this estate has the entire uncontrolled disposition of his property': B. Adkin, *Copyhold and Other Land Tenures* (London, Estates Gazette, 1907) 21.

[137] *Pollock & Maitland* vol. 2 13–14, Holdsworth, *HEL* vol. 3 107. There were special rules where the grant was to the heirs of the body of a particular person. See the next sub-section.

[138] *Bl.Comm.* Bk.II 318.

[139] De Donis Conditionalibus (1285), Coke, *2nd Inst.*, 331–337.

[140] Tail 'male', tail 'female', and tail 'general' were all possible: Simpson, *History of Land Law*, 85.

[141] Simpson, *History of Land Law* 77–80.

the condition was not satisfied, already existed and were common in 1285.[142] What was radical about a fee tail was not that the land might revert to the grantor at some point in the future, if the grantee's descendants died out. It was that the land could not be alienated away from the heirs of the original grantee in the meantime. Nobody could change the course of descent of the land, in order to prevent the next heir who was a descendant of the original grantee inheriting it on the death of the current heir, taking it free of whatever burdens the current heir might have tried to impose on it.[143]

In order to get around that restriction, it was necessary to invent a way of turning a fee tail into a fee simple.[144] From the middle of the fifteenth century, that could be done by a collusive common recovery,[145] and in 1833 that was replaced with a simple disentailing deed.[146] But, until it was converted, the owner of a fee tail could only grant a valid lease out of it for his or her lifetime. Any longer lease would be voidable by the descendants in tail,[147] and if the line became extinct, would be void against the original grantor's heir, to whom the land would revert.[148] By way of statutory exception to that rule, the Enabling Act 1540[149] gave a fee tail owner power, as against his own

---

[142] A grant to a man and his wife and the heirs begotten of their bodies (maritagium), for example, was a grant in fee simple, conditional upon the birth of issue within the prescribed class. See generally Holdsworth, *HEL* vol. 3 112–113, Simpson, *History of Land Law*, 60–63 and the notes in Halsbury's Statutes of England, *Real Property*, 2nd edn., vol. 20, 359–360.

[143] Holdsworth, *HEL* vol. 3 116.

[144] For the policy reasons for doing so, see F. Bacon, *The Use of the Law* (London, Moore, 1630) 53–54.

[145] *Doctor and Student*, 66–81, J. Biancalana, *The Fee Tail and the Common Recovery in Medieval England* (Cambridge, Cambridge University Press, 2001) 250–251.

[146] s.15 Fines and Recoveries Act 1833.

[147] M. Bacon, *A Treatise on Leases* (London, Strahan, 1798) 19, Preston, *Conveyancing*, vol. 2. 132. If the lease was granted to commence after the death of grantor, it was void as against the issue too, ibid 133, cf. *Viner's Abridgment*, 'Estates' I.a.2 pl.3.

[148] Platt, *Leases*, vol. 1 85.

[149] s.2.

issue,[150] to let corporeal land reserving at least the ancient rent for up to the longest of three lives in being or 21 years, provided that the lease was made by indenture.[151] Full leasing powers were conferred on tenants in tail in 1833,[152] but the same provision made it easy to bar the entail instead by a disentailing deed, which is what every sensible owner did.

Only the fee in land could be entailed. So it was not possible to create an entail of a lease for a term of years, nor any chattel.[153]

In 1926, a fee tail ceased to be a legal estate, and became an equitable estate instead.[154] Until the entail was barred,[155] the land would be subject to a strict settlement, regulated by the Settled Land Act 1925, so that the tenant in tail had the same statutory leasing powers as a tenant for life.[156]

It also became possible in 1926 to create an equitable fee tail in a leasehold estate and chattels,[157] without the resort to the subterfuge of the doctrine of conversion.[158] But it has not been

----

[150] *Co.Litt.* 44a, *Viner's Abridgment*, 'Estates', I.a.2, Preston, *Conveyancing*, vol. 2 136, Coote, *Leases*, 28.

[151] The power authorised the grant of a reversionary lease, if it would expire within 21 years of the date when it was made, rather than the date when it was due to commence: *Anon* (1565) Dyer 246a, *Viner's Abridgment*, 'Estates' I.a.2 pl.4.

[152] s.15 Fines and Recoveries Act 1833.

[153] So a devise of a leasehold term to the devisee and the heirs of his body, was an outright disposition of the term to the devisee: *Duke of Norfolk's case* (1681) 3 Ch.Cas 1, 14, 30, Holdsworth, *HEL* vol. 7 143–144. For devises of life terms in a leasehold estate, with remainders over (executory devises), see ch.8 heading 'Devolution on death'.

[154] s.130 Law of Property Act 1925.

[155] An entail can now be barred either by a disentailing assurance, executed during the lifetime of the tenant in tail (s.15 Fines and Recoveries Act 1833), or by the exercise of the testamentary power granted by s.176 Law of Property Act 1925. See generally Halsbury's Laws, *Real Property*, vol. 39 (2), 4th edn., ¶.121–133.

[156] s.20(i) Settled Land Act 1925. See sub-heading 'Tenants for life'.

[157] s.130 Law of Property Act 1925, *Re Hope's WT* [1929] 2 Ch 136.

[158] Before 1926, an entail could be achieved, indirectly, in equity, by directing the trustees to sell the lease and invest the proceeds in freehold land. The doctrine of conversion would do the rest. Other successive interests in a lease could be created in equity behind a trust, subject to the rule against perpetuities: see Halsbury's Laws, *Real Property* , vol. 39(2) 4th edn., ¶.104–105 and per Sjt Heale in *Scovell and Cavels' Case* (1588) 1 Leon 317, 318.

possible to create any new entailed interests since 1st January 1997.[159]

Foreigners: At common law, no foreigner could hold any freehold land nor bring any action in respect of it.[160] The theoretical justification for this was that fealty, ultimately to the Crown, was an essential part of tenure of a fee, and a foreigner was already bound in fealty to a foreign sovereign.[161]

A foreign merchant could take a lease of a house, but granting a lease of a house or shop to an alien manufacturer was made unlawful in 1540.[162] Blackstone thought that this prohibition had been 'virtually repealed' by a general statute dealing with importation of goods in 1562,[163] but only because, by the eighteenth century, it was starting to look decidedly silly. Other leases to foreigners were neither void nor voidable, but were forfeitable to the Crown if made without licence.[164]

Since 1870, foreigners have been able to hold and acquire land in the same way as subjects,[165] and only enemy aliens are prohibited from bringing actions in the courts.

Infants: For the purpose of determining the validity of a property transaction, an individual[166] was generally[167] an infant

---

[159] s.2(6) & para.5 sch. 1 Trusts of Land and Appointment of Trustees Act 1996.

[160] Scots ceased to be foreigners for this purpose when James the sixth of Scotland became James the first of England on 24th March 1603: *Calvin's Case* (1608) 7 Co.Rep 1a.

[161] K. Reid with ors., *The Law of Property in Scotland* (Edinburgh, LexisNexis UK, 1996) ¶.53.

[162] 32 Hen.8 c.16 s.13.

[163] 5 Eliz.1 c.7, *Bl.Comm*. Bk.I 360.

[164] Coote, *Leases*, 70.

[165] s.2 Naturalisation Act 1870.

[166] An ecclesiastical corporation was never treated as being underage, even if the incumbent was younger than 21 years. The same applied to the sovereign: *Duchy of Lancaster's Case* (1562) Plowden 212, Dyer's Notebook, 109 SS 30.

[167] An infant seised in fee of land which was subject to customary gavelkind descent (generally, land in Kent) could grant a lease for life at the age of 15 years by personal livery of seisin: *Anon* (1548) Bendloe 7 pl.26, *Robinson on Gavelkind*, 3rd edn. (London, Butterworths, 1822) 166.

at common law until the age of twenty-one.[168] Most lawyers, until 1765, thought that if an infant granted a lease which did not reserve any rent at all, it would be void,[169] but *Zouch* v. *Parsons*[170] decided that there was no special rule for rent free leases, and that all leases granted by or to an infant were merely voidable by the infant on obtaining majority.[171] If the infant died before becoming an adult, then the right to avoid it could be exercised by the infant's heir, in the case of a reversion which descended on the dead infant's heir,[172] and otherwise by the infant's personal representatives. But whoever exercised the right, it had to be exercised within a reasonable time of its accrual, or else it would be lost,[173] and even slight acts would amount to an affirmation.[174] There was, furthermore, never any right to avoid any act done by an infant, which the court would have compelled an adult in the same position to do, as a right and lawful act,[175] and even if the lease was avoided afterwards, a market rent was payable for any period during which the infant had enjoyed actual occupation of the property.[176]

An infant's guardian could make leases of the infant's

---

[168] For other purposes, the age varied according to the nature of the transaction and the sex of the individual; *Bl.Comm.* Bk.I 451. The age was reduced to 18 by s.1 Family Law Reform Act 1969.

[169] *Humphreston's Case* (1574) 2 Leon 216, *Anon* (1639) Bryson's Exch Case 119, J. Lilly, *The Practical Register*, 2nd edn. (London, Ward & Wickstead, 1735) vol. 1 673–674, M. Bacon, *A Treatise on Leases* (London, Strahan, 1798) 11, *Co.Litt.* 42b.fn(4), Coote, *Leases*, 19–20, cf. Chambers, *Leases*, 29.

[170] (1765) 3 Burr 1794, 1 Wm. Black 575. The same case decided that any deed executed by an infant was voidable, and not void, notwithstanding the reported dicta to the contrary in *Lloyd.* v. *Gregory* (1638) Cro Car 502, cf. the report of the same case at Sir W. Jones 405.

[171] *Ketsey's Case* (1613) Cro Jac 320 (sub nom *Keteley's Case*, 1 Brownlow 120), Preston, *Conveyancing*, vol. 2 249, *Pollock & Maitland*, vol. 2 445.

[172] See ch.8 heading 'Devolution on Death'.

[173] *Edwards* v. *Carter* [1893] AC 360.

[174] 'God give you joy of it' was held to be an affirmation in *Anon* (1582) 4 Leon 4.

[175] *Zouch* v. *Parsons* (1765) 3 Burr 1806, 1 Wm. Black 755.

[176] *Ketsey's Case* (1613) Cro Jac 320. A condition in a lease to an infant could be enforced, notwithstanding the infancy of the tenant: *Port's Notebook*, 102 SS 143 pl.7.

freehold socage[177] land, which would be binding during the guardianship, but not any longer.[178]

After 1830, the court could act on behalf of infants, for the purpose of authorising the surrender and re-grant of a lease, or the grant of a renewal lease, which would be binding on the infant afterwards.[179] In 1926 it became impossible for an infant to hold a legal estate in land at all. So an infant could no longer be the legal tenant of a lease. Instead, between 1926 and 1996, a purported grant of a legal estate to an infant,[180] took effect as an agreement to create a settlement of it, for the benefit of the infant, which would be a strict settlement regulated by the Settled Land Act 1925; with the result that, once executed, the trustees of the settlement could exercise leasing powers on behalf of the infant, and in the meantime the leasing power was vested in the public trustee.[181] Now, if an attempt is made to grant a lease to an infant, the grant takes effect as a declaration of trust, on the terms of the lease, in favour of the infant by the landlord.[182] Similarly, if an attempt is made to assign a lease to an infant, that takes effect as a declaration of trust by the assignor. But an infant can still disclaim the lease on becoming

---

[177] Before 1660, if the infant's land was held in knight service, then the guardian in chivalry was the lord, who was entitled to all the profits from the land of a male heir until the age of 21, and of a female heir until 16 or earlier marriage (unless she was already 14 at the death): *Bl.Comm.* Bk.II 67. See the discussion of wardship in ch.4 heading 'Fixed terms'.

[178] *Pigot* v.*Garnish* (1600) Cro Eliz 734. An infant could choose a guardian at 14. But by the Tenures Abolition Act 1660 any guardian appointed by a father's will could not be removed, and equity would restrain the appointment of an inappropriate guardian in any event: *Bl.Comm.* Bk.II 88. If the guardian died the lease ended: *Balder* v. *Blackbourne* (1618) Brownlow 79. The Tenures Abolition Act 1660 was reproduced in Ireland in 1662 by 14 & 15 Car.2 c.19 (Ir).

[179] s.12, s.16 Infants' Property Act 1830, extended to Ireland in 1835 by 5 & 6 Wm.4 c.17, s.2.

[180] If the grant was to an adult and an infant jointly, it took effect as a grant to the adult alone, but on trust so as preserve any beneficial interest of the infant: s.19(5) Law of Property Act 1925.

[181] Sch.1 pt.III Law of Property Act 1925, s.1(1)(ii)(d) Settled Land Act 1925, Halsbury's Laws, *Real Property* , vol. 39(2), 4th edn. ¶.54.

[182] Para.1(1) sch.1 Trusts of Land and Appointment of Trustees Act 1996, *Alexander-David* v. *Mayor and Burgesses of the London Borough of Hammersmith and Fulham* [2010] Ch 272.

an adult.[183]

Joint tenants and tenants in common: A 'joint tenancy' is where two or more persons[184] hold property, in which they all have an equal interest, as a single thing,[185] and which, on the death of any one of them, passes to the other or others of them by survivorship.[186] By contrast, a 'tenancy in common' is where property has already been divided up into separate shares, whether equal or not, each of which is held as the absolute property of its owner, so that the original property itself no longer exists as a single thing.[187]

Before 1926, a legal estate in land could be cut up into separate shares, so that each separate share would be held by a different tenant in common, as that person's own separate property. The owner of each share could grant a lease of that share, but even if all the owners came together and executed one lease, that instrument would still take effect as separate leases of their individual shares, rather than as one lease of the whole.[188]

The position where a lease was granted by joint tenants was more complicated. Since they were all owners of the same estate, they could join together and make a single lease of the property as a single whole.[189] Or, as an individual, each joint tenant could

---

[183] *Davies* v. *Benyon-Harris* (1931) 47 TLR 424.

[184] At common law a corporation aggregate could not be a joint tenant with anyone else at all, and a corporation sole could not be a joint tenant of freehold land: (1501) YB 16 Hen.7 f.15b pl.12, *Law Guarantee and Trust Society* v. *Bank of England* (1890) 24 QBD 406. Those disabilities were removed by s.1 Bodies Corporate (Joint Tenancy) Act 1899. See Halsbury's Laws, *Real Property*, vol. 39(2), 4th edn., ¶.192 and Halsbury's *Statutes*, 2nd edn., vol. 20 417–418.

[185] Littleton, *Tenures*, s.288.

[186] Littleton, *Tenures*, s.281, *Co.Litt.* 180b. A joint tenancy was 'odious in equity': *The Grounds and Rudiments of Law and Equity*, 2nd edn. (London, Osborne, 1751) 160.

[187] See, generally, Halsbury's Laws, *Real Property*, vol. 39(2), 4th edn., ¶.190–223.

[188] *Gyles* v. *Kempe* (1677) 1 Freeman 235, *Viner's Abridgment*, 'Estates' B.b.6 pl.11, Gilbert, *Rents*, 37, *Perks*, ¶.107.

[189] *Jurdain* v. *Steere* (1605) Cro Jac 83.

grant a lease of his or her undivided, equal share in the property.[190]

The grant of a lease for a term of years by a joint tenant was an exception to the normal rule that any separate dealing by a joint tenant with his or her interest would sever the joint tenancy, and turn it into a tenancy in common.[191] That lease could be made to bind the grantor's share in the property, even after the grantor's death,[192] without severing the joint tenancy or affecting the right of survivorship.[193] So if the grantor died before the other joint tenants, then the rent would be discharged,[194] but the deceased owner's share would accrue to the survivors, still subject to the lease.[195] Curiously, that rule seems to have been forgotten since 1926, so a lease by a beneficial joint tenant of his or her share is now a disposition which severs a beneficial joint tenancy.[196]

It was never possible to grant a single lease to persons as tenants in common. If the grant was made to them as tenants in common, then it followed that they must each have been granted separate leases of their shares.[197] So a single lease of one thing could only be granted to two or more people as joint tenants.[198] Once it had been granted, there was nothing to stop the tenants

---

[190] *Cartwright's case* cited in *Putt* v. *Nosworthy* (1671) 1 Vent 136, *Co.Litt.* 186a. So one joint tenant could lease to the other: *Viner's Abridgment*, 'Estates' B.b, Gilbert, *Rents*, 63.

[191] Challis, *Real Property*, 367. An assignment by one joint tenant would sever the joint tenancy, and the assignee would be a tenant in common with the other tenant or tenants: Littleton, *Tenures*, s.319.

[192] So a lease to commence on the grantor's death was valid against the grantor's share, even though that share would accrue to a survivor: *Harbin* v. *Barton* (1595) Moor 395, *Whitlock* v. *Horton* (1605) Cro Jac 91.

[193] 'One joint tenant may let his part for years or at will to his companion': *Co. Litt.* 186a.

[194] The rent would be discharged because the remaining joint tenants would take by survivorship, rather than as heirs or as purchasers of the share: *Anon* (1560) Dyer 187a.

[195] Littleton, *Tenures*, s.289.

[196] *Ahmed* v. *Kendrick* (1987) 56 P&CR 120, 124, *Bowers* v. *Bowers* (unrep Hoffmann J. 3.2.87) cf. *Penn* v. *Bristol & West Building Society* [1995] 2 FLR 938.

[197] Tenants in common 'come to such lands or tenements by several title, and not by one joint title': Littleton, *Tenures*, s.292.

[198] *Slingsby's Case* (1587) 5 Co.Rep 18b, *Scovell and Cavels Case* (1588) 1 Leon 317.

dividing it up amongst themselves into separate shares, at common law,[199] and dealing with those shares separately if they wished. But the covenants and conditions remained annexed to the whole, so that non-performance by the holder of one share would imperil all the others, and they could all be sued together as one tenant.[200]

Since 1926, it has been impossible for more than four people to hold a legal estate in land at the same time,[201] and they can only hold that legal estate as joint tenants. But behind the curtain of the legal title, they can hold it in trust for themselves, or any number of others, either as beneficial joint tenants or as beneficial tenants in common. So the legal estate will always pass by survivorship, but the beneficial ownership can be made to devolve differently. In addition to the other methods of severing a beneficial joint tenancy, since 1926 it has been possible to do so by serving a written notice to that effect.[202]

Mortgagor and mortgagee: Absent any express power conferred by the mortgage deed,[203] neither a mortgagor nor a mortgagee could create any tenancy binding on the other. Any tenancy granted by the lender would take effect subject to the borrower's equity of redemption, and so would be overreached on repayment of the mortgage debt.[204] Any tenancy granted by the borrower, after granting the mortgage, would take effect subject to the mortgage, with the result that the tenant would be at risk of eviction by the lender, if the lender chose to exercise its right to take possession,[205] or to sell the mortgaged estate free of

---

[199] Joint tenants for years could make a partition without a deed before the Statute of Frauds (1677): *Co.Litt.* 169a.

[200] *Ipswich* v. *Martin* (1616) Cro Jac 411.

[201] The legal estate vests in the first four named: s.34(2) Law of Property Act 1925.

[202] s.36(2) Law of Property Act 1925.

[203] Mortgages of substantial estates often contained powers allowing the borrower to create or renew leases, which were necessary for the proper management of the estate, on particular terms: Ashburner, *Equity*, 265.

[204] *Hungerford* v. *Clay* (1722) 9 Mod. 1. When the legal estate was reconveyed to the mortgagor, or on determination of the mortgage term, the lease would fall.

[205] *Keech d. Warne* v. *Hall* (1778) 1 Douglas 21. Hence, the mortgagee did not need to give any notice before evicting the tenant, *Thunder d. Weaver* v. *Belcher* (1803) 3 East 449; and if the mortgagee accepted rent from the tenant,

the tenancy.[206]

Consequently, the only safe course, if the lease was made by the borrower, was to join the lender to record its agreement to be bound, and vice versa.[207]

An attempt to remedy that problem was made in s.18 Conveyancing Act 1881, which gave the mortgagor or the mortgagee (whichever of them was in possession at the time) power to create agricultural and occupational leases of up to 21 years, and building leases for up to 99 years, at a rack rent, binding against the other. But the power did not apply if it was excluded in the mortgage deed,[208] and usually the borrower's power to grant leases was excluded. That power is now found in s.99 Law of Property Act 1925, and the same applies.[209] By contrast, the lender's power of leasing was and is often extended by the terms of the mortgage deed, so that there is rarely any need to join the borrower to a lease granted by the lender today. Indeed, the mortgage deed normally contains a security power of attorney authorising the lender to execute any document on behalf of the borrower.

Tenants for life: Between the Restoration and the First World War, both London and country estates were commonly tied up in strict settlements. The current, male, head of the family was a tenant for life,[210] whose 'interests were subordinate to those of the family, and the family was of more importance than he was.

---

that created a new periodic tenancy by conduct: *Corbett* v. *Plowden* (1884) 25 Ch.D 678.

[206] At the beginning of the nineteenth century, it was doubtful whether a power of sale (that is, to sell free of the mortgagor's right to redeem) could be attached to a mortgage at all. In order to get round that problem, mortgages were sometimes created by conveying the mortgaged property to trustees, to hold upon trust for sale, with power for the mortgagee to enter and apply the rents and profits towards the mortgage debt in the meantime: *In Re Alison* (1879) 11 Ch.D 284, 294.

[207] Stewart, *Practice of Conveyancing*, 325, 328.

[208] s.18(13).

[209] s.99(13). The power could not be excluded in relation to leases of agricultural land between 1948 and 1995; para.12 sch.14 Agricultural Holdings Act 1986.

[210] See ch.4 heading 'For life'.

He was the king in check'.[211]

Any underlease granted by a life tenant became void, at common law, on the death of that tenant for life.[212] Thereafter, the undertenant was a tenant at sufferance of the successor,[213] although if the successor did anything to acknowledge the tenancy, the court could imply the grant of a new parol tenancy, which, by the middle of the eighteenth century, would be a periodic tenancy.[214] The Settled Estates Acts of 1856 and 1877 empowered tenants for life to create leases for up to 21 years binding on the reversion out of court,[215] and more extensive general powers of leasing were conferred by the Settled Land Act 1882.[216] Those powers did not apply to the tenant of a lease for life held at a commercial rent. They only applied where the tenant for life was also beneficially entitled to the property for life under a strict settlement.[217]

In practice, however, strict settlements had usually given the tenant for life power to grant longer leases binding upon the reversion,[218] sometimes with, and sometimes without, the concurrence of others. But those powers were construed very

---

[211] B. English and J. Saville, *Strict Settlement, A Guide for Historians* (Hull, University of Hull Press, 1983) 11. For the mechanics of strict settlement, see ch.4 heading 'For life'.

[212] (1530/1) Brook's New Cases pl.16 (lease by doweress, a life tenant by law), (1532/3) Brook's New Cases pl.54 (generally), *Smith* v. *Widlake* (1877) 3 CPD 10. An executor of a tenant for life was entitled to sue in debt for any arrears of rent on the equity of s.3 Cestui Qui Vie Act 1540: *Hool* v. *Bell* (1696) 1 Ld.Raym 172, J. Lilly, *The Practical Register*, 2nd edn. (London, Ward & Wickstead, 1735) vol. 1 653. In *Turner* v. *Lee* (1637) Cro Car 471, it was held that this did not extend to a rent charge, but that was overruled in *Prescott* v. *Boucher* (1832) 3 Barn & Ad 849.

[213] See ch.4 heading 'At sufferance'.

[214] *Doe d. Calvert* v. *Frowd* (1828) 4 Bing 557, *O'Keefe* v. *Walsh* (1880) 8 LR Ir 184, cf. *Smith* v. *Widlake* (1877) 3 CPD 10.

[215] s.32 1856 Act, s.46 1877 Act.

[216] G. Cheshire, *The Modern Law of Real Property*, 5th edn. (London, Butterworths, 1944) 392–393, Holdsworth, *HEL* vol. 7 163.

[217] s.58(1)(iv).

[218] O. Bridgman, *Precedents of Conveyances* (London, Atkins, 1702) 265, *Winter* v. *Loveday* (1697) Comyn 37, 5 Mod 244, *Coventry* v. *Coventry* (1718) Comyn 312.

strictly. Edward Sugden, writing in 1811, warned:[219]

> If you have only a power to grant a lease, which is the
> case with every man whose property is settled on his family,
> you should communicate that circumstance to your solicitor,
> and furnish him with a copy of the power, because a very
> slight deviation from it—for instance, executing a lease in the
> presence of one witness, instead of two—may render the lease
> void, by which you may not only ruin your innocent tenant, but
> may, by the covenant which you must enter into with him, for
> the quiet enjoyment thereof, subject your estate to make good
> his loss, in case he is evicted by the person entitled to the estate
> after your death. This has too frequently happened.

The point was prescient. In 1821 the question of whether a
power, which authorised the grant of a lease containing 'a' right
of re-entry for non- payment for rent, had been validly exercised,
if the re-entry clause in the lease required the rent to be 15 days
in arrears first, took up nearly 250 pages in the law reports. By a
majority of six to five, the House of Lords eventually decided
that it was within the power.[220]

The problem was largely solved by the Leases Acts 1849
and 1850,[221] which turned a non-conforming lease into a contract
to create the nearest possible conforming one,[222] and the Leases
Act 1851, which continued any sub-lease at a rack rent, which
would otherwise fail on the death of the tenant life, until the next
anniversary of its grant.

In 1926, it became impossible to create a common law estate
for life. A lease for life at a rent or for other consideration

---

[219] 75–78. For the cases, see Coote, *Leases*, 176–211.

[220] *Smith* v. *Doe (lessee of Earl Jersey)* (1819) 7 Price Exc Rep 281–530. See
also *Loveday* v. *Winter* (1697) 5 Mod. 244, and E. Sugden, *Law of Property*
(London, Sweet, 1849) 496–499.

[221] Now s.152 Law of Property Act 1925.

[222] It was already the law that, if there was an executory contract to create a
non-conforming lease, specific performance could be obtained in equity so as
to require the landlord to grant the closest possible conforming lease: *Byrne* v.
Acton (1721) 1 Brown PC 186. Similarly, if the difficulty was only that the
length of the term was too long, in equity it would be treated as valid for the
shorter, authorised, term: *Pawcy* v. *Bowen* (1663) 1 Ch.Cas 23.

became a lease for a term of 90 years, determinable by notice one month after the relevant death.[223] Other leases for lives could only take effect in equity, behind the curtain of a strict settlement governed by the Settled Land Act 1925. An equitable tenant for life under the Settled Land Act 1925, however, would normally also be the legal owner of the trust property,[224] and was given wide leasing powers as such.[225] But it has not been possible to create any new Settled Land Act settlements since 1996. An equitable lease for life is now an ordinary equitable interest subsisting behind a trust of land.[226]

Women: A feme sole—an unmarried woman or widow—could always grant or take a lease in the same way as a man. But, before 1926,[227] on marriage a woman became a single legal person with her husband,[228] and that person, as it is often said, was the husband.[229] On their marriage (coverture) the husband's property remained his own, but all of his wife's freehold and leasehold property automatically became their joint property, and it was the husband alone who was entitled to deal with it during the marriage,[230] so that any legal act done by the wife whilst she

---

[223] s.149(6) Law of Property Act 1925.

[224] s.4(2) Settled Land Act 1925.

[225] ss.41–53 Settled Land Act 1925.

[226] s.2 Trusts of Land and Appointment of Trustees Act 1996.

[227] s.37 Law of Property Act 1925. See now s.1 Law Reform (Married Women and Tortfeasors) Act 1935.

[228] A married woman was a 'feme covert', the husband was her 'baron'.

[229] By marriage, the husband and wife are one person in law; that is, the very being or legal existence of the woman is suspended during the marriage, or at least consolidated into that of the husband': *Bl.Comm.* Bk.1 430. So, in 1440/1, a servant who murdered his master's wife was punished by being hung and drawn, instead of being simply hung, because that was the punishment for statutory treason, and it was statutory treason for a servant to kill his master; see *Partridge* v. *Strange* (1553) Plowden 77, 86. By the custom of London, however, a married woman carrying on a trade was liable in her own right for her own trade debts (*La Vie* v. *Philips* (1765) 1 Wm. Black 570). In litigation concerning the wife's freehold land, it was necessary for both husband and wife to be represented, and the wife was allowed to be heard: *Pollock & Maitland* vol. 2 408–409.

[230] So the wife could not deliver seisin by livery of seisin: *Perks*, ¶.186. The husband was bound by any deed which his wife had delivered in escrow, before

was married neither bound him[231] during the marriage nor her afterwards; for, so far as the common law was concerned, she was incapable of doing anything.[232]

During the marriage, the husband's power of disposition in relation to his wife's leasehold property was absolute. He could assign it[233] or surrender it, or otherwise deal with it[234] entirely as he saw fit, for his own benefit, and so as to bind his wife after his death.[235] The only thing he could not do with it, in the event that he died first, was dispose of it by his will; for, if he died before his wife, still holding the lease in right of his wife,[236] then it automatically became hers again by survivorship.[237] If, instead, his wife died first, the property was his by survivorship.[238]

A husband's power to grant leases out of his wife's freehold land[239] was much more limited. The basic rule was that the husband could only make a lease or other disposition out of it for the term of their joint lives, though, if any child of the marriage was born alive,[240] by the curtesy of England, anyone taking by inheritance from his wife, could not challenge it until he died.[241]

the marriage, even if the escrow condition was fulfilled afterwards: *Perks*, ¶9, ¶140–141.

[231] So if the wife demanded and received rent, the tenant had to pay it again to the husband, even if she had granted the lease before her marriage and the tenant had no notice of the marriage: *Tracey* v. *Dutton* (1621) Cro Jac 617.

[232] It followed that, during the marriage, only the husband could sue or be sued on the covenants binding on his wife: (1431) YB 10 Hen.6 f.11a–12a pl.38, (1467) YB 7 Ed.4 f.5b–7b pl.16, Platt, *Covenants*, 112–113, cf. *Anon* (1704) 6 Mod. 239 where an objection that the wife had been sued jointly with her husband, in respect of a lease made before they were married, was disallowed.

[233] *Anon* (1592) Poph 5.

[234] *Grute* v. *Locroft* (1592) Cro Eliz 287, *Steed* v. *Cragh* (1723) 9 Mod. 42, *Druce* v. *Denison* (1801) 6 Ves 385.

[235] *Grute* v. *Locroft* (1592) Cro Eliz 287.

[236] *Co.Litt.* 300a.

[237] *Bl.Comm.* Bk.II 434, cf. (1401) YB 2 Hen.4 f.19 pl.14.

[238] *Wrotesley* v. *Adams* (1558) Plowden 187, 192, *Hauchet's Case* (1565) Dyer 251.

[239] This included land freehold property given to the wife during the marriage: *Bennet* v. *Davis* (1725) 2 Peere Wms 316.

[240] What was needed was 'an heir, son or daughter, which shall be heard to cry within the four walls': Statute Concerning Tenants by the Curtesy of England (Time Uncertain), *Halsbury's Statutes*, 4th edn., vol. 20 363.

[241] *Bl.Comm.* Bk.II 126, 318, *Pollock & Maitland* vol. 2 403, D'Anvers, *Abridgment*, vol. 3 240, Holdsworth, *HEL* vol. 3 185–189. For gavelkind land

Otherwise, any lease granted during the marriage would be void when the marriage ended,[242] if granted by the husband alone,[243] or voidable[244] if his wife had actually joined in it.[245]

The inconvenience of the rule that anyone taking a lease of the wife's freehold property during her marriage, took it subject to the risk of premature, unpredictable and immediate determination on the death of the husband or the wife, or on their divorce,[246] even if the wife had joined in the grant, was recognised almost as soon as the rule was worked out.[247] At common law, the disposition could be confirmed by the wife during the marriage by levying a fine,[248] which required the wife to be interrogated by a judge, in her husband's absence, to see whether she really consented to the transaction.[249] Adopting this course also barred the wife's right to dower in that land.[250] But it involved difficulty and expense, and so leasing powers were gradually granted by statute instead. The Enabling Act 1540[251] empowered the husband and wife together to make a binding lease by deed for up to 21 years or three lives,[252] reserving rent to

---

(principally in Kent) the right applied even if the marriage was childless, but only extended to one half of the wife's land and ceased on re-marriage; Challis, *Real Property*, 342.

[242] By s.3 Cestui Que Vie Act 1540 a widower was given power to distrain for any arrears of rent which had accrued during the marriage.

[243] *Harvey & Thomas's Case* (1589) 1 Leon 15, *Walsal* v. *Heath* (1599) Cro Eliz 656, Brook's Abridgment 'Acceptance' 6, cf. *Jordan* v. *Wikes* (1613) Cro Jac 332, *Smallman* v. *Agborow* (1617) Cro Jac 417 which both hold it is voidable by entry.

[244] *Bragg* v. *Wiseman* (1614) 1 Brownlow 22, *Greenwood* v. *Tyber* (1620) Cro Jac 563, cf. *Brerton* v. *Evans* (1599) Cro Eliz 700, *Gardiner* v. *Norman* (1621) Cro Jac 617.

[245] So if the widow remarried, and the new husband accepted rent, the right to avoid the lease would be lost: *Anon* (1558) Dyer 159a. Originally, the right to avoid the lease was only lost by acceptance of rent if the lease had been made by deed; *Turney* v. *Sturges* (1553) Dyer 91a. But see 2 Wms Saund 180.fn(9).

[246] *Amice* v. *Clare* (1200) cited in S. Milsom, *The Legal Framework of English Feudalism* (Cambridge, Cambridge University Press, 1976) 45.

[247] Joint grants were made as late as 1223: *Pollock & Maitland* vol. 2 410.

[248] A 'fine' was a collusive compromise of a friendly action, as opposed to a 'recovery', which was a collusive judgment: F. Pollock, *The Land Laws*, 87.

[249] Littleton, *Tenures*, s.669, s.670.

[250] See ch.4 heading 'For life'.

[251] s.7.

[252] *Owen* v. *Ap-Rees* (1627) Cro Car 94.

the wife and the heirs of the wife.[253] After 1830, the court could authorise the surrender and re-grant of the wife's leasehold property,[254] or the renewal of a lease which had been granted out of the wife's property;[255] after 1833, a wife, with the consent of her husband or the court, could make any lease by deed that she wished;[256] and by s.46 Settled Estates Act 1877 husbands were given power to grant leases of all of their wives' freehold land, for up to 21 years in England or 35 years in Ireland, at a rack rent, excepting only any principal mansion house and any demesne land that was usually enjoyed with it.

The inconvenience of the rule that a feckless husband might ruin his wife by disposing of her leasehold property was not recognised until much later. In 1681, the husband's power to deal with his wife's leasehold property was absolute and extended to leases held in trust for her too.[257] But soon afterwards, courts of equity started protecting wives, by refusing to allow husbands to interfere where property had been settled on trustees to the wife's separate use;[258] and by the eighteenth century marriage settlements normally gave the wife the income from her property for life, with power for her to appoint the capital over by deed or will.[259] A married woman's equitable title to property held to her separate use was converted into a legal title by the Married Women's Property Act 1882, which also gave any woman married after 1882 the right to keep her pre-marriage property separate from her husband's, and deal with it

---

[253] Coote, *Leases*, 61.

[254] s.12 Infants' Property Act 1830.

[255] s.16 ibid.

[256] ss.77, 91 Fines and Recoveries Act 1833.

[257] *Sir Edward Turner's Case* (1681) 1 Vern 7. If the property was vested in trustees for the wife, the husband's power to deal with it ceased on her death: *Wytham* v. *Waterhowse* (1596) in J. Baker and S. Milsom, Sources of English Legal History, 2nd edn. (Oxford, Oxford University Press, 2009) 146–148. See also *Griffin* v. *Stanhope* (1617) Cro Jac 455.

[258] *Co.Litt.* 351a.fn(1), Eq. Ca. Abr. vol. 1 57 *et seq*, Holdsworth, *HEL* vol. 7 379. There is a precedent for a lease granted by a husband and wife to trustees for the wife's separate use in O. Bridgman, *Conveyances*, 3rd edn. (London, Atkins, 1699) vol. 1 115. See also ibid vol. 2 60.

[259] Ashburner, *Equity*, 231–234, 249.

as her own.[260]

In 1926, married women acquired legal personality, and a woman's property ceased to vest in her husband on marriage at all.[261] It belongs to her absolutely, in her own right, and any lease must be made by her, rather than by her husband.

In 1401, it was unclear whether a lease could be granted to a husband and wife jointly, so that it would pass to the survivor of them, or whether it would only take effect as a lease to the husband, so that he could devise it by will if he died first.[262] But by 1591, it was clear that leasehold property could be granted to them jointly. In that event, the husband had the same power of disposition during the marriage as if it had been granted to him alone, including the power to grant a reversionary lease, to commence on his death.[263] Any sub-lease granted by a husband, out of leasehold property which he and his wife had acquired jointly during the marriage, would be binding on his widow afterwards, because it would have been binding on her if the lease had been hers alone before the marriage.[264]

Where a freehold estate (including a lease for life) was granted to or devolved upon a husband and wife jointly prior to 1st January 1883,[265] then husband had the same, limited, powers to grant leases out of it, so as to bind his wife after his death, as if it had originally been hers alone.[266] Since the husband and wife were one person, no act of the husband could sever the joint

---

[260] Married Women's Property Act 1882, Ashburner, *Equity*, 236–237. 'Modern statutes have now given to every married woman a power of dealing freely with her property, and this was first evolved amongst the rich by means of marriage settlements': *Pollock & Maitland* vol. 2 403.

[261] s.37 Law of Property Act 1925. See now s.1 Law Reform (Married Women and Tortfeasors) Act 1935.

[262] *Abbot of Bermondsey's Case* (1401) YB 2 Hen.4 f.19 pl.14, (1401) YB 3 Hen.4 f.1 pl.4.

[263] *Grute* v. *Locroft* (1592) Cro Eliz 287.

[264] *Co.Litt.* 46b, 351a, per contra *Thetford* v. *Thetford* (1590) 4 Leon 50, *Viner's Abridgment*, 'Estates' I.a.2 pl.6.

[265] Halsbury's Laws, *Real Property*, vol. 39(2), 4th edn., ¶.227.

[266] But the formalities under the Enabling Act 1540 were less strict: *Smith* v. *Trinder* (1625) Cro Car 22. If the property was a freehold reversion, the husband could sue in his own name on the covenants contained in the lease, or he could sue jointly with his wife: *Brett* v. *Cumberland* (1616) Cro Jac 399.

tenancy, and this was called a 'tenancy by entireties'.[267] It was never clear whether the same prohibition on severance applied to a leasehold estate,[268] though that issue became a dead letter on the enactment of the Married Womens' Property Act 1882.

3. Lease or licence

In the eleventh century, all was clear. A lease for life was a freehold estate with a recognised place in the feudal system, so that a tenant for life had the same rights and legal protection as a fee simple owner. A tenant for a term of years, on the other hand, for all practical purposes, had nothing more than a contract, as had been the case in Roman law. The tenancy created obligations between the parties, but it was not enforceable against anyone else.

Had that simple scheme continued, there would never have been any difference between a lease for a term of years and a contractual licence. They would have amounted to the same thing.

But by the end of the sixteenth century, a lease for a term of years had become what it is now: an estate in land, enforceable against the world by the actions of trespass, nuisance and ejectment,[269] containing promises which are enforceable against successors in title and not simply the original parties.[270]

A licence, by contrast, confers no interest in the land at all. At its least, it was and is a mere permission, turning what would otherwise be a trespass, nuisance or eviction into a lawful act. At its most, it is a contractual right, the benefit of which is assignable by the licensee,[271] but the burden of which is enforceable only against the original contracting party, and

---

[267] *Co.Litt.* 326a, *Doe d. Freestone* v. *Parratt* (1794) 5 Term Rep 652, 654. *Pollock & Maitland,* vol. 2 434.

[268] Challis, *Real Property,* 377.

[269] See ch.9 headings 'Trespass quare clausum fregit', 'Nuisance' and 'Ejectment'.

[270] See ch.6.

[271] *Tolhurst* v. *Associated Portland Cement Manufacturers* [1903] A.C. 414.

nobody else.[272]

That being the difference in effect between a lease and a licence, it ought never to have been very hard to work out whether a particular agreement created a lease or a licence. If the agreement, objectively construed, passed enjoyment and control[273] of the land to the grantee,[274] for a definite time,[275] and was supposed to be binding on the grantor's successors in title, and if it complied with the necessary formalities for the time being,[276] then the parties must have created a lease, even though they might have labelled it as a licence. An agreement which passed enjoyment and control for the time being, but which was not for any definite period, or which was not supposed to be binding on the grantor's successors in title, or which failed to comply with the necessary formalities, created a tenancy at will.[277] An agreement which did not pass enjoyment and control at all created only a licence.[278]

The history of the point is, however, rather more complicated, and the law has inevitably been distorted by two factors: first, by the rule that a lease for a term of years must have a certain term (as to which, see chapter 4)[279] and secondly, by the various social contexts in which the issue has been relevant.

The social problems started with the rules for 'parish

---

[272] *Ashburn* v. *Arnold* [1989] Ch 1. What is sometimes called a 'licence coupled with an interest'—eg. a right to enter land which is ancillary to the exercise of a profit á prendre—is not really a licence at all. It is an appurtenant right which is part of that interest, and is enforceable as such. But see also *Mayor of London* v. *Hall* [2011] 1 WLR 501.

[273] *London and North Western Rly Co* v. *Buckmaster* (1874) LR 10 QB 70, 444, W. Fawcett, *The Law of Landlord and Tenant*, 3rd edn. (London, Butterworths, 1905) 85–86.

[274] So a covenant to 'permit and suffer' enjoyment created a licence: *Tooker* v. *Squire* (1607) 1 Rol Abr 848, 859.

[275] *Hall* v. *Seabright* (1669) 1 Mod. 14, *Right d. Green* v. *Proctor* (1768) 4 Burr 2208, *Jepson* v. *Jackson* (1677) 2 Lev 194.

[276] See ch.1 heading 'Formalities'.

[277] A tenancy at will is not binding on successors in title, because a transfer of the reversion revokes the tenancy at will. See ch.4 heading 'At will'.

[278] *Wells* v. *Kingston upon Hull* (1875) LR 10 CP 402.

[279] Heading 'Fixed terms'.

removal' under the poor rate first levied in 1601.[280] The idea was that the cost of providing for the poor of each parish should fall on the ratepayers of that parish, and parish removal was the process, formalised in 1662,[281] by which someone seeking assistance could be taken back to where he or she had come from, so that the cost would fall on the ratepayers of that parish instead. There was an enormous amount of litigation between parishes about this in the eighteenth and early nineteenth centuries, which all turned on whether the pauper had acquired a 'settlement' in a particular parish or not, the main test of which was 'renting a tenement of ten pounds a year'.[282] So someone paying £10 a year, even under a tenancy at will,[283] would have acquired a settlement in that parish, which could not have been acquired under a licence, no matter how expensive it might have been.[284] Since it was the policy of the Act that parishes should not be able to evade their responsibilities by exporting their poor elsewhere, there was always a temptation for judges to find that short term arrangements, made elsewhere for the purpose of business or employment, amounted to licences rather than tenancies.[285]

The rateable taxation of land also caused tensions on the separate question of who should be liable to contribute towards those rates. The class of rateable occupiers was gradually extended down to 1936, when the House of Lords decided that even a licensee could be rated.[286] In the meantime, short term

---

[280] The Poor Relief Act 1601.

[281] The Poor Relief Act 1662. In theory, by 22 Hen.8 c.12, vagabonds begging without a justice's licence could be whipped, and required to take an oath to return to the place where they were born or had last dwelt for a period of three years.

[282] *Anon* (1703) 6 Mod. 33. The decisions between 1732 and 1776 were collected in Burrows Settlement Cases, a volume of nearly 850 pages.

[283] *Cranley* v. *St Mary, Guildford* (1722) 1 Strange 502.

[284] *R* v. *Inhabitants of Minchinhampton* (1731) 2 Strange 874.

[285] *R* v. *Inhabitants of Tardebigg* (1801) 1 East 528, *R.* v. *Inhabitants of Mellor* (1802) 2 East 189. This is the origin of the 'during and for the more convenient performance of his duties' test for a service occupancy: *R* v. *Inhabitants of Chesunt* (1818) 1 Barn & Ald 475.

[286] *Westminster City Council* v. *Southern Rly Co* [1936] AC 511, 533, [1936] 2 All ER 322, 329.

business agreements[287] and agreements for housing the working classes were generally held to be licences, so that the liability would fall instead on the owner of the property, who was more likely to be able to pay, and against whom enforcement would be easier, in the event of default.[288]

In the twentieth century, the problem usually arose in the context of the Rent Acts. The history of those Acts is explained in detail in chapter 4. The crucial point, for present purposes, is that the protection of those Acts only ever applied to residential premises 'let' as a separate dwelling. Consequently, the protection could not apply to a contractual licensee. In *Lace* v. *Chantler*[289] Lord Greene MR decided that, if the parties to a contract thought they were creating a tenancy, the court had to strike out any terms which were inconsistent with the creation of a tenancy.[290] The court could not find that they had mistakenly created a contractual licence instead. Landlords immediately saw the potential in that argument, and began to say that because they had only ever intended to create a licence, the court could not find that the property was 'let' for the purpose of the Rent Acts. The courts grappled unsatisfactorily with that problem for 40 years. Sometimes the argument succeeded, and sometimes it did not, although judges struggled to offer any principled explanation of the distinction between those cases. The best the leading textbook could say on the subject was:[291]

---

[287] *Watkins* v. *Milton-next-Gravesend Overseers* (1868) LR 3 QB 350 (an exclusive right of mooring, terminable on one month's notice); *London and North Western Rly Co* v. *Buckmaster* (1875) LR 10 QB 444 (use of a stable at a monthly rent); *Rochdale Canal Co* v. *Brewster* [1894] 2 QB 852 (use of a dock determinable on six month's notice).

[288] . . . 'no lodger, though possessing the principal part of the house, was ever rated; but the owner, how small soever the part reserved for himself, is in the eye of the law the tenant of the whole, and is rated as the occupier': per Buller J in *R* v. *Eyles* (1784) Caldecott 407, 414. See also the Poor Relief Act 1819.

[289] [1944] KB 368.

[290] See also *Cobb* v. *Lane* [1952] 1 All ER 1199. Curiously, notwithstanding his adherence to that test, that did not prevent Lord Greene holding, in *Milmo* v. *Carreras* [1946] KB 306, that an underlease for the full term of the lease took effect as an assignment, notwithstanding the parties intended to create an underlease: see ch.2 heading 'Underletting'.

[291] R. Megarry, *The Rent Acts*, 10th edn. (London, Stevens & Sons, 1967) 60.

On one view, if the intention of the grantor, accepted by the grantee, is to create a licence and no tenancy, it would be wrong for the court to extract from the grantor an estate or interest in land in the teeth of the intention of the parties, at all events if the words or documents by which the transaction was effected are apt for a licence and not for a tenancy. On the other hand, if by being sufficiently careful in their drafting and explicit in their refusal to grant tenancies landowners could escape the Acts with ease, the social consequences would be grave. There have hitherto been enough flaws in the drafting or uncertainty in the surrounding circumstances to enable the courts to hold that tenancies have been created in all the reported cases where such a result seemed proper. . . . One day, however, the court will have to meet the challenge of well-drafted licences of a row of suburban villas.

Parliament even legislated on the premise that an agricultural licence could confer exclusive possession.[292]

The House of Lords finally made the point, in *Street* v. *Mountford*,[293] that the legal consequences of an agreement depend upon the objective effect of the terms which the parties have agreed, which are not necessarily the same as the consequences which the parties intended to achieve, with the result that an agreement for the grant of exclusive possession[294] for a term certain creates a tenancy, even if the parties thought that they were creating a licence.

4. Entry and interesse termini

A lease for life, granted before 1926, was a freehold estate, whether it was granted as a commercial lease at a rack rent or as

---

[292] s.2 Agricultural Holdings Act 1948, *Harrison-Broadley* v. *Smith* [1964] 1 WLR 456.

[293] [1985] 1 AC 809, 827.

[294] The term 'exclusive possession' is unfortunate, because 'possession' is, by its very nature, exclusive: 'exclusive enjoyment' would be a better description: M. Wonnacott, *Possession of Land* (Cambridge, Cambridge University Press, 2006) 68.

part of a family arrangement under a strict settlement.[295] As such the grant and completion of the grant were inseparable. Completion of the necessary formalities was, itself, the grant. Before that there was nothing. That was the case whether the grant was made by feoffment[296] and livery of seisin, or by bargain and sale or a covenant to stand seised under the Statute of Uses (1536),[297] or later by a simple deed under s.2 Real Property Act 1845.[298] Anyone in possession of the property under an uncompleted lease for life, even after the intended commencement date, could only be a common law tenant at will,[299] though some judges were willing to hold that a subsequent livery of seisin would amount to a new grant, and save the lease.[300]

A lease for a term of years of a corporeal hereditament,[301] however, could be created in two stages. It could be granted first, and then completed later, by an 'entry'.[302] Except where the lease

---

[295] See ch.4 heading 'For life'.

[296] A feoffment consisted 'simply and solely in the livery of the seisin', although the term was often used to refer to the preliminary charter: Challis, *Real Property*, 397 *et seq*. Technically, a feoffment only referred to a transfer of a fee simple by livery of seisin, 'and yet it is sometimes improperly called a feoffment when an estate of freehold only doth pass' (ie a lease for life): *Co.Litt.* 9a.

[297] F. Bacon, *The Use of the Law* (London, Moore, 1630) 61.

[298] 8 & 9 Vic. c.106.

[299] *Sharp's Case* (1599) 6 Co.Rep 26a. There was an exception where the lease for life was created pursuant to a power which owed its validity to the Statute of Uses (1536): Platt, *Leases*, vol. 1 53, Preston, *Conveyancing*, vol. 2 157.

[300] *Norton on Deeds*, 179. A deed could not be delivered twice. A second delivery would be void: *Perks*, ¶.154, *Stephens* v. *Elliot* (1596) Cro Eliz 484.

[301] A lease of an incorporeal hereditament could only be created by deed, and no 'entry' could be made on an incorporeal right: see below heading 'Leases of incorporeal hereditaments'.

[302] A lease could only be granted by someone who was in actual possession of an estate in the land: *Partridge* v. *Strange* (1553) Plowden 77, 88, *Jennings* v. *Bragge* (1595) Cro Eliz 447, 483, 3 Co.Rep 35a, *Co.Litt.* 214a, D'Anvers, *Abridgment*, vol. 3 165, Chambers, *Leases*, 19–21: 'If, therefore, a disseisee intends to make a lease for years in writing, he cannot deliver it as his deed until after entry and actual possession taken in his name; because if the deed could operate as a lease before entry, the only interest transferred would be a right of entry, which can no more be transferred than a right of action'. See also Coote, *Leases*, 21. A bare right to litigate remains unassignable, but rights of

was granted out of a freehold under the Statute of Uses (1536),[303] an entry by the tenant was necessary in order to complete the grant, and vest the completed lease in the tenant.[304] In the meantime, the grantee only had an 'interesse termini'; for, as Blackstone said: 'A bare lease does not vest any estate in the tenant, but only gives him a right of entry on the tenement (which is called an interest in the term, or interesse termini). But once he has entered, he acquires the estate'.[305]

An interesse termini was less than a legal lease but more than a mere right of entry.[306] It was an assignable legal interest in the land,[307] which the law recognised as a future term, coupled with a right to complete the lease by taking possession,[308] but not yet a full estate in the land.[309] So there was no lease capable of being assigned; only an assignable right to a lease,[310] which bound successors in title.[311]

The rule that an entry was necessary to complete a lease for years had important consequences. First, although the tenant could sue and be sued for debts due under the lease,[312] and on the covenants contained in the lease,[313] before the entry,[314] the tenant

---

entry were made transferable by s.6 Real Property Act 1845 (8 & 9 Vic. c.106). Since an entry was never necessary in order to complete a lease granted under the Statute of Uses (1536), it followed that such a lease could be assigned before an entry too: Coote, *Leases*, 22.

[303] See below.

[304] Littleton, *Tenures*, s.459, *Co.Litt.* 270a, *Bl.Comm.* Bk.II 144, 314. Contractual backdating of the term was always possible: *Mayne* v. *Beak* (1596) Cro Eliz 515, W. West *Simboleograph* (London, Stationers Co., 1610) pt.1 s.430, Coote, *Leases*, 116.

[305] *Bl.Comm.* Bk.II 144.

[306] Holdsworth, *HEL* vol. 7 247, *Viner's Abridgment*, 'Estates' B.b.5, Preston, *Conveyancing*, vol. 2 145.

[307] Hence it would bind a purchaser of the land, even one without notice, in the same way as a legal easement.

[308] *Gillard* v. *Cheshire Lines Committee* (1884) 32 WR 943.

[309] *Doe d. Rawlings* v. *Walker* (1826) 5 Barn & Cr 111, 118.

[310] *Bruerton* v. *Rainsford* (1583) Cro Eliz 15. Similarly, if the tenant entered and was ousted, the tenant could not assign the lease before re-entering (unless the immediate reversion was in the Crown): *Wyngate* v. *Marke* (1592) Cro Eliz 275.

[311] *Saffyn's Case* (1605) 5 Co.Rep 123b.

[312] *Alexander and Dyers' Case* (1589) 2 Leon 99.

[313] There could not be an 'interruption' to the tenant's enjoyment before the tenant had entered. Consequently, there could not be any breach of a landlord's

could not sue third parties whether in ejectment or trespass or nuisance for wrongs committed before the entry.[315] Secondly, it followed that the tenant technically needed to make an entry before bringing an action to be put in possession of the lease, against the landlord.[316]

Thirdly, there could be no reversion upon an interesse termini,[317] so if the landlord purported to release the reversion to the tenant before the tenant had entered, the release had no effect[318] other than as a release of the rent.[319]

Fourthly, a concurrent lease for years could not be completed without the co-operation of the prior tenant, for the concurrent tenant could not make an actual entry on the land whilst it was occupied by the prior tenant, and a notional entry could only be made if the prior tenant chose to attorn[320] to the concurrent tenant,[321] or allowed the concurrent tenant to enter 'saving his right' under the prior lease.[322] The tenant attorned by

---

covenant for quiet enjoyment before the tenant had entered: *Wallis* v. *Hands* [1893] 2 Ch 75, 85–86.

[314] *Cook* v. *Harris* (1698) 1 Ld.Raym 367, *Bellasis* v. *Burbriche* (1696) 1 Salk 209.

[315] *Scrope* v. *Hyk* (1511) 2 Caryll's Reps 116 SS 618, *Wheeler* v. *Montefiore* (1841) 2 QB 133, *Wallis* v. *Hands* [1893] 2 Ch 75, cf. *Gillard* v. *Cheshire Lines Committee* (1884) 32 WR 943. See also ch.5 heading 'Title and quiet enjoyment'.

[316] M.Bacon, *A Treatise on Leases* (London, A.Strahan, 1798) 183. In *Williams* v. *Bosenquet* (1819) 1 Brod & Bing 238, 245 Holroyd. J said that although an entry was necessary in order to bring an action in quare ejecit infra terminum, the fictions in the action of ejectment firmæ had done away with that. The point that he was making was that the real defendant, in an action in ejectment, was obliged to admit the notional claimant's entry, and the validity of the lease to the notional claimant, as a condition of being allowed to defend the action at all: see ch.9 heading 'Ejectment'.

[317] Littleton, *Tenures*, s.459, Challis, *Real Property* , 409.

[318] The covenants could, however, be released (*Co.Litt.* 270b) and the holder of the interesse termini could release it to the landlord before entry: *Doe d. Rawlings* v. *Walker* (1826) 5 Barn & Cr 111.

[319] *Co.Litt.* 270a.

[320] *Jones* v. *Weaver* (1556) Dyer 117b, *Bishop of Rochester's Case* (1572) 3 Leon 17.

[321] *Rawlyn's Case* (1587) 4 Rep 52a, 53b, *Edwards* v. *Wickwar* (1866) LR 1 Eq 403. The tenant of a reversionary lease could not attorn until it fell into possession: (1587) Gouldsborough 57 13.

[322] (1536/7) Brook's New Cases pl.97, Dyer 362, J.Lightwood, *Possession of Land* (London, Stevens, 1894) 31–32.

saying or doing anything which recognised the substitution of the new landlord.[323]

The Statute of Uses (1536)[324] solved all of those difficulties, except the first,[325] for leases created by deed out of a freehold estate.[326] In those circumstances, the interesse termini could be granted by bargain and sale,[327] or a covenant to stand seised to the use of the grantee, and turned into a legal lease, without an entry, at the election of the grantee.[328] The statute performed this useful conveyancing trick, because it deemed a grant made out of a freehold 'to the use of ' someone else, to be a grant of a legal estate to that person. It 'executed' the use,[329] so that, in the case of a lease granted out of a freehold, it was automatically a full lease without an entry.

The fourth problem was solved, for other cases, in 1705,[330] when the need for an attornment was abolished by statute, and even before then, it was sometimes possible to obtain an order in

---

[323] 'The most common attornment' was 'to say, Sir, I attorne to you by force of the said grant, or I become your tenant etc or to deliver to the grantee a penny, or a half-penny or a farthing, by way of attornment': Littleton, *Tenures*, s.551, s.567. For a memorandum of an attornment, see O. Bridgman, *Precedents of Conveyances* (London, Atkins, 1702) vol. 2 57.

[324] *Halsbury's Statutes*, 2nd edn., vol. 20 365–368. It was reproduced in Ireland by the Statute of Uses (1634) sess.2 c.1 (Ir).

[325] See *Lutwich* v. *Mitton* (1620) Cro Jac 604.

[326] Maitland, *Equity*, 37–38. Accordingly, it did not solve the problem where a tenant for years granted an underlease, because a tenancy for years was not a freehold estate, and so there was no seisin upon which the statutory magic could work.

[327] At common law, a mere bargain and sale could not convey a legal estate. But courts of equity took a different view, and under their maxim of considering that as done which ought to be done, they held that the vendor merely held to the use of the purchaser: B. Adkin, *Copyhold and Other Land Tenures* (London, Estates Gazette, 1907) 38.

[328] That applied even if the lease was granted at a peppercorn rent: *Barker* v. *Keete* (1677) 1 Freeman 249.

[329] *Iseham* v. *Morrice* (1628) Cro Car 109, 110. See per Neville J in *Mann, Crossman and Paulin* v. *Land Registry* [1918] 1 Ch 202, 207. See also F.Bacon, *The Use of the Law* (London, Moore, 1630) 61, Halsbury's Law, *Real Property* , 4th edn. vol. 39(2), ¶.20–21.

[330] s.9 Administration of Justice Act 1705. This provision appears to have been overlooked in *Edwards* v. *Wickwar* (1866) LR 1 Eq 403.

equity requiring a tenant to attorn.[331]

In 1926, the doctrine of interesse termini was itself abolished,[332] and since then, an entry has not been required in order to complete any lease.[333]

5. Registration

Although the doctrine of interesse termini has been abolished, there is now a very similar principle which applies to all leases which are registrable under the Land Registration Act 2002, which currently means all leases granted for a term of more than 7 years.[334] Between grant and registration, a registrable lease takes effect only in equity,[335] registration being retrospective to the date that the effective application to register the lease was lodged at the Land Registry, and not the date of grant.

It was the Land Registry Act 1862,[336] which first experimented with making the register itself the title to land. Previous registration schemes worked by requiring anyone taking an interest in land under an instrument to make a note of that instrument on a central, searchable register, or else risk losing priority to anyone taking under a later grant.[337] The theory

---

[331] *Philips* v. *Stanford* (1579) Cary 3, *Shute* v. *Mallory* (1607) Moore 805.

[332] s.149(1) Law of Property Act 1925.

[333] s.149(2) ibid.

[334] s.4 Land Registration Act 2002.

[335] s.34 Land Transfer Act 1875, s.22(1) Land Registration Act 1925.

[336] For Ireland, see the Local Registration of Title (Ireland) Act 1891, 54 & 55 Vic. c.66.

[337] The traditional view is that the Statute of Enrolments 1536 required registration of all conveyances of freeholds by bargain and sale for a different reason: it was so that the Crown would know who the current owner was, in order that feudal dues would be paid. It may be, however, that it was merely intended as a means of distinguishing indentures which would take effect as executory contracts from those which would take effect as conveyances: J. Kaye, *A Note on the Statute of Enrolments* (1988) 104 LQR 617, 633. The sanction for non registration was to make the conveyance void for the purpose of conveying a legal estate (that is, it could only take effect as a contract). But it quickly became a dead letter, as other methods of conveyance were adopted, which were not within the statute, and it was eventually repealed by sch.10 Law of Property (Amendment) Act 1924. See ch.7 heading 'Enlargement'.

was that anyone dealing with one of those parties later should either be able to discover the transaction by conducting a search against that person's name, or should otherwise take free of it.[338] That scheme had been adopted in 1663 when the Bedford levels were drained;[339] an anonymous pamphlet 'Reasons for a Registry', containing Sir Matthew Hale's proposals,[340] suggested that it should be adopted more widely in 1678; and it was adopted in Middlesex[341] between 1708 and 1936, and in parts of Yorkshire[342] from 1704 until as late as 1970.[343] The scheme was only abandoned in those counties as they became compulsory registration areas under the Land Registration Act 1925.[344]

Whilst it survived, the grant of a lease of land within those counties for a term of 21 years or more was registrable under those Acts, with the sanction of a loss of priority for non-compliance.[345]

Under the newer, and now universal, system of registration beginning with the Land Registry Act 1862, the register is itself the title, and takes the place the pre-registration deeds. Initially,

---

[338] That leads to the problem of what do with the purchaser who knows about an unregistered transaction. In the Yorkshire and Middlesex Registries, the doctrine of notice applied; *Le Neve* v. *Le Neve* (1748) 3 Atk 646. That rule was reversed in Yorkshire by the Yorkshire Registries Act 1884. Frederick Pollock thought that this made the Middlesex Registry 'worse than useless', F. Pollock, *The Land Laws*, 175.

[339] The Bedford Level Act 1663 required leases for seven years or more relating to land in the Bedford level to be registered, the consequence of non-registration being to deprive the land owner of the priority and privileges granted by the Act, rather than to make the lease void between the parties: *Hodson* v. *Sharpe* (1808) 10 East 350, *Willis* v. *Brown* (1839) 10 Sim 127.

[340] Registry of London (1756) L.I. Pamphlets vol. 24, W. Holdsworth, *The Reform of Land Law, An Historical Retrospect* (1926) 42 LQR 158. See also P. Hamburger, *The Conveyancing Purposes of the Statute of Frauds* (1983) 27 Am. J. Legal.. Hist. 354.

[341] The Middlesex Registry Act 1708.

[342] 2 & 3 Anne c.4 (1703), 6 Anne c.35 (1707), Yorkshire Registries Act 1884.

[343] It was also adopted in Ireland by the Registry of Deeds Act 1707, 6 Anne c.2 (Ir).

[344] S.1 Middlesex Deeds Act 1940, s.17 (1) Law of Property Act 1969. See also J. Howell, *Deeds Registration in England: A Complete Failure?* (1999) 58 CLJ 366.

[345] Registering an assignment of the lease was not good enough: *Honeycomb ex d. Halpern* v.*Waldron* (1736) 2 Strange 1064.

the Act was a complete failure. Registration was entirely voluntary, and depended on proving an unimpeachable 60-year root of title to every square inch of the land. Not surprisingly,[346] as a Royal Commission appointed to inquire into its failure reported in 1870, almost nobody registered[347] and the Land Registry was an office of sinecures.[348] The Commission's recommendations resulted in the Land Transfer Act 1875, which virtually repealed the 1862 Act,[349] which was, in turn, supplemented by a further Act of 1897, and which was then consolidated, with amendments, in the Land Registration Act 1925.

At first, the 1875 Act was as much of a failure as the 1862 Act, because registration remained entirely voluntary. But the 1897 Act changed that. Starting in London between 1899 and 1902,[350] over the next ninety years, registration became compulsory, throughout the whole of England and Wales, county by county.[351] Where unregistered land was within a compulsory registration area, the obligation to register arose on the next substantial dealing with it, with the sanction that the transfer would be ineffective as a disposition of the legal estate until it was registered.

Under the 1875 and 1925 Acts, the grant of a lease for a term of 21 years or more, and the assignment of a lease where 21 years or more of the term remained unexpired, were both sufficiently substantial dealings to require registration of the lease.[352] A lease for life or lives was also registrable under the

---

[346] 'It seemed the more prudent part to let sleeping lions alone': F.Pollock, *The Land Laws*, 173.

[347] J. Stuart Anderson, *Lawyers and the Making of English Land Law 1832–1940* (Oxford, Clarendon Press, 1992) 112–113.

[348] F. Pollock, *The Land Laws*, 173.

[349] The 1862 Act was finally repealed by s.135 Land Registration Act 2002.

[350] C. Fortescue-Brickdale and J. Stewart-Wallace, *The Land Registration Act 1925*, 3rd edn. (London, Stevens, 1927) 49–52.

[351] Eastbourne was next after London, in 1926, then Hastings and Middlesex followed in 1926 and 1928: J. Stewart-Wallace, *Introduction to the Principles of Land Registration* (London, Stevens, 1937) 30–31. The last surviving outposts of the unregistered system fell on 1st December 1990: Registration of Title Order 1989 (SI 1989 No.1347).

[352] s.11 Land Transfer Act 1875, s.8(1) Land Registration Act 1925.

1875 Act,[353] but a lease containing an absolute prohibition on assignment remained unregisterable before 1st January 1987,[354] even if the landlord had waived the covenant and allowed an assignment.

Leases for shorter terms granted at a rent without taking fine were overriding interests, and accordingly were not registrable.[355] Unregistered leases could be protected by actual occupation,[356] or entry of a notice or caution on the register. But a mortgage term[357] could not be registered as lease. It could only be registered as a legal charge.

It has not been possible to create a mortgage term since 13th October 2003, when the Land Registration Act 2002 came into force. A mortgage term automatically takes effect as a charge by way of legal mortgage.[358]

That Act also reduced the minimum length of the term necessary before a lease becomes registrable. All leases of more than seven years are now registrable.[359]

6. Equitable leases

A lease might be equitable, rather than legal, for one of two reasons.

The first reason might be that, although there is a specifically enforceable contract to grant a legal lease, the contract has not yet been completed.

In that situation, prior to the Judicature Acts 1873 to 1894, the contract would have been treated as unperformed for the purpose of determining the parties' status and rights in a common law court, but as having already been completed, for

---

[353] A lease for life became a defeasible lease for a term of 90 years when the 1925 Act came into force: see ch.4 heading 'For life'.

[354] s.11, 12 Land Transfer Act 1875; s.8(2) Land Registration Act 1925.

[355] s.18 Land Registration Act 1875, s.70(1)(k) Land Registration Act 1925.

[356] s.70(1)(g) Land Registration Act 1925.

[357] See ch.2 heading 'Mortgages as leases and of leases'.

[358] Ibid.

[359] s.4.

the purpose of determining the parties' status and rights in a court of equity, if and for so long as the person relying on the equitable right remained entitled to obtain a decree that the contract be performed specifically. Equity treated whatever it would have ordered a party to do, as having already been done, whereas common law courts ignored equity entirely.

So, in the case of a specifically enforceable contract to grant a lease, for the purpose of determining common law rights, in a common law court, the parties would be treated as if they were not yet landlord and tenant, whereas in a court of equity, the parties would be treated as if they were already landlord and tenant under the lease. The result was that unlike equitable rights, common law rights which depended on an existing relationship of landlord and tenant (for example, the right of distress) could not be enforced before the lease had actually been granted, whether voluntarily or under the compulsion of a decree for specific performance.

That, however, was changed by the Judicature Acts 1873 to 1894. As Jordan C.J. explained in *Dockrill* v. *Cavanagh:*[360]

> After the passing in England of the Judicature Acts, which invested the superior courts with jurisdiction in both equity and common law, it was held that in a court which possessed the combined jurisdictions (although not in a court which had only a common law jurisdiction: *Foster* v. *Reeves* [1892] 2 QB 255), a party to an agreement for a lease, if the lease was specifically enforceable (but not if it was not; *Coatsworth* v. *Johnson* (1886) 54 LT 520; *Inland Revenue Commissioners v. Derby* [1914] 3 KB 1186), could obtain against the other all the remedies which would be available to him if a proper lease had actually been executed: *Walsh* v. *Lonsdale* (1882) 21 Ch.D 9, although the agreement was not thereby converted into an actual lease: *Borman* v. *Griffith* [1930] 1 Ch 493, at pp 497–498.

The second reason why a lease might be equitable, rather than legal, is that it might be a lease of property which exists only in equity. It might, for instance, be a lease of a beneficial interest under a trust. This is not a true lease at all, because an

---

[360] (1944) 45 SR (NSW) 78, 83.

interest under a trust is not a hereditament, and legal rights cannot subsist in equitable property. Consequently, covenants could not run with the term or the reversion under an equitable lease. But from the mid-nineteenth century onwards, the law of estoppel prevented either party from alleging that a lease had been granted out of an equitable interest, unless that had been revealed beforehand,[361] and it may now be that the law of estoppel prevents that even where the equitable title of the grantor has been disclosed.[362]

7. Leases of incorporeal hereditaments

A hereditament is 'corporeal' if it was capable of being conveyed by livery of seisin at common law. All other hereditaments, which could only be granted by deed (in some cases, followed by an attornment)[363] were 'incorporeal'.[364] Since livery of seisin required a physical delivery of the land, it follows that the distinction is broadly between those interests in land which are capable of physical enjoyment and those which are not.[365]

An incorporeal hereditament has always been regarded as a 'tenement',[366] like corporeal land, which could therefore be leased or sub-leased.[367]

Since an incorporeal hereditament could not be conveyed by livery of seisin, but only by deed, it followed that a lease of an incorporeal hereditament could only be granted or assigned by

---

[361] *Oxford History of the Laws of England*, vol. 12 129–130.

[362] *Bruton* v. *London & Quadrant Housing Trust* [2000] 1 AC 406, cf. *Ministry of Agriculture and Fisheries* v. *Matthews* [1950] 1 KB 148, Platt, *Covenants*, 461–462.

[363] See ch.6.

[364] *Co.Litt.* 9a. Sweet's note in Challis, *Real Property*, 51, Holdsworth, *HEL* vol. 7 812–818.

[365] In Scotland, symbolic livery of incorporeal rights was possible: K.Reid with ors., *The Law of Property in Scotland* (Edinburgh, LexisNexis UK, 1996) ¶.90. In England, that was impossible: *Pannell* v. *Hodgson* (1576) Cary 52.

[366] *Co.Litt.* 19b, 20a, 154a.

[367] Coote, *Leases*, 14.

deed too; and, there being no physical thing which could be entered upon, no entry was necessary to complete it.[368]

Consequently leases of tithes,[369] tolls,[370] profits,[371] rights of common,[372] manors,[373] and ferries[374] have all been treated as being valid, if created by deed, but not otherwise. A rent, however, could not be reserved, as such, on the grant of an incorporeal hereditament before 1926.[375]

Leases of advowsons (a right to present a priest to a church) were prohibited by s.1 Benefices Act 1898.

Leases of public offices were void at common law,[376] unless the duties of the officer holder were purely administrative;[377] and even then, administrative offices which were connected with the courts could not be let for longer than the life of the tenant.[378] The objection to longer leases was that the duties attached to the office might go unperformed, in the gap between the tenant's death and the grant of probate or letters of administration.[379]

A reversion upon a lease looks a lot like an incorporeal

---

[368] *Bl.Comm.* Bk.III 206.

[369] *Anon* (1494) Caryll's Reps 115 SS 219, *Bally* v. *Wells* (1769) 3 Wils 25, *The Compleat Clerk*, 3rd edn. (London, Place, 1671) 749, O. Bridgman, Conveyances, 3rd edn. (London, Atkins, 1699) vol. 1 240. At common law, leases of tithes could only be granted for the life of the grantor (because the grantor only had a life interest in the tithe) but by 5 Geo.3 c.17 power was granted to make a lease of tithes for three lives in being or 21 years. The Tithe Acts 1836 to 1891 provided for the conversion of tithes into rent charges: see generally L. Shelford, *The Acts for the Commutation of Tithes*, 3rd edn. (London, Sweet, 1842). Tithes were a tenement at common law: *R* v. *Skingle* (1718) 1 Strange 100.

[370] *Egrmont* v. *Keene* (1837) 2 Jones Ir Ex 307.

[371] *Martyn* v. *Williams* (1857) 1 H&N 817, *Hooper* v. *Clark* (1867) LR 2 QB 200.

[372] *Sury* v. *Brown* (1623) Latch 99.

[373] *Gibson* v. *Searls* (1605) Cro Jac 84, 176.

[374] *R* v. *Nicholson* (1810) 12 East 330.

[375] *Jewel's Case* (1588) 5 Co.Rep 3a, Coote, *Leases*, 126, s.201 Law of Property Act 1925.

[376] *Meade* v. *Lenthall* (1640) Cro Car 587.

[377] *Sir George Reynel's Case* (1612) 9 Co.Rep 95a, 97a, *Veale* v. *Priour* (1665) Hard 351. See M. Bacon, *A Treatise on Leases* (London, Strahan, 1798) 8–9. The office of Marshal of the Marshalsea, and every inferior office in that prison, was made inalienable by 27 Geo.2 c.17 (1754).

[378] *The Case of Sutton, Marshal of the Court* (1703) 6 Mod. 57.

[379] M. Bacon, *A Treatise on Leases* (London, Strahan, 1798) 8.

hereditament, and there are certainly many statements in the books that it can only be conveyed by deed.[380] But it is, in law, a corporeal hereditament.[381] Otherwise, it would not have been possible to reserve a rent on the grant of a concurrent lease.[382] The reason why a deed was generally necessary had nothing to do with the supposed incorporeality of the reversion.[383] It was about the practical problem of conveying a freehold reversion by livery of seisin, or completing the grant of a concurrent lease by entry, when a tenant was already in occupation. Seisin could not be delivered, and an entry could not be made, without interfering with the rights of the tenant.[384] But if the tenant attorned, a deed was unnecessary;[385] and a tenant could agree to give up possession, for a moment, so that livery could take place, 'saving his own right'.[386]

Technically, an easement should never have been treated as an incorporeal hereditament either, for an easement is not an independent hereditament at all. It is a right which is appurtenant to a hereditament, whether corporal or not.[387] That is why an

---

[380] *Co.Litt.* 338a: 'yet because remainders and reversions, though they be of lands, are things that lie in grant, they cannot be surrendered without a deed'. F. Bacon, *The Use of the Law* (London, Moore, 1630) 60, Gilbert, *Rents*, 23–24, cf. *Butt's Case* (1600) 7 Co.Rep 23a, which acknowledges that a corporeal hereditament might exist 'in possession, reversion or possibility'. See also *Bl.Comm.* Bk.II 317.

[381] Challis, *Real Property*, 52–53 (a note by Sweet).

[382] At common law, a rent could not be reserved on the grant of a lease of an incorporeal hereditament: *Jewel's Case* (1588) 5 Co.Rep 3a, Holdsworth, *HEL* vol. 7 265–266. The rule was reversed by s.201 Law of Property Act 1925.

[383] The reason why so many writers treat a reversion as an incorporeal hereditament is the fact that it could be conveyed by deed followed by an attornment at common law. But a corporeal hereditament could be conveyed by a deed (a charter of feoffment) followed by livery of seisin, and an attornment was simply a substitute for the livery. So it was the attornment, not the deed, which did all the work. Attornment 'doe countervaile in law a feoffment by livery': *Co.Litt.* 315b.

[384] Littleton, *Tenures*, s.567, J. Lightwood, *Possession of Land* (London, Stevens, 1894) 31.

[385] *Anon* (1537) Dyer 33a, *Co.Litt.* 48b, Littleton, *Tenures*, s.60, Challis, *Real Property*, 52–53 (a note by Sweet).

[386] J. Lightwood, *Possession of Land* (London, Stevens, 1894) 31–32.

[387] S. Sweet, *The True Nature of an Easement* (1908) 24 LQR 259.

easement can be appurtenant to an incorporeal hereditament, without infringing the rule that incorporeal hereditaments cannot be appurtenant to each other.[388] But Blackstone mistakenly included private rights of way amongst his list of incorporeal hereditaments,[389] and easements have been treated as such ever since. That has produced some strange results, including the rule that an easement can be let,[390] even though it can only be enjoyed in connection with the estate to which it is appurtenant.

8. Prescriptive rights

Unlike adverse possession, which is founded on wrongful enjoyment of land, prescription is based on user as if of right. The long failure to complain about acts, which would otherwise be actionable by a land owner as trespasses or nuisances, is the evidential foundation from which the court concludes that the then owner of the land must have granted away the right to do those acts at some time in the past.

Originally, the evidence had to show use since time immemorial, meaning since the accession of Richard I in 1189.[391] In practice, that meant the only way in which a leasehold tenant could claim the benefit of a prescriptive right was if the right had already been vested in the owner of the fee[392] prior to the grant of the lease, and the landlord had let the right to the tenant along with the property demised by the lease.[393] No prescriptive right could be claimed by virtue only of use under a lease granted after 1189, for the later commencement of the lease would disprove the claim of use back to 1189.

In the mid eighteenth century, however, common law

---

[388] *Hanbury* v. *Jenkins* [1901] 2 Ch 422. Reversed by s.201 Law of Property Act 1925.

[389] *Bl.Comm.* Bk.II 35.

[390] *Land Reclamation* v. *Basildon Council* [1979] 1 WLR 767.

[391] The date was fixed by analogy with the period of limitation fixed for a writ of right: Simpson, *History of Land Law*, 103.

[392] *Baker* v. *Brereman* (1635) Cro Car 418.

[393] *Symonds* v. *Seabourne* (1633) Cro Car 325.

courts[394] relaxed the rule that someone claiming a right under a deed which was not in the possession of the opposing party, nor in court, nor rightfully in the possession of a third party,[395] had to produce it. The courts, instead, allowed secondary evidence to be given of the contents of lost deeds.[396] From there, it was a small step from directing a jury that a relevant post 1189 deed might have been lost,[397] to the 'revolting fiction'[398] that, after 20 years

---

[394] Evidence of the contents of lost deeds could be given in equity by filing an affidavit of loss: *Walmsley* v. *Child* (1749) 1 Ves Sen 341, 345, *Whitfield* v. *Fausset* (1750) 1 Ves Sen 387, 392, Holdsworth, *HEL* vol. 7 346. So in *Collet* v. *Jacques* (1669) 1 Ch.Cas 120 a claim for payment of rent succeeded in equity, even though the deeds had been lost and the claimant could not prove what sort of rent it was, or even what its origin had been.

[395] *The Grounds and Rudiments of Law and Equity*, 2nd edn. (London, Osborne, 1751) 20. If the original was lost, but the other party had a counterpart, an order could be made for production of the counterpart: *Anon* (1617) Cro Jac 429.

[396] *Read* v. *Bookman* (1789) 3 Term Rep 151, 156. Per Lord Kenyon: 'It is not a very pleasant thing for a court of law to say that it cannot administer justice on legal titles because they are fettered by certain forms'. This might, perhaps, explain a curiosity, namely, the 'custom' of London, allowing rebuilding to any height within the footprint of ancient foundations (*Plummer* v. *Bentham* (1757) 1 Burr 247). In 1189, the rule was that nobody could claim a right to light in London, except by showing a written grant (Fitz-Ailwyn's Assize of Buildings, 1189). In 1569 this was the custom of London (*Hale's Case* in J. Baker and S. Milsom, *Sources of English Legal History*, 2nd edn. (Oxford, Oxford University Press, 2009) 652–657) but the custom was held to be unlawful in the *Case of the City of London* (circa 1610) Calthorpe 1. The same case decided that, as a matter of general law, rebuilding within the footprint of ancient foundations could never be an actionable infringement with a right to light, irrespective of the height of the new building, which is not the law now. The Fire Courts, established after the fire of London in 1666, to regulate rebuilding and settle disputes, of necessity were obliged to act on informal evidence about property rights (M. Cooper, *Robert Hooke and the Rebuilding of London* (Sutton, Stroud, 2003) 137, 158). In cases where nothing at all had ever been built on an otherwise valuable development plot, it would have been easy to conclude that development must have been prohibited by a burned deed (Holdsworth, *HEL* vol. 7 346). But in cases where the land had previously been developed, it would have been much harder to infer the existence of a deed preventing redevelopment to a greater height, simply from the absence of previous redevelopment. So by 1757 the 'custom' had become what the general law had been in 1610, and the original rule had been lost.

[397] *Price* v. *Lewis* (1761) 2 Wms. Saunders 175n, *Darwin* v. *Upton* (1786) 2 Wms. Saunders 175n. Sometimes, the deed really has been lost. The author was

of otherwise unexplained use, the jury must find as a fact that the right had been granted by a lost deed more than 20 years ago, even when there was no evidence that was the case.[399]

Under this doctrine of lost modern grant, it was possible for one leasehold tenant to prescribe against another. The jury could find that the lost grant had been made by one leasehold tenant to another,[400] so that the benefit of the right and its burden could both be annexed to leasehold estates, and not affect the reversions at all. But, in 1834, Parke B expressed the view that this was no longer possible in *Bright* v. *Walker*,[401] probably because he thought, wrongly, that the doctrine of lost modern grant had been abolished entirely by the Prescription Act 1832. Although his comment was only obiter, and was ultimately disregarded in Ireland,[402] in England his dictum was followed in 1893[403] and now represents the law.[404]

Subject to a later exception for rights to light, *Bright* v. *Walker* also decided that prescription under the 1832 Act was only possible by and against the fee too, which had the following consequences where either tenement was let during the prescription period.

First, any use of the dominant tenement by a leaseholder is deemed to have been use for and on behalf of the ultimate fee simple owner, so that any prescriptive easement acquired by that use attaches to the fee simple and all derivative estates, and not the lease alone. Secondly, use by a leaseholder at a time when the ultimate fee in both tenements is held by the same person, cannot be the evidential basis of a prescriptive grant; for a fee simple owner cannot, by someone else's act, acquire a right against himself or herself. Consequently, a leasehold tenant cannot prescribe against its own landlord: if the landlord has a

---

once instructed in a 'lost modern grant' claim, which was compromised when a a relevant deed containing the necessary grant was found shortly before the trial.

[398] Per Lush J in *Dalton* v. *Angus* (1877) 3 QBD 85, 94.

[399] *Dalton* v. *Angus* (1881) 6 App.Cas. 740.

[400] Per Parke B in *Bright* v. *Walker* (1834) 1 CM & R 211, 218.

[401] Ibid.

[402] *Hanna* v. *Pollock* [1900] 2 IR 664.

[403] *Wheaton* v. *Maple & Co* [1893] 3 Ch 48. See also V. Delaney, *Lessees and the Doctrine of Lost Modern Grant* (1958) 74 LQR 82.

[404] *Simmons* v. *Dobson* [1991] 1 WLR 720.

leasehold estate, that is made impossible by the first rule; if the landlord has a freehold estate, that is made impossible by the second.[405] Thirdly, prescriptive use cannot commence at a time when the servient tenement is let. The prescription clock does not start ticking until that lease falls in,[406] except where the use is for forty years, and the use is not resisted within three years of the expiry of the lease.[407]

Rights to light are an exception to the rule that prescriptive easements can only be acquired by and on behalf of the fee, and to its consequences, for no good reason other than that the Exchequer Chamber so decided in 1861,[408] and the House of Lords held in 1907[409] that it was already too late to overrule the exception.[410]

In the meantime, it had already become common practice to include a covenant in a lease requiring the tenant to take steps to prevent third parties acquiring prescriptive rights against the landlord, by requiring them to report all encroachments, and join with the landlord in taking steps to prevent their acquisition. Such covenants are still commonly found in leases today, notwithstanding that, except in the case of rights to light, the landlord cannot be prejudiced by a use which commences during the term of the lease, unless it continues for 40 years and the landlord does not resist it within three years of the lease falling in.

It also became common practice to deal with the problems with rights to light by including provisions in the lease designed to ensure that the tenant would not be able to claim any right over the landlord's adjoining or neighbouring property. Broadly, two different techniques were and are used.

The first is to provide in the lease that the enjoyment of light over that property should be taken as being with the landlord's

---

[405] *Gayford* v. *Moffat* (1868) LR 4 Ch App 133.

[406] *Barker* v. *Richardson* (1821) 4 Barn & Ald 579. This includes the *scintilla temporis* between a surrender and re-grant.

[407] s.8 Prescription Act 1832.

[408] *Frewen* v. *Philips* (1861) 11 CB (NS) 449.

[409] *Morgan* v. *Fear* [1907] AC 425.

[410] An interference with a right to light was not originally actionable at common law at all, unless it was enjoinable in equity: *Attorney-General* v. *Nichol* (1809) 16 Ves 338, Ashburner, *Equity*, 472.

revocable consent. That works between the original parties, but it is hard to see how that provision can run with the term or the reversion. So time will start to run after the first transfer of either.

The second is for the landlord to reserve a right to build so as to interfere with any right of right of light or air as an easement out of the lease. That technique works well enough where the neighbouring land is owned by the landlord at the time of the lease, and it can be granted in favour of neighbouring land owned by third parties. But it cannot be granted in favour of such neighbouring land as the landlord might acquire in the future, for the identity of the dominant tenement has to be fixed at the date of grant.[411]

---

[411] *Voice* v. *Bell* (1993) 68 P&CR 441.

CHAPTER 2
Derivative Interests

1. Underletting

2. Reversionary leases

3. Concurrent leases

4. Mortgages as leases and of leases

5. Options and break rights

1. Underletting

An underlease is a lease which has, itself, been granted out of a lease.

A lease for life could never be granted out of a lease for a term of years, for a lease for life was a freehold estate, and a freehold estate could not be created out of leasehold tenure.[1] Nor could a lease for life be granted out of another lease for life, because freehold estates could only be granted in succession to each other.

There is also a well-established, if unsatisfactory and inconsistently applied, rule that a tenant for a fixed term cannot create a co-terminus or longer underlease, and that any attempt to do so automatically operates as an assignment of the tenant's

---

[1] Preston, *Conveyancing*, vol. 2 124. It might, however, have been valid between the parties as a contract: Coote, *Leases*, 32. For the implied right of forfeiture, where a tenant threatens the landlord's title, see ch.7 heading, 'Forfeiture'.

lease, and not as an underlease;[2] albeit an assignment which (as between the parties to it) is subject to all the covenants and conditions[3] contained in the purported underlease.[4]

The rule that a co-terminus or longer underletting automatically takes effect as an assignment never applied to an underletting by a tenant for life, even if the underlease was for 1000 years.[5] Nor does it apply to an underletting by a periodic tenant. A periodic tenant is able grant an underlease of whatever length he or she chooses,[6] which will continue as an underlease until the periodic tenancy comes to an end.[7] The rule has only ever applied where the underlease is purportedly granted out of a lease which was granted for a fixed term.

The supposed rational for the rule is that every lease must be granted so as to have a reversion. On expiry, it must fall back into the estate out of which it was carved,[8] for if there is no reversion, no 'rent' can be reserved on it.[9] But this ignores the

---

[2] It is not clear what happens in the case of a parol grant, which would have been valid as an underlease, being for less than three years and at a market rent, but which is void as an assignment (s.52, s.54(2) Law of Property Act 1925).

[3] *Baynes* v. *Lloyd* [1895] 1 QB 820.

[4] *Milmo* v. *Carreras* [1946] KB 306, *Grosvenor Estates* v. *Cochran* [1991] 2 EGLR 83.

[5] *Derby* v. *Taylor* (1801) 1 East 502, *Oxley* v. *James* (1844) 13 M&W 209.

[6] *Mackay* v. *Mackreth* (1785) 4 Doug 213, *Pike* v. *Eyre* (1829) 9 Barn & Cr 909, *Curtis* v. *Wheeler* (1830) Moo & M 493, *Oxley* v. *James* (1844) 13 M&W 209. In *William Skelton* v. *Harrison & Pinder* [1975] 1 QB 361 Judge Fay QC applied the periodic tenancy exception to a case where a business tenant for a fixed term had underlet part of the premises for a longer term, on the basis that, since the underletting was only of part, it was possible that the whole head-tenancy would be continued beyond the term date by the Landlord and Tenant Act 1954.

[7] At common law, the underlease will end at that same time. Some statutory provisions continue the underlease as against the head-landlord afterwards; eg. s.137 Rent Act 1977 (introduced by s.15(3) Landlord and Tenant Act 1954, overturning *Knightsbridge Estates* v. *Deeley* [1950] 2 KB 228), s.18 Housing Act 1988, s.24 Landlord and Tenant Act 1954.

[8] Platt, *Leases*, vol. 1 9–19, Preston, *Conveyancing,* vol. 2 124.

[9] Per Palles CB in *Ireland* v. *Landy* (1888) 22 LR Ir 403, 416. In *Langford* v. *Symes* (1857) 3 K & J 220, 228, Page-Wood VC said: 'The reason that a termor is a reversioner, where he has sub-let for a part only of his term, is that he has had the interest of the reversioner, that is of the freeholder, still in him during the rest of his term'.

fact that the immediate 'reversion' upon a lease is the estate into which it would merge, if the lease were to be determined today, and not the estate into which it might be expected to fall at the end of the term.[10] Otherwise it would be impossible to create a concurrent lease for a shorter fixed term than an existing lease,[11] or to surrender an existing lease to a shorter concurrent tenant; and it is not, and never has been,[12] the law that those things are impossible. Furthermore, a person without any title at all can create a lease, which is valid as a lease between the parties and their privies for all purposes by estoppel.[13] It is hard to think of any rational reason why an instrument, which would take effect between the parties as a lease at a particular rent, if the landlord had no title at all, should automatically make the grantee the tenant of an entirely different lease, at a different rent and on different terms, simply because the grantor happened to be the tenant of someone else for a shorter fixed term at the time of the grant. That is particularly so given that the grantee may have been told nothing about the landlord's title when accepting the 'lease', and had no way of finding out about it.

So there ought never to have been any conceptual problem in saying that a tenant who had purported to grant a co-terminus or longer underlease had retained a reversion.

In truth, the rule is simply an example of how the doctrine of precedent can produce bad law out of an unfortunate series of mistakes and misunderstandings.[14] Land law is particularly susceptible to this because those who deal with property rights have traditionally put a particularly high value on certainty and precedent.[15]

---

[10] The problem is that 'reversion' has a double meaning. It can refer to an interest which will commence in the future (eg a reversionary lease). Or it can refer to the current reversion.

[11] See below, heading 'Concurrent leases'.

[12] *Hughes* v. *Robotham* (1593) Cro Eliz 302.

[13] See ch.7 heading 'Estoppel and denial of title'.

[14] The rule was overturned in Ireland by s.3 Landlord and Tenant Law Amendment Act (Ireland) 1860. See *Seymour* v. *Quirke* (1884) 14 LR Ir 455.

[15] See, for example, Lord Browne-Wilkinson's remarks in *Prudential* v. *London Residuary Body* [1992] 2 AC 386, 397. *Co.Litt.* 395a.

The story begins in 1696 with *Hicks* v. *Downing*. [16] That was an action, in tort, by a tenant against an undertenant, for accidentally burning down the property.[17] The defendant took a pleading point. He said that only someone with a reversion could bring the action, and so the claimant should have pleaded expressly that the underlease had been granted so as to expire before the lease. Salkeld reports that the court agreed that a reversionary interest was necessary for this form of action, but held that this was implicit in the pleading that the defendant had an 'underlease', without any discussion about what the nature of a reversionary interest might be.

But according to Lord Raymond's collection of reports, the court also resolved that 'if a lessee for three years assigns his term for four years, or demises the house for four years, he does not by this gain any tortious reversion, and it does but amount to an assignment of his interest'. Whether the court actually said that is another matter. Lord Raymond's reports were compiled by others from his papers, ten years after his death; many of his early reports, like this, are known to have come from notes given to him by others;[18] and there is certainly one other error in this report.[19] It would not have been necessary for the court to make any finding or comment on the point in order to reach the decision which it did. Nor is it likely to have done so, when disposing of a bad pleading point. Nor is the actual decision reported in Lord Raymond's report. The suspicion must be that what is reported is a note of an interesting argument, and not the judgment of the court at all.

On its own, that might not have been enough to cause a problem. But the proposition appeared to have some support in Sheppard's Touchstones, which said[20] 'For when a lessee for life or years doth grant over all his estate or time unto another, this assurance is more properly called an assignment than a lease'.

---

[16] (1696) 1 Ld.Raym 99, 1 Salk 13, 12 Mod. 100.

[17] The tort was abolished, in the case of non-negligent accidents, in 1707. See ch.5 heading 'Repair'.

[18] J. Wallace, *The Reporters*, 3rd edn. (Philadelphia, Johnson, 1855) 249–251.

[19] It records that the defendant was an assignee of the underlease, when the pleadings show that he was the original grantee: 3 Ld.Raym 236.

[20] 266. See *Beardman* v. *Wilson* (1868) LR 4 CP 57.

Perhaps that was intended to be an observation on the correct
terminology to be employed when drawing a conveyance, but it
was capable of being read as a rule of law, and Sheppard's
Touchstones became an influential book.[21]

There was also the decision, in 1677, in *Loyd* v. *Langford*,[22]
that if a tenant granted a lease back to the landlord, reserving a
'rent' without any right of re-entry, that automatically took effect
as a surrender to the landlord, rather than as an underlease.[23] It
was easy to miss the crucial point that the disposition in that case
had been back to the landlord, and not out to a third party,[24] and
to think that it might be illustrative of a wider principle.

Some judges saw straight through this sort of nonsense. In
Poultney v. *Holmes*[25] it was held that a tenant could underlet for
the residue of the term of the lease, and the only consequence of
the absence of an end date reversion was that the tenant could
not distrain for the under-rent.[26] That was the first of a line of
cases,[27] culminating in *Pollock* v. *Stacy*,[28] where courts held that
there was nothing to prevent a tenant underletting for the whole

------

[21] Blackstone's language was even less felicitous. He copied this passage into
his Commentaries omitting the crucial verb: 'for if it be for the whole interest,
it is more properly an assignment than a lease': *Bl.Comm*. Bk.II 317.

[22] (1677) 2 Mod. 174, 1 Freeman 218. See also (1439) Statham's *Abridgment*,
Dette, 46.

[23] The landlord had died, without paying what was due, and it was common
ground that those sums were recoverable from the landlord's estate as a debt;
for, since 1557, even claims for breaches of simple contracts had been provable
against executors: *Norwood* v. *Read* (1558) Plowden 180. The issue was
whether the landlord's widow, by taking possession of the property, had
become personally liable for that debt as an executrix de son tort. An
underlease would have passed to her husband's executor: the freehold would
have passed to his heir (see ch.8 heading 'Devolution on death'). So her
liability for the debt, as an executrix de son tort, depended on establishing that
she had taken possession of an underlease, and not the freehold.

[24] In *Lewyn* v. *Forth* (1672) 1 Vent 185, 3 Salk 109, it was assumed that a
concurrent lease for the residue of the term of the headlease was valid.

[25] (1720) 1 Strange 404.

[26] A sum can be reserved as rent, even if there is no power to distrain: *CH
Bailey* v. *Memorial Enterprises* [1974] 1 WLR 728.

[27] *Preece* v. *Corrie* (1828) 5 Bing 24, Douglas 187, *Baker* v. *Gostling* (1834) 1
Bing NC 12, 246, *Pascoe* v. *Pascoe* (1837) Bing NC 898.

[28] (1847) 9 QB 1033.

of the residue of the term of the lease, if that was what the parties intended. As Denman CJ said in that case, 'we see no inconvenience in supporting as a lease that which was intended to be so, although it may pass all the lessor's interest'.

That line of cases was, however, ultimately overwhelmed by a contrary line, following the reported dicta in *Hicks* v. *Downing*. In *Beardman* v. *Wilson*[29] the Court of Common Pleas held that an underletting for the whole term could only take effect as an assignment, and in *Lewis* v. *Baker*[30] that rule was even applied to a case where the grantor also had a longer reversionary lease, leaving only a *scintilla temporis* in between.[31] Those cases were followed in *Milmo* v. *Carreras*[32] and *Grovesnor Estates* v. *Cochran*[33] and the principle is now only open to challenge in the new Supreme Court.

It remains in doubt what happens if a tenant for a term certain underlets to a periodic tenant, and then fails to give notice to quit to the periodic tenant before the head-term expires.[34]

2. Reversionary leases.

A reversionary lease is a lease which is granted now, to commence at some point in the future.[35]

At common law,[36] a lease for life could only take effect as

---

[29] (1868) LR 4 CP 57.

[30] [1905] 1 Ch 46.

[31] See also *Langford* v. *Symes* (1857) 3 K & J 220, where the grantor had an option, which was subsequently exercised, to acquire the fee simple reversion.

[32] [1946] KB 306.

[33] [1991] 2 EGLR 83.

[34] If the head-landlord grants a new tenancy to the head-tenant, then the periodic tenancy apparently continues as a periodic underlease: *Peirse* v. *Sharr* (1828) 2 Man & Ry1 KB 418.

[35] Preston, *Conveyancing*, vol. 2 146.

[36] The rule applied even after it became possible to create a lease for life by simple deed under s.6 Real Property Act 1845: Challis, *Real Property*, 109. But there was a statutory exception where the lease for life was created pursuant to a power which owed its validity to the Statute of Uses (1536): Platt, *Leases*, vol. 1 443–444, Preston, *Conveyancing*, vol. 2 157. For the other devices used to avoid the rule, see *Norton on Deeds*, 179. Since 1926, a lease for life has

from the date of grant.[37] So it was not possible to grant a lease for life, to take effect at some point in the future, even the very next day,[38] except where it was granted in reversion or remainder upon another lease for life, or as an equitable interest behind a trust.

But it has always been possible to grant other leases for a term which will commence at some point in the future,[39] including on the expiry of a lease for life.[40]

Between 1536 and 1925 it was possible to grant a reversionary lease for years by deed out of a freehold estate, which would take effect as a lease under the Statute of Uses (1536) without the need to make an entry.[41] Otherwise, before 1926 a reversionary grant could only ever take effect as an interesse termini, for an entry was necessary in order to complete the lease,[42] and the tenant could not enter until the term commencement date,[43] turning the reversionary interesse termini into a full lease.[44] That rule was abolished by s.149(1) Law of Property Act 1925,[45] and so since 1926 a reversionary lease has been treated as a full lease from its inception, which differs from a lease in possession only in the sense that the commencement date has been postponed.

A reversionary interesse termini for a term of years could be created orally until the enactment of the Statute of Frauds (1677). The exception in that Act for leases granted for a term of

---

taken effect as a lease for a term of 90 years, with a right to determine it on notice after the death of the relevant individual; see s.149(6) Law of Property Act 1925.

[37] *Barwick's Case* (1597) 5 Co.Rep 93b, Challis, *Real Property*, 107–109.

[38] *Greenwood* v. *Tyber* (1620) Cro Jac 563, *Goshawke* v. *Chiggell* (1629) Cro Car 154, D'Anvers, *Abridgment*, vol. 3 (London, Gosling, 1737) 159.

[39] 'A lease for years can be made to commence in futuro, because it is only a chattel interest, and hence is part of the personal estate (unlike a grant in fee, which has to be made immediately, so that it can pass to the heir at law)': *Bl.Comm.* Bk.II 143. See ch.8 heading 'Devolution on Death.'

[40] For a precedent for a lease for 100 years in reversion after a life, see *The Compleat Clerk,* 3rd edn. (London, Place, 1671) 741.

[41] *Perks*, ¶.62, *Mann, Crossman and Paulin Ltd* v. *Land Registrar* [1918] 1 Ch 202.

[42] *Smith* v. *Day* (1837) 2 M&W 684, 699 Per Parke B, *Lewis* v. *Baker* [1905] 1 Ch 46. See ch.1 heading 'Entry and interesse termini'.

[43] An entry before then was a tortious disseisin: *Mawle* v. *Cacyffr* (1619) Cro Jac 549.

[44] The reversionary interesse termini could be assigned: *Perks*, ¶.91.

[45] See ch.1 heading 'Entry and interesse termini'.

three years or less was held to apply to reversionary leases in 1725,[46] but only if the term would expire within three years of the date when the reversionary interesse termini was granted, rather than within three years of the commencement date of the lease. Since 1926, all reversionary leases must be made by deed.[47]

In the early 20th century,[48] lawyers started to doubt whether it was possible to create a reversionary lease which would fall into possession in more than 21 years time, on the grounds that the lease would infringe the rule against perpetuities. In *Mann, Crossman & Paulin* v. *Registrar of the Land Registry*[49] the Registrar refused to register such a lease, fearing that statutory compensation would be payable if he registered it, and it turned out to be void. Neville J decided that the lease was valid, because the rule against perpetuities is only concerned with the date upon which a property right becomes vested in interest, and a reversionary interesse termini vested as an interest in the land on the date of its grant. But s.149(3) Law of Property Act 1925 now makes void any reversionary lease where the term will commence more than 21 years after the grant of the lease, and any contract to grant a reversionary lease under which the term will commence more than 21 years from the date of completion of the lease.[50]

3. Concurrent leases.

A 'concurrent' or 'overriding'[51] is a lease of a reversion,[52] which has been granted out of the reversion upon a prior

---

[46] *Ryley* v. *Hicks* (1725) 1 Strange 651.

[47] s.52 Law of Property Act 1925.

[48] Challis, *Real Property*, 186, 472.

[49] [1918] 1 Ch 202.

[50] So a covenant to renew a lease in more than 21 years time is valid, because when the lease is granted, the term will commence within 21 years of the date of grant: *Strand and Savoy Properties* v. *Cumbrea Properties* [1960] 1 Ch 583. See however para.7(2) sch.XV Law of Property Act 1922, which invalidates covenants for renewal for a term of longer than 60 years.

[51] s.19 Landlord and Tenant (Covenants) Act 1995.

[52] Preston, *Conveyancing,* vol. 2 145–146.

lease, for a term which has commenced before that prior lease has expired.

A concurrent lease not the same thing as a headlease. The difference is that a headlease is a lease out of which the tenant has granted an underlease, whereas a concurrent lease is a lease of an existing reversion, carved out of that reversion.

In 1537 there was doubt about whether a concurrent lease could be granted at all,[53] but a concurrent lease granted for a longer term than the prior lease was recognised as valid in 1589,[54] and one for the same term in 1831.[55] The validity of a shorter concurrent lease was assumed in 1593,[56] but it was 1912 before there was any positive decision to that effect,[57] which was confirmed afterwards by statute.[58]

The rule that freeholds could only be granted in succession to each other meant that it was impossible for a tenant for life to grant an underlease for life. A tenant for life could only grant an underlease for years. But it did not prevent the grant of a concurrent lease for life, out of the reversion upon a lease for life; for the concurrent tenant would take the property by succession to a remainder, if the existing tenant died first.[59] In practice, a concurrent lease for life could only be granted under the Statute of Uses (1536), since the existence of the prior lease

---

[53] *Anon* (1537) Dyer 26a. Littleton assumed that both a concurrent lease for years and a concurrent lease for life could be granted: Littleton, *Tenures*, s.551, s.567.

[54] *Read* v. *Nash* (1589) 1 Leon 147, *Goodtitle* v. *Funucan* (1781) 2 Douglas 565, cf. per Gawdy J. in *Dove* v. *Wilmot* (1589) Cro Eliz 160.

[55] *Burton* v. *Barclay* (1831) 7 Bing 745.

[56] *Hughes* v. *Robotham* (1593) Cro Eliz 302.

[57] *Re Moore and Hulm's Contract* [1912] 2 Ch 105. Before then, the position had been in doubt. See *Shep.Touch.* 276.

[58] s.149(5) LPA 25.

[59] *Co.Litt.* 215a. In *Roe d. Brune* v. *Prideaux* (1808) 10 East 158, 185 Lord Ellenborough made the point that the doctrine of merger (see ch.7 heading 'Surrender and merger') would prevent the same person being both a tenant for life and a concurrent tenant for life (even if the lives were different), and it was not possible to avoid this problem by granting the concurrent lease as a reversionary lease instead, because of the rule that a lease for life cannot be granted as future interest.

for life made transfer by livery of seisin impossible.[60]

At common law, as has already been noted,[61] a concurrent lease for years could not be completed whilst the prior lease was still extant, unless and until the prior tenant agreed to attorn to the concurrent tenant.[62] In the meantime, the concurrent lease took effect only as a concurrent interesse termini.[63]

In 1836, in *Neale* v. *MacKenzie*, the Exchequer Chamber held that a deed was necessary, at common law, in order to create a concurrent lease.[64] It did so largely in deference to the views attributed to the late Chief Baron Gilbert, in Bacon's Abridgment, being a collection of the papers which he had left on his death.[65] The argument was that since an estate in land could not be conveyed by a person who was out of possession, and since the existence of the prior lease meant that a reversioner was not in possession, the consequence was that a concurrent lease could only take effect by estoppel,[66] and an estoppel could only arise by deed.

It is hard to see how any of that can have been right. At common law, it was quite possible to convey a freehold reversion by livery of seisin (without any deed) notwithstanding

---

[60] It was impossible because a tenancy for life was a freehold estate, and seisin passed to the tenant on the grant of a freehold estate. So the reversioner could not make a delivery of seisin (livery of seisin) to anyone else again afterwards, because it had already passed to the tenant of life.

[61] See ch.1 heading 'Entry and interesse termini'.

[62] Platt, *Leases*, vol. 2 57. A concurrent lease granted by deed out of the freehold could be completed without an attornment after 1535 under the Statute of Uses (1536), and the need for an attornment was abolished generally in 1705 (s.9 Administration of Justice Act 1705). Nonetheless, as late as 1820 it was argued that a concurrent lease took effect only as a concurrent interesse termini: *Grumbrell* v. *Roper* (1820) 3 Barn & Ald 711, 715.

[63] The covenants were, however, enforceable between the parties immediately: *Lewyn* v. *Forth* (1672) 1 Vent 185, 3 Salk 109 'Covenant'.

[64] *Neale* v. *MacKenzie* (1836) 1 M&W 747. See also *Wilson* v. *Sewell* (1762) 1 Wm.Black 617.

[65] M. Bacon, *Bacon's Abridgment*, 7th edn., 'Leases (N)' (London, Strahan, 1832) vol. 4 846–849, M. Bacon, *A Treatise on Leases* (London, Strahan, 1798) 186–187, Chambers, *Leases*, 25–26. Richard Preston too said that it could only be created by deed, though he admitted that this was not 'perfectly consistent': Preston, *Conveyancing*, vol. 2 149.

[66] *Ferrers* v. *Borough* (1599) Cro Eliz 665.

the possession of a leasehold tenant.[67] So it was simply wrong to say that the possession of the tenant meant that the reversioner had no power to make a disposition of the reversion. Nor, in truth, did that power infringe the rule that only a person in possession could make a disposition;[68] for the tenant and the reversioner were in possession of different things: the tenant was in possession of the lease, and 'the receipt of rent marks the landlord as being in present possession of his rights as owner'.[69] Indeed, in the case of a freehold reversion, the landlord had 'seisin' of it too.[70] So it ought to have been quite possible, at common law, for a landlord, who was enjoying the rights of a reversioner, to grant a parol concurrent lease out of it, which would then have taken effect as an interesse termini until the actual tenant attorned.[71]

Furthermore, whilst it might have been the law that a deed was necessary to create an estoppel as to title between landlord and tenant in 1726, when Baron Gilbert died,[72] that was no longer the case by 1836;[73] and if a lease of a reversion could only have been created by deed, then it would have been an incorporeal hereditament, with the result that it would have been impossible to reserve a rent upon it.[74]

The fundamental problem (as in so much of land law) appears to have been confusion about the concept of 'possession'. An estate in land is either 'vested in interest' or 'vested in possession'. If someone has a present fixed right only to begin enjoying it at some point in the future, then it is vested only 'in interest'. It is 'vested in possession' if someone has a

---

[67] (1536/7) Brook's New Cases pl.97, *Anon* (1537) Dyer 33a, *Co.Litt.* 48b, Littleton, *Tenures*, s.60, Challis, *Real Property*, 52–53 (a note by Sweet), Dyer 362. J. Lightwood, *Possession of Land* (London, Stevens, 1894) 31–32.

[68] Reversed by s.6 Real Property Act 1845.

[69] J. Lightwood, *Possession of Land* (London, Stevens, 1894) 187.

[70] Littleton, *Tenures*, s.58, *Brediman* v. *Bromley* (1606) Cro Jac 142.

[71] *Gilman* v. *Hore* (1692) 1 Salk 275, 3 Salk 152.

[72] D'Anvers, *Abridgment*, vol. 3 271, Holdsworth, *HEL* vol. 7 245–246.

[73] *Cooke* v. *Loxley* (1792) 5 Term Rep 4. See also *Veale* v. *Warner* (1669) 1 Wms Saund 323, 326.fn(f).

[74] *Jewel's Case* (1588) 5 Co.Rep 3a. See ch. 3 heading 'Rent reservation'.

present fixed right to enjoy it now.[75] In a sense, a reversion upon a lease for a term of years or for life is only vested in interest, because the right to enjoyment of the corporeal land itself is postponed until the termination of the lease.[76] But in another sense, it is vested in possession, because the right to receive the reserved rent and enforce the tenant's covenants is immediate.[77] The only thing that is deferred is the right to actual physical enjoyment of the land, and a person who is receiving rent is normally treated as being in possession of the estate to which it issues.

Consequently, the absence of any immediate right to physical enjoyment of the land ought never to have been a bar to the creation of a concurrent lease.

Today, there are statutory formality requirements, which mean that all leases,[78] excepting only leases for three years or less taking effect in possession at the best rent which can obtained without taking a fine,[79] must be made by deed.[80] But the decision in *Neale* v. *McKenzie* means that it is still not possible to grant a concurrent lease which takes advantage of that exception.[81]

4. Mortgages as leases and of leases.

In 1950 Waldock wrote:[82]
In English law the grant of a security in land has run the whole

---

[75] *Fearne's Contingent Remainders*, 4th edn. (London, Straghan & Woodfall, 1844) vol. 1 2, cited with approval in *Pearson* v. *IRC* [1981] AC 753, 772.

[76] So Fearne would have described it as 'vested in interest' (ibid).

[77] 'English lawyers regard an estate in reversion or remainder not as a future interest, but as a present interest, subject to the 'particular estate' which together with the reversion or remainder makes up the fee simple': F. Pollock, *The Land Laws*, 127. See also Preston, *Conveyancing*, vol. 2 145–146.

[78] s.52 Law of Property Act 1925.

[79] s.54(2) Law of Property Act 1925.

[80] See ch.1 heading 'Formalities'.

[81] A concurrent lease would otherwise be a lease 'in possession', because possession is defined so as to include the right to receive rent; s.205(xix) Law of Property Act 1925. So the words 'in possession' in s.54(2) exclude reversionary, not concurrent, leases.

[82] C. Waldock, *The Law of Mortgages*, 2nd edn. (London, Stevens & Sons, 1950) 19.

gamut of forms of security: the common method of giving security begins by being a pledge, turns into a true mortgage, and will probably end by being a charge.

Today, that prediction has become true.

In the twelfth and thirteenth centuries, land was normally mortgaged by way of leasehold pledge. The creditor took a lease of the land from the debtor, and applied the income either towards discharge of the principal and interest ('vivum vadium' or 'vifgage') or towards repayment of the interest alone ('mortum vadium' or 'vadimonium').[83] The latter was regarded as sinful, being usurious,[84] but was common nonetheless.[85] The length of the lease was not always specified,[86] but, where it was, if the full debt was not paid at the end of the term of the lease, the arrangement was usually that the creditor would automatically forfeit the whole of the debtor's interest in the land, and there were various means by which that could be done.[87]

By the fifteenth century doubts were being expressed about whether an estate could pass automatically in this way without a formal conveyance.[88]

---

[83] *Pollock & Maitland* vol. 2 119, *Co.Litt.* 205a, *Bl.Comm.* Bk.II 157.

[84] 'When an immovable is gaged and seisin of it is given to the creditor for a fixed term, the creditor and debtor will have agreed either that the profits and rents accruing shall count towards repayment, or that they shall not count. The former agreement is just and binding. The second, which is called mortgage, is unjust and dishonourable, but is not forbidden by the court of the lord king, although it deems it a kind of usury': Glanvill, *Treatise on the Laws and Customs of England*, ed. and trans. G. Hall (Clarendon, Oxford, 1965) 124. The Crown had a financial incentive to allow it, because the property of a usurer was forfeit to the Crown on death: W. Hawkins, *Pleas of the Crown*, 7th edn. (London, Robinson, 1975) vol. 1 374.

[85] See E. Tabuteau, *Transfers of Property in 11th Century Norman Law* (University of North Carolina Press, 1988) 81–82.

[86] Ibid 82.

[87] Simpson, *History of Land Law*, 132–134, Kaye, *Medieval English Conveyances*, 274–275, Plucknett, *Concise History*, 603–605.

[88] *Pollock & Maitland* vol. 2 122–123. Modern conveyancers face a similar problem, and adopt a similar solution, with rent deposit deeds. If a corporate tenant grants a charge to the landlord over the deposit, the charge will be void against a liquidator of that company, unless it has been registered under s.874 Companies Act 2006. In order to avoid the inconvenience of registering the

So the practice changed to a true mortgage.[89] The whole of the debtor's interest in the estate[90] forming the security would be conveyed to the lender at the outset, but the conveyance would be subject to a condition for reverter to the debtor, if the debtor re-paid the debt on a particular day.[91] It was called a 'mortgage' because, if the debtor did not repay on the prescribed day, the land was 'taken from him forever, and so dead to him'.[92]

By the seventeenth century,[93] the condition for reverter had become a covenant for re-conveyance instead.[94] The idea was to ensure that the redemption was documented, so that there could not be any doubt about in whom the legal estate was vested at any particular time.[95]

But this form of mortgage still had substantial disadvantages.

The disadvantage for the debtor was that people were reluctant to lend more money upon the security of second or subsequent mortgages; for until the first mortgage was redeemed, those securities could only take effect in equity, since the debtor no longer had a legal estate in the mortgaged property

---

charge, some rent deposit deeds provide that the deposit becomes the absolute property of the landlord immediately, but it is charged back to the tenant, to secure the landlord's obligation to repay it, if it becomes repayable.

[89] 'A mortgage is a conveyance of land or an assignment of chattels as a security for the payment of a debt or the discharge of some other obligation for which it is given': Per Lindley MR in *Santley* v. *Wilde* [1899] 2 Ch 474, 474.

[90] Littleton, *Tenures*, s.333: 'Also, as a man may make a feoffment in fee in mortgage, so a man may make a gift in tail in mortgage, or a lease for life or for a term of years in mortgage'.

[91] Littleton, *Tenures*, s.332. A lease could be assigned, in the same way. Hence if a term of years was granted over for the life of the assignee, it would take effect as an assignment subject to the condition for reverter on the death of the assignee: *Butt's Case* (1600) 7 Co.Rep 23a. This did not infringe the rule against creating lifetime successive interests in a lease for a term of years (see ch.4 heading 'For life') because that rule only made the grant over void. It did not prevent the reservation of a condition for re-entry in favour of the grantor, and a condition for re-entry could not be granted to any stranger.

[92] Littleton, *Tenures*, s.332.

[93] Plucknett, *Concise History*, 607. See e.g. the precedent for a mortgage of a lease in *The Compleat Clerk*, 3rd edn. (London, Place, 1671) 787, 789.

[94] By the nineteenth century, where the mortgage was of a freehold, this had generally become a covenant to convey or assign the mortgage on redemption to whomsoever the debtor might direct: Preston, *Conveyancing*, vol. 2 203.

[95] *Durham Bros* v. *Robertson* [1898] 1 QB 765, 772.

to offer,[96] and that was not a very desirable form of security.[97]

It was also inconvenient if the mortgaged property was freehold, that on the death of the lender, the mortgage went to the lender's legatee or heir, but the right to repayment of the mortgage debt went to the lender's personal representatives.[98]

But the really serious problem was if the mortgaged property was a lease, for the effect of assigning the lease to the lender was that the lender would become personally liable to the landlord for the rent, and on the covenants contained in the lease, as an assignee of the term.[99]

That might not have mattered very much whilst it was still the practice of lenders to take possession of the property as soon as the mortgage was granted, work it, and keep possession until the mortgage was redeemed, but it did matter from the late sixteenth century onwards[100] when the practice changed, and it became usual (as it is today) to leave the borrower in possession, pending a default on the mortgage debt.[101]

---

[96] All he or she could offer by way of further security was the equity of redemption (the right in equity to require the property to be reconveyed on payment of the existing mortgage debt).

[97] Maitland, *Equity,* 283.

[98] *Co.Litt.* 205a-b.fn(1). In London, by special custom, the mortgage went to the personal representatives too: Eq.Ca.Abr. vol. 1 150.

[99] Similarly, if a freehold was mortgaged in this way, the lender (as the current freeholder) would become liable to perform any customary obligations attached to that freehold: *Copestake* v. *Hooper* [1908] 2 Ch 10 (payment of a heriot on death). Of course, it was relatively rare for customary obligations to be attached to a freehold.

[100] *Powsley* v. *Blackman* (1645) Cro Jac 659, R.Turner, *Equity of Redemption* (Cambridge, Cambridge University Press, 1931) 89.

[101] In *Birch* v. *Wright* (1786) 1 Term Rep 378 Buller J held that the relationship between a mortgagor and mortgagee was not strictly a tenancy at will and nor was a mortgagor left in possession strictly a receiver, although the position was analogous to both. Mortgages afterwards often contained attornment clauses, by which the debtor covenanted to attorn to the lender as a tenant at will. The original purpose of those clauses was to give the lender a power of distress against the debtor, but that was outlawed by the Bills of Sale Act 1878. Subsequently, they were used because a landlord could apply for summary judgment for possession in the High Court, whereas a mortgagee could not (see R. Coote, *Law of Mortgages*, 9th edn. (London, Stevens and Sweet & Maxwell, 1927) vol. 1 685) and because a landlord of premises let for a term of less than

A decision in 1780 that the lender could not be made liable as an assignee of the lease unless he or she took possession[102] was quickly overruled,[103] and thereafter, if a lease was mortgaged in this way, the lender became liable as an assignee with or without an entry.[104]

There was, however, an alternative[105] method of creating a legal[106] mortgage which did not suffer from these problems. Instead of conveying the mortgaged property to the lender, the debtor would grant the lender a long lease or sub-lease of it, with a covenant to surrender it (or with a condition that it would become void) on repayment of the secured debt.[107] The idea was

---

seven years at rent of less than £20 pa. could recover possession in the Magistrates Courts under the Small Tenements Recovery Act 1838. See ch.9 heading 'Summary possession proceedings'.

[102] *Eaton* v. *Jacques* (1780) 2 Douglas 455. H.Bullow, ed. J. Fonblanque, *A Treatise on Equity*, 5th edn., vol. 1 (London, Clarke, 1820) 357.

[103] *Williams* v. *Bossnquet* (1819) 1 Brod & Bing 238.

[104] In *Sparkes* v. *Smith* (1692) 2 Vern 275 a landlord was refused equitable relief against a mortgagee on this ground, but it was pointed out that nothing could be done to prevent the landlord suing on the covenants at common law, and that it was 'folly' to mortgage a lease in this way. The same point was made refusing relief in *Pilkington* v. *Shaller* (1700) 2 Vern 374. See H.Bullow, ed. J. Fonblanque, *A Treatise on Equity*, 5th edn., vol. 1 356.

[105] At the beginning of the nineteenth century, it was doubtful whether a power of sale (that is, to sell free of the mortgagor's right to redeem) could be attached to a mortgage at all; T. Coventry, *Mortgage Precedents* (London, Brooke, 1826) 150, *Roberts* v. *Boze* (1825) cited ibid 152–153. In order to get round that problem, mortgages were sometimes created by conveying the mortgaged property to trustees, to hold upon trust for sale, with power for the mortgagee to enter and apply the rents and profits towards the mortgage debt in the meantime. In substance, this was just a variation on the first type of legal mortgage: *In Re Alison* (1879) 11 Ch.D 284, 294.

[106] Between 1783 (*Russel* v. *Russel* (1783) Brown CC 269, *Featherstone* v. *Fenwick* (1784) 1 Brown CC 270n, 14 Ves 606n) and 1990 (*United Bank of Kuwait* v. *Sahib* [1996] 3 All ER 215), it was possible to create an equitable mortgage simply by deposit of the title deeds, and this was frequently done for short term commercial borrowings. In *Lucas* v. *Comerford* (1790) 1 Ves Jun 235 it was suggested that a landlord could force the tenant to assign to an equitable mortgagee, but that was discountenanced in *Moores* v. *Choat* (1839) 8 Sim 508: see Platt, *Leases*, vol. 2 185, *Oxford History of the Law of England*, vol. 12 130–131.

[107] Littleton, *Tenures*, s.333, Holdsworth, *HEL* vol. 7 375. There is a precedent for a mortgage term for 500 years with a proviso that the lease would 'cease, determine, and be utterly void and of no effect, to all intents and purposes as if the same had never been made' in *The Compleat Clark*, 3rd edn. (London,

that the lender's lease would last only until the debt was repaid, and this was called a 'mortgage term'. The debtor retained the reversion upon the mortgage term, but in the meantime the lender had the right to possess the lease created by the mortgage. This meant that the debtor could create any number of subsequent legal mortgages by granting one or more concurrent mortgage terms out of the reversion, or the debtor could at least grant one more by transfer of the whole legal estate in the reversion to the subsequent lender in the traditional way.

This alternative method waxed and waned in popularity over the centuries. It was known to Bracton in the thirteenth century,[108] was often used in the seventeenth[109] and had become 'usual' by the eighteenth.[110] In the nineteenth century it was rare for mortgages of freeholds to be created in this way,[111] but it was still the usual way of mortgaging leases.[112]

The main advantage for the lender of mortgaging a lease in this way was that, because the mortgage term took effect as a sub-lease, the head-landlord could not sue the lender in debt for the rent nor in covenant or assumpsit on the promises contained in the mortgaged lease, for the lender would be an undertenant rather than a tenant.[113] But, before 1926,[114] there were disadvantages too.

First, unless the mortgage deed provided otherwise, the debtor (as owner of the reversion) was entitled to retain the title

---

Place, 1671) 816. At about the same time, Orlando Bridgman drew a mortgage term for 500 years which would become 'void, frustrate, and of none effect to all intents and purposes' on repayment: O. Bridgman, *Conveyances*, 3rd edn. (London, Atkins, 1699) vol. 1 36. Similarly, in Stewart, *Practice of Conveyancing*, 253, there is a precedent for automatic cesser on death, of a term of 500 years, created to secure a wife's rent charge.

[108] Bracton, vol. 2 74 (f.20).

[109] W. Holdsworth, *Historical Introduction to Land Law* (Oxford, Oxford University Press, 1927) 264.

[110] *Bl.Comm.* Bk.II 158.

[111] Stewart, *Practice of Conveyancing*, 154.

[112] Maitland, *Equity,* 164. See eg. *Bonner* v. *Tottenham and Edmonton BS* [1899] 1 QB 161.

[113] Holdsworth, *HEL* vol. 7 291. See ch.6 heading 'Underletting'.

[114] s.85(1), s.86(1), s.88(1), s.89(1) Law of Property Act 1925.

deeds.[115] Secondly, the lender could not sell[116] the reversion along with the mortgage term, unless the mortgage deed contained a declaration that the debtor held the reversion upon trust for the lender,[117] and even then it was unclear whether a power of attorney was sufficient to enable the lender to sell alone.[118] Thirdly, if the debtor did not perform the covenants in the mortgaged lease, it might be forfeited, and the lender might find it difficult to obtain relief from forfeiture as a sub-tenant.[119]

Whatever method was used, however, a lender with a legal security in land granted before 1926 necessarily acquired a right to possess an immediate legal estate in the lender's own name; for the debtor had either conveyed or assigned the legal estate in the property to the lender by creating the mortgage in the traditional way, or the debtor had granted the lender an actual lease or sub-lease of it by way of mortgage term.

On 1st January 1926 it became impossible to create a legal mortgage by outright conveyance or assignment.[120] If the parties attempted it, they would find that they had automatically created a mortgage term instead.[121] Now, for registered land, even this is prohibited. An attempt to create a mortgage term automatically creates a legal charge.[122]

Since 1926 legal mortgages of both freeholds and leaseholds have almost invariably been created as 'charges by way of legal mortgage'; the radical new method introduced, for registered

---

[115] C. Waldock, *The Law of Mortgages*, 2nd edn. (London, Stevens & Sons, 1950) 23, Halsbury's Laws, *Real Property,* vol. 39(2), 4th edn., ¶.87.

[116] Powers of sale became common in mortgage deeds after about 1800. Before then, the usual method of enforcement was foreclosure. See *Oxford History of the Laws of England*, vol. 12 135–136.

[117] *London & County Bank* v. *Goddard* [1897] 1 Ch 642.

[118] C. Waldock, *The Law of Mortgages*, 2nd edn. (London, Stevens & Sons, 1950) 29. There is a precedent in *The Compleat Clerk,* 3rd edn. (London, Place, 1671) for a mortgage term with a covenant by the borrower to convey the reversion if required, 729.

[119] See ch.7 heading 'Relief from forfeiture'.

[120] s.85(1) Law of Property Act 1925 (freeholds); s.86(1) Law of Property Act 1925 (leaseholds).

[121] s.85(2) Law of Property Act 1925 (freeholds); s.86(2) Law of Property Act 1925 (leaseholds).

[122] ss.23, 51 Land Registration Act 2002.

land by the Land Transfer Act 1875, and for unregistered land by the Law of Property Act 1925.[123]

A charge by way of legal mortgage does not convey the debtor's fee simple or assign the debtor's lease to the lender. The debtor retains the legal estate in both.[124] But the effect of a first legal charge of a fee simple is to grant the lender the same rights and powers as if the debtor had granted the lender a mortgage term for three thousand years,[125] and the effect of a first legal charge of a lease is to grant the lender the same rights and powers as if the debtor had granted the lender a sub-mortgage term for one day shorter than the lease.[126]

Although a charge by way of legal mortgage grants the lender the same rights and remedies as an actual mortgage term, it does not go further than that. It does not create an actual leasehold term, nor deem the lender to be subject to the liabilities of a tenant under such a lease. It simply gives the lender the same 'protection, powers and remedies' as if he or she were such a tenant.[127]

There being no actual mortgage term, it follows that charging a lease by way of legal mortgage is not a breach of a covenant against underletting.

Since, when the debtor grants a first charge by way of legal mortgage, the debtor retains his or her legal estate in the property, there is nothing to stop the debtor creating second or subsequent securities as legal charges too. A second or subsequent chargee has the same rights and powers as the holder of a concurrent mortgage term; that is, a mortgage term granted by the debtor subject to, and in reversion upon, any prior mortgage terms.

---

[123] In the case of unregistered land, it must be 'expressed' to be by way of legal mortgage. In the case of registered land, a profit á prendre in gross which has been registered in its own right may be charged in this way too: s.51 Land Registration Act 2002.

[124] s.95(4) Law of Property Act 1925.

[125] s.87(1)(a) Law of Property Act 1925.

[126] s.87(1) Law of Property Act 1925.

[127] *Weg Motors* v. *Hales* [1962] Ch 49, 73, 74, 77.

5. Options and break rights.

Options, in the law of landlord and tenant, tend to be one of three types. They can be options for the grant of a new term ('renewal' options).[128] Or they can be options to determine the term prematurely (sometimes called 'break' rights). Or they can be options to acquire the interest of the other party to the lease.[129]

Those options can be granted to either party. Even options for the grant of a new term, which are typically granted to tenants as a right of renewal, are sometimes granted as 'put' options to landlords, empowering them to force the tenant to take a new lease.[130]

In equity, options are construed in the same way as at common law,[131] so as to require strict compliance with any conditions precedent for their exercise.[132] So whereas the words 'the tenant paying the rent and performing the covenants' are mere surplusage in a landlord's covenant, in a tenant's option they have been construed since 1796[133] as creating a condition precedent, with which the tenant must comply in order to exercise the option, with the consequence that if there are any subsisting breaches on the date on which the option falls due for performance, the landlord is entitled to avoid it. But if the condition is not fulfilled as a result of unavoidable accident, fraud, surprise or 'ignorance not wilful', then equity can relieve against the consequences of the failure to perform that condition, and order specific performance of the option, with compensation

---

[128] Para.7(2) sch.XV Law of Property Act 1922 invalidates covenants for renewal for a term of longer than 60 years.

[129] A landlord's option to acquire the term of a business lease within pt.II Landlord and Tenant Act 1954 is made void by s.38.

[130] A landlord's option to require a previous tenant or a guarantor to take a new lease, in the event of a disclaimer by the ultimate tenant, was commonly used to avoid the effect of the decision in *Stacey* v. *Hill* [1901] 1 KB 690 (see ch.8 heading 'Bankruptcy and personal insolvency'). Similarly, in the 1970s there were tax advantages in granting a lease for 35 years, with an option to either party to require it to be renewed for a further 7 years, rather than granting a straight 42 year term.

[131] *Eaton* v. *Lyon* (1796) 3 Ves Jun 690, 693.

[132] *Pendred* v. *Griffith* (1744) 1 Brown PC 314.

[133] *Porter* v. *Shephard* (1796) 6 Term Rep 665.

for any loss caused by the failure to perform the condition if appropriate.[134]

It was unclear in 1561 whether a covenant for renewal would run with the term.[135] In 1565 it was decided that an option for renewal could be enforced by the tenant's executors,[136] and by the eighteenth century, it was clear that covenants for renewal were enforceable at the suit of an assignee of the term generally.[137] In *Woodall* v. *Clifton*[138] Romer LJ suggested that this was anomalous, and difficult to justify, but too late to question.

Covenants for perpetual renewal were held to be invalid in *Say* v. *Smith*[139] but upheld by the House of Lords in 1715 in *Bridges* v. *Hitchcock*,[140] as creating an equitable interest in the land binding from the time of the covenant's creation.[141] In Ireland, at the beginning of the nineteenth century, there was a strong presumption that any covenant for renewal would be treated as a covenant for perpetual renewal.[142] In England, however, the presumption was against perpetual renewal,[143] and

---

[134] *Eaton* v. *Lyon* (1796) 3 Ves Jun 660, 693, *Rawstone* v. *Bentley* (1793) 4 Brown CC 415, *Samuel Properties* v. *Hayek* [1972] 1 WLR 1296, 1306, Platt, *Leases*, vol. 1 753.

[135] *Skerne's Case* (1561) Mo KB 88.

[136] *Chapman* v. *Dalton* (1565) Plowden 284, *Hyde* v. *Skinner* (1723) 2 Peere Wms 196.

[137] *Richardson* v. *Sydenham* (1703) 2 Vern 447, *Tanner* v. *Florence* (1675) 1 Ch.Cas 259, *Finch* v. *Earl of Salisbury* (1675) 1 Eq Cas Ab 47, *Taylor* v. *Stibbert* (1794) 2 Ves Jun 437.

[138] [1905] 2 Ch 257, 279.

[139] (1564) Plowden 271.

[140] (1715) 5 Brown PC 6.

[141] Holdsworth, *HEL* vol. 7 260–261.

[142] See J.Finlay, *Leases of Lives Renewable Forever* (Dublin, Cumming, 1829), Platt, *Covenants*, 233.fn(a). If the tenant failed to pay the fine due on renewal in time, the Irish courts generally granted the tenant relief. That practice was upheld in the House of Lords in *Earl of Ross* v. *Worsop* (1740) 1 Brown PC 281 but overturned in *Vipon* v. *Rowley* (1774) 1 Ridge PC 194n, and then reinstated by s.1 Irish Tenantry Act 1779, 19 & 20 Geo.3 c.30 (Ir). But gross delay was still a bar to renewal: *Mountnorris* v. *White* (1814) 2 Dow 459.

[143] Platt, *Covenants*, 233–244, *Tritton* v. *Foote* (1789) 2 Brown CC 636, *Baynham* v. *Guy's Hospital* (1796) 3 Ves Jun 295, *Taylor* v. *Stibbert* (1794) 2 Ves Jun 437.

by sch.15 Law of Property Act 1922 any lease with a covenant
for perpetual renewal is automatically converted into a lease of
2000 years, and any perpetually renewable sub-lease is
converted into a term which is one day shorter than the headlease
(up to a maximum of one day less than 2000 years).[144]

Special rules have always applied to options to determine a
lease for breach of a condition, which are forfeitures, and these
are considered in chapter 7. Other options to determine are
technically limitations on the estate, rather than conditions
subsequent,[145] and there are no special rules for them. Options to
determine on paying a fine were known in the fifteenth
century[146] and a landlord's option to determine the lease at any
time on payment of sixpence was held valid against the tenant in
Lady Platt v. *Sleap*.[147] Six years later, in 1617, it was held that a
landlord's right to determine on payment of a nominal sum,
made the lease void, as fraudulent, against a purchaser from the
landlord,[148] but that was probably before it was appreciated that
the option would run with the reversion and so be enforceable by
the new landlord instead.[149]

Options to acquire the reversion or the term, however, do not
run with the land.[150] Although attempts have been made since the

---

[144] For conversion of perpetually renewable terms into fee farm tenure in
Ireland, see the Renewable Leasehold Conversion Act 1849, 12 & 13 Vic.
c.105.

[145] See ch.6 heading 'Conditions'.

[146] Kaye, *Medieval English Conveyances*, 266.

[147] (1611) Cro Jac 275.

[148] *Griffin* v. *Stanhope* (1617) Cro Jac 455.

[149] There is a precedent for a landlord's rolling break clause, conditional upon
the landlord paying a break premium calculated by reference to the unexpired
residue of the term, in W.West, *Simboleograph* (London, Stationers Company,
1610) pt.1 s.442, and for an unconditional tenant's right to break at the end of
the seventh and fourteenth years of the term in T. Williams, *Precedents in
Conveyancing*, vol. 3 (London, Kearsley, 1788) 982.

[150] In *Nichols* v. *Nichols* (1575) 2 Plowden 481 a lease for life had been
granted, with a condition that if the landlord died without issue the tenant
should have the fee simple. It was held that this bound the Crown, who took the
landlord's estate by forfeiture when the landlord was attained for treason, as a
fee simple conditional rather than a contractual option.

seventeenth century to make them do so,[151] those attempts all fell foul of the rule that a successor landlord is only bound to perform covenants which relate to things to be done on the demised land. So in *Woodall* v. *Clifton*[152] it was held that an option to acquire the reversion does not run with the lease, and is subject to the rule against perpetuities.[153]

At common law, even if the option was perpetuitous, so that it created no interest in the land,[154] the tenant could still recover damages against the original party for breach of covenant.[155] That rule was reversed by s.10 Perpetuities and Accumulations Act 1964, yet under the Perpetuities and Accumulations Act 2009, new options to acquire land are no longer subject to the rule against perpetuities at all.[156]

---

[151] See, e.g., the lease for a 1000 years of a garden, with an option to purchase the reversion in *The Compleat Clerk,* 3rd edn. (London, Brook,1671) 715.

[152] [1905] 2 Ch 257.

[153] J.Gray, *The Rule Against Perpetuities,* 3rd edn. (Boston, Little Brown, 1915) ¶.230.

[154] Options to purchase the reversion exercisable within one year of the determination of term were excepted from the rule against perpetuities by ss.9(1), 15(3) Perpetuities and Accumulations Act 1964.

[155] *Worthing Corpn* v. *Heather* [1906] 2 Ch 532.

[156] s.1.

CHAPTER 3
Rent

1. Rent reservation.

Modern leases still 'reserve' a rent because, in the medieval period, rent was 'treated as a thing; a tenement,[1] just like the land'.[2] Exactly the same remedies were available for interference with receipt of a rent as were available for interference with corporeal land. So as Pollock and Maitland said:[3]

---

[1] On the meaning of 'tenement' see Halsbury's Laws, *Real Property,* vol. 39(2), 4th edn., ¶.78.

[2] Holdsworth, *HEL* vol. 3 151.

[3] *Pollock & Maitland* vol. 2 128. See also *The Earl of Shrewsbury's Case* (1609) 9 Co.Rep 42a, 50b, and Littleton, *Tenures,* s.341 for novel disseisin of a rent seck.

Very often, however, there was no need for a proprietary action, because seisin of services is fully protected by possessory actions. It is protected by the same actions that protect a seisin of land. If 'M' has hitherto being paying his rent to 'A', and is coerced by distress into paying it to 'X', then 'A' has been disseised by 'X' and can bring an assize of novel disseisin against 'X' and recover his seisin . . . The wrong complained of is not in our modern phrase 'a malicious interference with contractual rights'; it is a disseisin, the ousting of another from that which he is possessed.

Yet it was never necessary to reserve a rent in order to create the relationship of landlord and tenant. Absent any rent, the fealty owed by the tenant to the landlord was sufficient.[4]

The common law recognised various types of rent, but the essential distinction was between rents 'reserved' to the grantor, on a disposition leaving a reversion in the grantor, on the one hand, and rents 'granted' or re-granted, on the other.[5] A rent reserved to the grantor, on a disposition which left a reversion in the grantor[6]—the subinfeudation of a fee simple,[7] or the grant of a fee tail, or the grant of a lease or underlease—was a 'rent

---

[4] Littleton, *Tenures*, s.132, *Co.Litt.* 67b, 93b, *Sury* v. *Brown* (1623) Latch 99, 100, 3 Bulstrode 328 Per Whitlock J: 'If one makes a lease, and no reservation of any rent in it, the law reserves fealty for him': Chambers, *Leases*, 1, *Ashburn Anstalt* v. *Arnold* [1989] Ch 1, contra *Perks*, ¶.536. In Ireland, fealty ceased to be part of the relationship by s.3 Landlord and Tenant Law Amendment Act (Ireland) 1860.

[5] C.Langdell, *Brief Survey of Equity Jurisdiction* (1896) 10 Harv L Rev 71, 79.

[6] 'No rent (which is properly said to be a rent) may be reserved upon any feoffment, gift or lease, but only to the feoffor, or to the donor, or to the lessor, or to their heirs, and in no manner may it be reserved to any strange person': Littleton, *Tenures*, s.346, (1436) YB 14 Hen.6 f.26 pl.77, *Co.Litt.* 213b, Gilbert, *Rents*, 54. There was an exception for the Crown. The Crown could reserve a rent to a stranger: Littleton, *Tenures*, s.346, *Cole* v. *Sury* (1626) Latch 264, 267, Platt, *Leases*, vol. 2 98.

[7] Further subinfeudation was prohibited by the Statute of Quia Emptores 1290. So any rent service due from an owner in fee simple to a superior lord (other than the Crown) must have been created before 30th November 1290: Halsbury's Laws, *Real Property*, vol. 39(2), 4th edn., ¶.7. These seigniorial rents, known as 'chief rents' or 'fee farm rents' were extinguished, at the latest, on 31st December 1935 by ss.128-140 Law of Property Act 1922; see Halsbury's Laws, *Real Property*, vol. 39(2), 4th edn., ¶.84. For an exception in Ireland, see the Renewable Leasehold Conversion Act 1849.

service'.[8]

A rent granted to a stranger out of freehold land was a 'rent charge', if it was granted with an express power to levy distress, and was otherwise a 'rent seck' (or a 'dry rent').[9] So was a rent granted back to the disponor on an outright conveyance of freehold land. But a rent charge or a rent seck could only issue out of freehold land. No rent charge or rent seck could be created out of a leasehold estate.[10]

A statutory power of distress for rents seck was granted by s.5 Landlord and Tenant Act 1730,[11] and thereafter there ceased to be any practical difference between the three types of rent.[12] All three were treated as tenements[13] and as incorporeal hereditaments.[14] But that did not change the rule that a rent charge or a rent seck could not issue out of a leasehold estate.

Where a rent service was reserved to a landlord, the landlord

---

[8] Littleton, *Tenures*, s.214. In 1310 rent due under lease for years was not a rent service, which meant that the landlord could only distrain by express agreement, but by 1370 it was settled that it had become a rent service: Kaye, *Medieval English Conveyances*, 265.

[9] Littleton, *Tenures*, s.218.

[10] *Brediman* v. *Bromley* (1606) Cro Jac 142, *Smith* v. *Mapleback* (1786) 1 Term Rep 441, *Langford* v. *Selmes* (1857) 3 Kay & J 220, cf. *Cartwright* v. *Pinkney* (1675) 1 Vent 272, 3 Keble 488.

[11] 'And whereas the remedy for recovering rents seck, rents of assize, and chief rents are tedious and difficult . . . from and after the twenty fourth day of June one thousand seven hundred and thirty one, all and every person or persons, bodies politick and corporate, shall and may have like remedy by distress and by impounding and selling the same, in cases of rents seck, rents of assize, and chief rents . . . as in case of rent reserved upon lease, any law or usage to the contrary notwithstanding'.

[12] Since a sum reserved on assignment of a leasehold estate cannot be 'rent' (*Smith* v. *Mapleback* (1786) 1 Term Rep 441), it follows that there is no right to distrain for it under this Act: *Langford* v. *Selmes* (1857) 3 Kay & J 220, *Lewis* v. *Baker* [1905] 1 Ch 46. But a creditor can distrain for sums due from a leasehold tenant if a special power to do so is contained in the instrument creating the debt: *Pollitt* v. *Forrest* (1847) 11 QB 949, 961, Platt, *Leases*, vol. 2 83.

[13] Holdsworth, *HEL*. vol. 3 151.

[14] *Bl.Comm*. Bk.II 41–43. See also s.205(ix) Law of Property Act 1925 which defines 'land' as including 'a rent and other incorporeal hereditament', and s.205(xxiii) which defines 'Rent' as including 'a rent service or a rent charge, or other rent, toll, duty, royalty, or annual or periodic payment in money or money's worth, reserved or issuing out of or charged upon land'.

could grant it away by deed[15] to a stranger later. Indeed, assignments of rents are still common today as part of security transactions.[16] The effect of separating a rent service from a freehold reversion was that it became a rent seck,[17] so that the assignee could bring an action in debt for it, but not, until 1705,[18] before the tenant had first attorned to the assignee.[19] Nor could the assignee distrain for it, before 1731,[20] because the implied right to distrain was lost by conveying the rent away from the reversion.[21] If it was separated from a leasehold reversion, then, before 1875,[22] the assignment would probably only have been regarded as being effective in equity, and then only if made for value.

In the same way as a grant of land, which did not refer expressly to heirs, would be construed merely as a grant for life,[23] so too a reservation of a rent made simply 'to the lessor' would be treated as a reservation for the life of the grantor,[24]

---

[15] See ch.1 headings 'Formalities' and 'Leases of incorporeal hereditaments'.

[16] Although a rent service can be assigned inter vivos, it cannot be left by will separately from the reversion, except by interposition of a trust: *Knolle's Case* (1534) Dyer 5b.

[17] Gilbert, *Rents* 6.

[18] s.9 Administration of Justice Act 1705.

[19] *Goodwin* v. *Parker* (1670) 1 Freeman 1.

[20] s.5 Landlord and Tenant Act 1730.

[21] This caused difficulties where the rent arrears were owed to a freehold reversioner who died before 1898. The arrears would pass to the personal representatives, but the reversion would vest automatically in the legatee or heir at law (see ch.8 heading 'Devolution on death'). Personal representatives were empowered by s.12 Cestui Que Vie Act 1540 to distrain for any arrears of 'rent service, rent charge, rent seck or fee farm', but this did not apply to arrears of rent owed by a leasehold tenant: Coote, *Leases*, 439–440. Power to do so was eventually granted by s.37 Civil Procedure Act 1833. There was no such difficulty with arrears of rent owed to a leasehold reversioner, for a leasehold reversion always vested in the personal representatives along with the arrears of rent, and since 1898, that has been the rule for a freehold reversion too.

[22] s.25(6) Judicature Act 1873. Now s.136 Law of Property Act 1925.

[23] Bracton vol. 2 267 (f.92b), *Perks*, ¶.243, *Bl.Comm.* Bk.II 121, *Pollock & Maitland* vol. 1 308, vol. 2 7, Halsbury's Laws, *Real Property*, vol. 39(2), 4th edn., ¶.147. The rule was abrogated by s.60(1) Law of Property Act 1925.

[24] *Anon* (1338) 2 Rol Abr 450 pl.2, *Anon* (1601) Gouldsborough 148 pl.68, Gilbert, *Rents*, 65, Preston, *Conveyancing*, vol. 2 186, cf. Platt, *Leases*, vol. 2 89.

which would abate on the grantor's death.[25] A landlord could get round the problem, by expressly reserving the rent to his 'heirs' or 'executors' as well, but if the landlord got it wrong, by reserving the rent to 'heirs' when the reversion would in fact pass to the landlord's 'executors',[26] or vice versa, then the rent would still abate on the landlord's death, because a reservation away from the reversion would contravene the rule that no rent could be 'reserved' to a stranger.[27] In 1535 it was decided that expressly reserving the rent 'during the term' would solve the problem, making the rent payable to the landlord's successors in title, after the original landlord's death,[28] whomever they might be,[29] and by 1671 that applied even where the lease mistakenly referred to the wrong successor,[30] which is why all modern leases still reserve rent 'during the term'.[31]

Strictly, it is said, that rent ought to be reserved as a yearly sum.[32] All that means is that it must issue out of the land by reference to some period of a year or less.[33] So a premium is not rent, even if it is payable in instalments.[34] But rent can never be reserved so as to be payable after the term has expired.[35] So the landlords of some modern leases, who attempt to evade the

---

[25] A reservation to the landlord and his 'assigns' would abate on the landlord's death too: *Co.Litt.* 215b.

[26] A freehold reversion passed to heirs, a leasehold reversion passed to executors: see ch.8 heading 'Devolution on death'.

[27] Similarly, if the reservation was made to the 'heir', but he took in a different capacity (eg. as remainderman) the rent would abate: *Huntley's case* (1627) Palmer 485, Gilbert, *Rents*, 59.

[28] (1535) YB 27 Hen.8 f.14b-18b pl.6, *Mallory's case* (1600) 5 Co.Rep 111b, Platt, *Leases vol.* 2 91.

[29] *Whitlock's Case* (1609) 8 Co.Rep 69b, 70b.

[30] *Sacheverell v. Frogatt* (1671) 2 Wms Saund 361, 367, 1 Vent 161, 1 Freeman 16, Gilbert, *Rents*, 68.

[31] Stewart, *Practice of Conveyancing,* 329n.

[32] *Co.Litt.* 47a.

[33] There is a precedent for yearly rent payable monthly in G. Jacob, *The Accomplished Conveyancer,* vol. 1 (London, Butt, 1714) 441.

[34] *Lord Hatherton v. Bradburne* (1843) 13 Sim 599, 611. If it is payable over the whole term, it may not truly be a premium: *Rush v. Matthews* [1926] 1 KB 492.

[35] *Barwick v. Foster* (1609) 1 Brownlow 105, 2 Brown PC 220, Cro Jac 227, 233, 1 Bulstrode 1, *Clun v. Fisher* (1613) 10 Co.Rep 127a, Cro Jac 309.

statutory[36] restrictions on the recovery of terminal dilapidations as damages, by reserving the post-termination loss as additional 'rent',[37] might find that the result is that nothing is recoverable at all.

It was not possible, at common law, to grant a rent out of an incorporeal hereditament, nor reserve a rent on a letting of an incorporeal hereditament,[38] except to the Crown.[39] That rule, however, was abrogated by s.201 Law of Property Act 1925.

2. Payment.

At common law, rent is payable in arrears, once a year, on the anniversary of the tenancy, unless the lease is for a shorter term, in which event it is payable on the expiration of the term or each period of the term. The theory was explained in *Clun's Case*:[40]

> . . . the rent reserved is to be raised out of the profits of the land, and is not due until the profits are taken by the lessee: for these words *reddeno inde*, or *reservando inde*, is as much as to say the lessee shall pay so much of the issues and profits at such days to the lessor . . . And that is the reason that the rent so reserved is not due or payable before the day of payment incurred, because it is to be rendered and restored out of the issues and profits.

In practice, most leases reserved an annual rent payable in arrears by equal instalments on the four usual quarter days,[41] or

---

[36] s.18 Landlord and Tenant Act 1927.

[37] See ch.5 heading 'Repair'.

[38] *Jewel's Case* (1588) 5 Co.Rep 3a, *Lovelace* v. *Reynolds* (1597) Noy 59, 60, Cro Eliz 563, *Co.Litt.* 47a, *Gardiner* v. *Williamson* (1831) 2 Barn & Ald 336, *Bl.Comm.* Bk.II 41, Holdsworth, *HEL* vol. 7 265–266, Gilbert, *Rents* 20–21.

[39] *Lord Mountjoy's Case* (1589) 5 Co.Rep 3b. The reason for the exception was that the Crown could levy distress for rent on land belonging to the tenant anywhere, and not just the demised premises: Statute of Marlborough 1267 c.15 (Coke, *2nd Inst*, 131–133). There was, perhaps, another exception in the case of tithes: Platt, *Leases*, vol. 1 70, cf. Gilbert, *Rents* 21.

[40] (1613) 10 Co.Rep 127a, 128a. See also Holdsworth, *HEL* vol. 7 267.

[41] See, e.g. the early sixteenth century lease of an Oxford brewhouse in J. Arnold, *The Customs of London* (London, Rivington, 1811) 109.

(in early leases) two of them,[42] until the twentieth century,[43] when the practice changed to paying quarterly in advance on those days instead.[44] The usual quarter days have been Ladyday (25th March), Midsummer (24th June), Michaelmas (29th September) and Christmas day (25th December)[45] since 1751.[46]

Before then, they were twelve days later, and those days continued to be customary quarter days in some counties afterwards.[47]

Unless the lease provides otherwise, rent technically becomes due for payment at sunset on the relevant day,[48] not before, and is 'in arrears' if it is not paid before midnight.[49] If the

---

[42] *Browning* v. *Beston* (1552) Plowden 130, 131, *Hill* v. *Grange* (1556) Plowden 164, 167, *Chapman* v. *Dalton* (1565) Plowden 284.

[43] The second edition of Key and Elphinstone's, *Precedents in Conveyancing* (London, Sweet and Maxwell, 1883) 624, contains alternative precedents for rents payable in arrears and rents payable in advance.

[44] As late as 1967 the editors of *Adkin's Law of Landlord and Tenant* could say: '. . . leases are occasionally found where all the rents are payable in advance e.g. at the commencement of every quarter, instead of at the end; and it is by no means uncommon for the last quarter's rent of a term to be made payable in advance so that the landlord may be sure of obtaining it without trouble': B. Adkin, *Landlord and Tenant*, 16th edn., eds R. Walton and M. Essayan (London, Estates Gazette, 1967) 83–84. There is a precedent for a rent payable in arrear, except for the last instalment, in the *Encyclopedia of Forms and Precedents*, 4th edn., vol. 11 (London, Butterworths, 1965) 303. The courts were hostile to attempts to make rent payable in advance in the nineteenth century. In *Holland* v. *Palser* (1817) 2 Stark 161 a covenant to pay the rent in advance was held to apply to the first instalment only.

[45] The 'two usual feasts' were Ladyday and Michaelmas (Gilbert, *Rents* 51–52, *Chapman* v. *Dalton* (1565) Plowden 284). The four usual feasts were those two plus Midsummer and Christmas. In Scotland the usual quarter days are 28th February, 28th May, 28th August and 28th November: Term and Quarter Days (Scotland) Act 1990.

[46] s.1, s.6 The Calendar (New Style) Act 1750, *Norton on Deeds*, 164–166.

[47] In *Doe d. Hall* v. *Benson* (1821) 4 Barn & Ald 588 it was held that evidence of the custom of the county could be given at trial to prove that 'Ladyday' meant Old Ladyday in a parol lease of land in Lincoln. The evidence was not admissible if the lease was in writing: *Norton on Deeds*, 166. The Crown still has its own quarter days which are 5th January, 5th April, 5th July and 10th October.

[48] *Wade's Case* (1601) 5 Co.Rep 114a.

[49] *Anon* (1588) Gouldsborough 98 pl.17, *Strafford* v. *Wentworth* (1722) 9 Mod. 21, *Rockingham* v. *Penrice* (1711) 1 Peere Wms 177, *Re Aspinall* [1961] Ch 526.

tenant pays on the due day, but before sunset, that satisfies the obligation to pay,[50] but a payment made on an earlier day did not discharge the obligation to pay later on the correct day at common law, nor prevent the landlord exercising a right to forfeit for failing to pay the rent again on the correct day.[51] By the nineteenth century, however, the acceptance of a pre-payment operated as an equitable satisfaction of the obligation to make the payment on a later date.[52] But equity only operates personally on the parties and those taking under them afterwards, so if a prior mortgagee takes possession before the rent day, the pre-payment to the mortgagor will be no defence, and the tenant will have to pay again.[53]

If a lease does not specify the place for payment of the rent, then the medieval rule was that any demand for or tender[54] of rent ought to be made at the land, because the land itself was the debtor.[55] So the landlord could not sue for the rent in debt[56] nor call on a rent guarantee[57] without making a demand at the land first. But the landlord could sue in covenant,[58] because a debtor who covenants to pay a sum is under an implied obligation to seek out the creditor, and a landlord could levy a distress for rent without any prior demand, since levying the distress was itself a demand at the demised property.[59]

There was never any need for the landlord to make a demand

---

[50] *Wade's Case* (1601) 5 Co.Rep 114a, *Southern* v. *Bellasis* (1701) 1 Peere Wms 180n, *Dibble* v. *Bowater* (1853) 2 E & B 564, Gilbert, *Rents*, 91, Platt, *Leases*, vol. 2 119.

[51] *Cromwell* v. *Andrews* (1583) Cro Eliz 15, sub nom *Fuller's Case* (1583) 4 Leon 4.

[52] *Nash* v. *Gray* (1861) 2 F & F 391.

[53] *De Nicholls* v. *Saunders* (1870) LR 5 CP 589.

[54] If the tenant tendered the rent, and it was refused, and the landlord still refused it after it was paid into court, 'he hath lost the money forever': *Co.Litt.* 207a.

[55] *Co.Litt.* 201b, *Sweton* v. *Cushe* (1603) Yelv 36, 37. There is a precedent for a lease requiring a demand to be made at the 'now mansion house of the premises' in W. West, *Simboleograph* (London, Stationers Co., 1610) pt.1 s.435.

[56] *Anon* (1626) Byrson's Exch Cas 24.

[57] The Notebook of Sir John Port (1514), ed. J. Baker (London, Selden Society, 1986) 102 SS 'Note' 18.

[58] *Anon* (1626) Byrson's Exch Cas 24, *Haldane* v. *Johnson* (1853) 8 Exch 689.

[59] *Maund's Case* (1601) 7 Co.Rep 28b.

for payment if the lease terms expressly dispensed with it,[60] nor if the landlord was the Crown.[61] Nor did the landlord need to make a demand if the place reserved in the lease for the payment of rent was the landlord's own residence. The corollary of this rule was that the tenant could make a valid tender of the rent at the place where the lease required it to be paid. So when the Bishop of Exeter let land with rent payable in Exeter, tender at the palace gate was good, 'whether the gate be open or shut'.[62] But a landlord is not obliged to accept tender of a part payment of rent, for if it is to be a good tender, it must be of the whole sum due.[63]

The rules about 'formal' demands, which are a common law pre-requisite of the right to forfeit for non-payment of rent,[64] are explained in chapter 7.

3. Rent control.

Residential premises: During the First World War, and for six months afterwards,[65] the Increase of Rent and Mortgage Interest (War Restrictions) Act 1915 froze the rent charged for any house, part of house, or flat, let as a separate dwelling,[66] except where the annual rent or rateable value was more than £35 in London and £26 elsewhere.[67] The limits were doubled, when that legislation was temporarily continued, in 1919,[68] and

---

[60] *Anon* (1626) Byrson's Exch Cas 24.

[61] Gilbert, *Rents*, 76. Crown debts were payable at the Exchequer, or to the bailiff or receiver general of the Crown, and not on the land: Gilbert, *Rents*, 89, Platt, *Leases*, vol. 2 100.

[62] *Anon* (1557) 3 Leon 4, Bendloe 14 pl.57.

[63] 3 Salk 2 'Acceptance'.

[64] (1366) YB 40 Ed.3 Lib. Ass. f.241 pl.11, *Co.Litt.* 202a.

[65] s.5(2).

[66] s.1(1). The Act was amended in 1917 to allow a tenancy for a term of 21 years or more to be granted for a premium: s.4(1) Courts (Emergency Powers) Act 1917.

[67] s.2(2).

[68] s.4 Rent and Mortgage Interest (Restrictions) Act 1919.

then tripled in 1920,[69] bringing about 98% of housing within the Acts. This subsequently came to be called 'old control'. Most properties were removed from old control between 1923 and 1938,[70] but in 1939 it still applied to about four million properties, which continued to be subject to the rent restrictions in the 1920 Act until 1957.

At the outbreak of the Second World War in 1939, any property where the rent or rateable value was less than £100 in London or £75 elsewhere, which was not still subject to old control, was swept into 'new control',[71] which was again most of the residential property in the country. The maximum recoverable rent for properties subject to 'new control' was based on the rent charged on 1st September 1939, instead of that charged on 3rd August 1914, which remained the case for properties subject to old control.[72]

Properties where the rateable value on 6th July 1956 exceeded £40 in London or £30 elsewhere, were removed from control by the Rent Act 1957,[73] which also made it impossible to create any new controlled tenancies.[74] The rent limit for remaining controlled tenancies was also changed, so that it was no longer based on 1914 or 1939 rental values. Instead, the landlord was generally allowed to charge twice the rateable value of the property, subject to adjustment for the terms of the tenancy.[75] Between 1972 and 1980 all those remaining controlled

---

[69] s.12(2) Increase of Rent and Mortgage Interest (Restrictions) Act 1920.

[70] For the details, see ch.4 heading 'Residential security'.

[71] s.3 Rent and Mortgage Interest Restrictions Act 1939.

[72] s.3. Where a property was subject to old control, but had not been let on 3rd August 1914, or was subject to new control, but had not been let on 1st September 1939, then the maximum recoverable rent was based on the rent last charged before it had been brought into control, or, if it had never previously been let, the rent charged on the first occasion on which it was let afterwards.

[73] s.11(1) Rent Act 1957.

[74] There were exceptions for new tenancies by way of surrender and re-grant or granted as a result of overcrowding: R. Megarry, *The Rent Acts*, 11th edn. (London, Stevens and Sons, 1988) vol. 1 219.

[75] s.1 Rent Act 1957. See generally L. Blundell and V. Wellings, *The Complete Guide to the Rent Acts* (London, Sweet and Maxwell, 1958) ch.4.

tenancies were converted into regulated tenancies instead.[76]

Regulated tenancies were introduced by the Rent Act 1965, which swept all the homes which had been decontrolled by the 1957 Act back into protection as new 'regulated' tenancies.[77] The 'fair rent' regime established under that Act, continues to apply to those residential tenancies which have Rent Act protection, being generally those where the original tenancy was granted for a term of less than 21 years before 15th January 1989.[78] The theory of 'fair rents' was that the landlord should not be allowed to charge more than whatever the open market rent would have been, had there been enough properties available to meet the demand. In other words, it was an open market rent discounted for scarcity. But the open market price of any commodity is a function how much of it is available to meet demand, and since few property owners actually wanted to devalue their investments by granting leases at less than the market rent,[79] there was almost no property available to meet the demand, with the result was that 'fair' rents often proved to be less than even half of open market rents. Rather than leave properties empty, landlords would sometimes grant short leases to companies, which were subject to the fair rent regime, but did not have security of tenure at the end of the contractual term. But more often, landlords would sell their properties off to owner occupiers by way of long leases granted for premiums instead.[80]

In 1980[81] an attempt was made to increase the number of properties available for letting, by introducing a scheme under which the landlord would have an absolute right to recover possession at the end of the term, or on any anniversary thereafter, by serving a statutory notice.[82] These were 'protected

---

[76] R. Megarry, *The Rent Acts*, 11th edn. (London, Stevens and Sons, 1988) vol. 1 221–223.

[77] The limits were £400 in London and £200 elsewhere on 23rd March 1965.

[78] s.34 Housing Act 1988.

[79] Rent Act reversions typically traded at a discount of between 30% and 45% to the vacant possession value.

[80] See ch.4 heading 'Fixed terms'.

[81] ss.51-55 Housing Act 1980.

[82] R. Megarry, *The Rent Acts*, 11th edn. (London, Stevens & Sons, 1988) vol. 1 212–217.

shorthold tenancies'. The attempt failed because the landlord could still only recover a fair rent, and it was very difficult to get the notices right.

That changed following the introduction of assured tenancies under the Housing Act 1988, which had no security of tenure at the end of the term (if a relatively simple notice was served at the beginning)[83] and under which the landlord was free to let the property at whatever rent the tenant might agree to pay. In *Spath Holme* v. *Manchester and Lancashire RAC*[84] it was pointed out that, since there was now a plentiful supply of private sector residential accommodation in the market, there could hardly any justification for continuing to apply a substantial discount for scarcity when setting fair rents for those tenancies which remained within the Rent Acts. The result was a substantial increase in fair rents, until statutory limits on the amount of any increase were imposed by order in 1999.[85]

Houses built and let by local authorities after the First World War were initially subject to a separate rent control regime, based on average rents charged for working-class dwellings in 1914. Since 1936 local authorities and housing associations have been entitled to charge whatever 'reasonable' rent they think fit, and from time to time to review and change those rents.[86]

Private sector furnished tenancies were outside the Rent Acts between 1920[87] and 1974[88] too. But under the Furnished Houses (Rent Control) Act 1946, a Rent Assessment Tribunal could reduce the rent payable for a furnished tenancy to such sum as it thought reasonable, and grant an indefinite number of six month

---

[83] Between 15th January 1989 and 27th February 1997 it was necessary to contract into the shorthold regime, by service of a notice at the beginning. Since 28th February 1997, an assured tenancy has automatically been a shorthold tenancy, without the need to serve any notice, unless the parties have contracted out: see generally T. Fancourt, *Megarry's Assured Tenancies*, 2nd edn. (London, Sweet and Maxwell, 1999) 111–124.

[84] [1995] 2 EGLR 80.

[85] Rent Acts (Maximum Fair Rent) Order 1999, SI 1999 No.69. The validity of the order was upheld by the House of Lords in *R* v. *Secretary of State for the Environment ex parte Spath Holme* [2001] 2 AC 349.

[86] s.83 Housing Act 1936, s.111 Housing Act 1957. Now s.24 Housing Act 1985.

[87] s.12(2) 1920 Act.

[88] s.1 Rent Act 1974.

extensions to the tenancy, if the landlord tried to evict the tenant as a result.

Agricultural land: Except for a brief period at the end of the First World War,[89] there was no rent control for leases of agricultural land before the enactment of the Agricultural Holdings Act 1948, which first gave tenants of agricultural holdings security of tenure,[90] under which either party had the right to demand an arbitration as to the rent after the first three years, and three yearly after that.[91] Originally, the review was simply to the open market rent.[92] That was changed in 1984,[93] and the changes were incorporated into the Agricultural Holdings Act 1986.[94] As a result of those changes there is no longer any express reference to the open market rent when setting the rent for an agricultural holding. That only comes in obliquely, because in determining the 'rent properly payable', the reviewer must take account of a number of factors, which include the rents achieved on lettings of comparable properties. But, crucially, the reviewer is obliged to discount the rent for scarcity.[95] Few farms are available for letting on the open market, notwithstanding the introduction of farm business tenancies in 1995, so rents set for agricultural holdings still tend to be well below open market rents.

Except in the case of an accidental surrender and re-grant of an earlier tenancy, and succession tenancies, new lettings of agricultural land since 1st September 1995 have been farm business tenancies, governed by the Agricultural Tenancies Act 1995, rather than by the previous agricultural holdings legislation. The parties are free to agree whatever initial rent they wish. There are restrictions on contractual rent review,[96] but the

---

[89] Corn Production Act 1917.

[90] See ch.4 heading 'Agricultural security'.

[91] s.8 Agricultural Holdings Act 1948.

[92] s.8 Agricultural Holdings Act 1948, s.2 Agriculture Act 1958.

[93] s.1 Agricultural Holdings Act 1984.

[94] s.12 Agricultural Holdings Act 1986.

[95] Para.1(3)(a) sch. 2 Agricultural Holdings Act 1986.

[96] s.9.

landlord is generally entitled to implement statutory reviews instead,[97] which are determined by arbitration[98] on an upwards or downwards to open market rent basis.[99] In practice, few farm business tenancies are granted for a term which is long enough to require a rent review. Indeed, few farm business tenancies are granted at all. If an agricultural landowner is not going to farm the land itself, the modern practice is to enter into a joint venture agreement with a farm contracting company, which enjoys all the benefits of economies of scale.

Business premises: There have only been two brief periods during which the rents of purely business tenancies have been controlled. Between 24th June 1920 and 24th June 1921 landlords were prohibited from raising the rent of business premises if the annual rent or rateable value was less than £105 in London or £78 elsewhere,[100] and between 6th November 1972 and 31st March 1976[101] there were statutory anti-inflation controls under which any increase in rent for all business premises was prohibited.[102] Otherwise, landlords and tenants of business premises have always been free to agree whatever rents they see fit, and on a compulsory renewal of a business tenancy having security of the tenure under the Landlord and Tenant Act 1954, the new rent set by the court is an open market rent.[103]

4. Variable rents and rent review.

Rent is now almost invariably reserved in money, and

---

[97] s.10.

[98] s.12.

[99] s.13.

[100] s.13 Increase of Rent and Mortgage Interest (Restrictions) Act 1920.

[101] s.2(4) Counter Inflation (Temporary Provisions) Act 1972, s.11 Counter Inflation Act 1973.

[102] Between 19th March 1975 and 31st March 1976 a landlord could raise the rent, if the landlord had first served a one month decontrol notice: The Counter-Inflation (Business Rents) (Decontrol) Order 1975 (SI 1975 No.21).

[103] s.34 Landlord and Tenant Act 1954.

money rents have always been common.[104] But, in the past, rent
was often reserved in a commodity instead[105]—there was never
any conceptual difficulty with this, since rent was supposed to
represent a share of the produce or profits of the land[106]—and
even an obligation to ring a church bell can be rent.[107]

In the eleventh century, rent was often reserved in grain,[108]
and that was still common at the end of the sixteenth.[109] If the
rent was in arrears, the landlord could bring a claim in debt based
on the market price of corn at the time the rent should have been
paid.[110] More romantically, nominal rents were sometimes
reserved in roses,[111] and a peppercorn rent is literally that.

Money rents based on the fluctuating price of a commodity

---

[104] A case in 1401 (YB 3 Hen.4 f.25b pl.2) involved a lease for 8 years granted
at a rent of £20 pa.

[105] Coal in a mining lease, *Buckley* v. *Kenyon* (1808) 10 East 139; 12 bottles of
Canary wine in *Pitcher* v. *Tovey* (1691) 4 Mod. 71; '200lbs of fine white sugar'
in a lease of land in Barbados, E.Wood, *Conveyancing,* vol. 3 (London,
Stratham & Woodfall, 1793) 125.

[106] It could not be a share of the actual produce of the demised property;
Co.Litt. 47a, *Bl.Comm.* Bk.II 41, Platt, *Leases*, vol. 2 101. A share of the actual
produce would be an *exception* of a profit á prendre, rather than a *reservation*
of a rent.

[107] *Doe d. Edney* v. *Billett* (1845) 7 QB 976.

[108] E. Tabuteau, *Transfers of Property in 11th Century Norman Law*
(University of North Carolina Press, 1988) 69.

[109] W. West *Simboleograph,* (London, Stationers Co., 1610) pt.1, s.433
(barley), s.439 (corn). Shakespeare's father held land at Asbies, at a rent of half
a quarter of wheat and the same of barley; see T. Blount *Tenures of Land and
Customs of Manors*, 5th edn., ed. W. Hazlitt (reprinted, Epsom, Barsby, 1999)
9. In *Woodland* v. *Mantel* ((1551) Plowden 94, 96) reference was made to rent
reserved in capons or eggs. Orlando Bridgman, in the seventeenth century,
drew a lease for three lives reserving hens, capons, and the average of two
days' harvests, as the rent: O. Bridgman, *Conveyances*, 3rd edn. (London,
Atkins, 1699) vol. 1 15. In *Master of St Cross Hospital* v. *Howard de Walden*
(1795) 6 Term Rep 338 the rent was 40 quarters of clean wheat.

[110] *Anon* (1590) 4 Leon 46.

[111] In 1604 a property in Billinghurst was held for 10,000 years at a yearly rent
of one red rose, and one in Peniston at a rent of 'a snowball at Midsummer and
red rose at Christmas': T. Blount *Fragmenta Antiquitatis* (*Blount's Jocular
Tenures*) 5th edn. (Reprint, Epsom, Barsby, 1999) 33, 278. The author has seen
a lease granted in the early twentieth century, where the rent was one rose
(colour not specified) to be rendered on Midsummer's Day.

were first introduced for college leases in 1576.[112] Even as late as the nineteenth century, these corn rents were still common in leases granted by colleges.[113] The same scheme was sometimes used for the commutation of tithes under Inclosure Awards during the eighteenth century. Tithes were typically commuted into money payments, subject to periodic review based on the local price of grain.[114]

In 1925 the Royal Mint stopped issuing gold coins[115] and in 1931 the value of sterling ceased to be related to the value of gold.[116] That resulted in an attempt, in 1932, to grant a lease where the sterling amount of the rent was pegged to the fluctuating value of gold,[117] but the drafting was held to be ineffective in 1956,[118] which prompted conveyancers to try an alternative approach.[119]

The fundamental fear, underlying the drafting of all rent review clauses in this period, was of contravening the rule that the rent reserved had to be 'certain' at every moment during the term of the lease, otherwise it could not be rent.[120] This was

---

[112] 18 Eliz.1 c.6 s.1, required one third of the rent of college leases to be paid in wheat or malt, or, in default, in money equivalent to the local market price. 'This is said to have been an invention of Lord Treasurer Burleigh, and Sir Thomas Smith, then principal secretary of state; who, observing how greatly the value of money had sunk, and the price of all provisions risen, by the quantity of bullion imported from the newfound Indies (which effects were likely to increase to a greater degree) devised this method for upholding the revenues of colleges': *Bl.Comm.* Bk.II 322, Reeves, ed. W. Finlason, *History of English Law* (London, Reeves and Turner, 1869) vol. 3 624.

[113] Stewart, *Practice of Conveyancing* 349.

[114] R. Kain, R. Oliver, R. Fry, S. Wilmot, *The Tithe Maps of England and Wales: A Cartographic Analysis and County-by-County Catalogue* (Cambridge, Cambridge University Press, 1995) 3.

[115] Gold Standard Act 1925.

[116] Gold Standard (Amendment) Act 1931.

[117] At common law, rent could be reserved in gold, and if a new lease was granted reserving the same monetary amount of rent in silver, that would not be treated as a lease at the same rent: *Mountjoy's Case* (1589) 5 Co.Rep 3b, 6a.

[118] *Treseder-Griffin* v. *Cooperative Insurance Society* [1956] 2 QB 127.

[119] R. Bernstein & K.Reynolds, *Handbook of Rent Review* (London, Sweet and Maxwell, 2004) ¶.1.2.3.

[120] Gilbert, *Rents* 9–10.

thought, on the authority of Coke,[121] to mean that the actual amount of the rent accruing due on each rent day had to be known on that day, rather than being ascertainable later, according to events happening afterwards.[122] In practice, mining leases had always been granted reserving a variable turnover rent, payable in arrears, and nobody had ever suggested that there was any problem with this, provided that the amount of the rent had become fixed by the relevant rent day. So the standard drafting technique used in rent review clauses throughout the 1960s and 1970s, in order to ensure that the amount of the rent due would be known on each rent day, was the 'trigger' type review. Commercial leases during that period were typically granted for terms in multiples of seven years, and the landlord was given the right to serve a written notice, triggering a review every seventh year, shortly before the review date. If the landlord did so, the market rent would be determined, either by an independent expert or by arbitration, and the rent would be increased to that sum, if it was higher than the passing rent. Pending the decision or award the rent would remain payable at the previous rate, but once the new rent had been determined, an amount equivalent to the difference between the new rent and the old rent, calculated back to the review date, would become due on the next rent date, and the new rent would be payable from that date, until the next review, too. So there would never be any question of contravening the certainty rule, for the sum of money payable by way of rent on any particular quarter day would always have been ascertained before that quarter day occurred, and there would never be any question of changing what was due on that date afterwards.

The disadvantage with this type of review was that it depended on the landlord remembering to serve the trigger

---

[121] *Co.Litt.* 96a. Coke gave this example: 'And yet in some cases there may be certainty in uncertainty; as a man may hold of his lord to sheer all the sheep depasturising without the lord's manor; and this is certain enough, albeit that the lord hath sometime a greater number and sometime a lesser number there; and yet this uncertainty, being referred to the manor which is certain, the lord may distrain for this uncertainty'.

[122] *Parker* v. *Harris* (1692) 4 Mod. 76, *In Re Essoldo* (*Bingo*) *Ltd's Underlease* (1971) 23 P&CR 1.

notice in time, which was normally during a five-month window commencing six months before the relevant review date. Throughout the 1970s there was litigation where the landlord had forgotten to do so, and then tried to serve the notice late, culminating in the decision of the House of Lords in *United Scientific Holdings* v. *Burnley BC*.[123] The effect of that decision was that time would not generally be treated as being of the essence for service of notices under rent review clauses, with the result that where one party had a right to implement a review by a particular date, and did not do so, in order to bar the right, the other party had to serve a notice making time of the essence, and the right to implement the review would only be barred if the landlord failed to serve the requisite notice within a reasonable time thereafter.[124] The general rule did not apply if time was expressly stated to be of the essence in the review clause, or if that followed as a matter of necessary implication; as the result, for instance, of a deeming provision.[125]

Various attempts were made to get round the problems inherent in the trigger type review clause: rolling review dates, so that a late trigger notice would take effect from the next anniversary of the missed review date; shorter review patterns, so that it would not matter so much if the landlord missed one; and, for short leases, fixed or index-linked increases, obviating the need for a review at all.[126]

But none of these solutions was entirely satisfactory. What was really required was automatic review, on each review date, with the amount of any increase being determined with retrospective effect afterwards, if necessary. Eventually, in

---

[123] [1978] AC 904.

[124] A tenant's notice making time of the essence for a landlord to implement a rent review is not effective to bar the right unless: the landlord has failed to comply with a contractual time limit for triggering the review (*Henry Smith's Charity* v. *Awada Trading* [1984] 1 EGLR 117, 120); the tenant, at the time it serves the notice, has performed all of its own outstanding obligations under the rent review clause (*Wood* v. *Berkeley Homes* (1992) 64 P&CR 311); and the notice allows the landlord a reasonable time thereafter to do whatever is necessary in order to implement the review (*Stickney* v. *Keeble* [1915] AC 386).

[125] *Starmark Enterprises* v. *CPL Distribution* [2002] Ch 306.

[126] There is a precedent for an index linked review clause in the *Encyclopedia of Forms and Precedents*, 4th edn., vol. 11 (London, Butterworths, 1965) 302.

1974,[127] it was decided that the feared problem about the certainty of the rent did not exist: whilst it was true that the landlord could not levy distress for the amount of any increase until that amount it had been ascertained, it did not follow that the increase had not been reserved as rent in the meantime.

Trigger type rent review clauses quickly fell into disuse afterwards, and all modern clauses are of the automatic type;[128] though there are, of course, still some old leases which contain trigger type clauses.

Some early rent review clauses provided for 'threshold' review: the rent could never fall below the original rent, but otherwise it could increase or decrease on each review. Yet these were an early aberration. The consistent drafting history since has been that the current rent can only remain the same or increase on each review; what is sometimes called a 'ratchet' review. The 1960s and early 1970s were times of increasing land values and high inflation, so it is not surprising or remarkable that this should have been the expectation of both parties.

When, however, commercial property values periodically crash, as they did in 1974, 1989 and 2008, there has been pressure to change the practice to allow downwards review too. Although such clauses have occasionally been forced on landlords, on renewals under part II Landlord and Tenant Act 1954,[129] they have generally resisted this pressure successfully, until the next rise in the market, when the issue recedes into the background again.

The statutory anti-inflation controls, which were in place between 6th November 1972 and 31st March 1976,[130] meant that the right to implement any review falling between those dates

---

[127] *CH Bailey* v. *Memorial Enterprises* [1974] 1 WLR 728, 731, confirmed in *United Scientific Holdings* v. *Burnley BC* [1978] AC 904.

[128] There is an early precedent for a semi-automatic review clause in the *Encyclopedia of Forms and Precedents*, 4th edn., vol. 11 (London, Butterworths, 1965) 300.

[129] *Boots the Chemist* v. *Pinkland* [1992] 2 EGLR 98.

[130] s.2(4) Counter Inflation (Temporary Provisions) Act 1972, s.11 Counter Inflation Act 1973.

was lost.[131] The lesson was learned, and rent review clauses since then have also provided for the review date to be postponed, during any period of statutory control, to the date when the control ends.

5. Insurance rent and service charge.

Fire insurance in England began in London at the end of the seventeenth century, after the great fire.[132] By the middle of the eighteenth century, covenants requiring the tenant to insure the property were common.[133] But having the tenant insure is not very convenient where a building is in multiple occupation, and there is always a risk that even a vigilant landlord might not find out about a breach until after the insurable event has happened, which is too late. So at the end of the nineteenth century some landlords started charging an additional variable insurance rent for the cost of insuring the property themselves.[134]

Leases of buildings in multiple occupation now also invariably contain provisions requiring the tenant to pay a proportionate part of the cost of maintaining the building and providing other services, by way of a variable service charge, which is sometimes reserved as an additional rent.[135] But this is a much later practice than charging an insurance rent. It was a

---

[131] Between 19th March 1975 and 31st March 1976 a landlord could implement a review, if the landlord had first served a one month decontrol notice: The Counter-Inflation (Business Rents) (Decontrol) Order 1975 (SI 1975 No.21).

[132] The 'Hand in Hand' or Amicable Contribution Society began as a mutual society in 1696.

[133] T. Williams, *Precedents in Conveyancing,* vol. 3 (London, Kearsley, 1788) 968, E. Wood, *Conveyancing,* vol. 3 (London, Stratham & Woodfall, 1793) 99, Stewart, *Practice of Conveyancing* 334.

[134] C. Bunyon, *The Law of Fire Insurance* (London, Layton, 1867) 132–133. A precedent for an insurance rent appears in the second, and every subsequent, edition of *Key and Elphinstone's Precedents in Conveyancing,* 2nd edn. (London, Sweet and Maxwell, 1883) vol. 1 625.

[135] In *Escalus Properties* v. *Robinson* [1996] QB 231 the Court of Appeal held that there was no conceptual difficulty in reserving a service charge to a landlord as additional rent. But see Platt, *Leases,* vol. 2 82–83.

'new' and 'modern' practice in 1972,[136] having been prompted, in the case of commercial property, by 'rapidly fluctuating and increasing prices',[137] and, in the case of residential property, by landlords granting longer leases for a premium in order to avoid the statutory controls on rent for short leases.[138]

Before the 1950s fixed service rents were sometimes encountered, but they were relatively rare.[139]

Early forms of service charge covenant required the tenant to pay the service charge to the landlord, in return for the landlord performing the services, and that arrangement is still common where commercial premises are let at a rack rent. But where flats were sold on long leases, leaving the landlord with an almost valueless reversion, landlords saw the advantage of making the tenants collectively responsible for the performance of the services and the collection of the service charge instead. That was done by issuing one share to each of the tenants in a specially incorporated service company, joining that company to the lease, and ensuring that the covenants to perform the services

---

[136] An early example is the lease in *Blatherwick (Services) Ltd* v. *King* [1991] Ch 218 which was granted in 1959. There is no precedent for a variable service charge in the twenty-fifth (1959) edition of *Prideaux's Precedents in Conveyancing*. The fifteenth (1953) edition of *Key and Elphinstone's Precedents in Conveyancing* contains a precedent for reserving the cost of gas and electricity consumed on the demised premises as rent (1095) and volume 11 of the fourth (1965) edition of the *Encyclopedia of Forms and Precedents* contains a precedent for reserving the variable cost of maintaining a garden as rent (304), but neither has a precedent for an all services rent.

[137] Per Buckley LJ in *Hayes* v. *Titan Properties* (1972) 24 P&CR 359, 361.

[138] See above heading 'Rent control'. There is a precedent for a complicated scheme for the sale of freehold flats, subject to leasehold easements over the common parts, which contain a variable service charge, in (1953) 17 Conv.(NS) 516–517. The first and second editions of E. George, *The Sale of Flats* (London, Sweet and Maxwell, 1957 & 1959) 121, 138, contained a primitive variable service charge covenant. The next edition, eleven years later (E. George and A. George, *The Sale of Flats*, 3rd edn. (London, Sweet and Maxwell, 1970) 255, contained a much fuller covenant.

[139] Encyclopedia of Forms and Precedents, 1st edn., vol. 7 (London, Butterworths, 1905) 432, *Barnes* v. *City of London Real Property Co* [1918] 2 Ch 18, *Property Holdings* v. *Clark* [1948] 1 KB 630, *Hayes* v. *Titan Properties* (1972) 24 P&CR 359, E. Foa, *Landlord and Tenant*, 8th edn. (London, Thames Bank, 1957) ¶.167.

and pay the service charge were made primarily[140] between that company and the tenants, and not the landlord and the tenants. Sometimes, to further distance the landlord from the obligations, the landlord granted the service company a lease of the common parts too.

There were two technical problems with reserving a service rent to a service company. First, since the obligation to pay the service charge, under that scheme, was owed to a third party, rather than to the landlord, the service charge could not technically be rent,[141] which meant that the service company could not levy distress for it, unless the tenant expressly granted the service company that right. Secondly, and more seriously, the burden of the obligation to pay service charge could not be made to run with the term of the lease, since it was not a covenant made between landlord and tenant. So it was necessary to alter the alienation covenant, so as to require the incoming tenant to give a fresh covenant to the service company on each assignment. That was made unnecessary, for leases granted after 1st January 1996, by s.12 Landlord and Tenant (Covenants) Act 1995.

Service charges cause more trouble between landlord and tenant than anything else. Commercial service charges are still largely unregulated, and the parties are left to make their own arrangements. But the recovery of residential service charge is regulated by three statutes, which make it all but impossible for an amateur landlord to recover it in the event of a dispute. The Landlord and Tenant Act 1985 contains provisions, originally introduced by the Housing Finance Act 1972[142] and amended by the Housing Act 1974, which impose mandatory consultation requirements for all but the most trivial of works,[143] and which absolve the tenant from paying unless the cost is reasonable and the works have been done or the services performed to a reasonable standard.[144] It also imposes an eighteen month

---

[140] Mortgage lenders normally insisted that the lease contain a landlord's covenant to perform the services, in the event of the service company being wound up or dissolved.

[141] See above 'Rent reservation'.

[142] ss.90-91A.

[143] s.20.

[144] s.19.

limitation period for making service charge demands[145] and invalidates any service charge demand that does not contain required information about the tenant's rights.[146] The Landlord and Tenant Act 1987 requires any demand for service charge payable to the landlord to contain the landlord's address for service[147] and requires any sinking fund to be kept in a trust account.[148] Any dispute about the service charge is fought out in the Leasehold Valuation Tribunal, where the tenant is at no risk of having to pay more than £500 towards the landlord's costs, no matter how unreasonable or trivial the complaints. The landlord cannot simply forfeit the lease instead, because the Housing Act 1996 prevents a landlord serving a notice under s.146 Law of Property Act 1925 or forfeiting for non-payment of service charge, unless the arrears have first been admitted or determined by a court or tribunal.[149]

6. Penalty rents.

Covenants to pay an increased rent, in the event that the tenant committed a breach of covenant, were common from the medieval period,[150] down to the beginning of the twentieth century.[151] Typically the penalties were made payable in the event of late payment of the rent[152] or, in the case of agricultural leases, if the tenant adopted prohibited courses of husbandry,

---

[145] s.20B.

[146] s.21B.

[147] s.47.

[148] s.42.

[149] s.81.

[150] (1422) YB 1 Hen.6 f.4 pl.17, (1431) YB 9 Hen.6 f.11b-12a pl.34, (1444) YB 22 Hen.6 f.57a-58b pl.7, (1481) YB Ed.4 f.18 pl.7, Stewart, *Practice of Conveyancing*, 342.

[151] As late as 1953 a precedent for a penal rent was published in *Key and Elphinstone's Precedents in Conveyancing*, 15th edn., vol. 1 (London, Sweet & Maxwell, 1953) 1005.

[152] In order to recover the penalty, an actual demand was necessary on the day the rent became due: (1481) YB 20 Ed.4 f.18 pl.7, Gilbert, *Rents* 140–144.

such as selling hay or straw off the holding.[153] These contractual penalty rents were popular because they were treated as liquidated damages[154] and were enforceable as such, even if they were really penalties.[155]

Penalty rents for adopting particular courses of husbandry were outlawed in 1908,[156] and the effect of the decision in *Dunlop Pneumatic Tyre Co* v. *New Garage and Motor Co*[157] is that it is unlikely that any penalty rent could be recovered today, unless it really did represent a genuine pre-estimate of the loss which the landlord would suffer by reason of the breach.[158] Accordingly, the only penalty which leases customarily contain today, apart from the right to forfeit, is the payment of interest at an agreed rate on any rent arrears.

There are, however, two eighteenth century statutes which still give a landlord a right to recover a penalty if the tenant wrongly holds over after the expiry of the lease. If a landlord makes a written demand for possession after a lease for life, lives or years[159] has expired, and the tenant refuses to give up possession, knowing that there is no right to remain, then by s.1. Landlord and Tenant Act 1730 the landlord is entitled to bring a claim in debt to recover double the rental value of the land from the former tenant, for the period of the former tenant's occupation thereafter.[160] If, instead, the tenant gives notice of

---

[153] T. Williams, *Precedents in Conveyancing,* vol. 3 (London, Kearsley, 1788) 951, T. Jackson, *The Agricultural Holdings Act 1908* (London, Sweet & Maxwell, 1912) 51.

[154] *Rolfe* v. *Peterson* (1772) 2 Brown PC 436, 6 Brown PC 410, Platt, *Leases,* vol. 2 107.

[155] *Jones* v. *Green* (1829) 3 Y & J 298, *Oxford History of the Laws of England,* vol. 12 115.

[156] s.25 Agricultural Holdings Act 1908. There were originally exceptions for breaking up pasture and underwoods, damaging trees, and failing to burn heather. For agricultural holdings, see now s.24 Agricultural Holdings Act 1986.

[157] [1915] AC 79.

[158] *Wilson* v. *Love* (1896) 65 LJQB 474, *O'Neill* v. *Murphy* [1948] IrR 72.

[159] This has been interpreted including yearly periodic tenancies (*Clayton* v. *Blakley* (1798) 8 Term Rep 3) but as excluding weekly and quarterly tenancies: *Lloyd* v. *Rosbee* (1810) 2 Camp 453, *Wilkinson* v. *Hall* (1837) 3 Bing NC 508. It probably also excludes a fixed term tenancy of one year or less: *Land Settlement Association* v. *Carr* [1944] 1 KB 657.

[160] *Cobb* v. *Stokes* (1807) 8 East 358, Coote, *Leases* 404–406.

'his, her or their intention to quit the premises by him, her, or them holden, at a time mentioned in such notice, and shall not deliver up possession,' then, by s.18 Distress for Rent Act 1737, the landlord is entitled to levy distress for a double rent, or recover it by action. Taking a single rent afterwards is not necessarily a waiver of the right to double rent.[161]

7. Apportionment.

This section deals with apportionment of rent if the lease determines between rent days. Apportionment on a transfer of part of the reversion or part of the term is dealt with in chapter 6.

The basic rule, at common law, was that no apportionment of rent was possible on a determination[162] of the term between rent days, because the obligation to pay each gale of rent was a whole obligation 'to be rendered and restored out of the issues and profits'[163] of the land. So if rent was payable quarterly in arrears, and a landlord ended a tenancy (whether by forfeiture or otherwise)[164] between rent days, or terminated a tenancy at will between rent days, the landlord lost the right to claim any rent for that quarter.[165]

Originally, if a landlord accepted a surrender of part of the

---

[161] *Ryal* v. *Rich* (1808) 10 East 48.

[162] On an assignment of a lease between rent days, the assignor could, in equity, be made to pay an apportioned part of the rent, if the assignment had been made to a beggar or insolvent person, with a view to avoiding liability for that quarter's rent: *Treakle* v. *Cook* (1683) 1 Vern 165, H. Bullow ed J. Fonblanque, *A Treatise on Equity,* 5 edn. (London, Clarke, 1820) 359.fn(y).

[163] *Clun's Case* (1613) 10 Co.Rep 127a, 128a. In equity, apportionment was possible where part of the land had been acquired compulsorily by a third party: *Adams* v. *Brown* (1676) 1 Nottingham's Chancery Cases 73 SS 378. See also H. Bullow, ed J. Fonblanque, *A Treatise on Equity,* 5th edn. (London, Clarke, 1820) 383–387.

[164] In 1586 it was suggested that the rent due under a tenancy for years would be apportioned, if the tenant committed a forfeiture by purporting to convey the freehold reversion to a third party; Gouldsborough 29 pl.2. For such forfeitures, see ch.7 heading 'Forfeiture'.

[165] For the same reason, where rent is payable in advance, the tenant cannot recover any of that rent, if the landlord forfeits between rent days.

premises, that would extinguish the whole rent for that quarter too, for the same reason,[166] but in 1675 it was decided that there could be an apportionment in that circumstance, except where the landlord accepted the surrender from an assignee of part, and no apportionment of the rent had been agreed between the tenants of the two parts beforehand.[167]

The absence of any possibility of apportionment on a termination between rent days meant that it was necessary to make a special rule for tenancies at will, if the tenant chose to end the tenancy before the rent day. In that event the tenant had to pay for the whole of the period up to the rent day,[168] provided that the landlord had not retaken possession by the end of it.[169] Or the court could bring about the same result by saying that, as a matter of construction of the agreement, the landlord could terminate it at any time, but the tenant could only terminate it at the end of the year.[170] Whether a landlord could be prevented from terminating it before a rent day was a point 'left to sleep' in *Dunsdale* v. *Iles*.[171] The invention of the periodic tenancy in the middle of the eighteenth century, solved the problem in this type of case, by turning arrangements which had previously been terminable at the will of either party into interests which could only be determined by due notice on both sides, expiring on an anniversary of the tenancy.[172]

There was also a problem where a sub-lease had been granted by a tenant for life. Unless the lease for life had been granted pursuant to a power which bound the reversioner or remainderman,[173] an underlease granted by a tenant for life

---

[166] Brook's Abridgment 'Extinguishment' 48; *Rawlyns's case* (1587) 4 Co 52a, Gouldsborough 93 pl.8.

[167] *Hodgkins* v. *Robson* (1675) 1 Vent 276, Platt, *Leases*, vol. 1 134, Gilbert, *Rents*, 152, 165.

[168] *Sir Thomas Bowe's Case* (1670) Alyen 4.

[169] (1505/6) Keilw 65, *Carpenter* v. *Colins* (1605) Yelv 73, *Sir Thomas Bowe's Case* (1646) Alyen 4, *Layton* v. *Feild* (1701) 3 Salk 222 'Lease at will'.

[170] *Anon* (1505) Caryll's Rep, 115 SS 457, *Co.Litt.* 56a, *Title* v. *Grevett* (1703) 2 Ld.Raym 1008.

[171] (1673) 3 Keb 166.

[172] See ch.4 heading 'Periodic'.

[173] See ch.1 heading 'Capacity' sub-heading 'tenants for life'.

would determine automatically when the tenant for life died,[174] meaning that the last gale of any rent payable in arrears would never become due, unless the tenant for life was considerate enough to die between sunset and midnight on a rent day.[175] In *Strafford* v. *Wentworth*[176] the tenant for life died ten hours before sunset on the rent day. It was only because the sub-tenant had, in fact, paid the rent to the wrong person that morning, that the executor of the tenant for life was able to trace it into the hands of the recipient. If the sub-tenant had not paid it at all, the right to sue for it would have been lost. That prompted parliament to interfere, and by s.15 Distress for Rent Act 1737 the personal representatives of a tenant for life were given a right to recover an apportioned part of the rent if the tenant for life died before the rent day, or the whole of the rent if the tenant for life died on the rent day. In 1753 that was interpreted as extending to a lease made by a tenant in tail, who had died without issue,[177] and the Act was extended to cover all doubtful cases where the lease was in writing in 1834.[178]

The rule that a sub-lease granted by a tenant for life would determine on the death of the tenant for life was altered, for sub-leases at a rack rent, by s.1 Landlord and Tenant Act 1851, which prolonged the sub-lease until the end of the year instead, and apportioned the rent for that year between landlord's executors and the succeeding owner of the reversion.[179]

Apportionment in all cases where the rent was payable in arrears, was made possible by s.3 Apportionment Act 1870, which provides that all periodic payments are treated as accruing from day to day, and which allows an apportioned part to be recovered where a lease determines before the whole rent becomes due. But it does not apply to advance payments. Consequently, apportionment is still not possible where the rent

---

[174] See ch.7 heading 'Expiry'.

[175] *Clun's case* (1613) 10 Co.Rep 127a, 128a, Platt, *Leases*, vol. 2 139.

[176] (1722) 9 Mod. 21.

[177] *Pagget* v. *Gee* (1753) 9 Mod. 482, Platt, *Leases*, vol. 2 141.

[178] s.1 Apportionment Act 1834.

[179] Automatic expiry at the end of the year was changed to expiry after service of a 12 month notice to quit by s.14 Agricultural Act 1920.

is payable in advance, except where there is an express or implied term to the contrary. Of course, often there is. Rent is frequently expressly reserved so as be payable on an apportioned basis for any period of less than a quarter, usually at the beginning and end of the term, and a term to like effect can often be implied.[180]

8. Abatement and set-off.

A debtor is allowed to plead three broad excuses for non-payment of a debt otherwise due to the creditor: first, that although the debt is owing, there is a separate debt which the creditor owes back, and the two debts ought to be set-off against each other (mutual set-off); secondly, that the debt has been reduced in amount or extinguished by reason of events which have that effect at common law (abatement); and thirdly, that notwithstanding the absence of any defence to the claim for the debt at common law, in equity, payment of the debt ought to wait until a cross-claim has been litigated out, so that the two judgment debts can be set-off against each other later (equitable set-off).[181]

Mutual set-off: The first type of defence is called mutual set-off, and it was first allowed under the Statutes of Set-Off,[182] at a time when it was still possible to imprison an individual for debt. The purpose of the Acts was to ensure that neither party would be at risk of imprisonment, at the suit of other, except for the net outstanding balance owed between them, and for this purpose the defendant was allowed to plead and give evidence of the mutual debt, so that the plaintiff could only obtain judgment against the defendant for the balance owing to him, if any.[183]

The Statutes of Set-Off were, in fact, repealed by the Civil Procedure Acts (Repeal) Act 1879 and the Statute Law Revision

---

[180] *York* v. *Casey* [1998] 2 EGLR 25.

[181] *Hanak* v. *Green* [1958] 2 QB 9, 23, s.72 County Courts Act 1984.

[182] The Insolvent Debtor's Relief Act 1728 and the Set-Off Act 1734.

[183] *Stein* v. *Blake* [1996] AC 243, 251.

and Civil Procedure Act 1883, but their effect was preserved by s.24(7) Judicature Act 1873, and that provision is now found in s.49(2) Senior Courts Act 1981. So where a landlord owes a debt to a tenant, the tenant can rely on this as a defence by mutual set-off to the landlord's claim to the rent.[184] But the defence is only available for debts and equivalent fixed amounts. It is not available where the cross-claim is an unliquidated cross-claim for damages.[185] So if a landlord sued in debt or covenant for rent, the tenant could not set up a cross-claim for damages as a defence to that claim by way of mutual set off. After 24th June 1738, however, claims for rent under parol leases were often brought in assumpsit,[186] and since assumpsit, was technically a claim for damages for breach of a later promise to pay the debt, a tenant could dispute the amount of damages, on the basis of an unliquidated cross-claim, even if the original promise was to pay in 'ready money'.[187]

Abatement: The second type of defence to a claim for a debt is called abatement, of which there are three broad types.

The first type of abatement is where the tenant has been lawfully evicted by someone claiming by title paramount to the landlord[188] or has been unlawfully evicted by the landlord itself. In both cases, the whole rent is suspended,[189] unless and until the tenant is re-admitted[190] If the eviction is from only part of the property, a proportionate part of the rent is suspended if the

---

[184] *Gower* v. *Hunt* (1734) Barnes 290.

[185] *Howlett* v. *Strickland* (1774) 1 Cowp 56.

[186] For the reasons why, see ch.9 heading 'Debt'.

[187] *Eland* v. *Karr* (1801) 1 East 375.

[188] *Day* v. *Austin* (1595) Cro Eliz 398, *Dalston* v. *Reeve* (1696) 1 Ld.Raym 77, E. Sampson, *De Bon Pleading* (London, Atkins, 1677) 109, Platt, *Covenants*, 198.

[189] Holdsworth, *HEL* vol. 7 270, 274.

[190] *Read* v. *Lawnse* (1562) Dyer 212b, *Co.Litt.* 148b. In calculating damages for breach of a landlord's covenant for title or quiet enjoyment, credit has to be given for the rent which would otherwise have been payable: *Coulter's Case* (1598) 5 Co.Rep 30a, 31a. For a contractual right to abate in these circumstances, see W. West, *Simboleograph*, (London, Stationer's Co., 1610) pt.1 s.434.

eviction is by title paramount,[191] but the whole rent is suspended if the eviction is by the landlord.[192] In both cases, an actual eviction is required in order to suspend the rent. A mere intrusion does not have that effect.[193]

The second type of abatement is where the tenant has been compelled to spend money discharging one of the landlord's obligations under the lease. Most of the cases involve landlords who have failed to carry out some covenanted work of repair to the property.[194] In that circumstance, 'the lessee may do it, and pay himself by way of retainer of so much out of the rent'.[195] But the same principle also applies if, in order to avoid a distress, the tenant pays the landlord's property taxes or arrears of head-rent.[196] In each case, the money is treated as having been expended to the landlord's use or at the landlord's implied request, out of the rent. For this right to arise, however, the amount must have been paid and be unchallenged or unchallengeable.[197]

The third type of abatement is where the parties have agreed

---

[191] *Smith* v. *Malings* (1607) Cro Jac 160, *Boodle* v. *Campbell* (1844) 7 Man & Gr 386. If some adverse right, falling short of an eviction, is established against the land, then it is possible that the rent can be apportioned in equity, but not if the open market rent would still be more than the rent reserved by the lease: *Jew* v. *Thirkwell* (1663) 1 Ch.Cas 31, cf. *Duckenfield* v. *Whichcott* (1674) 2 Ch.Cas 204.

[192] *Walker's Case* (1587) 3 Co.Rep 22a, 22b, *Sibill* v. *Hill* (1588) Gouldsborough 80 pl.18, *Hodgkins* v. *Robson* (1675) 1 Vent 276, Platt, *Leases*, vol. 2 127–128, cf. Gilbert, *Rents*, 178. The rule was reversed, in Ireland, by s.44 Landlord and Tenant Law Amendment Act (Ireland) 1860, and at common law the tenant remains liable on the non-rental covenants in the lease, notwithstanding an eviction from part: *Morrison* v. *Chadwick* (1849) 7 CB 266, 283.

[193] *Hunt* v. *Cope* (1775) 1 Cowper 242.

[194] The right, of course, does not apply if the tenant would have been liable to do the repairs in any event: (1455) YB 34 Hen.6 f.17a-18a pl.32.

[195] *Browne* v. *Elmer* (1520) YB 12 Hen.8 pl.1, 119 SS 2, 4, (1413) YB 14 Hen.4 f.27a pl.35, Statham's Abridgment, 'Barre' f.275 pl.42, *Beale and Taylor's Case* (1591) 1 Leon 237, Cro Eliz 222, *Weigall* v. *Walters* (1795) 6 Term Rep 488, *Lee Parker* v. *Izzet* [1971] 1 WLR 1688. For an express covenant to like effect, see E.Wood, *Conveyancing,* vol. 3 (London, Stratham & Woodfall, 1793) 85.

[196] *Sapsford* v. *Fletcher* (1792) 4 Term Rep 511.

[197] *British Anzani* v. *International Marine* [1980] 1 QB 137 148.

the rent shall abate in particular circumstances;[198] usually today where the property is destroyed or otherwise becomes useless to the tenant, without the fault of either party;[199] and the necessity of an express agreement about these matters is a consequence of the rule that a tenant's obligation to pay rent, and perform the covenants or contractual obligations[200] in the lease, is absolute, even if the property is accidentally destroyed, and the landlord has insured against the risk of destruction and pocketed the proceeds of the policy.[201]

Equitable set-off: The third type of defence to a claim for a debt is called equitable set-off. Prior to the Judicature Acts 1873 to 1894, courts of equity would sometimes grant an injunction, to prevent a creditor obtaining or enforcing a judgment for a debt, until the debtor had been given a chance to litigate out an unliquidated cross-claim for damages. The idea was to give the debtor time to turn the unliquidated cross claim into a judgment debt, so that then there could be a mutual set-off between the two judgment debts.[202]

The Judicature Acts 1873 to 1894 made the application for the injunction unnecessary: instead, in cases where courts of equity would have granted an injunction before the Judicature

---

[198] In *Baylye* v. *Hughes* (1628) Cro Car 137 it was decided that the right to such an abatement ran with the term.

[199] Stewart, *Practice of Conveyancing,* 333.

[200] In the case of obligations imposed by law, rather than voluntarily undertaken by act of the parties, inevitable accident or act of war is a defence. So if a property is destroyed by an act of god, the tenant has no defence to a claim for rent, but (absent any repairing covenant) the tenant is not liable to rebuild the property, because the tenant's liability in waste is an obligation which is imposed by law, rather than by voluntary act of the tenant.

[201] *Paradine* v. *Jane* (1671) Aleyn 27, *Monk* v. *Cooper* (1727) 2 Strange 762, *Hare* v. *Groves* (1796) 3 Anstr 687, *Holtzapffle* v. *Baker* (1811) 18 Ves Jun 115, *Leeds* v. *Cheetham* (1827) 1 Sim 146, Platt, *Covenants,* 278–282. In the case of damage by fire, the tenant can sometimes require the insurer to lay out the insurance monies remedying the damage; see s.83 Fires Metropolis Act 1774.

[202] In *Hamp* v. *Jones* (1840) 9 LJ (NS) Ch 258, an injunction was granted to prevent a tenant enforcing a judgment for damages for an illegal distress, on the grounds that the landlord was entitled to an equitable set-off for subsequent rent arrears.

Acts, the injunction is now to be taken as read, so that the same facts can be pleaded as an equitable defence to the claim to enforce the debt. In effect, the plea is that the court should not adjudicate on the common law claim until the unliquidated counterclaim has been decided, thereby turning it into a judgment debt for a fixed amount, which can be set-off against the landlord's claim.

The practice before the Judicature Acts 1873 to 1894 was to grant the injunction in any case where the cross-claim for damages was so closely connected with the claim that it would have been unfair to require the claim to be paid without deduction.[203] Of course, ideas of fairness tend to change over time. In 1916 there was no doubt that it would be unfair to make a landlord wait for the rent whilst the tenant litigated out a counterclaim.[204] But by 1979 that had changed. In *British Anzani (Felixstowe)* v. *International Marine Management*[205] Forbes J. extended the rule that account could be taken of an unliquidated cross-claim when deciding the terms on which to grant relief from forfeiture,[206] so as to allow equitable set-off against claims for rent generally. Whilst he acknowledged, the 'important qualification is that the equity must impeach the title to the legal demand, or in other words go to the very foundation of the landlord's claim,' he held that meant only that there has to be a close connection between them.[207] Since then, in effect, any counterclaim arising out of the lease has been treated as capable of being set-off in equity, except where there is contractual exclusion of the right.[208]

---

[203] *Morgan & Son Ltd* v. *S. Martin Johnson & Co Ltd* [1949] 1 KB 107.

[204] *Hart* v. *Rogers* [1916] 1 KB 646, *Monk* v. *Cooper* (1727) 2 Strange 763, Platt, *Covenants*, 197–201, Platt, *Leases*, vol. 2 121–124.

[205] [1980] QB 137.

[206] *O'Mahony* v. *Dickinson* (1805) 2 Sch & Lef 400, *Beasley* v. *Darcy* (1800) 2 Sch & Lef 403n, *O'Connor* v. *Spaight* (1804) 1 Sch & Lef 305.

[207] 152.

[208] See ch.5 heading 'To pay rent'.

9. Distress and replevin.

Distress is the process by which a landlord personally or the landlord's bailiff[209] can seize, impound, and ultimately sell, chattels which are present on the land, in order to satisfy a rent which issues out of that land.[210]

It is a historical curiosity that the right ever applied to leasehold terms at all, for its origins lie in the enforcement of feudal obligations between lord and vassal,[211] whereas a lease for a term of years was conceived as being a purely contractual relationship. But by the end of the fourteenth century it was clear that it did apply,[212] although as with every power of distress at common law,[213] there was no power of sale. The right was simply a right in the nature of a lien, to seize and hold the property until the debt was paid.

Since the right was in the nature of a lien, it followed that it could only be exercised over things which could be returned to the tenant afterwards in the same condition as before, and it was the distrainor's duty to return them in that condition, when the tenant 'replevied' them by paying the arrears of rent.[214] The right

---

[209] Statute of Westminster II (1285) c.37. Consequently, even a court appointed receiver cannot distrain in his or her own right, unless the tenant has attorned: *Shelley* v. *Pelham* (1747) 1 Dick 120, *Pitt* v. *Snowden* (1752) 3 Atk 750, *Hughes* v. *Hughes* (1790) 1 Ves Jun 161. For attornment, see ch.6 heading 'Rent and attornment'.

[210] If the landlord distrains, the landlord cannot sue for the rent in debt, for so long as he continues to hold unsold goods under the distress: *Lehain* v. *Philpott* (1875) LR 10 Ex 242. Similarly, the landlord cannot distrain after obtaining judgment for the rent, because the rent merges in and is extinguished by the judgment: *Chancellor* v. *Webster* (1893) 9 TLR 568.

[211] F. Pollock, *The Land Laws*, 146.

[212] Kaye, *Medieval English Conveyances*, 265. An express power to distrain was only included in leases for the elucidation of 'common people', who might not know about the implied right: Littleton, *Tenures*, s.331, *Doctor and Student*, 125.

[213] *Pollock & Maitland* vol. 2 576.

[214] *Wilson* v. *Ducket* (1675) 2 Mod. 61. Corn in sheaves could be impounded on the premises, but not taken away, for some of it would have been lost in carriage; *Pitt* v. *Shew* (1821) 4 Barn & Ald 206, J. Lilly, *The Practical Register*, 2nd edn. (London, Ward & Wickstead, 1735) vol. 1 654. Removable

could not be exercised at night,[215] for the taking was a security for the rent, and the tenant could not be expected to prevent the distress by tendering the rent at night. Christian piety also prevented a landlord levying a distress on a Sunday.[216]

Various things were and are privileged from distress, as a matter of policy, at common law: things in actual use at the time of the distraint; goods belonging to third parties which are temporarily in the custody of a tenant exercising a public trade;[217] straying cattle, which have not broken any fences, until they have been present on the land for one night;[218] and property belonging to the Crown. Tools of a tenant's trade, oxen and sheep[219] might only be taken in the absence of other goods of sufficient value.

At common law, the landlord had no right to use, work or deal with the distrained goods, except as a matter of necessity.[220] Taking excessive distress was made unlawful by the Statute of Marlborough 1267,[221] as was distraining elsewhere than at the premises out of which the rent issued.[222] Nor was it possible to distrain for a rent seck,[223] nor any sum reserved upon a lease of an incorporeal hereditament, for rent could only issue out a

---

fixtures cannot be distrained upon at common law, because returning them would not re-fix them to the property, so they would not be in the same condition as before.

[215] *Shakelton* v. *Gay* (1491) Caryll's Rep 115 SS 63, *Doctor and Student*, 127.

[216] *Werth* v. *London Discount Co* (1889) 5 TLR 521.

[217] *Read* v. *Burley* (1598) Cro Eliz 596, *Simpson* v. *Hartopp* (1744) Willes 512.

[218] In 1466 there was no right to distrain for rent on straying cattle at all: *Hulle* v. *Orynge, The Thorns case* (1466) YB 6 Ed.4 f.7 pl.18 per Littleton J. But by 1518 the rule was that the landlord could distrain once the cattle had been levant and couchant upon the ground: *Doctor and Student*, 23, J. Lilly, *The Practical Register*, 2nd edn. (London, Ward & Wickstead, 1735) vol. 1 652.

[219] Distress Act 1266.

[220] *Bagshawe* v. *Goward* (1607) Cro Jac 147. F. Pollock, *The Land Laws*, 147, *Bl.Comm.* Bk.III 10.

[221] c.4, Coke, *2nd Inst*, 106–107. Taking an excessive distress is not actionable in trespass (*Lynne* v. *Moody* (1729) 2 Strange 851) unless the excessiveness appears on the face of the pleadings: *Hutchins* v. *Chambers* (1758) 1 Burr 579, 590.

[222] 52 Hen.3 c.15, *Anon* (1311) 6 SS 126, *Capel* v. *Buszard* (1829) 6 Bing 150.

[223] Brook's Abridgment 'Dette,' pl.39: 'If a man hath a term for years, and grants all his estate of the term, rendering rent, he cannot distrain'. See also *Lewis* v. *Baker* [1905] 1 Ch 46.

corporeal hereditament.[224] Furthermore, if a landlord did any unlawful act in the course of distraining, the landlord became a trespasser *ab initio*[225] and the distress would be void.[226]

The tide started to turn against tenants in the sixteenth century when the pleading rules in a tenant's action to replieve the distrained goods were relaxed, so that the landlord no longer had to prove its own title or the name of the current tenant,[227] and executors of a landlord were granted the right to distrain for arrears incurred during the deceased landlord's lifetime.[228]

But it was a series of Acts of Parliament between 1689 and 1737 which really changed things. The Distress for Rent Act 1689 empowered landlords to distrain on crops which had already been cut, by impounding them on the premises, and gave landlords a right to triple damages for any pound breach or rescue of impounded goods.[229] The Landlord and Tenant Act 1709[230] gave landlords the right to distrain off the premises, for goods which the tenant had removed from the premises on[231] or after the rent day, in an attempt to protect them from distress,[232] and empowered landlords to distrain for arrears up to six months after the lease had expired.[233] The Landlord and Tenant Act 1730 made rents seck distrainable.[234] The Distress for Rent Act 1737 imposed a penalty of double the value of the goods, if the tenant had removed them to avoid a distress,[235] empowered landlords to

---

[224] *Co.Litt.* 47a, 142, *British Mutoscope and Biograph Co* v. *Homer* [1901] 1 Ch 671. Reversed by s.201 Law of Property Act 1925.

[225] There was an exception if the landlord refused a tender of the rent during the distress. Although this made the taking unlawful, it did not make the landlord a trespasser, because it was a negative act: *Six Carpenters' Case* (1610) 8 Co.Rep 146a, 146b 'not doing is not trespass', cf. Littleton, *Tenures*, s.484.

[226] *Welsh* v. *Bell* (1669) 1 Vent 36.

[227] 21 Hen.8 c.19 (1529).

[228] s.1 Cestui Que Vie Act 1540.

[229] See below.

[230] s.6.

[231] *Dibble* v. *Bowater* (1853) 2 E & B 564.

[232] s.2.

[233] s.7. Coote, *Leases*, 441.

[234] s.5.

[235] ss.3-4.

take ripe crops and fruit by way of distress,[236] granted landlords a general right to impound on the premises rather than carrying the goods away,[237] and reversed the rule that any unlawful act done in the course of the distress made it void and the distrainor a trespasser *ab initio*.[238] But the most important change was that a combination of those Acts gave the landlord a power of sale. If the tenant did not repleve the goods within five days, the distrainor could cause the value of the goods to assessed by two sworn appraisers, and then sold, in satisfaction of the arrears and charges.[239]

The tide turned back in the nineteenth century, as the political power of the merchant classes waxed and that of the landed gentry waned. In the course of that century, protection from distress was given to those who provided goods and equipment to the cloth manufacturing industry,[240] and then to the property of water,[241] gas[242] railway[243] and electricity[244] companies, and finally to those who provided hired machinery or breeding stock for use in agriculture.[245] Limited protection was given also to anyone who paid a tenant to feed their livestock. The landlord could only levy distress on their animals if there was nothing else available, and could not recover more than the unpaid price for feeding them,[246] so that in order to recover them, the owner of the animals needed to pay the landlord only the agistment debt that he or she already owed to the tenant. The same Act made it generally unlawful to levy distress on

---

[236] s.8.

[237] s.10.

[238] s.19.

[239] *Bl.Comm.* Bk.III 14. The Law of Distress Amendment Act 1888 by s.5 dispensed with appraisement, except where the tenant or owner of the goods required it in writing, and extended the minimum period before sale to fifteen days, where that was required in writing too. For the form of the appraiser's oath, see *The Young Clerk's Magazine*, 5th edn. (London, Strahan & Woodfall) 89.

[240] s.18 Hosiery Act 1843.

[241] s.44 Waterworks Clauses Act 1847.

[242] s.18 Gas Clauses Act 1871.

[243] Railway Rolling Stock Protection Act 1872.

[244] s.25 Electric Lighting Act 1882.

[245] s.45 Agricultural Holdings Act 1883.

[246] Ibid.

agricultural land for arrears of rent that were more than a year old.[247] The Law of Distress Amendment Act 1888 required any bailiff, executing a distress on behalf of a landlord, to be certified by a County Court judge, and the Law of Distress Amendment Act 1895 gave the judge power to cancel the certificate.

By the end of the twentieth century, the right to distrain was, for all practical purposes, confined to business tenants, who were not yet technically insolvent.[248] It ceased to be used for agricultural holdings after 1948, because the vacant possession value of agricultural land was generally well in excess of its value subject to an agricultural holding. So if the tenant got into arrears with the rent, then the landlord would serve a case D notice to quit,[249] in the hope of getting the property back, instead of distraining. Similarly, no landlord of a long lease of

---

[247] s.44.

[248] A landlord may distrain, notwithstanding the presentation of a bankruptcy petition against the tenant and the subsequent making of a bankruptcy order. But a landlord cannot distrain for arrears accruing due earlier than six months before the bankruptcy order was made (s.347(1) Insolvency Act 1986) and if the landlord has done so between presentation of the petition and the making of the order, the balance is held for the bankrupt's estate (s.347(2) Insolvency Act 1986). Furthermore, if the landlord distrains within the period of three months prior to the making of the order, the whole of the proceeds of the distraint are, in any event, deemed to be charged with payment of the preferential creditors in the bankruptcy (s.347(3) Insolvency Act 1986). So, by distraining in the three months prior to the making of the order, the landlord only obtains priority over the unsecured creditors. Similar provisions apply on a compulsory winding up of a company (ss.128, 176 Insolvency Act 1986). A landlord needs permission from the court before levying distress against a tenant whilst an interim order is in force, giving the tenant a moratorium in which to make proposals for a voluntary arrangement (s.252 Insolvency Act 1986). The same applies if an application is made to put the tenant into administration or if the tenant is already in administration, except that the administrator can give permission too (ss.10-11 Insolvency Act 1986). A landlord cannot levy distress against a dissolved company, because all the property of a dissolved company vests in the Crown as bona vacantia (s.1012 Companies Act 2006) and distraint against the Crown is prohibited. If, however, the Crown exercises its statutory power of disclaimer, the property is deemed never to have vested in the Crown (s.1014 Companies Act 2006) distraint is once again permitted, and any unlawful distraint in the meantime is retrospectively validated.

[249] See ch.4 heading 'Agricultural security'.

residential property would ever attempt to levy distress to recover arrears of rent, if there was a chance of getting the property back by forfeiting instead. Rent Act tenants[250] (and their agricultural equivalents), assured tenants,[251] and tenants who were full- time servicemen[252] were all protected from distress by a requirement that the landlord had to seek permission from the court first. Local authority secure tenants were not protected,[253] but the common law rule that distraining landlords must either enter buildings through an unlocked door, or be invited in by their victims, was enough to ensure that the right was rarely exercised in practice.

Ultimately, the Law Commission recommended that distress should be abolished[254] and judges too became increasingly hostile to the right, and started to worry that it might involve a breach of the Human Rights Act 1998.[255]

In *Eller* v. *Grovecrest Investments*[256] the Court of Appeal even overturned the long established rule that a landlord was entitled to levy distress for the full amount of any rent owed, irrespective of any set-off which the tenant might have been able to plead, had the landlord brought an action in debt for the rent instead.[257] Now, the Tribunals, Courts and Enforcement Act 2007 provides for the right to be abolished, and replaced with a

---

[250] s.6 Increase of Rent and Mortgage Interest (Restrictions) Act 1920, s.147 Rent Act 1977.

[251] s.19 Housing Act 1988.

[252] s.1(2) Reserve and Auxiliary Forces (Protection of Civil Interest) Act 1951.

[253] Local authority tenants were first given security of tenure by the incoming Conservative government in the Housing Act 1980. That was done out of a fear that Labour controlled local authorities might sabotage the 'right to buy', which had been a central plank of the Conservative manifesto, by serving notices to quit on all their tenants, and then allowing them to remain only as tenants at sufferance. Accordingly, the scheme of security provided the minimum protection necessary, and that did not extend to protecting tenants from distraint.

[254] Distress for Rent, (1991) Law Com No.194.

[255] *Fuller* v. *Happy Shopper* [2001] 1 WLR 1681. The point was not argued, and nothing was said about human rights in the original draft judgment.

[256] [1995] QB 272.

[257] *Absolon* v. *Knight* (1743) Barnes 450, *Townrow* v. *Benson* (1818) 3 Madd 203, *Briant* v. *Pilcher* (1855) 16 CB 354. There was a statutory exception in the case of ascertained compensation due to a tenant of an agricultural holding: s.22 Agricultural Holdings Act 1948.

statutory process called 'commercial rent arrears recovery'. The relevant provisions are not yet in force.

At common law a landlord could levy distress on goods found on the demised premises, irrespective of who owned them,[258] unless they were already in the custody of the law.[259] The owner of the goods could bring an action against the tenant for suffering the distress, but had no remedy against the landlord. Victorian concern for the deserving poor meant that lodgers[260] obtained a measure of protection, by the Lodgers' Goods Protection Act 1871, which allowed them to protect and recover their goods from superior landlords distraining for unpaid head-rents, by service of a statutory form of notice.[261] The Act was subsequently extended to undertenants and innocent third parties generally by the Law of Distress (Amendment) Act 1908. But landlords were given a valuable right in return. As an alternative to levying distress, landlords were given the right to serve a notice on any lodger or sub-tenant, which would transfer the right to receive the sub-rent to the head landlord, so that it could be applied towards the arrears of the head-rent instead.[262] Any sub-tenant or lodger who claimed the benefit of the Act to recover their goods had to do that automatically.

A landlord cannot enter land to levy a distress if the tenant has tendered the rent. If the landlord attempts to do so, the tenant may use physical force to prevent the entry, and if the landlord actually does so, the tenant can rescue the goods at any time

---

[258] *Humphry* v. *Damion* (1612) Cro Jac 300.

[259] In 1793 a court in South Carolina decided that a slave of a third party, found on the land, could be taken by way of distraint: *Bull* v. *Horlbeck* (1793) 1 Bay (S Car) 301.

[260] If the tenant and undertenant lived in the same building, then the undertenant was a 'lodger' within the original enactment, even if the two parts were entirely separate: *Phillips* v. *Henson* (1877) 3 CPD 26. So, at least in 1877, Lord Templemann's dichotomy between a lodger and a tenant did not exist; see *Street* v. *Mountford* [1985] 1 AC 809.

[261] As an additional protection for the working classes, s.4 Law of Distress Amendment Act 1888 prevented landlords from levying distress upon bedding, wearing apparel, and tools of the tenant's trade, all of which would have been exempt from execution under s.96 County Courts Act 1846.

[262] s.6. There was already legislation in Ireland to this effect: (1826) 7 Geo.4 c.29, s.6.

before they are impounded, or bring an action in trespass later.[263] Similar rules apply if the tender is made after the landlord has entered but before the goods have been impounded, except that, in that event, the tender must include the costs of the distress, and the lawful application of physical force will be to evict the landlord afterwards, rather than to prevent the original entry. But once the goods have been impounded, further resort to self-help is prohibited.[264] They are in the custody of the law; the landlord can, if he wishes, impound them on the premises;[265] and treble damages are payable if the tenant breaks the pound (even after an illegal distress).[266]

A tenant who wishes to recover impounded goods, in order to prevent their sale, must apply to repleve the goods. This requires the tenant to provide security for the value of the goods taken, and give an undertaking to bring an action against the landlord to try the issue of the lawfulness of the levy or the continued detention of the goods. If the tenant does that, the court makes an immediate order for the return of the goods. This is an extremely old form of action, which is preserved in schedule 1 to the County Courts Act 1984. If the tenant, instead, wants to prevent a threatened distress, the application is by injunction, which is normally granted on condition that the tenant brings the disputed rent into court or otherwise gives security for it. That condition is imposed because the tenant would have do that, in order to repleve the goods, if the injunction were not granted and the landlord levied a distress.

Alternatively, the tenant can allow the landlord to sell the impounded goods, and bring an action for the unlawful detention and sale afterwards.[267] A wrongful distress is either 'illegal',

---

[263] *Bennett* v. *Bayes* (1860) 5 H&N 391.

[264] *Co.Litt.* 160b. 'Note reader this difference. That tender upon the land before the distress makes the distress tortious, tender after the distress and before the impounding makes the detainer, and not the taking wrongful . . . tender after the impounding makes neither the one nor the other wrongful, for then it comes too late, because then the cause is put to the trial of the law, to be there determined': *Six Carpenters' Case* (1610) Co.Rep 146a, 147a.

[265] s.10 Distress for Rent Act 1737.

[266] s.3 Distress for Rent Act 1689.

[267] The action can be brought against any agent who arranges the distress and sale too: *Bennett* v. *Bayes* (1860) 5 H&N 391.

'irregular' or 'excessive'. A distress is 'illegal' if there was no right to distrain at all, or if some unlawful act is committed in the course of the levy (for example, breaking a lock in order secure entry to the demised premises).[268] The recoverable damages are double the value of the goods, if the landlord has sold the goods and the reason for the illegality is that no rent was owing at all;[269] otherwise it is the full value of the goods, plus any special damages, without deduction for the rent. A distress is 'irregular' if the landlord does some unlawful act after the original levy, such as selling the goods after the tenant has tendered the arrears and costs of the distress. Until 1737,[270] that would have made the landlord a trespasser *ab initio*, so that the tenant could recover the full value of the goods. Since then, the tenant has only been able to recover its actual loss, taking account of the rent arrears. A distress is 'excessive' if the landlord seizes more, in number or value, than the goods which are reasonably necessary in order to satisfy the arrears, and the recoverable loss is the amount of the excess (the 'over-plus') which is repayable to the tenant in any event, together with any special damages.

---

[268] It is not wrongful for landlord to remain on premises for a reasonable time for the purpose of selling distrained goods, after the minimum period of five days in s.2 Distress for Rent Act 1689 and s.10 Distress for Rent Act 1737 has expired: *Pitt* v. *Shew* (1821) 4 Barn & Ald 208. But it is illegal physically to evict tenant from the property in order to levy the distress: *Etherton* v. *Popplewell* (1800) 1 East 139.

[269] s.4 Distress for Rent Act 1689.

[270] s.19 Distress for Rent Act 1737. For Ireland, see 9 & 10 Vic. c.111, s.14.

CHAPTER 4
Term

---

1. For life

2. At will

3. Fixed terms

4. Periodic

5. At sufferance

6. Agricultural security

7. Residential security

8. Business security

This chapter is about leases of different lengths.

It is about the commercial and legal reasons why landlords chose to grant, and tenants chose to take, leases of particular lengths, and the consequences which followed from their decisions.

It also examines how, during the twentieth century, the autonomy of the parties about the length of the term came to be displaced by statute, giving agricultural, residential and business tenants security of tenure.

1. For life.

Littleton, writing in the fifteenth century, said:[1]

---

[1] Littleton, *Tenures*, s.56.

> A tenant for a term of life is where a man lets lands or tenements to another for term of the life of the lessee, or for the term of the life of another man. In this case the lessee is tenant for a term of life. But by common speech, he who holdeth for a term of his own life, is called a tenant for the term of his life, and he who holds for the term of another's life is called tenant for 'pur terme d'autre vie'.

In that passage, even in the original law-french, Littleton twice called a tenant for life a 'lessee', and a life tenancy was often known as a 'lease for life'. But it would be wrong to conclude that a lease for life created a leasehold estate, or that a life tenancy was a form of leasehold tenure;[2] for the only leasehold tenures known to Littleton were tenancies for a fixed term and tenancies at will. Periodic tenancies are an eighteenth century invention.[3]

A tenancy for life was a form of freehold[4] tenure.[5] It was a freehold estate with a reversion or remainder. So a tenant for life acquired an immediate freehold, which included actual seisin of the fee. That remained the case, even after the Statute of Quia Emptores in 1290 prohibited subinfeudation, because the Act only applied on a complete disposal of the fee simple. In sharp distinction, when a freeholder granted a lease for a term of years, seisin of the fee remained with the landlord throughout, and the tenant only acquired a chattel interest.

Tenancies for life were probably the most common form of aristocratic land holding immediately after the Norman Conquest. Against the background of the constant threat of native rebellion, grants of land were typically made for life in

---

[2] There was never any doubt that a lease for life was a freehold estate: *Pollock & Maitland* vol. 2 9, Littleton, *Tenures*, s.381, *Bl.Comm.* Bk.II 120. When Littleton was writing, it was still an open question whether a tenancy pur autre vie was a freehold estate (see Kaye, *Medieval English Conveyances* 250–251, Simpson, *History of Land Law*, 67) though Littleton himself treated it as such: Littleton, *Tenures*, s.381.

[3] See below heading 'Periodic'.

[4] The term 'free' refers to the fixity, rather than the presence or absence, of any rent or services. *Pollock & Maitland* vol. 2 113.

[5] 'Everyone who has an estate in any lands or tenements for the term of his own or another man's life is called a tenant of the freehold, and none other of a lesser estate can have a freehold': Littleton, *Tenures*, s.57.

return for military service, without any presumption of heritability;[6] for warrior fathers do not always produce a warrior son.[7] Two hundred years later, when heritable grants in fee simple had become common, life tenancies for relicts[8]—that is, dower for widows[9] and curtesy for widowers[10]—were already being implied by law,[11] and the important practical consequences, which followed from the fact that a life interest was a freehold estate, meant that tenancies for life or pur autre vie were often granted even up to the beginning of the nineteenth

---

[6] S. Milsom, *English Feudalism and Estates in Land*, [1959] C.L.J. 193.

[7] This accounts for the ancient rule of construction, reversed by s.60(1) Law of Property Act 1925, that a conveyance to an individual which did not expressly refer to heirs, took effect only as lease for life: Bracton, vol. 2, 267 (f.92b), *Bl.Comm.* Bk.II 121, Challis, *Real Property,* 341, Halsbury's Laws, *Real Property, vol.* 39(2), 4th edn., ¶.147. Similarly, where the grant was made by deed under the Statute of Uses (1536), in the absence of the word 'heirs', a grant to a person and his assigns would only carry a tenancy for the life of the grantee: *Co.Litt.* 42a. There was originally an exception where the grant was made by a tenant in tail, which would be construed as a grant for the life of the grantor, rather than of the grantee, but that was probably no longer the law by the beginning of the nineteenth century: Coote, *Leases* 4, *Doe d. Pritchard* v. *Dodd* (1838) 5 Barn & Ad 689, 692–694.

[8] See generally Simpson, *History of Land Law* 65–66.

[9] On the death of her husband, a widow was entitled to enjoy one-third of any fee simple land which had belonged to him at any time during the marriage, for the rest of her life: *Pollock & Maitland* vol. 2 404, *Bl.Comm.* Bk.II 129 *et seq*, Holdsworth, *HEL* vol. 3 189–197. It was a charge on the land, which took priority to any disposition made during the marriage, other than one made by fine, ibid 420–423, *Doctor and Student* 138–142, Holdsworth, *HEL.* vol. 3 189–197. But there was no entitlement to dower out of a leasehold estate (*Anon* (1278–1289) 112 SS 360), even one of 10,000 years: *Countess of Radnor* v. *Vandebendy* (1697) Shower 70. It was abolished by the Dower Act 1833.

[10] See ch.4 heading 'For life'. The right to the curtesy of England (a widower's life estate in his late wife's freehold land) only applied if a child of the marriage had been born alive: Statute Concerning Tenants by the Curtesy of England (Time Uncertain), *Halsbury's Statutes*, 2nd edn., vol. 20 363. Different rules applied to gavelkind land, principally in Kent: Challis, *Real Property*, 342. For the origin of the right, see *Pollock & Maitland* vol. 2 414–418, Holdsworth, *HEL* vol. 3 185–189. Courtesy extended to incorporeal hereditaments, and, after 1882, to the wife's separate property, provided that she herself had not disposed of it during her lifetime or by will: *Hope* v. *Hope* [1892] 2 Ch 336. It was abolished in 1926 (s.56 Administration of Estates Act 1925), except in relation to equitable interests in entailed property.

[11] Simpson, *History of Land Law,* 65–66.

century, in circumstances where the grant of a tenancy for a fixed term would otherwise have been much more natural and appropriate.[12]

Those practical consequences were as follows. First, a tenant for life could recover possession against strangers using one of the real actions such as novel disseisin,[13] and secondly, the landlord of a tenancy for life could not destroy it by suffering a collusive recovery. It was 1499 before a tenant for a term of years acquired an equivalent power to recover the term against strangers by bringing ejectment,[14] and collusive recoveries remained possible against leasehold tenants until 1529.[15] Thirdly, before the Parliamentary Reform Act 1832, the parliamentary franchise in the country (rather than in towns) was generally confined to those holding freehold estates worth at least 40s pa.[16] So a tenant for life had social position and political power which a tenant for a leasehold term of years lacked.[17] Fourthly, before 1710,[18] the actions of debt and covenant could not be brought for arrears of rent under a lease for life, until after the lease had ended; for the obligation to pay rent under a lease for life was a single obligation, whereas the obligation to pay each instalment of rent under a lease for years was a separate obligation.[19] Fifthly, an underlease for a term of years, granted by a tenant for life, would always take effect as an underlease, irrespective of the length of the term, and not as an assignment.[20] Sixthly, a term of years would always merge in and be extinguished by a lease for life held by the same tenant, even if the lease for years was

---

[12] Holdsworth, *HEL* vol. 7 240.

[13] See ch.9 heading 'Ejectment'.

[14] Ibid.

[15] s.3 Recoveries Act 1529, *Pollock & Maitland* vol. 2 109–110, *Pledgard* v. *Lake* (1599) Cro Eliz 718. See below heading 'Fixed terms'.

[16] *Bl.Comm.* Bk.I 166–168.

[17] *Rattle* v. *Popham* (1734) 2 Strange 992.

[18] s.4 Landlord and Tenant Act 1709.

[19] See Lutwych 'Debt' 165, part of William Nelson's 'ridiculous and abusive' (yet accurate) 'running commentary on each case, which made Mr. Viner call the book "a reproach and dishonour to the profession, and rather adapted to Billingsgate than Westminster Hall"': J. Wallace, *The Reporters*, 3rd edn. (Philadelphia, Johnson, 1855) 245.

[20] See ch.2 heading 'Underletting'.

for longer than anyone could possibly live.[21] Seventhly, a lease for life could not be forfeited automatically. If it was to end prematurely for breach of a condition, that required a re-entry.[22] A term of years, however, could end automatically on the breach of a condition.

There were conveyancing consequences and traps, which followed from the fact that a lease for life was a freehold estate, too. A lease for life was not simply a contract. It was a conveyance of a freehold estate. So, even before the Statute of Frauds (1677),[23] it could not be made simply by an oral contract followed by an entry. It had to be made by a ceremonial feoffment, the essence of which was livery of seisin,[24] or by a bargain and sale or a covenant to stand seised under the Statute of Uses (which effected a statutory transfer of seisin to the tenant for life) or in a court of record by a fine. It also followed that a lease for life could not be granted or reserved[25] out of a term of years, for a freehold could not be carved out of a leasehold.[26]

Nor could a lease for life be granted out of another lease for life, for freehold estates could only be granted in succession to each other.[27] Nor could a lease for life be created so as to take effect from a future date, even the very next day,[28] except upon

---

[21] Challis, *Real Property*, 367.

[22] *Co.Litt.* 214b. A lease for life could be limited, so as to expire on the earlier happening of an event. For the technical difference between a limitation and a breach of condition, see ch.6 heading 'Conditions'.

[23] See ch.1 heading 'Formalities'.

[24] *Jones* v. *Weaver* (1556) Dyer 117b.

[25] Hence an assignment of a lease for years to commence on the death of the assignor would be invalid: J. Gray, *The Rule Against Perpetuities*, 3rd edn. (Boston, Little Brown, 1915) ¶.71, 809–812.

[26] *Butt's Case* (1600) 7 Rep 23, Viner's Abridgment 'Estates' Q.a.2, Preston, *Conveyancing*, vol. 2 124. If a tenant for years purported to grant a lease for life or other freehold estate by livery of seisin or by fine or recovery, that would amount to a disclaimer of the lease, and the landlord could forfeit. See ch.7 heading 'Forfeiture'.

[27] So it was possible to create a concurrent lease for life (a lease for life carved out of the reversion upon a lease for life), for the new concurrent tenant would take by succession, if he or she outlived the occupational tenant: *Co.Litt.* 215a.

[28] *Barwick's Case* (1597) 5 Co.Rep 93b, Challis, *Real Property* 107–9, Preston, *Conveyancing*, vol. 2 156–7. The peculiar and inconvenient rule that the words 'from' and 'henceforth' meant 'starting on the next day' was held to be

the determination of another lease for life,[29] or where it was created pursuant to a power which owed its validity to the Statute of Uses (1536).[30] So, at common law, a lease for life could not be granted to commence on the expiry of a lease for a term of years. If there was an extant term of years, it could only be granted as an immediate concurrent lease,[31] not as a reversionary lease, and a person holding under an uncompleted lease for life could only be a common law tenant at will.[32]

The most significant disadvantage of a lease for life, as a commercial or business arrangement, was its unpredictable termination date. That un-predictability could be, and often was, ameliorated by pegging the lease to the lives of two or three family members, so that it would last until the death of the survivor of them,[33] or by granting a lease for life together with a reversionary term for a fixed number of years, to commence on the relevant death.[34] In the medieval period, either alternative was plainly better, from the tenant's point of view, than taking a lease for a straight term of years, which the landlord could overreach simply by transferring the reversion to a third party or by failing to defend a collusive action.[35] By the middle of the sixteenth century, however, a tenant for years was secure against

---

controvertible in *Llewellyn* v. *Williams* (1610) Cro Jac 258, and was deprecated by Lord Mansfield in *Doe d. Bayntun* v. *Watton* ((1774) 1 Cowp 189, Platt, *Leases*, vol. 2 55–57). He held subsequently, in *Pugh* v. *Duke of Leeds* ((1777) 2 Cowp 714) that those words could be either inclusive or exclusive of the current day, depending on the context, which has been the law ever since.

[29] Challis, *Real Property,* 104.

[30] G.Gray, *The Rule Against Perpetuities*, 3rd edn. (Boston, Little Brown, 1915) ¶.52, Platt, *Leases*, vol. 2 52–53, Preston, *Conveyancing,* vol. 2 157. For the other devices used to avoid the rule, see *Norton on Deeds*, 179.

[31] *Winter* v. *Loveday* (1697) 2 Salk 537.

[32] *Sharp's Case* (1599) 6 Co.Rep 26a. Some judges were willing to hold that a subsequent livery would save the lease: *Mellow* v. *May* (1602) Moor 636, 1 Keb 285, *Norton on Deeds* 179.

[33] The peg-lives had to be people living at the time the lease was granted.

[34] In *Hemmings* v. *Brabason* (1660) O.Bridg Rep 1, 1 Lev 45, the court disagreed about whether this created one lease, or a lease for life and a reversionary term of years. See also *Goodwin* v. *Clark* (1661) Lev 35, and *Jermyn* v. *Orchard* (1695) Shower 199. There are precedents in *The Compleat Clerk,* 3rd edn. (London, Place, 1671) for a lease of 100 years in reversion upon one life, and for a lease of 21 years in reversion upon two lives, 741, 745.

[35] So, in *Haywood* v. *Abbess of Wherwell* (1384) YB 8 Ric.2 (Ames) f.12 pl.4, a building lease was granted as a lease for life.

collusive recoveries,[36] could sue for trespass,[37] and could recover possession from the landlord and third parties, if evicted unlawfully, by bringing ejectment.[38] So, afterwards, business leases tended to be granted for fixed terms of up to 21 years, rather than for a life or lives.[39] Yet, for the emerging middle classes, there was still social cachet as well as political power in being a tenant for life, and so in agricultural districts, tenancies for the longest of three lives were not uncommon as business arrangements, even down to the Victorian period,[40] especially on estates owned by the church and charities.[41]

As a family rather than business arrangement, the grant of a tenancy for life suited the needs of wealthy landowners exactly, from the middle of the seventeenth century until the beginning of the twentieth century,[42] when changes in the system of taxation on death made it inefficient. During that period it was extremely common for land to be held upon a 'strict settlement', under which the current male head of the family was a tenant for life. This suited landowners' needs because the dearest wish of most them was that their lands should descend, passing from eldest male son to the next male heir, until the day of judgment, and their greatest fear was always that a profligate heir (and most of them were) might be forced to sell the land, in order to pay his debts, disinheriting future generations.

---

[36] Supra.

[37] See ch.9 heading 'Trespass'.

[38] See ch.9 heading 'Ejectment'.

[39] Holdsworth, *HEL* vol. 7 241.

[40] The 'ancient notion of the inferiority of an estate for years is still in great measure attached to it': Coote, *Leases*, 6. The first edition of the *Encyclopedia of Forms and Precedents*, published in 1905, contained a precedent for a lease for three lives: *Encyclopedia of Forms and Precedents*, 1st edn., vol. 7 (London, Butterworths, 1905) 272.

[41] *Attorney-General* v. *Crook* (1836) 1 Keen 121.

[42] B. English and J. Saville, *Strict Settlement, A Guide for Historians*, (Hull, University of Hull Press, 1983) 15–18. There was at least one firm of solicitors in the north of England who were still re-settling land in this way, up to 1996: Law Com 181, *Transfer of Land, Trusts of Land* 12 fn.72.

In theory, after the Statute of Westminster II in 1285,[43] this could be achieved easily enough by creating a fee tail,[44] for individuals holding land in fee tail could not make any lifetime disposition of it which would alter the course of its descent after their deaths.[45] But judges resisted this, and by the middle of the fifteenth century it was relatively easy for a fee tail owner to bar (or 'dock') the entail, turning it into a fee simple, by a collusive recovery.[46]

So a more sophisticated solution was needed, and the Civil War provided the necessary prompt. Anyone fighting on what might later turn out to be the losing side risked not only forfeiture of his life but also of all of his estates,[47] and when a fee tail was forfeited for treason, by statute, the issue in tail were barred too.[48] So it was a sensible precaution to ensure that the current head of the family, and any living male children, only had successive life estates, and not a fee simple or tail.[49] Instead, a remainder in fee tail was generally granted to trustees, for the next unborn heir,[50] in the hope that he would inherit in less

---

[43] De Donis Conditionalibus (1285) c.1. 'Wherefore our lord the King, perceiving how necessary and expedient it should be to provide remedy . . . hath ordained, that the will of the giver, according to the form in the deed of gift manifestly expressed, shall be from henceforth observed; so that they to whom the land was given under such condition, shall have no power to aliene the land so given, but it shall remain unto the issue of them to whom it was given after their death, or shall revert unto the giver or his heirs, if issue fail, [either by reason that] there is no issue at all or if any issue be and fail by death or the heir of the body of such issue failing'. See generally Coke, *2nd Inst*, 331–337, *Pollock & Maitland*, vol. 2 19–29, Simpson, *History of Land Law*, 77–80.

[44] See ch.1 heading 'Capacity' sub-heading 'fee tail owners'.

[45] Holdsworth, *HEL* vol. 3 116.

[46] *Taltarum's (or Talkarum's) Case* (1472) YB 12 Ed.4 f.19 pl.25, J.Biancalana, *The Fee Tail and the Common Recovery in Medieval England* (Cambridge, Cambridge University Press, 2001) 250–251, F. Pollock, *The Land Laws*, 80–89, *Co.Litt*. 379b.fn(1). If a fee tail owner attempted to convey the fee simple without first barring the entail, it took effect as a base fee, which would continue until the entry by the next tenant in tail: *Machell v. Clark* (1700) 2 Ld.Raym 778.

[47] *Co.Litt*. 392b. There was an exception for gavelkind land in Kent, where the rule was 'father to the bough, son to the plough': *Doctor and Student*, 35.

[48] 26 Hen.8 c.13, s.5, Holdsworth, *HEL* vol. 3 70.

[49] Holdsworth, *HEL* vol. 7 197–198.

[50] It had been settled law since 1343 that a grant could not be made directly to an unborn child: Kaye, *Medieval English Conveyances* 242–243, *Perks*, ¶.52.

troubled times, and in default of an heir, the fee was granted over to some living relative or relatives.[51]

By this means of 'strict' settlement, it was possible to tie up the land for as much as a hundred years, until eventually, with luck, the last life tenant would produce a son who would be presumptive entitled to the fee tail. The trick, in order to perpetuate the arrangement afterwards, was to persuade the son, as soon as he reached the age of 21, to join with his father, in re-settling the whole estate on similar terms, for the next unborn generation.[52] The son, of course, did not have to go along with this. He could choose to wait it out until his father died instead, at which time the land would come to him as tenant in fee tail, and he would be able to bar the entail on his own, and do what he liked with the land. But the eldest son was normally kept deliberately poor, by making no cash provision for him in the current settlement, so that even a difficult son[53] could be bribed into agreeing a resettlement of the land when he reached 21, with a cash advance to pay his outstanding debts and an annuity to be paid during his father's lifetime.[54]

The settlement normally granted the current tenant for life

Nor could it be made to a man and his unnamed future wife: *Trecarram & Friendship's Case* (1585) 4 Leon Case 64.

[51] J. Williams, *On the Present Mode of Family Settlements of Landed Property*, in *Papers Read Before the Juridical Society 1855–1858* (London, Stevens, 1858) 47, B. English and J. Saville, *Strict Settlement, A Guide for Historians*, 15–16. The credit for this is normally given to Orlando Bridgman (1608–1674), who was the 'father of conveyancers' (Douglas 568), and to Geoffrey Palmer (1598–1670); B. English and J. Saville, *Strict Settlement A Guide for Historians* 118 fn.13, F. Pollock, *The Land Laws*, 116, Holdsworth, *HEL* vol. 7 112, 376–377. It could only be done with a freehold estate. A life tenancy could not be created out of a term of years, except by way of executory devise: *Lord North* v. *Butts* (1557) Dyer 139b, 140b. For executory devises, see ch.8 heading 'Devolution on death'.

[52] For actual mechanics by which that was done, see G. Cheshire, *The Modern Law of Real Property*, 5th edn. (London, Butterworths, 1944) 387.

[53] There was rarely any difficulty in persuading the eldest son to agree a re-settlement, although: 'He might have become the full owner . . . if he had possessed the means of waiting, the independence of thought and the will to break with the tradition of his order and the bias of his education, and the energy to persevere in his dissent against the counsels and feelings of his family': F. Pollock, *The Land Laws* 9.

[54] B. English and J. Saville, *Strict Settlement, A Guide for Historians* 21–22, Simpson, *History of Land Law* 220–222.

appropriate management powers, including power to grant leases on commercial terms, which would be binding on the remainder after his death, if made on the terms specified in the power,[55] thus overcoming the problem that any under-lease would determine automatically on his death.[56] The settlement would also normally protect 'jointures' for widows and 'portions' for daughters by granting (or reserving powers to grant) leases at a peppercorn rent over parts of the settled estate, charged with the payment of those sums for that purpose to trustees.[57]

In 1926, it became impossible to create a common law tenancy for life. A lease for life at a rent or for other consideration became a lease for a term certain of 90 years, determinable by notice one month after the relevant death.[58] Other leases for lives could only take effect in equity, behind the curtain of a strict settlement governed by the Settled Land Act 1925, under which the equitable tenant for life, however, would normally also be treated as the legal owner of the trust property for the time being,[59] and was given wide leasing powers as such.[60] It has not been possible to create any new Settled Land Act settlements since 1997. Instead, an equitable life interest is now an ordinary interest under a trust of land.[61]

2. At will.

The common law originally knew of no estates less than a freehold. A tenancy for a term of years was just a contract[62] and a tenancy at will was a mere possession.[63] Tenancies at will were

---

[55] See ch.1 heading 'Formalities', sub-heading 'tenant for life'.
[56] See ch.1 heading 'Capacity' sub-heading 'tenant for life'.
[57] O. Bridgman, *Precedents of Conveyances* (London, Atkins, 1702) vol. 2 36, Holdsworth, *HEL* vol. 7 380. See below heading 'Fixed terms'.
[58] s.149(6) Law of Property Act 1925.
[59] s.4(2) Settled Land Act 1925.
[60] ss.41-53 Settled Land Act 1925.
[61] s.2 Trusts of Land and Appointment of Trustees Act 1996.
[62] For a discussion of the nature of these contracts in Hebrew, Greek and Roman Law, see R. Hunter, *The Law of Landlord and Tenant*, 4th edn. (Edinburgh, Bell & Bradfute, 1896) 1–38.
[63] Viner's Abridgment 'Estates' S.b.

known in both Norman and Anglo-Saxon law before the conquest,[64] and Littleton in the fifteenth century said of them:[65]

> Tenant at will is where lands or tenements are let by one man to another, to have and to hold to him at the will of the lessor, by force of which lease the lessee is in possession.

At this time, the distinction between a freehold estate and tenancy at will broadly corresponded with the social distinction between freemen and villeins. Freemen held their freeholds as property: villeins had a mere possession at the will of their lords.[66] So it was natural for Littleton to refer to a tenancy at will as being a holding according to the will of the landlord, and it was originally thought that an actual re-entry by the landlord was needed to determine a tenancy at will. By 1511, however, it was clear that the tenancy could only last for so long as both parties wished,[67] and Coke pointed out that a tenant could hardly re-enter upon himself or herself.[68] So the rule instead became that the tenancy would end when one party informed the other that he or she no longer wished the tenancy to continue[69] or when one of them otherwise did something that was wholly inconsistent with the continuation of the relationship of landlord and tenant between them.[70]

Since death ends all personal relationships, it follows that the death of either the landlord[71] or the tenant[72] terminates a tenancy

---

[64] E. Tabuteau, *Transfers of Property in 11th Century Norman Law* (Chapel Hill, University of North Carolina Press, 1988) 72, R. Hunter, *The Law of Landlord and Tenant*, 4th edn. (Edinburgh, Bell & Bradfute, 1896) 41.

[65] Littleton, *Tenures*, s.68. See ch.7 heading 'Emblements'.

[66] Challis, *Real Property* 63. See ch.1 heading 'Capacity' sub-heading 'copyholders'.

[67] *Scrope* v. *Hyk* (1511) 2 Caryll's Rep 116 SS 618, Spelman 135 pl.1, cf. (1440) YB 18 Hen.6 f.1a pl.1, (1480) YB 20 Ed.4 f.9 pl.4.

[68] *Co.Litt.* 55a.

[69] *Dunsdale* v. *Iles* (1673) 3 Keb 207.

[70] *Countess of Shrewsbury* v. *Crompton* (1600) 5 Co.Rep 13b, Cro Eliz 784, D'Anvers, *Abridgment*, vol. 3 233, *Bl.Comm.* Bk.II 146.

[71] *Co.Litt.* 57b.

[72] *Co.Litt.* 62b.

at will.[73] Any disposition of the landlord's interest,[74] or purported assignment by the tenant,[75] also terminates the tenancy, the point being that such a disposition is inconsistent with a wish that the parties should remain as landlord and tenant. Similarly, any act done by the landlord, which would be unlawful against a tenant, terminates the tenancy, because it demonstrates the landlord's desire to end it.[76] The tenancy also determines if the tenant does any act (such as committing waste or purporting to underlet)[77] which the landlord cannot have intended the tenant should be permitted to do, as a tenant at will,[78] because that too would be inconsistent with a joint desire that the tenancy should continue. A tenant at will, however, cannot claim that the tenancy has ended prior to the date on which the landlord first had notice of the circumstances which caused the tenancy to determine,[79] and the same no doubt applies the other way around.

Proceedings to recover possession in ejectment, before 1852, involved the landlord granting an actual or notional lease to a third party, in whose name the claim was made.[80] So a landlord who wished to recover possession from a tenant at will had to make sure that the pleaded date for the grant of the new, notional, lease was after the tenancy at will had ended. If it had not ended automatically, and no prior demand for possession or its equivalent[81] had been made, the claim would fail as being

---

[73] A tenancy at will granted by or to joint tenants did not end on the death of one of them, and nor did a tenancy at will granted by or to a woman end on her marriage, because, in both cases, there would still be an original party alive on both sides who might wish it to continue: *Henstead's Case* (1594) 5 Co.Rep 10a.

[74] *Doe d. Davies v. Thomas* (1851) 6 Ex 857.

[75] *Co.Litt.* 57a, *Shaw v. Barbor* (1601) Cro Eliz 831.

[76] *Co.Litt.* 55b, *Doe d. Hanley v. Wood* (1819) 2 Barn & Ald 724.

[77] Since a tenant at will had no estate in the land, just a possession, a tenant at will could not underlet: (1506) YB 21 Hen.7 f.26 pl.3, *Anon* (1573) 4 Leon 35.

[78] *Walgrave v. Somerset* (1586) Gouldsborough 72.

[79] *Pinhorn v. Souster* (1853) 8 Ex 763.

[80] See ch.9 heading 'Ejectment'.

[81] An actual physical entry would be sufficient: Cole, *Ejectment* (London, Sweet, 1857) 59. But, in contrast to the position where what was being alleged was a forfeiture (see ch.7 heading 'Forfeiture') the fictional entry by the notional claimant, which the tenant was required to admit as a condition of defending the action, was not sufficient: *Right d. Lewis v. Beard* (1811) 13 East 210.

premature.[82] Hence, even today, a landlord must make a demand for possession, or otherwise ensure that the tenancy at will has already been determined, before issuing proceedings for possession.

A tenant who enters under a void lease[83] becomes a tenant at will. Originally, the subsequent acceptance of rent from that person made no difference; he or she would remain a tenant at will,[84] whose tenancy could be determined by a moment's notice on either side. There was a similar rule if a landlord accepted rent from a tenant at sufferance (a former tenant whose lease had expired). Acceptance of the rent turned the tenancy at sufferance into a tenancy at will, but nothing more.[85]

But those rules changed, at the same time and in step with, judicial acceptance of the concept of the periodic tenancy.[86] In 1646, payment of rent still made no difference.[87] By 1700, however, the court could imply an agreement to renew the tenancy for a fixed term of one year, from the subsequent acceptance of an instalment of rent,[88] and by the end of that century, the inference was of a yearly periodic tenancy instead.[89] Although the inference to be made was ultimately a question of fact for the jury,[90] the natural inference to be drawn from the acceptance of rent, in the case of a void lease, was an agreement

---

[82] *Goodtitle d. Herbert* v. *Galloway* (1792) 4 Term Rep 680, *Denn d. Brune* v. *Rawlins* (1808) 10 East 261, *Doe d. Newby* v. *Jackson* (1823) 1 Barn & Cr 448, *Doe d. Nicholl* v. *M'Kaeg* (1830) 10 Barn & Cr 721, Adams, *Action in Ejectment*, 4th American edn. (New York, Banks Gould & Co, 1854) 145.
[83] *Braythwayte* v. *Hitchcock* (1842) 10 M&W 494.
[84] *Tooker* v. *Squire* (1607) 1 Rol Abr 848, 859.
[85] *Co.Litt.* 55a, *Bl.Comm.* Bk.II 145.
[86] See the heading 'Periodic' below.
[87] *Sir Thomas Bowe's Case* (1646) Aleyn 4.
[88] *Leighton* v. *Theed* (1700) 2 Salk 413, 3 Salk 222, 1 Ld.Raym 707, Viner's Abridgment, 'Estates' S.b.2.
[89] *Richardson* v. *Langridge* (1811) 4 Taunton 128, *Bishop* v. *Howard* (1823) 2 Barn & Cr 100, Coote, *Leases*, 10, Holdsworth, *HEL* vol. 7 244–245.
[90] *Roe d. Brune* v. *Prideaux* (1808) 10 East 158, 185, *Caulfield* v. *Farr* (1873) IR 7 CL 469. In Ireland, s.5 Landlord and Tenant Law Amendment Act (Ireland) 1860 gave the landlord an election to treat any tenant holding over for more than one month as a tenant from year to year.

to confirm it as a periodic tenancy,[91] subject to automatic termination at the end of the agreed term;[92] and in the case of an expired lease, was an agreement to renew it as a periodic tenancy,[93] even if the rent was accepted only on a mistaken premise of law;[94] so that as early as 1765 Wilmot J could be reported as having said:[95] 'In the country, leases at will in the strict legal notion of a lease at will, being found extremely inconvenient, exist only notionally; and were succeeded by another species of contract, which was less inconvenient'.[96]

So now, tenancies at will tend to exist only in cases where the occupier has not paid any rent at all,[97] or otherwise where it is, in practical terms, objectively impossible to infer that the parties have yet impliedly agreed to create a periodic tenancy;[98] as, for instance, is the case where the parties are still negotiating the terms of a written lease,[99] or where the agreed terms of the lease require the tenant to provide a guarantor, and the landlord is still waiting for the tenant to do so.[100]

At the end of the twentieth century, the rule that acceptance of rent from a former tenant created a periodic tenancy, rather than a tenancy at will, caused enormous difficulties where courts had exercised statutory powers to make suspended possession orders in favour of local authorities and other social landlords. The problem was that the effect of the order was to terminate the

---

[91] *Clayton* v. *Blakley* (1798) 8 Term Rep 3. The result, in that case, was that the landlord was able to claim a penalty rent under s.1 Landlord and Tenant Act 1730 which would not have been payable if the tenancy had been at will. *Roe d. Jordan* v. *Ward* (1789) 1 H.Black 97.

[92] *Doe d. Tilt* v. *Stratton* (1828) 4 Bing 444.

[93] *Doe d. Martin* v. *Watts* (1797) 7 Term Rep 83, cf. *Smith* v. *Widlake* (1877) 3 CPD 10.

[94] *Morrison Low* v. *Patterson* 1985 SLT 255.

[95] *Timmins* v. *Rowlinson* (1765) 3 Burr 1603, 1609. See also Holdsworth, *HEL* vol. 7 245 which mistakenly attributes the quote to Lord Mansfield.

[96] Blackstone's report of the same case attributes a much more restrained comment to Wilmot J; namely, that the tenancy from year to year had almost extinguished the tenancy at will, which was a most unreasonable and inconvenient tenure to both parties: 1 Wm. Black 535.

[97] *Rex* v. *Collett* (1823) Russ & Ryan CC 498.

[98] *Doe d. Knight* v. *Quigley* (1810) 2 Camp 505.

[99] *Goodtitle d. Galloway* v. *Herbert* (1792) 4 Term Rep 680, *Doe d. Hollingsworth* v. *Stennet* (1799) 2 Esp 717.

[100] *Doe d. Bingham* v. *Cartwright* (1820) 3 Barn & Ald 326.

tenancy automatically as soon as the tenant breached it afterwards,[101] although the tenancy was capable of being revived later, on an application made by the tenant, with retrospective effect.[102] In practice, however, few social landlords were so unreasonable as to enforce the order after one, trivial breach. But instead of applying to reinstate their tenancies, tenants started arguing that, if their tenancies had ended automatically, and if the landlord had accepted rent afterwards, then their landlords must have impliedly granted them new periodic tenancies instead, to which the original possession orders would no longer apply. The judicial answer to this was an oxymoron:[103] for so long as there remained a possibility that the former tenancy might be revived by further order of the court, the former tenant would be treated neither as a tenant nor as trespasser, but as a 'tolerated trespasser'.[104]

This solved the problem in the sense that the court could find that the landlord had not granted the tenant a new tenancy, and that the original order remained enforceable unless it had been revoked or varied subsequently. But it left the problem that the former landlord owed the tenant no continuing obligations under the lease in the meantime. The extraordinary answer to this was to decide that a trespassing former tenant, whose possession against the former landlord was treated as being wholly wrongful, could nonetheless sue the former landlord in nuisance for interfering with that possession.[105]

Eventually, the problem was resolved by statute,[106] and the Supreme Court later decided that it had all been an unfortunate mistake, albeit one that it was too late to put right.[107]

Where a tenancy at will expressly reserves a rent, the landlord can bring an action in debt or levy distress at the

---

[101] *Thompson* v. *Elmbridge BC* [1987] 1 WLR 1425.

[102] *Pemberton* v. *Southwark LBC* [2000] 1 WLR 1762.

[103] *Austin* v. *Southwark LBC* [2010] UKSC 28, per Lady Hale ¶45.

[104] *Burrows* v. *Brent LBC* [1996] 1 WLR 1448, *Stirling* v. *Leadenhall Residential* [2001] 3 All ER 645.

[105] *Pemberton* v. *Southwark LBC* [2000] 1 WLR 1672.

[106] sch. 11 Housing and Regeneration Act 2008.

[107] *Austin* v. *Southwark LBC* [2010] UKSC 28.

landlord's election.[108] In 1440 it was held that a tenant at will who had never entered was liable in debt for the agreed rent,[109] but by 1536 a tenant at will was only liable for any period of actual occupation.[110] In the absence of an express agreement to pay rent, a tenant at will is impliedly obliged to pay compensation for use and occupation instead.[111]

3. Fixed terms.

In the thirteenth century, there was already a clear distinction between a lease granted for an uncertain length of time and a lease granted for a fixed, certain period of time.

A lease granted until the happening of an event, the date of which was unknown,[112] was automatically a lease for the life of the grantee,[113] defeasible by re-entry if the uncertain event happened within the grantee's lifetime, provided that it was made with the formality[114] appropriate for a lease for life.[115] Otherwise, it was a tenancy at will.[116]

---

[108] Littleton, *Tenures*, s.72.

[109] (1440) YB 18 Hen.6 f.1a pl.1.

[110] *Goddale's case* (1536) Dyer 14a, *Bellasis* v. *Burbrick* (1696) 1 Salk 209, E.Sampson, *De Bon Pleading* (London, Atkins, 1677) 109.

[111] See ch.9 heading 'Assumpsit'.

[112] Eg. 'I give and grant to you so much land until you have taken thence forty pounds': Bracton, vol. 3 50 (f.176b). Or a lease for so long as the grantor remained the abbott of a religious house: Littleton, *Tenures*, s.382, *Bl.Comm.* Bk.II 121.

[113] This followed, first from the rule that a grant which did not mention heirs was impliedly a lease for life (reversed by s.60(1) Law of Property Act 1925), and secondly from the rule that it is impossible to create a lease in perpetuity (*Sevenoaks Maidstone and Tonbridge Rly Co* v. *London Chatham and Dover Rly* (1879) 11 Ch.D 625, 635), as opposed to a perpetually renewable fixed term: see sch. 15 Law of Property Act 1922.

[114] See ch.1 heading 'Formalities'.

[115] *Co.Litt.* 42a, M. Bacon, *A Treatise on Leases* (London, A.Strahan, 1798) 177, *Blamford* v. *Blamford* (1615) 3 Bulstrode 98, 100, D'Anvers, *Abridgment*, vol. 3 203.

[116] Bracton, vol. 3 50 (f.176b), (1440) YB 18 Hen.6 f.16b pl.6, Littleton, *Tenures*, s.382, Viner's Abridgment 'Estates' P.a pl.9, *Kusel* v. *Watson* (1878) 11 Ch.D 129, *Austin* v. *Newham* [1906] 2 KB 167, 170. 'If a man leases lands of value 20s pa. till one and twenty pounds be levied out of the issues and

By contrast, a lease granted for a fixed, certain length of time was called a lease for a term of years. At common law, a lease for a fixed term was a lease for a 'term of years', even if it was for a fixed period of less than a year, for, as Blackstone said:[117]

> If the lease be but for half a year, or a quarter, or any less time, this lessee is respected as a tenant for years, and is styled so in some legal proceedings; a year being the shortest term which the law in this case takes notice of.

This was a 'middle kind of interest between an estate for life and a tenancy at will',[118] which 'grew up later than the feudal settlement upon which the estates of freehold were based; and it never acquired any definite place in the feudal system'.[119] It was a chattel real.[120]

In the sixteenth century, the boundaries between a determinable lease for life and a lease for a certain term of years, were staked out in *Say* v. *Smith*:[121]

> Every contract sufficient to make a lease for years ought to have certainty in three limitations, viz: in the commencement of the term, in the continuance of it, and in the end of it: so that all these ought to be known at the commencement of the lease, and words in a lease which do not make this appear are but babble . . . And these three are in effect but one matter, shewing the certainty of time for which the lessee shall have the land, and if any of these fail, it not a good lease, then there wants certainty.

---

profits, it is but a lease at will without livery': *Bishop of Bath's Case* (1605) 6 Co.Rep 34b, 35b.

[117] *Bl.Comm.* Bk.II 140. A lease for a fixed term of less than one year is also a lease for a 'term of years' within the meaning of the Law of Property Act 1925: s.205(xxvii) Law of Property Act 1925. But for the purpose of other statutes, not incorporating that definition, a 'term of years' means a term of at least two years: *Land Settlement Association* v. *Carr* [1944] 1 KB 657.

[118] M. Bacon, *A Treatise on Leases* (London, Strahan, 1798) 1.

[119] Challis, *Real Property,* 63.

[120] See ch.1 fn.3.

[121] (1564) Plowden 269, 272. See also *Partridge* v. *Strange* (1553) Plowden 77, 85, (1554/5) Brook's New Cases pl.462, pl.468, *Foot* v. *Berkley* (1667) 1 Vent 83, *Bishop of Bath's Case* (1605) 6 Co.Rep 34b, 35b, Viner's Abridgment 'Estates' P.a pl.2.

But the rule does not apply to a lease granted to an executor to pay debts,[122] and nor did it apply to leases made by traders under statute merchant or statute staple, or imposed by elegit to enforce a judgment debt.[123] Where it does apply, the rule does not require the actual commencement date of a lease for years to be known in advance. The lease could be granted so as to commence on the happening of a contingent event,[124] or on one of a number of dates, at the option of the grantee,[125] and if granted to take effect from an impossible date, it would be construed as taking effect immediately.[126]

Nor does the rule prohibit premature or collateral determination on the happening of contingent or uncertain events.[127] Nor, provided that the actual length of the term is known, is there anything to stop the lease being granted for

---

[122] *Sir Andrew Corbet's Case* (1599) 4 Co.Rep 81b, *Blamford* v. *Blamford* (1615) 3 Bulstrode 98, 100, D'Anvers, *Abridgment*, vol. 3 162.

[123] *Bl.Comm.* Bk.II 160–162, Holdsworth, *HEL* vol. 3 128–132.

[124] *Chedington's Case* (1598) 1 Co.Rep 153b, 155a, *The Bishop of Bath's Case* (1605) 6 Co.Rep 34b, 35a. If the expiration date was a fixed calender date (rather than a fixed length of time calculated from its commencement: Platt, *Leases*, vol. 2 51) then, in order for the lease to be valid, the contingent event had to happen within the lifetime of both parties; ibid 155, cf. *Child* v. *Baylie* (1618) Cro Jac 459. An assignment of a lease cannot be made to take effect from the death of the assignor, for a life estate is treated as a greater estate than a leasehold term, and so a reservation of a life estate is necessarily a reservation of the whole term: J. Gray, *The Rule Against Perpetuities*, 3rd edn. (Boston, Little Brown, 1915) ¶.71, ¶.809–812, *Savell* v. *Badcock* (1594) 3 Leon 84, *Jermyn* v. *Orchard* (1695) Shower 199, Platt, *Leases*, vol. 2 52.

[125] *Anon* (1591) 1 Leon 227 involved a lease granted to begin 'at the feast of our Lady Mary', without saying in which year.

[126] *Foot* v. *Berkley* (1667) 1 Vent 83. The example given in that case was a lease where the commencement date was supposed to be 'the feast of the nativity of the lord' (i.e. Christmas Day), and the words 'the feast of' had been accidentally omitted. Today, such an obvious mistake would be corrected as a mater of construction, so that the lease would commence on Christmas Day of the current year, rather than on a day 2011 years ago, or thereabouts: *Mannai Investment Co Ltd* v. *Eagle Star Life Assurance Co Ltd* [1997] 3 All ER 352. But the formal and literalist rules of construction which applied in the sixteenth century, meant that it was only possible to disregard the date entirely, and treat the lease as commencing forthwith, as if no commencement date had been specified at all, cf. *Fish* v. *Bellamy* (1605) Cro Jac 71, Dalison's Reps 124 SS 26 pl.15.

[127] Preston, *Conveyancing* vol. 2 168.

discontinuous periods.[128] All the certainty rule requires is that the maximum length of the lease has to be fixed and knowable if and when the lease does commence.[129] So a lease 'for the duration of the war' would be incapable of being a grant for a term of years, whereas a lease for a duration of 1000 years, subject to immediate determination at the end of the war, would be perfectly valid.[130]

The certainty rule was relaxed in the eighteenth century, to bring 'running' or 'periodic' tenancies within the scheme for fixed term tenancies.[131] They were treated as being leases for a term certain, even though the length of the term was uncertain at their commencement, and depended on the future acts of the parties.[132] In 1926, leases for lives were brought within the scheme for fixed term tenancies too: in 1845 it had become impossible to create a lease for life by livery of seisin without a charter of feoffment made by deed,[133] and the Law of Property Act 1925 abolished livery of seisin entirely,[134] and turned a lease for life at a rent from a freehold estate into a leasehold term of 90 years.[135]

So the distinction between leases for certain and uncertain terms should simply have fallen away, at least where the original tenant was an individual. A lease granted for an uncertain term should, thenceforth, have taken effect automatically as a lease for 90 years, subject to earlier defeasance on the death of the grantee or the happening of the uncertain event, and an agree-

---

[128] Preston, *Conveyancing* vol. 2 164–167. This happened automatically where a wife's right to dower took priority to a term granted by her husband during his lifetime. The lease was automatically suspended for the remainder of her life, and extended for an equivalent period afterwards; *Co.Litt.* 46a, *Shep. Touch.* 275.
[129] So a lease for so long as JS shall name, is a good lease if it commences on the date that JS names the length: *Bl.Comm.* Bk.II 143, *Bishop of Bath's Case* (1605) 6 Co.Rep 34b, 35b.
[130] *Lace* v. *Chantler* [1944] KB 368.
[131] See the next section.
[132] See below heading 'Periodic'.
[133] s.3 Real Property Act 1845, Platt, *Leases*, vol. 2 8. There was an exception for customary leases for life of gavelkind land by infants which survived until 1926. For the formalities before 1845, see ch.1 heading 'Formalities'.
[134] s.51.
[135] s.149(6).

ment to grant such a lease should likewise have been treated as a contract to grant that term.[136] But the courts lost sight of the original rule that a grant for an uncertain period complying with the necessary formalities created a defeasible life interest,[137] with the result that in *Prudential* v. *London Residuary Body*[138] the House of Lords mistakenly held that a grant for an uncertain term was void, and did not create a tenancy at all.[139]

In the early medieval period, short leases for a fixed term were sometimes granted as part of money-lending transactions, in order to avoid prohibitions on usury,[140] much as Islamic mortgages are granted today. Short leases were also granted to farmers, 'who every year rendered some equivalent in money, provisions, or other rent, to the lessors or landlords; . . . And yet their possession was esteemed of so little consequence, that they were rather considered as the bailiffs or servants of the lord, who were to receive and account for the profits at a settled price, than as having any property of their own'.[141]

Fixed term long leases did exist, but were much rarer,[142]

---

[136] In *Zimbler* v. *Adams* [1903] 1 KB 577 the Court of Appeal held that an agreement to create a lease for an uncertain term was an agreement to create a lease for life.

[137] So, in *Great Northern Rly Co* v. *Arnold* (1916) 33 TLR 114, Rowlatt J held that a lease for an uncertain term was an agreement to create a term of 999 years, and, on similar facts, in *Lace* v. *Chantler* [1944] 1 KB 368, the Court of Appeal held that it was simply void. As a result of that decision, leases made for the duration of the Second World War were converted, by the Validation of Wartime Leases Act 1944, into leases for a term of 10 years, determinable on one month's notice after the end of the war. But in *Siew Soon Wah* v. *Yong Tong Hong* [1973] AC 836 the Privy Council followed two cases (*Kusel* v. *Watson* (1879) 11 Ch.D 129 and *In Re King's Leasehold Estates* (1873) LR 16 EQ 521) in which an uncertain term had been enforced, as such, in equity.

[138] [1992] 2 AC 386.

[139] Since it was void, the House of Lords was able to say that an implied periodic tenancy, on such of those terms as were consistent with a periodic tenancy, was created on entry and payment of rent instead.

[140] This was 'vifgage'. See ch.2 heading 'Mortgages as leases and of leases'. Plucknett, *Concise History*, 572–573.

[141] *Bl.Comm* Bk.II 141–142. See also Kaye, *Medieval English Conveyances*, 267–268.

[142] Coke thought leases for 40 years or more were anciently outlawed, but only because he took that assertion in Andrew Horne's, *Mirror of Justice*, seriously. On the unreliability of the *Mirror of Justice*, see P. Winfield, *The Chief Sources of English Legal History* (Cambridge Mass, Harvard University Press, 1925)

usually having been granted to the church in order to avoid the restrictions on gifts in mortmain.[143] The problem with long fixed terms in the medieval period was that they could be destroyed by a collusive, fictitious recovery by title paramount. If the landlord allowed a stranger to recover the land by action, the term was destroyed.[144] The Statute of Gloucester (1278) provided a very partial remedy.[145] Where the lease was made by deed, the tenant was entitled to intervene in the action and prove that the recovery was collusive rather than by right, in which event execution would be postponed until the expiry of the lease. But this was easy to evade. It only applied to a default judgment, and the tenant had to intervene before the judgment was entered.[146] It was not until 1529[147] that all the gaps were filled and a tenant for years was completely protected against fraud or collusion by those who held freehold estates.[148] Afterwards 'estates for years became more permanent, and for that reason the lessees took

---

266–268. Coke also thought long leases were never without some suspicion of fraud, which was a more serious point: *Co.Litt* 46a, *Bl.Comm* Bk.II 142.

[143] See ch.8 heading 'Mortmain'.

[144] There were various practical ways around this problem. One was to deliver seisin on a charter of feoffment of the reversion, which was expressed to take effect only if the tenant's possession was disturbed. This was a fee simple conditional: Littleton, *Tenures*, s.330, (1336) YB 10 Ed.3 f.39 pl.33, 32 Ed.3 tit Gar 30, *Colthirst* v. *Bejushin* (1550) Plowden 20, 34. But its validity was controversial: *Co.Litt.* 216b–218a. The second was not to grant a lease at all, but instead to convey the whole of the landlord's estate to the tenant, on terms that it would revert at the end of the term. The third was to grant the tenant a right of pre-emption: Kaye, *Medieval English Conveyances*, 261–263.

[145] In Scotland, the Leases Act 1449 c.17 solved the problem at a stroke, by turning what had been a personal contract into an indefeasible estate in land. It provided 'for the safety and favour of poor people that labour the ground, that they and all others that have taken or shall take lands in time to come from lords, and have terms of years thereof; that suppose the lords sell or alien that land or lands, the takers shall remain with their tacks (leases) unto the issue of their terms, into whose ever the lands come to, for suchlike as they took them for'. See further *Styles of the Juridical Society* vol. 1 (Edinburgh, Elliot, 1787) 389–395.

[146] *Co.Litt.* 46a, (1507) Keilway f.92 pl.6. 'These inconveniences so effectually obviated the benefits which were intended to flow from the statute, that no great change seems to have been produced by it. The remedy provided fell into disuse, and feigned recoveries became as great instruments of oppression as before': Chambers, *Leases*, 8, cf. *Pollock & Maitland* vol. 2 109–110.

[147] s.3 Recoveries Act 1529, *Bl.Comm.* Bk.II 142.

[148] See *Co.Litt.* 46a, Challis, *Real Property*, 64, *Chambers*, Leases 9.

long terms',[149] so that, by the Tudor period, terms of 21 or 99 years were being granted as investments for premiums.[150]

From the sixteenth century onwards, long terms were not being granted simply as investments or as mortgages.[151] They were often used for the purpose of estate planning and development too.

They could, for instance, be used to deprive a superior lord of the benefit of wardship.

If a boy inherited land held in knight service, the lord's right of wardship gave him all the profits of the land until the boy reached the age of twenty one. If a girl younger than 14 inherited the land instead, the lord was entitled to the profits until she reached the age of 16 or married.[152] Until the beginning of the sixteenth century, any term of years previously granted out of that land would be suspended during the lord's wardship.[153] Afterwards, the courts reversed that rule,[154] and so the profits of the freehold could be reduced to nothing, by encumbering the land with a lease to the use of the heir at a peppercorn rent, so that the lord would only receive the rent.[155] Francis Bacon apparently described this as an abuse without a remedy,[156] and Lord Ellesmere, who was Lord Chancellor at the beginning of the seventeenth century, would never grant equitable relief to a

---

[149] *Theobalds* v. *Duffoy* (1724) 9 Mod. 102, 103.

[150] *Oxford History of the Law of England*, vol. 6 632. There is a precedent in O. Bridgman, *Conveyances*, 3rd edn. (London, Atkins, 1699) vol. 1 103 for a lease for a term of 1000 years granted for a premium and reserving a peppercorn rent, with a sub-lease back to grantor reserving a rack rent.

[151] See ch.2 heading 'Mortgages as leases and of leases'.

[152] *Co.Litt.* 88.fn(11), *Bl.Comm.* Bk.II 67, Simpson, *History of Land Law*, 17–18.

[153] J. Baker and S. Milsom, *Sources of English Legal History*, 2nd edn. 203–205.

[154] *Sir Andrew Corbet's Case* (1599) 4 Co.Rep 81b.

[155] Until the practice was outlawed by the Statute of Marlborough 1267 c.6 (Coke, *2nd Inst*, 109–112), it was common to grant the land to a family member or friend, reserving a nominal rent charge until the heir achieved majority, and a rent of more than the annual value of the land afterwards, so that the grantee would have no interest in holding it after the heir came of age: *John de Boys* v. *Philip fr Burnr* (1285) 122 SS 212-217. This also seems to have been used as a technique for avoiding dower. *Anon* (1278–1289) 112 SS 360.

[156] Nottingham, *Prolegomena of Chancery and Equity*, ed D.Yale (Cambridge, Cambridge University Press, 1965) 223.

long lessee for this and other reasons.[157] In *Cotton's Case*[158] it was held that, if an infant inherited a lease of a 1000 years, the lord could have the profits of the lease instead, but apparently, by a subsequent direction of the court, that decision was not followed afterwards.[159] The problem went away when military tenures were abolished by the Tenures Abolition Act 1660, which turned them into common socage, out of which an infant's guardian could make no personal profit.

Or long leases could be used as a convenient way to mitigate the effects of primogeniture.[160]

Where an estate was held in strict settlement, in the hope that it would ultimate pass to the eldest male heir, long leases of parts of it would be granted to trustees to secure portions for younger children[161] and jointures for widows.[162] The settlor would grant the term to the trustees of the settlement,[163] charged with payment of the portion or jointure. Once the portion or jointure had been paid,[164] by accumulating the profits from the lease, the

---

[157] *Risden* v. *Tuffin* (1597) Tothill 122, Nottingham, *Prolegomena of Chancery and Equity,* ed. D.Yale (Cambridge, Cambridge University Press, 1965) 222. See also Platt, *Leases* vol. 2 2.

[158] (1612) Godbolt 191.

[159] Nottingham, *Prolegomena of Chancery and Equity,* ed. D.Yale (Cambridge, Cambridge University Press, 1965) 223 fn.4. In *Hemmings* v. *Brabason* (1660) O.Bridg Rep 1, 1 Lev 46, it was suggested that a lease for a term longer than 70 years would be subject to wardship.

[160] *Bl.Comm.* Bk.II 142.

[161] *Goodwin* v. *Clark* (1661) Lev 35.

[162] See eg. the precedent for a lease for a term of 99 years to secure an annuity in O. Bridgman, *Conveyances,* 3rd edn. (London, Atkins, 1699) vol. 1 43. See also ibid vol. 2 197.

[163] See e.g. *Doe d. Budett* v. *Wright* (1819) 2 Barn & Ald 716.

[164] The sums were generally relatively small. 'The descendants of younger sons, who on the continent, would all be counts or barons, in England have no titles and sit even below knights. Furthermore, the younger sons and daughters of the very richest lords receive, by English custom, but little money from their families, barely enough to live on. The sons are given the same education as their eldest brother and then turned out, as soon as they are grown up, to fend for themselves; the daughters are given no education at all, the general idea being that they must find some man to keep them—which, in fact, they usually do. The rule of primogeniture has kept together the huge fortunes of the English lords; it has also formed our class system': N. Mitford, *The English Aristocracy,* in *Noblesse Oblige* (London, Hamish Hamilton, 1956) 41.

term would be held on the same trusts as the fee: it 'attended the inheritance'.[165] The difficulty that caused was that these long leases lay about the title like unexploded bombs. A purchaser of any part of the estate would have to investigate them all, for fear that any one of them might still be extant, affect the purchased land, and be enforceable against him after the purchase. Although there was a presumption that, once the portion or jointure had been paid in full, and the original purpose of the lease had been exhausted, the term would be held in trust to attend the inheritance,[166] so that a disposition of a fee simple would also impliedly carry the lease with it,[167] that presumption could be rebutted.[168] So, in order to be safe, at completion the purchaser would also have to take an express assignment of any of these leases that might conceivably still be extant and affect the land.[169] The problem was eventually solved by the Satisfied Terms Act 1845.[170]

Leases were useful in the family context for another reason. At common law, only the testator's personal estate vested in his or her personal representatives, and the personal representatives had to pay all of the testator's debts out of the personal estate alone. Where a fee simple descended to an heir, it was automatically charged with payment of any debts which the testator had expressly covenanted would be paid by 'heirs'.

---

[165] *Huddlestone* v. *Lamplugh* (circa 1530) Ch R 36, Preston, *Conveyancing,* vol. 2 129. 'The person who possesses the legal estate is seldom entitled to the beneficial interest; and consequently, subject to any particular charge,' the leases 'follow the limitations of the freehold, or, in the language of the books, are attendant on the inheritance': Chambers, *Leases*, 10. The lease would then merge in the fee in equity, and the person in whom the term was vested would be prevented from setting it up as a defence to a possession action by the heir: Ashburner, *Equity, 72, Tiffin* v. *Tiffin* (1680) 1 Vern 1, Viner's Abridgment 'Estates' B.b.2.

[166] Stewart, *Practice of Conveyancing* 13.

[167] Ashburner, *Equity* 71.

[168] Nottingham, *Prolegomena of Chancery and Equity,* ed. D.Yale (Cambridge, Cambridge University Press, 1965) 231-232, J. Williams, *The Law of Ejectment*, 2nd edn. (London, Sweet & Maxwell, 1911) 4–5.

[169] There is a precedent for this in O. Bridgman, *Conveyances*, 3rd edn. (London, Atkins, 1699) vol. 1 230. See also *Co.Litt.* 290b.fn(1).

[170] See now s.5 Law of Property Act 1925 and Halsbury's Laws, *Real Property,* vol. 39(2) 4th edn., ¶.51, ¶.112–113.

Otherwise, freehold land simply was not available for the purpose of paying the testator's debts at all at common law, although statute gradually changed that.[171] Creating a lease for a term of years, which would vest in the testator's personal representatives as part of the personal estate until the debts were paid,[172] was a way altering the priority rules, and charging the freehold land with the testator's debts.[173]

Long leases were also useful as a means of producing long term capital growth for a family estate. Much of the urban residential development which took place after the Restoration of Charles II down the end of the nineteenth century, took place under building leases. The pattern was set by the Earl of Southampton's development of Bloomsbury Square in 1661.[174] Typically, the owner of the land would lay out the roads, and then grant leases of the individual plots to investors and speculative builders, with a rent free period of one year[175] at the beginning and a ground rent afterwards, in return for which the tenant would agree to build a house to particular specifications on each plot and leave it there for the landlord at the end of the term. The tenant would then build out to the required specifications[176] (or, more often, whatever the tenant thought he could get away with)[177] as quickly and cheaply as possible, and

---

[171] See ch.8 heading 'Liability of the heir and personal representatives'.

[172] A lease for the payment of debts made by will to a personal representative was an exception to the rule that the term of a lease for years had to be certain: *Sir Andrew Corbet's Case* (1599) 4 Co.Rep 81b, *Blamford* v. *Blamford* (1615) 3 Bulstrode 98, 100.

[173] There are precedents for leases of land in trust to pay debts in O. Bridgman, *Conveyances* (London, Atkins, 1702) vol. 2 58 & G. Jacob, *The Accomplished Conveyancer* vol. 1 (London, Butt, 1714) 1714.

[174] J. Summerson, *Georgian London* (London, Pleiades, 1945) 23, S. Jenkins, *Landlords to London* (London, Constable, 1975) 30–31. See also M. Davey, *Long Residential Leases: Past and Present*, in S. Bright, *Landlord and Tenant, Past, Present and Future* (Oxford, Hart, 2006).

[175] Stewart, *Practice of Conveyancing* 329.

[176] See e.g. *The Young Clerk's Magazine*, 5th edn. (London, Strahan & Woodfall) 79, Stewart, *Practice of Conveyancing* 339.

[177] *City of London* v. *Nash* (1747) 3 Atk 512 is illustrative of the typical sharp practices of the time. One of the reasons why stucco façades were so popular with London builders, was that the stucco concealed all the shoddy workmanship underneath.

then grant underleases at a rack rent in order to make a return on the investment. At the end of the term of the head-lease,[178] the property would revert to the landlord, with the house on it, by then normally in very poor condition.

Originally, residential building leases were typically granted for terms of 42 years, but the period gradually lengthened first to about 60 years in the eighteenth century,[179] and then to 80 or 99 years[180] in the nineteenth.[181]

In the twentieth century, building leases were sometimes granted for specialised commercial developments, such as hotels and cinemas. But the long lease for a fixed term normally encountered today is a lease of a residential flat within a larger building. Separate self-contained flats were uncommon, until the Victorians started building mansion blocks in the late nineteenth century, and few attempts were made to sell off separate flats within buildings to owner-occupiers before the middle of the twentieth century.[182] Where that had been done in the past, either no proper attempt had been made to deal with the problem of regulation and maintenance of the rest of the building,[183] or it

---

[178] Some building leases were granted as underleases. In *Simpson* v. *Clayton* (1836) 4 Bing NC 758 the head-tenant had covenanted to use his best endeavours to obtain a renewal of the headlease, which was determinable on lives. The head-landlord refused to renew the lease, except on payment of a premium representing the full improved value of the property, and the judge held that the covenant did not oblige the head-tenant to pay an unreasonable amount, so the underleases were lost.

[179] *City of London* v. *Nash* (1747) 3 Atk 512, 513, T. Williams, *Precedents in Conveyancing*, vol. 3 (London, Kearsley, 1788) 962, E. Wood, *Conveyancing* vol. 3 (London, Stratham & Woodfall, 1793) 128, 130.

[180] In *Calthorpe* v. *McOscar* [1924] 1 KB 716 the building lease had been granted in 1825 for a term of 95 years.

[181] F. Pollock, *The Land Laws* 142. *The Encyclopedia of Forms and Precedents*, 1st edn., vol. 7 (London, Butterworths, 1905) contained precedents for 99 and 999 year building leases; 337, 357.

[182] Some mansion blocks built between 1918 and 1939 were sold off in this way: D. Piercy, *A Surveyor Looks at the Sale of Flats*, in E. George, *The Sale of Flats*, 2nd edn. (London, Sweet and Maxwell, 1959) 210. But, in the Victorian period, 'probably nine-tenths' of houses were let from year to year: W.A. Holdsworth, *The Useful Library: The Law of Landlord and Tenant*, (London, Routledge, 1863) 23.

[183] It was necessary to enact the Lincoln's Inn Act 1860, to give statutory force to an agreement made in 1682, regulating the flying freeholds in New Square, for this reason.

had been dealt with by vesting the freehold in the building in a committee of trustees, so that each flat owner would only have an equitable title to the flat,[184] neither of which was very satisfactory.

The fundamental problem with trying to sever a freehold laterally, so as to create a freehold flat, was that the burden of repairing and other positive covenants could not be annexed to freehold land.[185] But there was no difficulty with annexing a repairing covenant to a leasehold term or reversion.[186]

So when, in the twentieth century, rent control[187] made it impossible for owners of buildings to continue letting flats at an open market rent on short leases, they generally chose to sell off the flats by means of long leases, granted for a substantial initial premium,[188] instead. An attempt to change this in 2002, by the introduction of a statutory alternative of 'commonhold',[189] proved to be an embarrassing failure: developers could not see any advantage in making the change, mortgage lenders were suspicious of it, and estate agents did not think that people would be willing to pay a premium for anything 'common'.[190]

---

[184] This was the scheme adopted when Albany in London was converted into flats in 1803.

[185] *Austerberry* v. *Corporation of Oldham* (1885) 29 Ch.D 750.

[186] In theory, the covenants could be annexed to a necessary leasehold easement, and there is a precedent for a complicated scheme for the sale of freehold flats, with the benefit of leasehold easements over the common parts, in (1953) 17 Conv.(NS) 516–517.

[187] See ch.3 heading 'Rent control'.

[188] After 25th March 1949 a landlord could not demand a premium for the grant of a Rent Act tenancy: s.2(1) Landlord and Tenant (Rent Control) Act 1949. To avoid that prohibition, it was necessary to grant a term of at least 21 years or at a low rent instead. There is a precedent for such a lease in (1953) 17 Conv.(NS) 558.

[189] Commonhold and Leasehold Reform Act 2002.

[190] There is, curiously, additional value if a long lease is being sold with 'a share of the freehold', meaning a share in a management company which owns the reversion or a lease of the common parts. That is odd because something is much more likely to go wrong with the performance of the services, if the decisions are being been made by a committee of well-meaning amateurs; and when things do go wrong, instead of everyone in the building having a common interest in fighting a third party, they will instead be fighting amongst themselves with their neighbours.

4. Periodic.

By the middle of the fifteenth century most of the manorial demesne land in the country was leased to yeoman farmers,[191] and an arrangement that lasted from year to year had become common. As Sir John Baker points out,[192] that is hardly surprising, after the plague of 1349, and two hundred years of harsh winters during the 'Little Ice Age'. Lords simply did not have the villein man-power to be able to continue farming it themselves.

That remained the usual practice down to the end of the nineteenth century,[193] when most of the agricultural land in England and Wales was still let to tenant farmers,[194] on annual tenancies,[195] and the relationship between the landlord and tenant was still more feudal than commercial. It was the 'constant practice'[196] for a proportion of the rent to be remitted in bad years, but:[197]

> The landlord in return expects a certain amount of deference and compliance in various matters from his tenant. Not only does the farmer meet him half-way on questions of shooting rights, and allow free passage to the hunt, but his political support of the landlord is not unfrequently reckoned on with as much confidence as the performance of the covenants and conditions in the tenancy itself. In the case of holdings from year to year it may be not unfairly said that being of the landlord's political party is often a tacit condition of the tenancy.

---

[191] *Oxford History of the Laws of England,* vol. 6 632, Plucknett, *Concise History,* 574.

[192] *Oxford History of the Laws of England,* vol. 6 643. See also Holdsworth, *HEL* vol. 7 243 and G. Brodrick, *English Land and English Landlords* (London, Cassell, 1881) 17–18, 201.

[193] Holdsworth, *HEL* vol. 7 288–289.

[194] 'A large owner who farms his own land is now met with only as an occasional exception': F. Pollock, *The Land Laws,* 137.

[195] In 1880 the average farm size was fifty-six acres and it was mostly let under yearly tenancies, without security of tenure: G. Brodrick, *English Land and English Landlords* (London, Cassell, 1881) 198–200. See also F. Pollock, *The Land Laws* 154.

[196] F. Pollock, *The Land Laws,* 155.

[197] Ibid.

Yet there was no place for periodic tenancies in medieval land law. There is no mention of periodic tenancies in Bracton, Littleton and Coke. For them, leases were either a freehold estate for life, or a chattel interest for a fixed term of years, or a mere possessory holding at will. A tenancy for a rolling term simply did not fit into the scheme at all.

As a result, in 1511 either party could determine a tenancy from year to year at the end of any year, without prior notice.[198] In 1522[199] the Court of Common pleas was divided about whether, if the landlord allowed the tenancy to continue afterwards, the tenant would hold over as a tenant at will or as a tenant for a fixed term of another year.[200] Nobody thought that the tenant held over for a rolling term. Fitzherbert and Broke JJ thought that the tenant held over as a tenant at will, because the length of the further term had been uncertain at its commencement, and the tenancy did not comply with the formalities for a lease for life.[201] Pollard J and Brudenell CJ thought that the tenancy was for a fixed term of another year, because the arrangement could be made certain, at the beginning of each year, by the act of the parties.[202]

This difficulty produced some absurd rules of construction, as the courts struggled to find ways to decide that the parties had originally created a fixed term of longer than a year.[203] Although

---

[198] *Scrope* v. *Hyk* (1511) 2 Caryll's Rep 116 SS 621, Spelman 135 pl.1.

[199] *Burgh* v. *Potkyn* (1522) YB 14 Hen.8 f.10 pl.6, 119 SS 125, 120 SS 82.

[200] The issue arose in the context of an action for waste, which could be brought against a tenant for a fixed term but not against a tenant at will: see ch.9 heading 'Waste'.

[201] Per Fitzherbert J (119 SS 129): 'This cannot be a lease for years, for there is no certain point of termination, and so it shall be lease at will'. See also *Bishop of Bath's Case* (1605) 6 Co.Rep 34b, 35b.

[202] There is a precedent in W.West, *Simboleograph* (London, Stationers Co., 1610) pt.1 s.451 for a lease for 'one whole year . . . and so from year to year at the will and pleasure' of the parties.

[203] In 1564 it was said that a lease for three years, and so from three years to three years, would create a fixed term of six years; *Say* v. *Smith* (1564) Plowden 269, 272. In 1606 a term of one year, and thereafter from year to year, was held to create a fixed term of three years, and a tenancy at will afterwards; *Bishop of Bath's Case*, (1605) 6 Co.Rep 34b, 35b. In 1612 a lease for a year, and thereafter from year to year (excepting the last day of each year) for so long as the grantor lived, was held to be a lease of two years less two days;

in 1641 Noy thought that it was it was necessary to give 'warning . . . to depart',[204] as late as 1700 Holt CJ held that no notice was required to determine a lease from year to year at the end of any year, although once any year had started, the original lease would continue until the end of that year.[205] As was explained in Bacon's Abridgment:[206]

> A parol lease was made de anno in annum, *quamdiu ambabus partibus placuerit*; it was adjudged that this was but a lease for a year certain, and that every year after it was a springing interest, arising upon the first contract and parcel of it; so that if the lessee had occupied eight or ten years, or more, these years, by computation from the time past, made an entire lease for so many years; and if rent was in arrear for part of one of those years, and part of another, the lessor might distrain and avow as for so much rent arrear upon one entire lease, and need not avow as for several rents due upon several leases, accounting each year a new lease.

By 1765,[207] though the law on the need to give notice was

Lutterel v. *Weston* (1610) Cro Jac 308. See also *Shep.Touch.* 271, Platt, *Leases*, vol. 1 659.

[204] W. Noy, *Grounds and Maxims of the Law of England*, 9th edn. (Reprinted Oxford, Professional Books Ltd, 1985) 165. In *Taylor* v. *Seed* (1696) Comberbach 383, Skin 649, it was said that there was a special custom in London that six months notice would be given to terminate a tenancy at a rent of 40s pa. or more, and three months notice would be given to terminate a tenancy at a lower rent, which was upheld.

[205] *Leighton* v. *Theed* (1700) 2 Salk 413, 3 Salk 222, 1 Ld.Raym 707. *Agard* v. *King* (1600) Cro Eliz 775, is to the same effect, though in *Sir Thomas Bowe's Case* (1646) Aleyn 4) it was held that if a tenant for years held over, paying rent, that only created a tenancy at will, which could be determined without notice. See also Holdsworth, *HEL* vol. 7 244.

[206] 7th edn., vol. iv 839. See also Platt, *Leases* vol. 1 660 *et seq* on the question of whether a demise 'from year to year' created a term of one or two years.

[207] *Timmins* v. *Rowlinson* (1765) 3 Burr 1603, 1609 Per Wilmot J: 'In the country, leases at will, in the strict legal notion of a lease at will, being found extremely inconvenient, exist only notionally; and were succeeded by another species of contract, which was less inconvenient. At first, it was indeed settled to be for a year certain: and then the landlord might turn the tenant out at the end of the year. It is now established that if a tenant takes from year to year, either party must give reasonable notice, before the end of the year; though that reasonable notice varies, according to the custom of different counties'.

changing.[208] Blackstone, the second volume of whose *Commentaries* were published the following year, caught the change.[209] He said:[210]

> . . . courts of law have of late years leant as much as possible against construing demises, where no certain term is mentioned, to be tenancies at will; but have rather held them to be tenancies from year to year so long as both parties please, especially where an annual rent is reserved; in which case they will not suffer either party to determine the tenancy even at the end of the year, without reasonable notice to the other.

The development of the consequent rules about service of a notice to quit, and the length of the notice required, is discussed in chapter 7.

5. At sufferance.

A tenant at sufferance is 'he that at the first came by lawful demise, and after his estate ends continues in possession wrongly holding over'.[211] In short, a tenant at sufferance is a former tenant who has become a trespasser, but against whom the

---

[208] Chambers, *Leases* (1811) states the law as per *Leigton* v. *Theed* (supra) 72. But it has to be remembered that, like Bacon's Abridgment, that book was an arrangement of materials left by Chief Baron Gilbert on his death in 1726.

[209] The earliest hint of a change in the case law, apart from the custom of London, is in *Legg* v. *Strudwick* (1709) 2 Salk 414, where it was said that a tenancy from year to year fell within the exception for leases of three years or less in the Statute of Frauds (1677), because there would never be more than two years of the term in existence at any one time. The idea that notice would be required to determine at the end of any one year was implicit in the idea that there might be a time when more than one year of the term remained unexpired.

[210] *Bl.Comm.* Bk.II 147. *Gulliver d. Tasker* v. *Burr* (1766) 1 Wm. Black 596 decided that reasonable notice was needed to terminate at the end of the year, even where the tenant had died during the term. See also *Doe d. Dagget* v. *Snowden* (1778) 2 Wm. Black 1224 and cf. *Mackay* v. *Mackreth* (1785) 4 Doug 213.

[211] *Co.Litt.* 57b.

person next entitled has not yet entered.[212]

There is no privity of estate between a landlord and a tenant at sufferance. So the landlord's estate cannot be conveyed to a tenant at sufferance by a release.[213]

If land is in the possession of a tenant at sufferance, then the landlord cannot bring an action in trespass against a third party without having entered on the tenant at sufferance first,[214] and strictly the landlord formerly had to enter before bringing ejectment to evict a tenant at sufferance,[215] though the fictional entry made in the action of ejectment was, itself, sufficient by the end of the seventeenth century.[216]

If a landlord gives a tenant at sufferance permission to remain, then the tenant becomes a tenant at will. The effect of a permission implied from the subsequent acceptance of rent is discussed under the heading 'At will' above. But there is a difference between giving the former tenant permission to remain and giving the former tenant extra time to get out. In the latter case, the former tenant remains a trespasser.[217]

6. Agricultural security.

Between the seventeenth century and the end of the First World War, most agricultural land was let to tenant farmers from

---

[212] It is impossible to be a tenant at sufferance of the Crown. Anyone who would otherwise be a tenant at sufferance is simply an intruder on the royal demesne: see ch.9 heading 'Crown proceedings'.

[213] *Butler* v. *Duckmanton* (1606) Cro Jac 169.

[214] *Trevillian* v. *Andrew* (1697) 5 Mod. 384.

[215] *Doe d. Moore* v. *Lawder* (1813) 1 Stark 308. Per Lord Ellenborough: 'If the party went upon the premises indicating his intention to take possession, he did all that the law requires'. In *Doe d. Harrison* v. *Murrell* (1837) 8 Car & P 135, Lord Abinger is reported as having said that 'a tenant by sufferance, turned out by his landlord without a demand for possession, could not maintain ejectment, because he has no interest in the land; but he might maintain trespass'. But the context shows that he was contemplating an action in trespass against a third party, with no title, not the landlord. In fact, a tenant at sufferance could maintain ejectment against third parties with no title too, for an earlier squatter can recover possession from a later squatter, relying solely on prior possession.

[216] See ch.9 heading 'Ejectment'.

[217] *Whiteacre d. Boult* v. *Symmonds* (1808) 10 East 13.

year to year. It was very common for the letting to be made by a tenant for life of a strict settlement,[218] and that caused a particular problem if the landlord died part way through the year. Most settlements gave the tenant for life a special power to bind the reversion when granting annual agricultural sub-leases, but if the settlement did not contain this power, or if the terms of the power were not complied with strictly, the sub-tenancy to the tenant farmer would end automatically on the death of the tenant for life; for absent any such power, a tenant for life could not sub-let for longer than his own interest.[219]

Where this happened part way through the year, an agricultural sub-tenant had an ancient common law right called emblements,[220] to enter the land again at harvest time, and reap any annual crops previously sown. But as agricultural processes and techniques became more sophisticated in the nineteenth century, that ceased to be satisfactory compensation for the loss of the tenancy,[221] and so by s.1 Landlord and Tenant Act 1851,[222] if a sub-tenancy at a rack rent would otherwise have ended on the death of a tenant for life, it was automatically continued against the person next entitled, until the end of that year instead.[223]

Nor was it very satisfactory that an annual tenancy of agricultural land could be determined by as little as six months notice to quit, to expire on the anniversary of the tenancy. So the

---

[218] For the reasons why, see above, heading 'For life'.

[219] See ch.1 heading 'Capacity' sub-heading 'tenants for life'.

[220] See ch.7 heading 'Emblements'.

[221] By s.26 Agricultural Holdings Act 1908 agricultural tenants were given power to adopt any system of cropping of arable lands that they saw fit, the 'Norfolk' or 'four course' system of crop rotation having been made antiquated in the nineteenth century by the use of phosphates and nitrogen.

[222] This provision was repealed by s.1 Statute Law (Repeals) Act 1971. It had been made unnecessary by the changes made to the status of a tenancy for life in 1926 (see heading 'For life' above) and by s.14 Agriculture Act 1920 (subsequently, s.4 Agricultural Holdings Act 1948) which provided for an automatic extension until after the expiry of a 12 month notice to quit instead.

[223] In *Haines* v. *Welch* (1868) LR 4 CP 91 it was held that this provision applied to a cottage with about an acre of land, only part of which was sown with corn and potatoes.

Agricultural Holdings Act 1883[224] changed that to twelve months notice, except where the parties had expressly agreed otherwise.[225] The Agricultural Act 1920 removed that power to contract out,[226] and automatically continued expired tenancies of agricultural land which had been granted for a fixed term of at least two years, as annual periodic tenancies afterwards, unless that notice to quit had been given.[227]

Apart from that, there was no statutory security of tenure before 1948. The tenancy could be brought to an end in any of the ways in which it could be determined at common law, albeit that customary or statutory compensation might be payable on quitting.[228]

During the Second World War there were detailed emergency regulations governing almost all aspects of agricultural practice. Afterwards, most of the agricultural land in England and Wales was still let to tenant farmers,[229] and it was thought that if they were given security of tenure, then they would have an incentive to invest capital with a view to carrying out long term improvements, which would improve farm productivity and enable the government to end the post-war rationing of foodstuffs. Accordingly, part III of the Agriculture Act 1947, which came into force on 1st March 1948, provided a general scheme of security of tenure for tenants of agricultural land. It was re-enacted following year as the Agricultural Holdings Act 1948.

It applied wherever land was let for the purpose of agriculture for a term of years or from year to year, and it also

---

[224] s.33.

[225] *Barlow* v. *Teal* (1885) 15 QBD 501. s.23 Agricultural Holdings Act 1908 gave the landlord power to serve a notice to quit part of the holding for eight specified purposes, which the tenant could adopt as a notice for the whole. That right was replicated in subsequent legislation, down to and including, the Agricultural Holdings Act 1986.

[226] s.28.

[227] s.13 Agriculture Act 1920, ss.25(1), 57(1) Agricultural Holdings Act 1923, *Land Settlement Association* v. *Carr* [1944] 1 KB 657.

[228] See ch.7 heading 'Compensation on quitting'.

[229] In 1950 62% of agricultural land in England and Wales was rented, compared with the remaining 38% which was farmed by the owner: F. Dovring, *Land and Labour in Europe 1900–1950* (The Hague, Martinus Nijhoff, 1956) 150.

applied to any agricultural licence or tenancy for a fixed or periodic term of a year or less (other than a grazing licence) as if it were a tenancy from year to year.[230] The purpose of this provision was to prevent the 1948 Act being circumvented in the same way as the 1920 Act had been, by the practice of granting successive fixed term tenancies of 364 days.[231] But that still left a gap in the scheme—tenancies granted for a fixed term of more than one year[232] but less than two years—which was never filled, with the consequence that those tenancies never acquired security of tenure as agricultural holdings.[233]

The scheme under the Agricultural Holdings Act 1948, and under the 1986 Act which replaced it, was to prevent the landlord terminating those tenancies, otherwise than by service of a notice to quit, and to give the tenant the right to serve a counter-notice, requiring the landlord to obtain the consent of the Agricultural Land Tribunal[234] to the termination of the tenancy,[235] which could only be obtained on certain discretionary grounds.[236]

There was an exception if the landlord's notice to quit specified one of seven grounds as the reason for its service, known to agricultural lawyers as the seven deadly sins.[237] They were,[238] in order: that the Tribunal had given its consent to the operation of the notice on a discretionary ground; that the land was required for non-agricultural use for which planning permission had been granted; that the Tribunal had decided that the tenant was guilty of bad husbandry; that arrears of rent had been outstanding for at least two months, or the tenant had failed to remedy some other remediable breach of the tenancy

---

[230] s.2 Agricultural Holdings Act 1948.

[231] *Land Settlement* v. *Carr* [1944] KB 657.

[232] *Bernays* v. *Prosser* [1963] 2 QB 592.

[233] *Gladstone* v. *Bower* [1960] 2 QB 384.

[234] Originally, consent was required from the Minister of Agriculture. The change was made by s.5 Agriculture Act 1958 as a result of the Report of the Franks Committee (1957 Cmnd 218).

[235] s.24 1948 Act, s.26 1986 Act.

[236] ss.25-6 1948 Act, s.27 1986 Act.

[237] The term was coined by a Bristol solicitor, W. Scammell.

[238] s.24 1948 Act. They were subsequently consolidated in the Agricultural Holdings (Notice to Quit) Act 1977. In the 1986 Act they appear in pt.1 sch. 3.

agreement; that the tenant had committed an irremediable breach of the tenancy agreement, causing the landlord harm; that the tenant had become insolvent; and that the original tenant[239] had died less than three months before service of the notice. An eighth sin of termination for the purpose of amalgamation or re-shaping of agricultural units required by the Minister of Agriculture was added in 1967,[240] and the tenant of a smallholding reaching retirement age became an additional ground for possession in 1984.[241]

In each of those cases, if the tenant disputed the grounds for serving the notice to quit, the tenant was allowed to refer that dispute to arbitration,[242] but only so that the arbitrator could decide whether the ground had been proved or not. The arbitrator had no discretion to allow the tenancy to continue if the ground was made out.

In 1976 it became possible for close relatives of a deceased agricultural tenant to apply to the Agricultural Lands Tribunal for a succession tenancy,[243] and up to two successions are possible. Succession upon retirement became available as an alternative in 1984, but at the same time, the right was limited, so that statutory successions are only possible where the original tenancy was granted before 12th July 1984.

On 1st September 1995, lettings of agricultural land went from being one of the most regulated and secure forms of tenancy, to one of the least. For lettings since then, the law has basically reverted to the scheme which had been introduced by the Agriculture Act 1920, and which was in place prior to the enactment of the Agriculture Act 1947. Now, a farm business tenancy for a fixed term of two years or less expires automatically by effluxion of time, and is not continued. If the fixed term is longer than two years, then the tenancy is

---

[239] *Woodward* v. *Earl of Dudley* [1954] 1 Ch 283. By s.7 Agriculture (Miscellaneous Provisions) Act 1954, this was changed, in the case of joint original tenants, to the death of the survivor of them. In 1976 this was changed again to the current tenant, or the sole surviving current tenant: s.16 Agriculture (Miscellaneous Provisions) Act 1976.

[240] s.29(4) Agriculture Act 1967.

[241] s.6 Agricultural Holdings Act 1984.

[242] s.26 1948 Act.

[243] s.18 Agriculture (Miscellaneous Provisions) Act 1976.

continued, as an annual periodic tenancy afterwards, unless notice has been given to terminate it on its term date between 12 and 24 months beforehand.[244] An annual farm business tenancy can be terminated by a notice to quit, to expire on an anniversary of the tenancy, served between 12 and 24 months beforehand.[245] The common law governs the length of the notices required to terminate shorter periodic farm business tenancies.[246]

7. Residential security.

Residential tenants had no security of tenure before the First World War. During that war, and for six months afterwards,[247] the Increase of Rent and Mortgage Interest (War Restrictions) Act 1915 required the landlord of a house, part of a house or flat, let as a separate dwelling,[248] to prove specified grounds for recovering possession following determination of the contractual term, except where the annual rent or rateable value was above £35 in London and £26 elsewhere.[249] Those limits were doubled by legislation which temporarily continued the 1915 Act after the war.[250]

Further legislation followed in 1920,[251] which was designed to last for three years. In fact, it lasted, as part of the 'tapestry' of Rent Acts, until 1968. It tripled the original value limits, bringing 98% of housing within the Acts. But whereas, for security purposes, the 1915 Act did not distinguish between long

---

[244] s.5. Agricultural Holdings Act 1995.

[245] s.6.

[246] See ch.7 heading 'Expiry'.

[247] s.5(2).

[248] s.12(2). The 1933 Act referred to 'a house let as a separate dwelling or a part of a house being so let': s.16(1). A 'house' included a 'flat' (see *Wimbush* v. *Cibulia* [1949] 2 KB 564) for: 'The Acts were passed in a hurry, the language used was often extremely vague': Per Scrutton LJ, *Skinner* v. *Geary* [1931] 2 KB 546, 561. In *Vaughan* v. *Shaw* [1945] 1 KB 400, 401 MacKinnon LJ described the Acts as an 'obscure mass of words' and 'that welter of chaotic verbiage'.

[249] s.2(2).

[250] Rent and Mortgage Interest (Restrictions) Act 1919.

[251] The Increase of Rent and Mortgage Interest (Restrictions) Act 1920.

leases and short leases, the 1920 Act and all subsequent Rent Acts did. A tenant of a lease of residential property, which had originally been granted for a term of 21 years or more, at a rent that was less than two thirds of its rateable value, ceased to have security of tenure in 1920, and did not acquire any form of security again until 1951.[252]

Short leases: The 1920 Act established the framework for the security of tenure provisions of all subsequent Rent Acts, by introducing the concept of a 'statutory' tenancy. The idea was that when the original contractual term of the tenancy expired, whether pursuant to a common law notice to quit or otherwise, then if the tenant was occupying the property as a residence at that time,[253] the contractual tenancy would immediately be replaced by a statutory right of irremovability, which would continue if and for so long as the tenant occupied the property as a residence,[254] and which could otherwise only be terminated by the court on statutory grounds. On the death of the tenant, a resident spouse or other member of the tenant's family could succeed to the tenancy,[255] and after 1965, that could happen twice.[256]

Houses built or converted into flats after 2nd April 1919 were exempt from the 1920 Act,[257] as were all new tenancies granted between 31st July 1923 and 18th July 1933.[258] On 29th

---

[252] See below sub-heading 'long leases'.

[253] Only an individual could occupy a property as a residence. So whilst a corporate tenant was entitled to the benefit of the restrictions on rent during the contractual term of the tenancy, it could not claim the protection a statutory tenancy afterwards: *Hiller* v. *United Diaries* [1934] 1 KB 57.

[254] s.2 Rent Act 1977. This applies even to a tenant's notice to quit. But service of a tenant's notice to quit is a discretionary ground for possession if the landlord has relied upon it; case 5 sch. 15 Rent Act 1977.

[255] s.12(g) 1920 Act.

[256] Second successions were possible by agreement under s.17 of the 1957 Act. They became a right for deaths after 7th December 1965 by s.13 of the 1965 Act. Second successions have been impossible since 15th January 1989, and only a *de jure* or *de facto* spouse of a Rent Act tenant can now acquire a statutory, rather than an assured, tenancy by first succession: pt.1 sch. 4 Housing Act 1988.

[257] s.12(9).

[258] Rent and Mortgage Interest Restrictions (Continuance) Act 1923.

September 1933, any tenant of a high value house (Class A) who still had protection, lost it,[259] but lettings of low value houses (Class C) made afterwards were brought back within the Acts.[260]

Middle value houses (Class B) were left alone, until 1938, when the top half of the band was moved into Class A and the bottom half into Class C.

On the outbreak of the Second World War, the clock was put back to 1920. Properties where the rent or rateable value was less £100 in London or £75 elsewhere, were swept back into protection,[261] which left only a few mansion-houses outside.

The next decontrolling measure was the Rent Act 1957, which stopped any new tenancy granted after 6th July 1957 from acquiring protection, and took existing tenancies of most large houses out of control too,[262] subject to 'standstill' protection for a minimum of fifteen months. Peter Rachman, at that time working as an estate agent's clerk, realised that there was money to be made buying slum properties which were still subject to controlled tenancies cheaply,[263] and then 'persuading' the existing tenants to leave, so that they could be relet at market rents, giving his name to a new noun. In the end, it did him no good. He died young and the counter-reaction was the Rent Act 1965, which brought all those properties which had been decontrolled by the 1957 Act back into the Rent Acts as 'regulated' tenancies instead.[264]

The original grounds for recovering possession in the 1915 Act were the non-payment of rent or some other breach of the tenancy agreement, the commission of acts of waste, nuisance or annoyance to neighbours, and a reasonable requirement for the landlord's own occupation, or for the occupation of an employee

---

[259] s.2(2) Rent and Mortgage Interest (Restrictions) Act 1933.

[260] s.1(2) Rent and Mortgage Interest (Restrictions) Act 1933.

[261] Rent and Mortgage Restrictions Act 1939. Crown leases were exempt, including any sub-tenancy created out of a crown lease, even if the Crown had sold the reversion (*Rudler* v. *Franks* [1947] KB 530) until crown sub-tenancies were brought within the Acts by the Rent Act 1952.

[262] The rateable value limits were fixed at £40 in London and £30 elsewhere.

[263] Most of these slum properties were in the now fashionable and expensive Notting Hill.

[264] The rateable value limits were £400 in London and £200 elsewhere.

of the landlord, or an employee of some other tenant of the landlord. There was also a general sweeping up discretion to make a possession order on any ground which might be deemed satisfactory to the court,[265] which was not repeated afterwards.

The power to make a possession order on the ground that the landlord had agreed to sell the property with vacant possession, relying upon a tenant's notice to quit, was added in 1920;[266] assignment or sub-letting of the whole without consent was added in 1923;[267] and sub-letting at an excessive rent,[268] and the availability of suitable alternative accommodation, became grounds for possession in 1933.[269] At the same time, an overriding requirement was added that it had to be reasonable to make a possession order, so that making the order would always ultimately be a matter of discretion for the court.[270] In 1936 overcrowding was added as a discretionary ground for obtaining possession[271] and in 1965 the first three 'mandatory' grounds were added. Those were cases where the court would be obliged to make possession order, whether it was reasonable to do so or not. The most important one was where the letting had been by an owner occupier, who wished to resume residence, having served notice on the tenant at the start of tenancy that possession might be recovered on that ground.[272] The other two mandatory grounds were limited to recovery of possession from church ministers and agricultural workers.[273] Farmhouses which became redundant on amalgamation of agricultural units could be recovered under a mandatory ground which was added in 1967,[274] and the Rent Act 1974 added mandatory grounds for very short fixed terms and landlords who wished to retire to the property.[275]

---

[265] s.2(3).
[266] s.5(c).
[267] s.4 1923 Act.
[268] s.4 1933 Act.
[269] s.3 Rent Restrictions (Amendment) Act 1933.
[270] Ibid.
[271] s.65 Housing Act 1936.
[272] s.14 Rent Act 1965.
[273] s.15 Rent Act 1965.
[274] s.38 Agriculture Act 1967.
[275] ss.2–3.

Furnished tenancies were excluded from the Rent Acts from the beginning.[276] In 1946, it became possible to obtain an indefinite series of six-monthly extensions to a furnished letting,[277] which would otherwise qualify for Rent Act protection, but furnished tenancies were not properly brought within the Rent Acts until 1974,[278] when an exception for resident landlords was also introduced.[279]

By s.33 Rent Act 1965[280] the court acquired a similar power to defer the operation of notices to quit given to agricultural workers of tied accommodation, who generally had no statutory protection because they occupied under service licences or at a low monetary rent.[281] They acquired protection equivalent to the protection enjoyed by Rent Act tenants under the Rent (Agriculture) Act 1976, and the following year, the remaining Rent Acts were consolidated into the Rent Act 1977.[282] But that proved to be the high-water mark for short lease residential security of tenure, for the incoming Conservative government in 1979 was keen to stimulate the rental market by giving landlords a guarantee that they would be able to recover their properties at the end of the agreed term.

The first attempt at this was in the Housing Act 1980, which introduced a new mandatory ground for the recovery of possession, where the landlord had given notice that the tenancy would be a 'protected shorthold tenancy'. It failed because it proved almost impossible to get the notices right.

The next attempt was more successful. The Housing Act

---

[276] s.2(2) Increase of Rent and Mortgage Interest (War Restrictions) Act 1915.

[277] Furnished Houses (Rent Control) Act 1946. The provisions were repeated in pt.VI Rent Act 1968.

[278] s.1 Rent Act 1974.

[279] Para.1 sch. 2 Rent Act 1974. The power to defer the operation of a notice to quit for these 'restricted contracts' was retained, but not for any contract made after 28th November 1980: s.72(3) Housing Act 1980.

[280] A more limited power had been granted the previous year under s.2 Protection from Eviction Act 1964. See now, s.4 Protection from Eviction Act 1977.

[281] s.12(7) 1920 Act, s.3(1) 1939 Act.

[282] The earlier consolidating Act was the Rent Act 1968, which consolidated the 'tapestry' of previous Acts, except for s.16 Rent Act 1957 (minimum length of notices to quit) and part III Rent Act 1965 (protection from eviction otherwise than by court process).

1988 introduced 'assured tenancies' which (if the right notices were served at the beginning) would be 'shorthold' tenancies having no security of tenure. The need to serve that preliminary notice was abolished with effect from 27th February 1997,[283] with the result that private sector short-term lettings now automatically have no security of tenure, unless the parties choose to contract into the non-shorthold regime. Otherwise, all the landlord has to do, in order to be entitled to recover possession on the expiry of the contractual term, or at any time afterwards, is give two months written notice to quit.[284]

From 1936, new tenancies granted by local authorities, or by institutions which are now called social housing associations,[285] were excluded from the Rent Acts[286] Those which remained within the Rent Acts lost protection in 1954.[287] Their tenancies were common law tenancies until 1980. Ironically, the incoming Conservative government of 1979 was forced to grant security of tenure to local authority residential tenants in the Housing Act 1980; for a central plank of the manifesto had been that tenants of local authorities should be allowed to purchase their homes at a substantial discount to the open market value, and the fear was that, unless they were granted security of tenure, some local authorities would seek to frustrate this by serving notices to quit. The scheme for secure tenancies is now found in the Housing Act 1985.

Long leases: Between 1920 and 1951, leases of houses and flats which had been granted for a term of more than 21 years, and which reserved a rent of less than two thirds of the rateable value, had no statutory security of tenure. When the lease expired, the landlord was entitled to recover possession. The

---

[283] Between 15th January 1989 and 27th February 1997 it was necessary to contract into that shorthold regime, by service of the notice at the beginning. Since 28th February 1997, an assured tenancy has automatically been a shorthold tenancy, unless the parties have agreed otherwise: see generally T. Fancourt, *Megarry's Assured Tenancies*, 2nd edn. (London, Sweet and Maxwell, 1999) 111–124.

[284] s.21.

[285] s.93 Housing Act 1936.

[286] s.83 Housing Act 1936.

[287] s.33(1) Housing Repairs and Rent Act 1954.

Leasehold Property (Temporary Provisions) Act 1951 was enacted to provide a temporary scheme of protection in this situation, which was continued by part 1 Landlord and Tenant Act 1954.[288] If, but for the fact that the lease was a long lease,[289] it would have qualified for Rent Act protection, then the effect of those Acts was to continue the original contractual tenancy until the landlord served a notice, either to resume possession or proposing a statutory tenancy. The landlord could only resume possession on grounds which broadly corresponded with some of the Rent Act grounds,[290] and otherwise the tenant became entitled to a statutory tenancy. That was changed to an assured periodic tenancy for long leases expiring after 15th January 1999, which was the tenth anniversary of the coming into effect of the Housing Act 1988.[291]

Tenants of private houses (but not flats) held under long leases, were given the right to buy-in every reversionary interest, at value, and also the right to acquire fifty-year ground-rent extensions to their existing leases,[292] in 1967. In the case of flats within a building, held on similar terms, the tenants were collectively given a right of pre-emption for most dealings with the reversion in 1987,[293] which was easily evaded; and in 1993 they were given a collective right of compulsory purchase of the reversion in the building, equivalent to that enjoyed by a tenant of a house,[294] and individual rights to buy ninety year extensions to their leases at peppercorn rents.[295] Originally, there were low rent and residence requirements for all of these rights, but they were largely abolished in 2002.[296] Tenants of local authorities acquired the right to purchase long leases of their flats or the

---

[288] S. Magnus, *The Leasehold Property (Temporary Provisions) Act 1951* (London, Butterworths, 1951) 6–8.
[289] The requirement that the long lease be at a low rent was removed by s.21 Housing Act 1957.
[290] s.12 and sch. 3 Landlord and Tenant Act 1954.
[291] sch. 10 Local Government and Housing Act 1989.
[292] Leasehold Reform Act 1967.
[293] Pt.1 Landlord and Tenant Act 1987.
[294] Ch.I Leasehold Reform and Urban Development Act 1993.
[295] Ch.II Leasehold Reform and Urban Development Act 1993.
[296] s.141 Commonhold and Leasehold Reform Act 2002.

reversions upon their houses under the Housing Act 1980.

8. Business security.

Business tenants had to wait until the middle of the twentieth century before acquiring security of tenure, despite well-organised campaigns in the nineteenth.[297]

The protection given to residential tenants during the First World War[298] applied, almost by accident, where those premises were also used partly for business purposes—typically, a small shopkeeper living above the shop—provided that there was also a substantial element of residential use.[299]

The residential scheme of protection continued to apply to those mixed use premises until 1957,[300] and between 24th June 1920 and 24th June 1921 all business tenants (except those occupying premises having a very high rateable value) had temporary protection from eviction under the Rent and Mortgage Interest Restrictions Act 1920.[301]

Purely business tenants had no protection thereafter until the enactment of the Landlord and Tenant Act 1927,[302] which came into force on 25th March 1928,[303] and which provided a weak form of security. The court could force the landlord to grant the tenant a new lease, if the tenant could satisfy the court that the compensation payable for loss of 'inherent' goodwill would be inadequate compared with the loss of the 'personal' goodwill.[304]

---

[297] The best account of the history is in M.Haley, *The Statutory Regulation of Business Tenancies* (Oxford, Oxford University Press, 2000) ch.1. On the influence of the Leasehold Enfranchisement Association see A. Offer, *Property and Politics 1870–1914* (Cambridge, Cambridge University Press, 1981) 153–158.

[298] See the heading 'Residential security' above.

[299] *Colls* v. *Parnham* [1922] 1 KB 325.

[300] The Rent Act 1957 brought mixed use tenancies within the scheme of part.II Landlord and Tenant Act 1954.

[301] s.13 1920 Act.

[302] For the provisions of that Act dealing with alteration, alienation and improvements, see ch.5.

[303] s.26.

[304] For the operation of these provisions, see ch.7 heading 'Compensation on quitting'.

Even then, no new tenancy could be granted, if the landlord could show a wish to redevelop the property, or where the landlord, or the landlord's son or daughter, wished to occupy the property, or where that would have been inconsistent with good estate management.

Between 1951 and 1954, tenants of retail shops had, in addition, the right to apply to the county court for yearly extensions to their tenancies.[305] In 1954, the compensation and renewal provisions of the 1927 Act were repealed, and were replaced by a new scheme, which applied to all business tenancies (except where the business was agriculture), and under which the general presumption was in favour of renewal. That is the scheme in part II of the Landlord and Tenant Act 1954, which, with modifications, is still in force today.

It gives most business tenants security of tenure by continuing their tenancies after the contractual expiry date.[306] Provided that the tenant is in business occupation[307] on that date,[308] the lease is continued beyond that date, first to the termination date specified in the landlord's s.25 termination notice or in the tenant's s.26 request for a new tenancy;[309] and then, if an application is made to the court, to the date which is three months after the final disposal of those proceedings.[310]

The landlord is entitled to oppose the grant of a new tenancy, on a number of grounds:[311] if the opposition is successful on a ground that does not involve the tenant's fault, the tenant is entitled to statutory compensation for disturbance, being a multiple of the rateable value. If the landlord does not oppose renewal, or its opposition is unsuccessful, then the tenant is entitled to a new tenancy, at a market rent, and otherwise on

---

[305] Leasehold Property (Temporary Provisions) Act 1951. S. Magnus, *The Leasehold Property (Temporary Provisions) Act 1951* (London, Butterworths, 1951) 8–10.

[306] s.43 of the Act contains various exceptions.

[307] A flexible concept: *Pointon* v. *Poulton* (2007) L&T Rep 7.

[308] *Surrey County Council* v. *Single Horse Properties* [2002] 1 WLR 2106.

[309] s.24. Only a tenant for fixed term can make a s.26 request.

[310] s.64.

[311] s.30. For the origin of these grounds, see s.13 Rent and Mortgage Interest Restrictions Act 1920.

terms fixed by the court. There are various anti-avoidance provisions.[312]

The Act has been amended substantially twice.

The first set of substantial amendments was made by the Law of Property Act 1969, in response to recommendations made by the Law Commission.[313]

Landlords were given power to apply for an 'interim rent', so that the rent payable during the continuation period would no longer be fixed at the old rate;[314] a power was given to the court to authorise the parties to enter into fixed term tenancies, to which the Act would not apply;[315] tenants improvements made during the term of a previous tenancy were to be disregarded when fixing the new rent;[316] and where a landlord opposed a new tenancy on a non-fault ground, the tenant no longer needed to go through the charade of applying for a new tenancy in order to claim compensation.[317]

The second set of substantial amendments were made by the Regulatory Reform (Business Tenancies) (England and Wales) Order 2003.[318] The application to the court following service of a s.25 notice or a s.26 request can now be made by either party; where a new lease is granted, the interim rent is normally now automatically the same as the new rent; and instead of applying to the court to exclude the grant of a tenancy from the Act, the parties can now do it themselves, using the appropriate form of notice or declaration.

---

[312] s.24(2) Landlord and Tenant Act 1954.
[313] (1969) Law Com 17.
[314] s.24A.
[315] s.38(4).
[316] s.34(2).
[317] s.37(1).
[318] SI 2003 No.3096.

CHAPTER 5
Covenants and Contractual Promises

1. Express, implied and usual

2. Title and quiet enjoyment

3. Repair

4. To pay rent

5. Alteration

6. Alienation

7. User

This chapter deals with the types and content of the promises commonly made between a landlord and a tenant in a lease. The transmission of the benefit and burden of those promises is the subject of the next chapter.

1. Express, implied and usual.

A promise is a 'covenant' if it is made in an instrument which the promisor has executed and delivered[1] as a deed. Other promises are only enforceable as part of a contract supported by consideration, either as promissory conditions or warranties or innominate terms.[2] The common law cause of action for the

---

[1] On the need for a delivery, even where the covenant is made by a corporation, see *Norton on Deeds* 11–13. For corporations which are companies, see now s.44(1)(b) Companies Act 2006.

[2] See ch.7 heading 'Repudiation and Frustration'.

enforcement of promises made by deed was 'covenant': the cause of action for the enforcement of contractual promises was 'assumpsit'.[3]

An instrument was only a person's deed, at common law, if it was written on paper or parchment[4] and it had been sealed[5] and delivered by that person.[6]

Sealing, in an age when most people were illiterate, was a serious business. Glanvill, writing in about 1180, noted that where someone 'acknowledges his seal publicly in court, he is strictly bound to warrant the charter, and to observe without question the agreement as set out in the charter as it is contained therein; and he should blame his own poor custody if he suffers damage because his seal was poorly kept'.[7]

A signature became necessary in 1926 for individuals making covenants,[8] reflecting the general move away from formalistic sealing during the nineteenth century,[9] and the need for a witness replaced the need for a seal in 1990.[10] In the meantime, the rules about what physically counted as a seal had been judicially relaxed in 1952.[11] It is still the law that a corporation can make a deed simply by application of its

---

[3] See ch.9 headings 'Covenant' and 'Assumpsit'.

[4] *Co.Litt.* 229a. 'For if it be written on stone, board, linen, leather or the like, it is no deed': *Bl.Comm.* Bk.II 297, *Co.Litt.* 229a. But a wooden tally with a seal attached was held to be a deed in *Finchingfeld* v. *Byrcho* (1311) YB 4 Ed.2 26 SS 153, 154, cf. (1378) YB 2 Ric.2 f.33 pl.8. See also T.Plucknett, *Deeds and Seals* (1950) 32 TRHS (4th series) 1419, Kaye, *Medieval English Conveyances*, 14–16, C. Fifoot, *History and Sources of the Common Law* (London, Stevens, 1949) 223–224.

[5] *Perks*, ¶.150.

[6] 'A covenant is the agreement or consent of two or more by deed in writing, sealed and delivered, whereby either or one of the parties doth promise to the other, that something is done already, or shall be done afterwards': *Shep.Touch.* 160.

[7] Glanvill, *Treatise on the Laws and Customs of England*, ed. and trans. G. Hall (Oxford, Clarendon, 1965) 127.

[8] s.73 Law of Property Act 1925. On what counts as a delivery, see *Chamberlain* v. *Stauton* (1588) 1 Leon 140.

[9] O.W. Holmes, *The Common Law*, ed. M Howe (Boston, Little Brown & Co., 1963) 215.

[10] s.1 Law of Property (Miscellaneous Provisions) Act 1989.

[11] *Stromdale and Ball Ltd* v. *Burden* [1952] Ch 223.

common seal, but since 1926[12] the signature of two officers (or now, one officer whose signature is witnessed) has provided additional protection for purchasers, which also makes sealing unnecessary.[13]

There are three, ancient, exceptional cases, where a deed is not necessary in order to make a covenant. First, by custom, a deed is not necessary for contracts made in the City of London.[14] Hence, the motto of the London Stock Exchange '*dictum meum pactum*' is literally true. Secondly, a similar custom previously applied in Bristol,[15] although it might now have fallen into desuetude.[16] Thirdly, obligations owed to the Crown under letters patent have the force of covenants even though not executed by the subject.[17]

Leases today are normally made by lease and counterpart: the landlord executes the lease as a deed and delivers it to the tenant; at the same time, the tenant executes the counterpart as a deed, and delivers it to the landlord. Until 1845[18] the lease and counterpart were normally written on the same piece of parchment, which was then cut with a jagged line, so as to make it an indenture, or, in the medieval period, through the word 'Cyrographum' (a cyrograph) as a protection against forgery.[19] The two halves would not match unless both were genuine. But

---

[12] s.74(1) Law of Property Act 1925.

[13] s.44 Companies Act 2006.

[14] *Prior of Bingham's Case* (1482) YB 22 Ed.4 f.2a pl.6, *Port's Notebook* (1986) 102 SS 10, S. Milsom, *A Natural History of the Common Law* (New York, Columbia University Press, 2003) 40.

[15] *Wade* v. *Bemboes* (1583) 1 Leon 2. Both customs were probably a survival from a period when the action of covenant did not require a seal. See S. Milsom, *Studies in the History of the Common Law* (London, Hambledon, 1985) 154. Only the highest echelons of society had seals in the time of Hen.II: O.W. Holmes, *The Common Law,* ed. M Howe (Boston, Little Brown & Co, 1963) 214.

[16] Customary law only remains law for so long as the custom is continued: *Bl.Comm.* Bk.1 77.

[17] *Brett* v. *Cumberland* (1616) Cro Jac 399, 1 Rol Abr 517 pl.1, Platt, *Covenants,* 9–10.

[18] s.5 Real Property Act 1845. Now, s.56(2) Law of Property Act 1925.

[19] *Co.Litt.* 229a.fn(1), Kaye, *Medieval English Conveyances,* 256, R.Hunter, *The Law of Landlord and Tenant,* 4th edn. (Edinburgh, Bell & Bradfute, 1896) 46.

even down to the nineteenth century, simple leases were sometimes executed by the landlord alone as a deed poll.[20] The parchment was cut with a straight or 'polled' edge, in which event the landlord's only remedies during the term were to levy distress or bring an action in debt for the reserved rent.[21]

There are four different types of leasehold covenant.

An 'express' covenant is a covenant the terms of which are written in the deed. This is the first type.

The second is a covenant which is imported or implied, as a matter of law, whenever a person delivers a deed that uses particular words, or which creates a particular relationship.[22]

The third is a covenant implied as a matter of construction, where there is a gap in the wording of the express covenants, and that gap is filled either as a matter of necessity or as a matter of business common sense, based on the objective, assumed intention of the parties.[23]

The fourth type are 'usual' covenants. These are the express covenants, which the court would incorporate into a lease, if making an order for specific performance of an 'open' contract; that is, a contract which did not specify the particular terms of the lease, other than the extent of the demised property, its commencement date, duration and rent.[24] Anything less than that, and the contract would be too uncertain to be enforceable at all. The usual covenants change in accordance with conveyancing practice from time to time.[25] They are not the covenants which

---

[20] Platt, *Covenants* 54.

[21] See Platt, *Leases* vol. 2 6, Kaye, *Medieval English Conveyances*, 9, 256. See also ch.9 heading 'Debt' and ch.3 heading 'Distress and replevin'.

[22] 1 Rol Abr 'Covenant (G): 'In which cases, the law will create a covenant', 520, Platt, *Covenants* 36–55. These implied covenants do not extend to things which were not in existence when the lease was made; *Huddy* v. *Fisher* (1586) 1 Leon 278.

[23] *Baynes* v. *Lloyd* [1895] 1 QB 820, 823, *Belize Communications* v. *Belize Telecom Ltd* [2009] UKPC 11.

[24] See generally L. Crabb, *Leases: Covenants and Consents* (London, Sweet and Maxwell, 1991) 197–202.

[25] *Hampshire* v. *Wickens* (1878) 7 Ch.D 555. At that time the usual covenants in a lease of a building were (561): 'Covenants by the lessee: 1. To pay rent. 2. To pay taxes, except such as are expressly payable by the landlord. 3. To keep and deliver up the premises in repair, and 4. To allow the lessor to enter and

are usual in a particular locality.[26] They are the covenants which are usual in general for that type of property, without regard to its special features,[27] unless the agreement expressly provides otherwise,[28] or unless the usual covenant everywhere is to comply with whatever the local custom might be.[29]

A contractual promise is the contractual equivalent of a covenant, where the promisor has not made it by covenant, but has made it in an enforceable contract instead.[30] So an 'express' contractual term in a tenancy is one, the terms of which the parties have agreed by express words, and an 'implied' contractual term is either a promise which is imported as a matter of law from the use of particular words or the creation of a particular relationship, or a promise which is imported to fill a gap in one of the express terms. The 'usual' contractual terms of a tenancy not made by deed are the equivalent of the 'usual' covenants for one which is made by deed.

2. Title and quiet enjoyment.

The essential difference between a covenant for title and a covenant for quiet enjoyment 'is that the former provides an assurance that the conveying party has at the date of the conveyance the very estate in quantity and quality which he purports to convey, whilst the latter provides an assurance against the consequences of that defect . . . Accordingly, whilst breach of the former covenant occurs at the date of the conveyance, breach of the latter occurs only when the

---

view the state of repair. And the usual qualified covenant by the lessor for quiet enjoyment by the lessee'.

[26] *Burwell* v. *Harrison* (1691) Prec Ch. 25.

[27] *Church* v. *Brown* (1808) 15 Ves Jun 257, 261.

[28] Platt, *Covenants* 441.

[29] So, for example, on a letting of agricultural land in the nineteenth century, one of the landlord's usual covenants would be to pay compensation for disturbance in accordance with the custom of the country, but the custom of the country varied from county to county: see ch.7 heading 'Compensation on quitting'.

[30] For the formalities necessary to make a lease, or an agreement for a lease, see ch.1 heading 'Formalities'.

disturbance of the enjoyment takes place'.[31]

The covenant implied as a matter of law on the grant of a lease was originally both a covenant for title and a covenant for quiet enjoyment. It was a guarantee that the landlord had the necessary title to grant the lease and a warranty that the tenant would be able to enter and enjoy the property during the term without anyone else's permission.[32] It was implied by analogy to the warranty that would be implied on a conveyance of freehold land, if the grantor used the words '*dedi et concessi tale tenementum*',[33] and express covenants to this effect were apparently common by the mid-thirteenth century.[34]

What was never clear was whether these implied obligations depended on the use of particular words or whether they were inherent in the creation of the relationship of landlord and tenant.[35] In 1598 it was settled that both covenants would be implied from the use of the words '*dedi, concessi, demisi*, or *assignavi*',[36] and shortly afterwards the English 'demise'[37] was held to be sufficient too. In 1845 Parliament legislated on the premise that the implication of the covenants depended on the use of particular words, excluding 'give' and 'grant' from the

---

[31] E.Scammell, *Land Covenants* (London, Butterworths, 1996) 601. See also *Howell* v. *Richards* (1809) 11 East 633, 642–643. Consequently a covenant for quiet enjoyment in a reversionary lease cannot be breached until the lease falls into possession: *Ireland* v. *Bircham* (1835) 2 Bing NC 90. An absolute covenant for title is inconsistent with a qualified covenant for quiet enjoyment, because an absolute covenant for title is a guarantee that the landlord's power to grant the lease is unimpeachable (*Smith* v. *Compton* (1832) 3 Barn & Ad 189), but a landlord whose title is defective, and who cannot give an absolute covenant for title without immediately being in breach, might nonetheless be willing to risk guaranteeing that the tenant will not be disturbed, by giving an absolute covenant for quiet enjoyment: *Howell* v. *Richards* supra at 633.

[32] Platt, *Leases*, vol. 2 285, cf. *Baynes* v. *Lloyd* [1895] 2 QB 610, 616.

[33] Statute De Bigamis (1276), Coke, *2nd Inst.*, 274–276.

[34] Kaye, *Medieval English Conveyances* 260.

[35] 'The doctrine that a demise for years implies a warranty seems to flow as a natural consequence from the original character of such a demise. The lessor gives the lessee no right in the land, but covenants that the lessee shall enjoy the land; this covenant he must fulfil in specie, if that be possible: otherwise he must render an equivalent': *Pollock & Maitland* vol. 2 107 fn.1.

[36] *Nokes's Case* (1599) 4 Co.Rep 80b.

[37] *Holder* v. *Taylor* (1613) Hob 12, *Howell* v. *Richards* (1809) 11 East 633, *Lines* v. *Stephenson* (1838) 5 Bing NC 183, *Shep.Touch.* 165.

list,[38] and the leading contemporary text on covenants said that no covenant could be implied from the use of the words 'bargain and sale'.[39] There was also authority that no covenant could be implied on the demise of an equitable estate.[40] But Parke B suggested, in *Hart* v. *Windsor*,[41] that the covenants (or contractual terms to like effect) could be implied on any letting, and there was some support for that view subsequently.[42] Lord Russell CJ, at first instance in *Baynes* v. *Lloyd*,[43] took a middle position. He thought that the rule was that the covenant for quiet enjoyment could be implied on any letting, but that a covenant for title depended on particular words. Although that was doubted on appeal,[44] his view was eventually vindicated in *Budd Scott* v. *Daniel*.[45] So the law now appears to be settled that particular words are necessary to imply a covenant for title but not in order to imply a covenant for quiet enjoyment.

The implied covenants, however, only bound the landlord for the length of the landlord's own estate.[46] So, if a tenant accidentally granted a sub-lease for a longer term,[47] there was no implied covenant as to the residue.[48] Nor did the implied

---

[38] s.4 Real Property Act 1845, cf. *Co.Litt.* 384a.fn(1). The implied covenants for title in the Law of Property Act 1925 worked in the same way; see s.76(4). See also Platt, *Covenants*, 38–39 for the statutory implication of particular covenants in instruments registered in the Yorkshire Deeds Registries. For the history of these registries, see ch.1 heading 'Registration'.

[39] Platt, *Covenants*, 49.

[40] *Smith* v. *Pocklington* (1831) 1 Crompt & Jerv 445.

[41] (1844) 12 M&W 68.

[42] *Mostyn* v. *The West Mostyn Coal and Iron Co* (1876) 1 CPD 145, 152–153, 154.

[43] [1895] 1 QB 820.

[44] [1895] 2 QB 610.

[45] [1902] 2 KB 351, cf. *Malzy* v. *Eichholz* [1916] 2 KB 308, 314.

[46] *Swan* v. *Stransham* (1567) Dyer 257, *Cheiny* v. *Langley* (1589) 1 Leon 179. So a husband, who granted a lease out of his wife's freehold land, did not impliedly warrant that it would bind his wife after his death: *Bragg* v. *Wiseman* (1614) 1 Brownlow 22. For the limits on a husband's power to bind his wife, see ch.1 heading 'Capacity' sub-heading 'women'. An express covenant could be limited in the same way: *Gervis* v. *Peade* (1598) Cro Eliz 615.

[47] For the proprietary effect of this, see ch.2 heading 'Underletting'.

[48] *Adams* v. *Gibney* (1830) 4 Moore & Payne 491, *Baynes* v. *Lloyd* [1895] 1 QB 820 affirmed on this point [1895] 2 QB 610. An express covenant 'during

covenants extend to tortious acts by a stranger.[49] Yet they did originally extend not only to the acts of the landlord and those claiming under the landlord, but also those claiming by title paramount.[50] In 1444, Newton CJ explained this on the basis that it was proper that a tenant who was lawfully evicted by a stranger, with a better claim to the land than the landlord, should have a remedy against the landlord who had let the property to the tenant, for there could be none against anyone else.[51]

By the beginning of the sixteenth century, however, doubts were being expressed about whether the implied covenants for title and quiet enjoyment extended to this sort of interruption by title paramount.[52] The point was debated for about four hundred years, until it was eventually resolved that the doubts were right, and the implied covenants for title[53] and quiet enjoyment did not extend to interruption or eviction by title paramount. Covenants which do not extend to eviction by title paramount are called 'qualified' rather than 'absolute' covenants,[54] and the risk under them that the landlord has no title falls on the tenant.

An express covenant for quiet enjoyment, it was decided in 1598, would oust both implied covenants,[55] except in the case of

---

the term' applies during the whole term purportedly granted, and does not determine with the grantor's estate: *Lanning* v. *Lovering* (1603) Cro Eliz 917, *Evans* v. *Vaughan* (1825) 4 Barn & Cr 261. Express covenants in this form were common from the mid-thirteenth century onwards: Kaye, *Medieval English Conveyances*, 260.

[49] *Andrew's Case* (1591) Cro Eliz 214, 2 Leon 104, *Dudley* v *Folliott* (1790) 3 Term Rep 584. The land, in that last case, was in New York, and the tortious act was the seizure of the land by insurgents during the American Revolution.

[50] *Brancaster* v. *Wallis* (1383) 6 YB Ric.2 (Ames, 1996) f.208 pl.2.

[51] (1444) YB 22 Hen.6 f.52b pl.26. See also (1534) 26 Hen.8 f.3 pl.11 where Englefield JCP made the same point in respect of an express covenant and (1454) YB 32 Hen.6 f.32 pl.27.

[52] *Sir John Port's Notebook* (1493–1503) 102 SS 151 pl.36, *Mountford* v. *Catesby* (1573) Dyer 328a, *Andrew's Case* (1591) Cro Eliz 214, *Style* v. *Hearing* (1605) Cro Jac 73, *Major* v. *Grigg* (1677) 2 Mod. 213, *Jones* v. *Lavington* [1903] 1 KB 253.

[53] Hence the implied covenant for title is a covenant that the grantor has not, itself, granted anyone else a better right: *Broughton* v. *Conway* (1565) Dyer 240a.

[54] A covenant to 'suffer' the tenant peaceably to enjoy is a qualified covenant: *Anon* (1566) Dyer 255a pl.4.

[55] *Nokes* v. *James* (1599) 4 Co.Rep 80b, Cro Eliz 674, *Deering* v. *Farrington* (1674) 1 Mod. 113, *Line* v *Stephenson* (1838) 4 Bing NC 678, (1838) 5 Bing NC 183.

a lease for life,[56] and it has always been possible to covenant expressly even against tortious acts by third parties having no right at all.[57] In practice, well drawn leases always contain an express, qualified covenant for quiet enjoyment,[58] with the exception only of those granted by the Crown Estate Commissioners,[59] who usually, but not invariably, refuse to give express covenants, on the quaint ground that they act on behalf of the crown government and the sovereign personally does not give covenants, as if the business of government were still conducted by the sovereign personally. Attempts by landlords to make the covenant conditional upon strict compliance by the tenant with the terms of the lease are nearly as old as the express covenant itself, and are invariably unsuccessful.[60]

Whether the covenant for quiet enjoyment was absolute or qualified, express or implied, it originally only extended to physical acts[61] that were done on the land in exercise of a claimed lawful right[62] in or over the demised land,[63] which

---

[56] *Co.Litt.* 384a, *Shep.Touch.* 165.

[57] In *Southgate* v. *Chaplin* (1715) 1 Comyn 230 there was a conditioned bond where the covenant for quiet enjoyment was against 'any person having or claiming or pretending to have any right'. Similarly, in *Perry* v. *Edwards* (1720) 1 Strange 400, a covenant to 'hold harmless' was held to extend to tortious acts. Some of the covenants for quiet enjoyment in *The Compleat Clerk,* 3rd edn. (London, Place, 1671) were of the absolute type, 707, 712, 726. Others were of the qualified type, 758. By the Victorian period, the covenant was usually in qualified form, notwithstanding that the tenant was rarely shown the landlord's title deeds: Platt, *Leases,* vol. 2 292.

[58] For the practice in respect of covenants for title, see the end of this section.

[59] *Commissioners of Crown Lands* v. *Page* [1960] 2 QB 274.

[60] *Allen* v. *Babbington* (1666) 1 Sid 280 'subject to payment of rent and performance of covenants', *Hays* v. *Bickerstaffe* (1675) 2 Mod. 34 'paying the rents and performing the covenants', *Edge* v. *Boileau* (1885) 16 QBD 117, *Yorkbrook Investments* v. *Batten* (1986) 52 P&CR 51.

[61] 'A entry or other actual disturbance' was required: *Shep.Touch.* 171, *Howard* v. *Maitland* (1883) 11 QBD 695.

[62] After 1667, this included equitable rights: *Ashton* v. *Martyn* (1667) 2 Keb 288 (a bill in equity held to be a 'suit'), *Hunt* v. *Danvers* (1680) T. Raym 370, cf. *Selby* v. *Chute* (1613) Moore 859, 1 Brownlow 23.

[63] The landlord was not permitted to say that it was deliberately committing a wrong: *Cave* v. *Brookesby* (1635) W Jones 360, *Markham* v. *Paget* [1908] 1 Ch 697, 718, Platt, *Covenants,* 320.

affected the tenant's title or possession, rather than a particular mode of enjoying it.[64] So someone did not breach a covenant not to 'molest, vex or put out' any copyholder by beating one of them in a cowshed on the property.[65] Nor was an accidental trespass whilst hunting a breach of the covenant.[66]

The meaning changed, however, at the end of the nineteenth century. In *Sanderson* v. *Berwick*[67] Fry LJ said:

> It appears to us to be in every case a question of fact whether the quiet enjoyment of the land has or has not been interrupted; and where the ordinary and lawful enjoyment of the demised land is substantially interfered with by the acts of the lessor, or those lawfully claiming under him, the covenant appears to us to be broken, although neither the title to the land nor the possession of the land may be otherwise affected.

So even mere threats to evict the tenant are now actionable.[68] In short, any act that would be a trespass or a nuisance if committed by a stranger, is now a breach of the covenant for quiet enjoyment, if committed or authorised by the landlord.

That, however, is as far as it goes. The covenant for quiet enjoyment has never been a covenant to repair[69] nor of fitness for purpose. As Parke B said in *Hart* v. *Windsor*:[70]

> There is no authority for saying that these words imply a contract for any particular state of the property at the time of the demise: and there are many [cases] which clearly show that there is no implied contract that the property shall continue to be fit for the purpose for which it is demised; as the tenant can neither maintain an action, nor is he exonerated from payment of rent, if the house demised is blown down or destroyed by fire, *Monk* v. *Cooper* (2 Strange 763), *Balfour* v. *Weston* (1 Term Rep 310), and *Ainsley* v. *Rutter* there cited; or

---

[64] *Mogan* v. *Hunt* (1690) 2 Vent 213.

[65] *Penn* v. *Glover* (1595) Cro Eliz 421.

[66] *Lloyd* v. *Tomkies* (1787) 1 Term Rep 671.

[67] (1884) 13 QBD 547, 551.

[68] *Kenny* v. *Preen* [1963] 1 QB 499.

[69] *Pomfret* v. *Ricroft* (1669) 1 Wms Saund 321.

[70] (1844) 12 M&W 68, 86–87. See also *Sutton* v. *Temple* (1843) 12 M&W 52.

gained upon by the sea, *Taverner's case* (Dyer 56a); or the occupation is rendered impracticable by the king's enemies, *Paradine* v. *Jane* (Aleyn 26); or where a wharf demised was swept away by the Thames, *Carter* v. *Cummins* (cited in 1 Chanc Ca 84). In all these cases, the estate of the lessor continues, and that is all the lessor impliedly warrants.

Standard form implied covenants for title were introduced by s.7 Conveyancing Act 1881, as a word saving measure, and were repeated in the Law of Property Act 1925.[71] They were incorporated into any conveyance (including a lease) made between 1st January 1881 and 30th June 1995, in which the grant was expressed to have been made by the grantor acting in a particular capacity.[72] In practice, however, it was rare for a lease to contain an express statement about the capacity in which the landlord had made the grant, and tenants were content to rely on the qualified covenant for quiet enjoyment alone.[73]

In 1995, however, the statutory basis of implication was changed, from words descriptive of the capacity of the grantor, to words that were descriptive of the quality of the grantor's title.[74] The Law Commission had recommended that this change should be made in 1991,[75] specifically so that covenants for title would be implied on the grant of a lease. That, combined with the prominence of the title guarantee in Land Registry prescribed forms, means that many leases are now thoughtlessly granted with 'full title guarantee', notwithstanding that a full title guarantee is wholly inconsistent with the qualified nature of the covenant for quiet enjoyment which they invariably contain.[76]

---

[71] s.76, sch. 2.

[72] Eg. 'as trustee' or 'as beneficial owner'.

[73] On an assignment of the term, or a conveyance of the reversion, the capacity of the conveying party was, of course, expressed, and the relevant covenant for title implied.

[74] Law of Property Miscellaneous Provisions Act 1994, E.Scammell, *Land Covenants* (London, Butterworths, 1996) 613.

[75] Law Com No.199.

[76] *Smith* v. *Compton* (1832) 3 Barn & Ad 189.

3. Repair.

In the medieval period, it was usual for a tenant to covenant to return the property at the end of the term in the same condition as when the lease had been granted,[77] except in London,[78] Norfolk and Ely,[79] where the custom was that the landlord repaired instead.[80] By the nineteenth century, those customs were obsolete,[81] and the usual tenant's covenant had become what it is today, namely a full covenant to 'keep and deliver up' the demised premises in repair,[82] without any exception for damage by fire or tempest.[83] But in the last twenty years or so, landlords have found it increasingly difficult to let second-hand industrial, warehouse and office buildings, except on 'schedule of condition' terms: the full repairing obligation is expressly qualified by a proviso that the tenant shall not be obliged to return the property at the end of the term in any better condition than at its commencement. If the trend continues, the standard commercial repairing covenant may become again what it was in the medieval period.

In the absence of any express tenant's repairing obligation,

---

[77] *Doctor and Student*, 113, Kaye, *Medieval English Conveyances*, 266, (1366) YB 40 Ed.3 f.5 pl.11. In *Wood* v. *Tirrell* (1576/7) Cary 59, the landlord covenanted to put the house in repair by a certain date, and the tenant covenanted to keep it in repair thereafter. See also (1413) YB 14 Hen.4 f.27a pl.35 where the landlord covenanted to put the property into repair at the commencement of the term.

[78] Fitz Barre 47, Brook's Abridgment 'Dette' pl.18.

[79] *Burwell* v. *Harrison* (1691) Prec Ch. 25.

[80] (1455) YB 34 Hen.6 f.17a-18a pl.32.

[81] In *The Compleat Clerk,* 3rd edn. (London, Place, 1671) 756, there is a precedent for a lease of a house in London with a full tenant's repairing covenant.

[82] *Hampshire* v. *Wickens* (1878) 7 Ch.D 555. A covenant to keep property in repair implies an obligation to put it in repair, if it is not already in that condition at the commencement of the term: *Lurcott* v. *Wakely* [1911] 2 KB 905. A full tenant's repairing covenant, and an obligation to repair on notice, were both implied as standard covenants whenever a lease was made in the short form authorised by the Leases Act 1845.

[83] *Sharp* v. *Milligan* (1857) 23 Beav 419. This exception was sometimes included in express covenants to repair: see eg. G. Jacob, *The Accomplished Conveyancer,* vol. 1 (London, Butt, 1714) 439.

all tenants (including tenants at will) are under an implied duty
to use the premises in a tenantlike manner; that is, to use them
appropriately and responsibly.[84]

In the case of a tenant of agricultural land, that meant
cultivating the land in a husbandlike manner, and according to
local custom from time to time, whilst there were still such
customs.[85] Periodic tenants are (statute apart) also under an
implied obligation to keep any demised buildings wind and
watertight,[86] and to carry out fair and tenantable repairs—such as
repairing fences[87]—but not to remedy fair wear and tear,[88] nor
rebuild, nor carry out substantial works.[89] In the case of tenancy
for a fixed term of a year or longer, there is additionally an
implied obligation to deliver up the property at the end the term
in the same condition as when demised,[90] fair wear and tear
excepted.[91] But none of those implied covenants or terms
extended to carrying out repairs to the main structure of any
building, unless the damage had been caused by the tenant's
neglect.[92]

Apart from any covenant or contractual obligation, a tenant
can also be obliged to carry out repairs by virtue of the law of
waste.[93] Waste is a tort: its history, and the extent of a tenant's

---

[84] *Marsden* v. *Edward Heyes Ltd* [1927] 2 KB 1, Platt, *Covenants*, 266–267.

[85] *Powley* v. *Walker* (1793) 5 Term Rep 373, *Oxford History of the Laws of
England*, vol. 12 114. For an express covenant to the same effect, see Stewart,
Practice of Conveyancing, 344.

[86] *Auworth* v. *Johnson* (1832) 5 Car & P 239.

[87] *Cheetham* v. *Hampson* (1791) 4 Term Rep 318.

[88] *Torriano* v. *Young* (1833) 6 Car & P 8-12.

[89] *Leach* v. *Thomas* (1835) 7 Car & P 327, *Wedd* v. *Porter* [1916] 2 KB 91,
100, S. Grady, *The Law of Fixtures*, 2nd edn. (London, Wildy & Son, 1866)
350–352.

[90] J. Lilly, *The Practical Register*, 2nd edn. (London, Ward & Wickstead,
1735) vol. 2 194.

[91] *Marsden* v. *Edward Heyes Ltd* [1927] 2 KB 1.

[92] *Anon* (1537) Dyer 26a, *Mint* v. *Gold* [1951] 1 KB 517, Viner's Abridgment
'Estates' B.b.17.

[93] Coote, *Leases* 237: 'Permissive waste to buildings consists in omitting to
keep them in tenantable repair: suffering the timbers to become rotten by
neglecting to cover the house; or the walls to fall into decay for want of
plastering; or the foundation to be sapped by leaving a moat or ditch unscoured.

obligations under it, are discussed in detail in chapter 9. The important point here is that the law of waste does not oblige anyone to remedy damage done by acts of god, such as storms or fires caused by lightning.[94] But, after the Statute of Marlborough (1267),[95] the law of waste did oblige tenants to remedy damage done by fires started by any other means. Liability in tort for damage caused by fires without negligence was removed in 1707[96] but that did not affect any contractual liability. So an express covenant to repair binds a tenant to remedy damage caused by fire, no matter how the fire started.[97] An act of god can, nonetheless, discharge even an express covenant or condition,[98] if it makes performance impossible.[99] So, for instance, it was said in 1366 that a covenant to sustain a wall would oblige the tenant to rebuild it, even if it was blown down in a storm, because it would be possible to rebuild it, whereas a covenant to sustain trees would be discharged, if a storm blew them down, because it would be impossible for the tenant to put them back up again.[100]

Merely suffering the house to remain unroofed (provided it were so at the commencement of the tenancy) will not be waste; but then the tenant must take the consequences of any other part thereby becoming ruinous or decayed. To permit walls, built to exclude water, to remain in a dilapidated state as to cause the lands to be overflowed and injured, is waste.'

[94] *Colthirst* v. *Bejushin* (1550) Plowden 20, 28, *Rook* v. *Worth* (1750) 1 Ves Sen 460, 462. Holdsworth, *HEL* vol. 3 122.

[95] c.24, Coke, *2nd Inst*, 143–144.

[96] 6 Anne c.31 s.6. This was originally a temporary provision, but it was made permanent in 1711 by 10 Anne c.14 s.1. The relevant provision now is s.86 Fires Metropolis Act 1774.

[97] (1366) YB 40 Ed.3 f.5 pl.11, *Chesterfield* v. *Bolton* (1739) 2 Comyn 627, *Bullock* v. *Dommitt* (1796) 6 Term Rep 650, *Pym* v. *Blackburn* (1796) 3 Ves Jun 34, 38, *Walton* v. *Waterhouse* (1672) 2 Wms Saund 420.

[98] H. Bullow, ed. J. Fonblanque, *A Treatise on Equity*, 5th edn., vol. 1 (London, Clarke, 1820) 400.

[99] An act of state or by enemy aliens does not. Hence, during the Second World War, it was necessary to enact statutes absolving tenants from liability for damage done to requisitioned property (Landlord and Tenant (Requisitioned Land) Act 1944) and giving them a right to disclaim property damaged or destroyed by bombs (Landlord and Tenant (War Damage) Acts 1939 and 1941). There is a precedent for a contractual exclusion of liability for damage done by the King's enemies in W. West, *Simboleograph* (London, Stationer's Co., 1610) pt.1 s.442.

[100] (1366) YB 40 Ed.3 f.5 pl.11.

Originally, a landlord owed a tenant no implied repairing obligations at all. There was no law against letting a tumbledown house,[101] and a landlord, by letting property, did not make any implied covenant, promise or representation about its condition or fitness for purpose.[102] Even where a tenant's repairing covenant contained an express exception, the court could not imply any correlative obligation on the landlord to repair the excepted property.[103]

Nor was a landlord obliged to keep any retained property in repair, even if the tenant had been granted a right to use it.[104] That last rule was reversed, for essential access routes, by the House of Lords in *Liverpool City Council* v. *Irwin*,[105] and the absence of any implied contractual obligation did not preclude a claim in nuisance, for which purpose the landlord was treated like any other neighbouring landowner.

The rule for furnished lettings of residential accommodation changed in 1843, so as to give the tenant a right to terminate the tenancy if the premises were not fit for human habitation at the commencement of the term.[106] The full story of how that happened is told in chapter 7.[107] That implied condition for termination became unexcludable, in 1885, for lettings at a low rent.[108] The rental value limits were raised, in 1909, to £40 in London, £26 in other urban areas, and £16 elsewhere,[109] and, at the same time, an unexcludable landlord's obligation to keep the property fit for human habitation during the term was added.[110]

---

[101] *Cavalier* v. *Pope* [1906] AC 428.

[102] *Hart* v. *Windsor* (1844) 12 M&W 68.

[103] *Weigall* v. *Waters* (1795) 6 Term Rep 488.

[104] *Pomfret* v. *Ricroft* (1645) 1 Wms Saund 321.

[105] [1977] AC 239.

[106] *Smith* v. *Marrable* (1843) 11 M&W 5, *Sutton* v. *Temple* (1843) 12 M&W 52.

[107] Heading 'Repudiation and frustration'.

[108] s.12 Housing of the Working Classes Act 1885. The annual rental limits were £20 in London, £13 in Liverpool, £10 in Manchester and Birmingham, £4 in Ireland, and £8 elsewhere.

[109] s.14 Housing, Town and Country Planning Act 1909, s.10 Housing Act 1923, s.6 Housing Act 1957.

[110] s.15 Housing, Town and Country Planning Act 1909. A covenant to put property into a habitable state of repair, is a covenant to make it safe and

Most working class housing was within those limits then, but the current annual limits are just £80 in London and £52 elsewhere,[111] and so they no longer catch even weekly tenancies of the meanest lodgings. They do, however, occasionally catch long leases granted for a premium, where the ground rent has been incautiously reserved as a purely nominal sum.

Since 1957 it has been a statutory term of every letting of residential premises for a term of seven years or less, that the landlord will carry out structural and other repairs,[112] and where a landlord has a duty to repair, or a right to enter and repair, an additional duty of care to occupiers and visitors is imposed by s.4 Defective Premises Act 1972.

Absent any statutory obligation to repair, an express covenant ousts all implied contractual obligations, including even the implied obligation to use in a tenant like manner.[113] But it does not exclude tortious liability in waste.[114]

Express covenants to repair have been common from the earliest times. A covenant to 'keep' the demised property in repair is now construed as a covenant to put and keep it in that condition throughout the term,[115] but that is a relatively recent development. In 1596, in *Sir Anthony Main's Case*, it was said that a covenant to keep the houses of a manor in repair during the term, could be fully performed simply by delivering them up in that condition at the end of the term, and by doing nothing to prevent that until then.[116] That was presaged on an older idea that a covenant only needs be performed once, and that if a covenant required something to be done during a period of time, the covenantee could choose the date of performance. That rule was repudiated by the Court of King's Bench in 1818, in *Luxmore* v.

---

comfortable for the purposes of the class of tenant likely to take it: *Belcher* v. *McIntosh* (1839) 2 Mood & Rob 186, 8 Car & P 720.

[111] s.8 Landlord and Tenant Act 1985.

[112] ss.32-33 Housing Act 1957, s.11 Landlord and Tenant Act 1985.

[113] *Standen* v. *Christmas* (1847) 10 QB 135, cf. *White* v. *Nicholson* (1842) 4 M & Gr 95.

[114] See ch.9 heading 'Waste'.

[115] *British Telecommunications* v. *Sun Life* [1996] Ch 69.

[116] *Sir Anthony Main's Case* (1596) 5 Co.Rep 20b, 21a, *Englefield's Case* (1591) 7 Co.Rep 11b, 15a, *Walter* v. *Montague* (1623) 2 Rol Reps 332, 347, Godbolt 335.

Robson,[117] on the grounds that it was contrary to common sense, and it has never been in doubt since that the covenant is broken by a failure to repair during the term.[118] But in the meantime two drafting techniques were adopted to circumvent the problem. The first was to separate out the repairing covenants, so that the obligation to repair at all times during the term, and the obligation to yield up in repair at the end of the term were two distinct obligations.[119] The second was to include an 'enter and repair' clause.

An enter and repair clause combines a reservation to the landlord of a right to enter and inspect the property during the term, with a covenant by the tenant to remedy any disrepair discovered and notified to the tenant as a result.[120] Provisions of this type are found even before 1596.[121] But the influence of *Main's case* can be seen in cases such as *Harflet* v. *Butcher*,[122] where the covenant was to repair on notice during the term and

---

[117] (1818) 1 Barn & Ald 584.

[118] Platt, *Covenants*, 288–289, Platt *Leases* vol. 2 190.

[119] See eg. *Wrotesley* v. *Adams* (1558) Plowden 187, 188, W. West, *Simboleograph* (London, Stationers Co., 1610) pt.1 ss.430, 436, O. Bridgman, *Conveyances*, 3rd edn. (London, Atkins, 1699) vol. 1 16, 261. By 1827, there was no longer any point in separating the covenants out (although it is still customarily done today), and so Stewart could say that a yield up covenant 'in strictness might be omitted; but they are often beneficial to persons, ignorant of their rights at law': Stewart, *Practice of Conveyancing,* 335. One case where a separate yield up covenant would have been necessary, is the lease of a rabbit warren in W. West, *Simboleograph* pt.1 s.440, where the covenant was to leave the warren stocked with five hundred black rabbits and five hundred gray ones. The rabbits would have been reared in artificial mounds above ground, cared for by a warrener, so it would have been possible to tell whether the covenant had been performed or not.

[120] See e.g. the precedents in W.West, *Simboleograph* (London, Stationers Co., 1610) pt.1 s.430 and *The Compleat Clerk* (London, Place, 1671) 3rd edn. 704, 725, 758.

[121] In *Mascal's Case* (1587) 1 Leon 62 it was held the covenant was breached when the notice expired, and in *Swetman* v. *Cush* (1603) Cro Jac 8 it was held that the notice must be given to the tenant and not an undertenant. By contrast, there is no 'enter and repair' clause in the early sixteenth century lease of an Oxford brewhouse in J. Arnold, *The Customs of London* (London, Rivington, 1811) 109.

[122] (1622) Cro Jac 644.

yield up in repair at the end of the term.[123] By the middle of the nineteenth century, these covenants were usually coupled with a right of re-entry in the event of breach,[124] and after 1938, a right for the landlord to enter and do the work itself, and recover the cost of doing so as a debt, in what was ultimately held to be a successful[125] attempt to circumvent the restrictions in the Leasehold Property (Repairs) Act 1938, considered at the end of this section.

Absent any express right to enter and repair, a landlord has an implied right to inspect the demised property to see whether the tenant has committed any waste.[126] In the case of a weekly tenancy, the implied right extends to carrying out repairs too.[127] There are also various statutory rights allowing landlords of residential accommodation to inspect and repair,[128] which include the right to require the tenant to vacate whilst the repairs are carried out, if necessary.[129]

In 1590 it was decided that a covenant to 'maintain, sustain and repair'[130] would be breached by rebuilding, even if the state of the property was ruinous at the time of the demise.[131] As a result, most repairing covenants now include the words 'renew' and 'rebuild' too.

During the nineteenth century, it was decided that, in construing a covenant to repair, regard must be had to the state and condition of the property at the commencement of the term,

---

[123] The actual decision was that the notice requirement did not apply at the end of the term. Covenants to yield up in repair were common by the middle of the seventeenth century: O. Bridgman, *Conveyances*, 3rd edn. vol. 1 34.

[124] Platt, *Leases*, vol. 2 216.

[125] *Jervis* v. *Harris* [1996] Ch 195.

[126] *Hunt* v. *Dowman* (1618) Cro Jac 478, sub nom *Hunt* v. *Dadvers* 2 Rol Reps 21, S. Grady, *The Law of Fixtures*, 2nd edn. (London, Wildy & Son, 1866) 435–436.

[127] *Mint* v. *Gold* [1951] 1 KB 517.

[128] s.8(2), s.11(6) Landlord and Tenant Act 1985, s.148 Rent Act 1977, s.16 Housing Act 1988.

[129] *McGreal* v. *Wake* (1984) 13 HLR 107.

[130] The tendency to include as many synonyms as possible in the covenant is at least 400 years old: W. West, *Simboleograph* (London, Stationers Co., 1610) pt.1 s.430 includes a covenant to 'repair, sustain, maintain, scour and cleanse'.

[131] *Wood and Avery's Case* (1590) 2 Leon 189.

and the age of the property at the end. The point was that the landlord is not entitled to a new building back at the end.[132] That was carried so far as to say that a tenant did not have to remedy the consequences of any inherent defect in the building,[133] though that doctrine was repudiated in *Ravenseft Properties* v. *Davstone Holdings*.[134]

Prior to the decision in *Jeune* v. *Queen's Cross Properties*[135] in 1973 it had always been thought that neither a landlord nor a tenant could obtain specific performance of a repairing obligation.[136] But, in that case, whilst acknowledging that the rule applied to claims by landlords, Pennycuick VC made an order for specific performance in favour of a tenant. Parliament confirmed that decision, in favour of tenants of dwelling houses, in 1985,[137] and, in truth, the absence of any jurisdiction to grant specific performance of a repairing obligation had always sat uncomfortably with the rule that it was possible to get specific performance of a covenant to build a new building, if the plans and specifications were sufficiently clear.[138] In *Rainbow Estates* v. *Tokenhold*[139] an order for specific performance of a repairing obligation was finally made in favour of a landlord.

In the absence of specific performance, the measure of loss in a claim for breach of a repairing obligation was originally simply the cost of the necessary works, whether the claim was

---

[132] *Young* v. *Mantz* (1838) 6 Scott 277.

[133] *Lister* v. *Lane* [1893] 2 QB 212.

[134] [1980] QB 12.

[135] [1974] Ch 97.

[136] *Dean and Chapter of Ely* v. *Stewart* (1740) 2 Atk 44, *City of London* v. *Nash* (1747) 3 Atk 512, 1 Ves 12, *Rayner* v. *Stone* (1762) 2 Eden 128, *Lucas* v. *Comerford* (1790) 1 Ves Jun 235, *Mosely* v. *Virgin* (1796) 3 Ves Jun 184, *Lane* v. *Newdigate* (1804) 10 Ves 192, *Flint* v. *Brandon* (1803) 8 Ves Jun 159, *Hill* v. *Barclay* (1810) 16 Ves Jun 402, E. Bullow, ed. J. Fonblanque, *A Treatise on Equity*, 5th edn., vol. 1 (London, Clarke, 1820) 355.fn(r), Platt, *Covenants* 293–4, Platt, *Leases*, vol. 2 209–210.

[137] s.17 Landlord and Tenant Act 1985.

[138] Platt, *Covenants* 297–298.

[139] [1999] Ch 64.

brought during the term or afterwards.[140]

But in 1841 Coleridge J held that the damages recoverable during the term were an amount equivalent the diminution in the value of the landlord's reversion.[141] For claims brought after the expiry of the term, the measure of loss remained the cost of works, and the loss of rent whilst the works were being done,[142] until that loss was capped at the diminution in the value of the landlord's reversion by s.18 Landlord and Tenant Act 1927.[143]

The Leasehold Property (Repairs) Act 1938 made it harder for a landlord to claim damages for failure to repair a house, or to forfeit the lease of the house, if more than five years of the term of the lease remained unexpired and the rateable value was not more than £100, by requiring the landlord to serve a notice first, and by empowering the tenant to serve a counternotice, which would make it necessary for the landlord to obtain consent from the court, on one of a number of grounds, before bringing the action or forfeiting.[144] In 1954, that was altered so as to cover all properties (other than agricultural holdings) where the original term of the lease had been for seven years or more, and three years or more remained unexpired.[145] Those provisions do not prevent a landlord entering and repairing the demised property itself, and then recovering the cost of doing so as a debt from the tenant, where the lease contains an enter and repair clause authorising that,[146] but, in practice, it is often difficult to exercise that right, if the tenant is in occupation and is opposed to the entry.

---

[140] *Vivian* v. *Champion* (1705) 2 Ld.Raym 1125, 1126 per Holt CJ: 'We always enquire in these cases, what it will cost to put the premises in repair, and give so much as damages, and the plaintiff ought in justice to apply the damages to the repair of the premises'.

[141] *Doe d. Worcester Schools* v. *Rowlands* (1841) 9 Car & P 734, *Turner* v. *Lamb* (1845) 14 M&W 412, Platt, *Leases*, vol. 2 121–123.

[142] *Woods* v. *Pope* (1835) 6 Car & P 782.

[143] Although s.18 Landlord and Tenant Act 1927 does not apply to a remediation covenant in a licence, it is likely that the common law measure of loss is now the same, as a result of the decision of the House of Lords in *Ruxley* v. *Forsyth* [1996] AC 344.

[144] s.1.

[145] s.51 Landlord and Tenant Act 1954.

[146] *Jervis* v. *Harris* [1996] Ch 195.

4. To pay rent.

A tenant's covenant[147] to pay rent is implied as a matter of law from the words 'yielding' or 'paying' in the reddendum of the lease.[148] But, like all covenants which are implied as a matter of law, it can only be enforced against any particular tenant for the period during which the lease is vested in that tenant. As a matter of privity of contract, the implied covenant is only binding on the original tenant until the first assignment,[149] and as a matter of privity of estate, it is only binding on assignees for the period during which the lease is vested in them.[150]

Nonetheless, landlords were generally[151] content to rely on the implied covenant, until the middle of the eighteenth century.[152] Indeed, the cases which established the principle that an original tenant remained liable on express covenants after assignment of the term were all cases about repairing covenants, rather than covenants to pay rent.[153]

There was an express covenant in *Pitcher* v. *Tovey*,[154] and in that case the court pointed that it was folly for a landlord to

---

[147] A 'covenant' is only implied, of course, if the tenant executes the lease as a deed. Otherwise, it is a contractual promise which is implied from those words.

[148] *Newton* v. *Osborn* (1653) Style 387, Platt, *Covenants*, 50–54, Platt *Leases*, vol. 2 87.

[149] *Brett* v. *Cumberland (No.2)* (1619) Cro Jac 521, *Bachelour* v. *Gage* (1630) Cro Car 188, W Jones 223, *Auriol* v. *Mills* (1790) 4 Term Rep 94.

[150] See ch.6 heading 'Rent and attornment'.

[151] The precedents for leases in W. West *Simboleograph* (London, Stationers Company, 1610) did not include an express covenant to pay rent. Nor did the precedents in *The Compleat Clerk*, 3rd edn. (London, Place, 1671) although they did include express covenants dealing with the discharge of obligations to pay quit rents, charges and heriots to third parties, 714, 725, 728. There appears to have been an express covenant in *Jenkins* v. *Hermitage* (1674) 1 Freeman 377 and there was an express covenant in the lease made in 1697 in *Monroe* v. *Lord Kerry* (1710) 1 Brown PC 67.

[152] See eg. *Hornby* v. *Houlditch* (1737) Andrews 40.

[153] (1533/4) Brook's New Cases pl.74, *Fisher* v. *Ameers* (1611) Brownlow 20, *Barnard* v. *Goodscall* (1612) Cro Jac 309.

[154] (1692) 4 Mod. 71, 12 Mod. 23. The quality of the Modern reports is very uneven, but 12 Mod. is generally reliable: see J.Wallace, *The Reporters*, 3rd edn. (Philadelphia, Johnson, 1855) 219–227. The argument is better reported in 1 Shower 340.

allow an assignment unless the lease contained such a covenant. The point was that the permitted assignment would discharge the original tenant's liability for the rent both in debt and on any implied covenant,[155] whilst the assignee could avoid liability afterwards by assigning over to a pauper, for the rule in *Dumpor* v. *Syms*[156] meant that a second assignment would not require the landlord's consent.[157]

So by the middle of the eighteenth century, it had become standard practice to include an express covenant to pay rent,[158] in order to ensure that the liability of the original tenant to pay would continue, notwithstanding the assignment,[159] and the point was sometimes reinforced by adding the words 'throughout the term' or their equivalent to the covenant, as well as to reddendum reserving the rent.[160] A hundred years later,[161] and it had become standard practice to include those reinforcing words, as it is today.

Those reinforcing words are normally followed by a promise to pay 'without any deduction or abatement' or its equivalent. The origin of those words lies in land tax. Originally, a tenant had no right to recover the tax from the landlord, unless by express agreement.[162] But as Holt CJ explained in *Brewster* v.

---

[155] See ch.6 heading 'Rent and attornment'.

[156] (1603) 4 Co.Rep 119b, Cro Eliz 815.

[157] See the heading 'Alienation' below.

[158] See eg. G.Jacob, *The Accomplished Conveyancer, vol.* 1 (London, Butt, 1714) 438, *The Young Clerk's Magazine*, 5th edn. (London, Strahan & Woodfall, 1772) 79, 83, T. Williams, *Precedents in Conveyancing,* vol. 3 (London, Kearsley, 1788) 952.

[159] Platt, *Covenants*, 195, cf. C. Barton, *Modern Precedents in Conveyancing* vol. 4 Leases, 3rd edn. (London, Hunter, 1821) 69.fn (12).

[160] Some of the precedents in M. Bacon, *A Treatise on Leases* (London, A. Strahan, 1798) are in this form (247, 273) whilst others are not (257, 262). The precedents for payment covenants in E. Wood, *Conveyancing*, 6th edn., vol. 5 (Dublin, Lynch, 1793) included those words. For inclusion of those words in the reddendum, see ch.3 heading 'Rent Reservation'.

[161] The standard covenants implied on making a lease in the short form authorised by the Leases Act 1845 included a covenant to pay the rent throughout the term and without any deductions.

[162] (1477) YB 17 Ed.4 f.5b–6a pl.4, *Chapman* v. *Dalton* (1565) Plowden 284, 295.

Kitchel:[163]

> The assessment or tax according to the pound rate came in 17
> Car.1. In these assessments there was a clause to empower the
> tenant to deduct. So it was in 1642, 1644, 1649. And then, on
> this account it was, that in conveyances it came to be provided
> that there should be no deduction for taxes.

So, in a case in 1691,[164] the rent had been reserved 'free and
clear from all manner of taxes, charges and impositions
whatsoever', and there was a seventeenth century precedent for a
tenant's covenant to bear taxes in times of war in *The Compleat
Clerk*.[165] When, during the eighteenth century, covenants to pay
rent became common, the covenant was naturally drafted as one
expressly requiring the tenant to pay without any deduction or
abatement.[166]

In *Cranston* v. *Clarke*[167] it was held that simply reserving the
rent 'without any deduction or abatement' did not amount to an
agreement by the tenant to bear taxes charged in the property,[168]
but similar words were held to effective in *Bradbury* v. *Wright*[169]
and in *Parish* v. *Sleeman*.[170] Ironically, in *Connaught
Restaurants* v. *Indoor Leisure*[171] the Court of Appeal held that
the effect of those words was practically confined to taxes and
other impositions, with the result that they did not prevent
tenants exercising their newly acquired rights of set-off.[172] The

---

[163] (1697) 2 Salk 615. Land tax was a temporary imposition in times of crisis,
until it was made a permanent annual tax in 1798 (38 Geo.3 c.5 and c.60).

[164] *Giles* v. *Hooper* (1691) Carthew 135. See also *Marshall* v. *Wisdale* (1674) 1
Freeman 148.

[165] 3rd edn. (London, Place, 1671) 728. See also G. Jacob, *The Accomplished
Conveyancer* vol. 1 (London, Butt, 1714) 438, 441.

[166] M. Bacon, *A Treatise on Leases* (London, A.Strahan, 1798) 280, Coote,
Leases 277–278.

[167] (1753) Sayer 78.

[168] For a covenant designed to avoid this result, see E. Wood, *Conveyancing,*
6th edn., vol. 5 (Dublin, Lynch, 1793) 175.

[169] (1781) 2 Douglas 624.

[170] (1860) 1 De Gex F & J 326.

[171] [1991] 1 WLR 501.

[172] For the right of set-off, see ch.3 heading 'Abatement and set off '.

result of that decision is that most covenants now expressly exclude any right of set-off too.

5. Alteration.

Leases rarely contained any express covenant forbidding the tenant from making alterations before the middle of the eighteenth century.[173] The landlord was generally content to rely on an express covenant to repair, and to leave the tort of waste to do the rest of the work.[174] Making any alteration which changed the character of the property was voluntary waste, which could be restrained by injunction,[175] and damages for it could be obtained at common law. Indeed, so strict was the law of waste that when it was intended that the tenant should be able to make alterations, as for instance, would be the case when a lease for life was being granted as part of a strict settlement,[176] it was necessary to disapply the law of waste by providing that the tenant would hold without impeachment for it. In the late eighteenth century, however, the rules about waste became less fierce, as the courts started refusing to interfere where alterations would improve the value of the property ('meliorating' waste). Landlords responded by including express covenants against alterations in their leases, so that by 1971 a covenant against structural alterations and changing the external appearance of a property had become a usual covenant.[177]

In 1927, the court acquired the power to authorise business tenants to make improvements to the demised property, in

---

[173] Express restrictions against felling trees are an exception, no doubt because of the value of timber in the Tudor economy. J. Lilly, *The Practical Register*, 2nd edn. (London, Ward & Wickstead, 1735) vol. 2 201–202.

[174] *Co.Litt.* 53a. See generally ch.9 heading 'Waste'.

[175] *Cregan* v. *Cullen* (1864) 16 IR Ch R 339 (conversion of a field to a burial ground), *Maunsell* v. *Hort* (1877) IR 11 Eq 478 (conversion of stable to butcher's shop). On the poor quality of Irish law reporting in this period, see W. Osborough, *Puzzles from Irish Law Reporting*, in P. Birks ed., *The Life of the Law* (London, Hambledon Press, 1993) 89, 105.

[176] See ch.4 heading 'For life'.

[177] *Chester* v. *Buckingham Travel* [1981] 1 WLR 96.

defiance of any express prohibition on making alterations contained in the lease.[178] At the same time, any lease (other than a mining lease or lease of agricultural land) containing an express prohibition against making improvements without licence of consent, was made subject to a statutory proviso that consent could not be refused unreasonably.[179]

6. Alienation.

At common law, a lease has always been freely alienable, whether by assignment or by sub-letting.[180] There is no covenant implied as a matter of law against doing either of those acts,[181] and in 1443 it was doubted whether a lease could be made subject to an absolute condition against assignment at all.[182] The debate on that point continued on into the sixteenth century[183] before reaching the unhappy compromise that an absolute prohibition could be enforced by forfeiture, but it could not prevent the tenant vesting the estate in the assignee in the meantime.[184]

---

[178] s.3(4), s.21 Landlord and Tenant Act 1927.

[179] s.19(2) Landlord and Tenant Act 1927.

[180] In *R* v. *Inhabitants of Aldborough* (1801) 1 East 597 Kenyon CJ said that the law gave a tenant authority to assign his interest. In Scotland, the opposite rule applied: *Styles of the Juridical Society* vol. 1 (Edinburgh, Elliot, 1777) 406.

[181] *Hampshire* v. *Wickens* (1878) 7 Ch.D 555, Platt, *Leases*, vol. 2 239–248. By way of exception, by custom a copyholder could underlet for a year without consent, but needed the lord's licence to underlet for longer. But the explanation for that lies in the origins of copyhold as a tenancy at will; see ch.1 heading `Capacity' sub-heading `Copyholders.'

[182] (1443) 21 Hen.6 f.33 pl.21.

[183] *Oxford History of the Laws of England*, vol. 6 639.

[184] An assignment of a lease containing an absolute prohibition on assignment is effective to vest the term in the assignee (albeit subject to the risk of forfeiture or an injunction requiring re-assignment) because a leasehold term was assignable property at common law. By contrast the assignment of purely contractual rights was long prohibited by the rules against maintenance of actions. Although those rules have been greatly relaxed, that was originally effected in equity by allowing the assignee to sue in the name of the assignor (*Co.Litt.* 232b.fn(1), 265a.fn(1)). But equity never allowed that in the case of

In practice, prohibitions on assignment or subletting, or doing so without consent, were not uncommon, from as early as the thirteenth century,[185] through to the seventeenth century.[186] But leases, in this period, were still frequently made without any restriction on assignment or sub-letting at all, especially where the lease was granted as an investment or by way of mortgage term.[187] Prohibitions on assignment and sub-letting were the exception, rather than the rule, in the leases in seventeenth century precedent books.[188]

By the end of the eighteenth century, however, a prohibition on assignment without consent had become so common[189] that it was possible to argue that it had become a 'usual' covenant. That argument was rejected, after some doubt,[190] in 1808,[191] and it followed that other restrictions on the transmission of possession and disposition were not usual covenants either.[192]

---

personal contractual rights or contractual rights which were expressed to be unassignable. Accordingly, a purported assignment of those rights still vests nothing in the assignee.

[185] Kaye, *Medieval English Conveyances*, 256, 258.

[186] *Parry* v. *Harbert* (1539) Dyer 45b (not to assign 'without consent'), *Moor & Farrand's case* (1583) 1 Anderson 123, 1 Leon 3 ('in any manner demise, assign or set over without consent'), *Curtis* v. *Marsh* (1598) 1 Rol Abr 427 pl.5 ('shall not parcel out the land, nor any part thereof from the house'), *Wilkinson* v. *Wilkinson* (1818) 3 Swanst 515, 525.

[187] *Oxford History of the Laws of England*, vol. 6 639.

[188] Most of the precedents in W. West, *Simboleograph* (London, Stationers Company, 1610) pt.1 under the heading Leases do not contain any restriction on alienation. There are, however, precedents for restrictions prohibiting all alienation without consent (s.442) or the same excepting only a sub-tenancy 'at will from year to year' (s.430). For the meaning of that expression, see ch.4 heading 'Periodic'. The only precedent in *The Compleat Clerk*, 3rd edn. (London, Place, 1671) which prohibits alienation without consent, is a lease of a windmill, 717, 722. Similarly, most of Orlando Bridgman's precedents allowed free alienation. By way of exception, he produced a precedent for a right of re-entry if the tenant should 'let, set or assign' without written consent: 260. There is a similar precedent in Woodfall, *Landlord and Tenant*, 663–664. See also *Blacker* v. *Mathers* (1759) 1 Brown PC 334.

[189] *Roe d. Hunter* v. *Galliers* (1787) 2 Term Rep 133, 139. It was, nonetheless, still treated as an optional extra at that time in E. Wood, *Conveyancing*, vol. 3 112.

[190] Coote, *Leases*, 145, *Henderson* v. *Hay* (1792) 3 Brown CC 632, *Folkingham* v. *Croft* (1796) 3 Anstr 700, *Browne* v. *Raban* (1808) 15 Ves 528.

[191] *Church* v. *Brown* (1808) 15 Ves Jun 258, Platt, *Covenants*, 430–8, Platt *Leases* vol. 2 239–248.

[192] Ibid, 265.

In Ireland, by statute,[193] every lease granted between 1st June 1826 and 1st May 1832 contained an implied prohibition on assignment or sub-letting without the landlord's written consent, except where the lease expressly provided otherwise, and ss.10 and 18 Landlord and Tenant Law Amendment Act (Ireland) 1860 made any assignment or sub-letting which required consent void, unless that consent had been given in writing. In England and Wales, however, even as late as 1971,[194] a covenant against assignment without consent was still not a usual covenant,[195] although a fully qualified covenant against assignment and sub-letting is undoubtedly now a usual covenant in all commercial leases, and is sometimes even seen in long residential leases.

Restrictions on disposition have always been construed strictly.[196] So a covenant against assigning the lease is not broken by granting an underlease[197] nor by an assignment of an underlease.[198] Nor is a disposition which takes place by process of law, rather than by voluntary act of the parties, a breach of that covenant. So the automatic vesting of an unmarried woman's leasehold property in her husband on marriage[199] was

---

[193] 7 Geo.4 c.29 (1826), s.3.

[194] *Chester* v. *Buckingham Travel* [1981] 1 WLR 96.

[195] The correctness of this might be open doubt, given that the standard covenants implied on a lease granted in the short form authorised by the Leases Act 1845 included a covenant not to assign without consent.

[196] *Church* v. *Brown* (1808) 15 Ves Jun 258, 264. In a Scottish appeal, *Montgomery* v. *Charteris* (1813) 5 Dow PC 293, the House of Lords held that the grant of a lease for a term of 97 years at a premium by a tenant in tail was a breach of a condition against alienation or disposal.

[197] *Crusoe d. Blencowe* v. *Bugby* (1771) 3 Wills 234. In *Doe* v. *Payne* (1815) 1 Stark 86 it was held that proving that a third party was carrying on business at the premises was not sufficient to prove a breach of a covenant against assigning, setting over, or otherwise letting the premises. Anomalously, covenants against underletting have been held to prohibit assignment: *Greenaway* v. *Adams* (1806) 12 Ves Jun 395, 400. It is unlikely that case would be followed today.

[198] Consequently, whilst the lord's licence was required before a copyholder could grant a lease for more than a year (see ch.1 heading 'Capacity' sub-heading 'copyholders') no further licence was required if the copyholder's tenant wished to assign or underlet: *Johnson* v. *Smart* (1614) 1 Rol Abr 508 pl.14.

[199] See ch.1 heading 'Capacity' sub-heading 'women'.

not a breach of a disposition covenant.[200] Nor was the vesting of the lease in personal representatives on the death of the tenant.[201] Nor was the vesting in a creditor who seized it under process of the law, unless the seizure was collusive.[202] Express covenants tend to be drafted in the widest possible terms as a result: they tend to restrict assignment and underletting and parting with or sharing possession[203] or occupation.

It was long in doubt whether a covenant against assignment of a lease prevented the tenant disposing of the lease by will.[204] In 1782, in *Lord Stanhope* v. *Skeggs*,[205] the court was divided about the legality of a restriction on alienation by an executor, but it was upheld in *Weatherall* v. *Geering*.[206] The initial vesting in the personal representatives was no breach of the covenant, because it was an involuntary act. So the question was whether a subsequent assent out to the legatee was a breach.[207] Early cases held an assent was a breach, except in cases where the executor was also the legatee; that is, where the executor was assenting to himself, so that the lease remained vested in the same person afterwards as before, albeit held in a different capacity.[208] But in 1655 it was decided that an assent was not an 'assignment' at

---

[200] In *Thornhill* v. *King* (1600) Cro Eliz 757 a widow inherited a lease. She re-married, and her new husband assigned the lease on to a third party. The court held that the covenant was broken on the assignment, and not on the re-marriage.

[201] *Anon* (1554) Dalison's Reps 124 SS 70 pl.29, *Crusoe d. Blencowe* v. *Bugby* (1771) 2 Wm.Black 766, 3 Wils 234, cf. *Parry* v. *Harbert* (1539) Dyer 45b, 4 Leon 5 where the vesting in the tenant's executors was held to be a breach of a condition not to 'grant over the land by will or otherwise'.

[202] *Doe d. Mitchinson* v. *Carter* (1798) 8 Term Rep 57, 300.

[203] *Roe d. Hunter* v. *Galliers* (1787) 2 Term Rep 133.

[204] Platt, *Covenants*, 412–417, *Knight* v. *Mory* (1587) Cro Eliz 60, *Barry* v. *Stanton* (1594) Cro Eliz 331, *Horton* v. *Horton* (1605) Cro Jac 74, *Fox* v. *Swann* (1655) Styl 483, *Crusoe d. Blencowe* v. *Bugby* (1771) 3 Wils KB 234.

[205] Cited in *Roe d. Hunter* v. *Galliers* (1787) 2 Term Rep 133. See also *Doe d. Mitchinson* v. *Carter* (1798) 8 Term Rep 57, 59, 300.

[206] (1806) 12 Ves Jun 504, 513.

[207] So in *Anon* (1549) Dyer 66a, there was no breach because the covenant only prohibited a 'gift, sale or grant', and not a devise.

[208] *Knight* v. *Mory* (1587) Cro Eliz 60, *Coke* v. *Taunton* (1594) Cro Eliz 330, *Windsor* v. *Burry* (1581/2) Dyer 45b.fn(3).

all,[209] which settled the point.[210] An assent is, however, caught by wider prohibitions, such as prohibitions against 'setting over or otherwise doing away with' the term.[211]

Similarly, because the statutory assignment on bankruptcy was involuntary,[212] it was not caught by a covenant against assignment, and nor did the assignees in bankruptcy, who were authorised by statute to realise the bankrupt's estate, need to obtain consent when assigning the lease on.[213] So it became the practice to alter the re-entry clause, so as to insert a proviso for re-entry on bankruptcy instead, and a proviso in those terms was upheld in 1787.[214]

Just as, to the medieval mind, a repairing obligation was an obligation to be performed once,[215] so too, where a lease contained a covenant or condition against doing something without consent, that was an obligation to be performed once as well. In *Dumpor* v. *Syms*[216] the lease contained a condition that the tenant and his assigns should not alienate without licence. The court accordingly held that when the landlord gave the original tenant licence[217] to assign, that discharged the condition, so that no licence was required for subsequent assignments. Lord Eldon rightly described this as 'extraordinary', but followed it as 'the law of the land' in *Brummell* v. *MacPherson*,[218] and it was

---

[209] *Fox* v. *Swann* (1655) Style 482, *Crusoe d. Blencowe* v. *Bugby* (1771) 3 Wils KB 234.

[210] *Crusoe d. Blencowe* v. *Bugby* (1771) 3 Wills 234.

[211] Ibid.

[212] See ch.8 heading 'Bankruptcy and personal insolvency'.

[213] *Goring* v. *Warner* (1724) 2 Eq.Ca.Abr 100, *Weatherall* v. *Geering* (1806) 12 Ves Jun 504, 512, *Doe d. Goodbeher* v. *Bevan* (1815) 3 M & S 353, 361.

[214] *Roe d. Hunter* v. *Galliers* (1787) 2 Term Rep 133. Consequently, in *Doe d. Mitchinson* v. *Carter* (1798) 8 Term Rep 57, 300, the court held that a covenant against assignment was not breached by a taking in execution, principally because the usual condition for forfeiture on bankruptcy was missing.

[215] See the discussion of *Maine's* case under the heading of 'Repair' supra.

[216] (1603) 4 Co.Rep 119b, Cro Eliz 815. It was presaged by a difference of opinion in an anonymous case of 1557, Dyer 152a.

[217] An indulgence was not equivalent to an actual licence: *Doe d. Bosacawen* v. *Bliss* (1813) 4 Taunton 735.

[218] (1807) 14 Ves 173.

not until 1859[219] that the rule was reversed by statute for conditions and 1860 for covenants.[220] In practice, by then, every well drawn lease already avoided the problem, by requiring the incoming assignee to give a fresh covenant to the landlord.

At common law, the effect of a restriction on disposition 'without consent' is exactly the same an absolute prohibition on that disposition. There is no implied term that the landlord will give consent in particular circumstances. So the landlord could give or withhold consent, as the landlord saw fit, in precisely the same way as if the restriction had been absolute. But, in 1892, a statutory implied term was added, where the covenant was expressed to be against disposition 'without consent', that no fine could be extracted for giving consent,[221] and in 1927 a statutory proviso that consent would not be withheld unreasonably (or at all, in the case of many building leases) was added too.[222] In 1995, the terms of that proviso were changed,[223] in order to allow the parties to agree in advance the circumstances in which it would, and would not, be reasonable to withhold consent. But that was a change of form rather than substance, for exactly the same result could already be achieved as a matter of drafting, simply by making those matters pre-conditions to the application for consent.

A proviso against withholding consent unreasonably is, however, exactly that. It means that the tenant can assign, without consent, if the landlord withholds it unreasonably, but it is not a cross-covenant to give consent, sounding in damages if the landlord breaches it.[224] Nor could an undertenant force its

---

[219] ss.1–2 Law of Property (Amendment) Act 1859. Now s.143 Law of Property Act 1925. In Ireland, it was reversed in 1826 by 7 Geo.4 c.29, s.4.

[220] s.6 Law of Property (Amendment) Act 1860. Now s.148 Law of Property Act 1925. It was never clear whether the rule applied to a covenant too. In *Jones* v. *Jones* (1803) 12 Ves Jun 186, 191 it was suggested that it did. See too 3rd Report, *Real Property Commissioners*, 49, cf. Platt, *Leases*, vol. 2 271–3. Richard Preston advised that the rule could be avoided by making the right of re-entry conditional upon first giving written notice: Preston, *Conveyancing*, vol. 2 198.

[221] s.3 Conveyancing Act 1892. Now s.144 Law of Property Act 1925.

[222] s.19(1) Landlord and Tenant Act 1927.

[223] s.22 Landlord and Tenant (Covenants) Act 1995.

[224] *Treloar* v. *Bigge* (1884) LR 9 Ex 151.

immediate landlord to seek any necessary consent from superior landlords. Those defects in the law were remedied by statutory duties imposed by the Landlord and Tenant Act 1988.[225]

7. User.

Express repairing obligations, and in their absence, the implied duty to use the property in a tenant like manner and the law of waste, often had the practical effect of limiting the use to which the demised property could be put. A tenant, for instance, who was under an implied obligation to cultivate agricultural land in a husband-like manner, could hardly do anything else with it; and from the eighteenth century onwards, leases of agricultural land often forbade particular courses of husbandry, reinforcing that obligation.[226]

But there was not always that difficulty. The front room of a medieval town-house could serve as a perfectly adequate shop or beerhouse, without breaching any repairing or other obligations. Express prohibitions on particular uses are sometimes found in medieval leases, usually to deal with local problems. For instance in 1456 the Royal Foundation of St Katharine (which still exists) let three houses near Southwark subject to an express condition that no prostitute[227] be allowed to live there.[228] But it was rare for leases to contain any general prohibition on particular uses before the end of the eighteenth century,[229] when general prohibitions on carrying on any business,[230] or particular

---

[225] See generally D.Kidd and G.Higgins, *Landlords' Consents* (London, RICS, 2009).

[226] Stewart, *Practice of Conveyancing*, 344–348.

[227] A 'feme puteine'.

[228] (1456) Fitzherbert, 'Barre' pl.162, f.119. See also the prohibition on using a house for selling coals in *Chinsley* v. *Langley* (1610) 1 Rol Abr 427 pl.7.

[229] So, for instance, there is a precedent for a lease of a shop without any user covenant in G. Jacob, *The Accomplished Conveyancer* vol. 1 (London, Butt, 1714) 440.

[230] Stewart, *Practice of Conveyancing*, 333–334, Platt, *Covenants*, 443 *et seq.* In the Leases Act 1845 a standard covenant against using the property as a

offensive trades,[231] or using the property so as to cause a nuisance or annoyance to adjoining occupiers,[232] began to appear in building leases for residential developments,[233] in order to preserve the amenity of the neighbourhood and in the hope of attracting high-class residential tenants.

Accordingly, covenants restrictive of user were not 'usual' covenants, even as late as the middle of the nineteenth century.[234] By 1971, a covenant against change of use without the landlord's consent, such consent not to be unreasonably withheld,[235] had become a usual covenant in business leases. In practice, for most of the twentieth century, the structure of the user clause in business leases tended to be that one type of use was positively authorised at the outset, other uses would be forbidden absolutely, and a change to anything in between would be permitted, but only with the landlord's prior written consent, not to be unreasonably withheld.[236] After 1963, the initial permitted use was often expressed as one of the 'use classes' contained in statutory instruments relating to Town and Country Planning,[237] so that minor changes in use, which did require planning permission, would not need the landlord's consent either.

'shop' meant that no business use was permitted at all, and that the property could only be used as a private dwelling house.

[231] In 1793 the offensive trades were a 'butcher, poulter, fishmonger or farrier': E.Wood, *Conveyancing,* vol. 3 (London, Stratham & Woodfall, 1793) 112. By 1804 they had expanded (Woodfall, *Landlord and Tenant,* 681) to: 'a maker of sedan or other chairs, baker, brewer, butcher, currier, distiller, dyer, founder, smith, soap boiler, school master or school mistress, sugar-baker, auctioneer, pewterer, tallow chandler or tallow maker, working brazier, tinman, tripe-boiler, pipe-maker, pipe-borer, plumber'. See also Stewart, *Practice of Conveyancing,* 334. A covenant not to exercise the trade of a butcher was held to be breached by selling any meat, even if animals were not killed on the premises in *Doe d. Gaskel* v. *Spry* (1818) 1 Barn & Ald 617.

[232] *Macher* v. *Foundling Hospital* (1813) 1 V & B 188.

[233] *Roe d. Hunter* v. *Galliers* (1787) 2 Term Rep 133, 141, C. Barton, *Modern Precedents in Conveyancing,* vol. 4 *Leases,* 3rd edn. (London, Hunter, 1821) 215, Wm. Blythwood and T. Jarman, *Precedents,* vol. 4 (London, Sweet, 1827) 433.

[234] *Van* v. *Corpe* (1834) 3 Myl & K 269, *Wilbraham* v. *Livesey* (1854) 18 Beav 206, 210.

[235] *Chester* v. *Buckingham Travel* [1981] 1 WLR 96.

[236] See Stewart, *Practice of Conveyancing* 334 for an early version of this form of covenant.

[237] 1963 SI No.708.

Landlords had an interest in ensuring that the permitted use was not defined too tightly, because, if it were, that would have an adverse impact on the rental value of the property for rent review purposes later on.

Positive covenants by tenants to trade from the premises—what are now called 'keep open' covenants—were originally found only in mining leases and leases of public houses. They were included in mining leases[238] because there was usually a turnover rent, and so if the tenant failed to work the mines, the rent would fall.[239] They were included in leases of public houses[240] because most public houses were owned by breweries, and the brewer had an interest in making a profit by selling as much beer as possible to the tenant,[241] and in preserving the goodwill by ensuring that the tenant could not remove trade to another public house.[242] Already, by 1828, a covenant not to trade other than as a licensed victualler was a 'usual' covenant in a lease of a public house for that reason.[243] Keep open covenants, however, have never been enforceable by injunction.[244]

In 1926, the court acquired the power to discharge or alter user covenants in long leases,[245] where fifty years of the lease had already expired and the covenant had become outdated,

---

[238] C. Barton, *Modern Precedents in Conveyancing*, vol. 4 Leases, 3rd edn. (London, Hunter, 1821) 55, 327, 329, Key and Elphinstone, *Precedents in Conveyancing*, vol. 1 (London, Sweet and Maxwell, 1878) 627–628.

[239] *Smith* v. *Morris* (1788) 2 Brown CC 311.

[240] Key and Elphinstone, *Precedents in Conveyancing*, vol. 1 (London, Sweet and Maxwell, 1878) 561.

[241] The fixed rent reserved by the lease is customarily called the 'dry' rent. The rent made by way of profit on sales of beer, wines and spirits to the tenant is called the 'wet' rent. Breweries invariably let their public houses on 'tied' terms; that is, on terms which required the tenant to purchase beer (and sometimes wine and spirits) exclusively from that brewery: e.g. C. Barton, *Modern Precedents in Conveyancing*, vol. 4 Leases, 3rd edn. (London, Hunter, 1821) 47. It was long in doubt whether a beer tie was a covenant which was capable of running with the term.

[242] *Linder* v. *Pryor* (1838) 8 Car & P 518.

[243] *Bennett* v. *Womack* (1828) 3 Car & P 96, 7 Barn & Cr 627.

[244] *Hooper* v. *Broderick* (1840) 11 Sim 47.

[245] Originally, a lease granted for a term of 70 years or more. Since 1969, a lease granted for a term of 40 years or more.

obsolete or useless.[246] That power was transferred to the Lands Tribunal in 1949, and the fifty year period was reduced to twenty-five years in 1954.[247] In 1927, any lease (other than a mining lease or lease of agricultural land) which contained a prohibition against change of use without licence or consent, was made subject to a statutory proviso that the landlord could not charge a fine or premium for giving that permission, except where the change of use also involved structural alteration to the premises.[248] But that does not apply to absolute prohibitions on changes of use, and nor does it prevent the landlord refusing consent unreasonably, both of which a landlord is still entitled to do.

---

[246] s.84 Law of Property Act 1925.
[247] s.52 Landlord and Tenant Act 1954.
[248] s.19(3) Landlord and Tenant Act 1927.

CHAPTER 6
Transmission and Disposition

The most remarkable thing about a lease is not that it confers rights which are enforceable against strangers, for so do all estates and interests in land. Nor is it that the benefit of the covenants in the lease can be made to run with the reversion and the term, for it is possible to annex the benefit of other covenants to land too.[1] Rather, it is the fact that the burden of the covenants can be made to run, so as to be enforceable against successors in title, who were never parties to the covenant. It is this ability to bind successors in title to perform promises made by a predecessor which makes the

---

[1] *Pakenham's Case* (1369) YB 42 Ed.3 f.3 pl.14 (a covenant to perform divine service), *Noke* v. *Awder* (1595) Cro Eliz 373, 436 (a covenant for title), *Swift Investments* v. *Combined English Stores* [1989] 1 AC 632 (a surety covenant).

relationship of landlord and tenant so unusual.[2]

This chapter is about how the rules for enforcement by and against successors in title developed.

1. Rent and attornment.

From the earliest times,[3] rent has been payable, as and when it falls due, by the current tenant to the current landlord, whether those persons were the original parties to the lease or not; for the technical problems about the enforcement of promises by and against third parties, which have bedeviled the law of contractual obligations ever since, never applied to the obligation to pay rent.

None of those problems applied because, to the medieval mind, the obligation to pay rent was not so much a contractual promise but more an almost physical part of the land,[4] which had been retained by the landlord out of the grant of the lease.[5] At the time, it must have been natural for lawyers, dealing with a multitude of

---

[2] For a brief period in the thirteenth century, the burden of a warranty as to title could be enforced against a purchaser of the covenantor's other land (Kaye, *Medieval English Conveyances* 53–56. O.W. Holmes, *The Common Law*, ed. M Howe 271) and there continued to be special rules about the enforcement of the burden of covenants against heirs down to the end of the nineteenth century: see ch.8 heading: 'Liability of the heir and personal representatives'. The ability of a landowner to make a covenant prohibiting a particular use of the land binding on successors, was a very late development of the rules of equity: *Keppel* v. *Bailey* (1834) 2 My & K 517, 540–549.

[3] Pollock & Maitland suggested that leases for years were uncommon before 1200: (*Pollock & Maitland* vol. 2 111). See also R. Faith, *The English Peasantry and the Growth of Lordship* (London, Leicester University Press, 1997) 180–182. But it may be that there are other explanations for the absence of records: see E. Tabuteau, *Transfers of Property in Eleventh Century Norman Law*, 66, Kaye, *Medieval English Conveyances* 255.

[4] As late as 1603 it was said that a rent demand 'ought to be made on the land only, because the land is the debtor': *Sweton* v. *Cushe* (1603) Yelv 36, 37. Coke said (*Co.Litt.* 201b): 'The land is the principal debtor, for the rent issueth out of the land'. 'Rent' is, in itself, an incorporeal hereditament, *Bl.Comm.* Bk.II 41.

[5] Rent reserved on a lease for years of a corporeal hereditament is a rent service, and therefore incident to the reversion. See Simpson, *History of Land Law* 99–100, Simpson, *History of the Common Law of Contract* 84–86.

tenures held in return for various services,[6] which were frequently commuted to an annual money payment,[7] to think about rent in this way; and it does not seem entirely strange, even to modern conveyancers. Leases still 'reserve' a rent in the 'reddendum', although for the reasons explained below, they now also contain a positive covenant to pay rent too.

The procedural consequence of viewing the obligation to pay rent in this way, was that the current tenant of a lease, whether in writing or not,[8] was required to pay the rent to the current landlord, as and when it fell due, and none of the conceptual difficulties about the enforcement of other promises by and against third parties ever applied to it.[9] By 1430, it was already well established that, if the tenant assigned the term, the original landlord could bring an action in debt against the assignee, for rent falling due after the assignment, on the grounds that the debt had been reserved out of the land, and so went with it,[10] albeit that, if the lease was a lease for life, the landlord had to wait patiently until the end of the term before bringing the action.[11] In 1490, it was put beyond doubt that a successor to the original landlord could bring an action in debt for the rent,[12] provided that the tenant had attorned,[13] during

---

[6] Freehold tenures reserving services were all converted into common socage by the Tenures Abolition Act 1660, with the exception of frankalmoign (land granted to the church in return for prayers said for the grantor's soul: Holdsworth, *HEL* vol. 3 34–37.). Frankalmoign tenure is now impossible, except where the death of the last incumbent occurred before 1926, by reason of the repeal of s.7 Tenures Abolition Act 1660 by s.56 Administration of Estates Act 1925. See Halsbury's Laws, *Real Property*, vol. 39(2), 4th edn., ¶.10.

[7] Gilbert, *Rents* 2, F. Pollock, *The Land Laws*, 3rd edn. (London, Macmillan, 1896) 140.

[8] Simpson, *History of the Common Law of Contract*, 171–173.

[9] *Prior of Bradstock's case* (1369) YB 44 Ed.3 f.42 pl.46, *Ernely v. Garth* (1491) 115 SS 65.

[10] *Prior of Marie Spittle's case* (1430) YB 9 Hen.6 f.52, pl.35, (1431) YB 10 Hen.6 f.11 pl.38, 1 Rol Abr 592 pl.1, Simpson, *History of the Common Law of Contract* 85.

[11] The rule that rent payable under a lease for life was a single obligation, and that whilst the landlord could recover instalments by distress, the landlord could not bring an action in debt or covenant until all the rent was due, was eventually reversed by s.4 Landlord and Tenant Act 1709 with effect from 1st May 1710.

[12] *Ernley v. Garth*, (1490) YB 5 Hen.7 f.18 pl.12, *Sir John Port's Notebook* (1986) 102 SS 96, *Walker's Case* (1587) 3 Co.Rep 22a, 22b. In 1431 the point was still in

the grantor's lifetime,[14] by saying or doing anything which recognised the substitution of the new landlord. The most common attornment, at this time, was 'to say, Sir, I attorne to you by force of the said grant, or I become your tenant, or to deliver to the grantee a penny, or a half-penny or a farthing, by way of attornment'.[15]

Shortly afterwards it became possible to convey a freehold reversion[16] in a way that avoided the need for an attornment afterwards.[17] That could be done by conveyance to the use of the new landlord, made by bargain and sale or a covenant to stand seised under Statute of Uses (1536),[18] the effect of which was that the new landlord would automatically have a right to rent accruing afterwards. Even in those cases where an attornment was still necessary, as for instance, was the case where the reversion was conveyed by levying a fine[19] or by way of a recovery,[20] a court of

---

doubt: see (1431) YB 9 Hen.6 f.16b pl.7, Simpson, *History of the Common Law of Contract*, 86.

[13] *Pollock & Maitland* vol. 2 132, Littleton, *Tenures*, s.572, *Humble* v. *Glover* (1594) Cro Eliz 328, *Vandeput* v. *Lord* (1718) 1 Strange 78. 1 Rol Abr 591 pl.2 says: 'If a man lease for years reserving a rent, and then grants over the reversion, and the tenant attorns, the grantee shall have an action of debt for the rent accruing afterwards,' adding that this had been doubted in (1431) YB Hen.6 f.16b pl.7. In *Apleton* v. *Baily* (1608) 1 Brownlow 102, a claim for arrears of rent by an executor of an assignee of the reversion was dismissed, for failure to plead any attornment to the testator. An attornment by one joint tenant bound the other: *Tooker's Case, Rudde* v. *Tucker* (1600) 2 Co.Rep 66b, Cro Eliz 737, 802.

[14] Otherwise, the deed transferring the reversion was void: Littleton, *Tenures*, s.551. The rule that the attornment had to take place during the grantor's lifetime did not apply if the reversion was transferred by fine or recovery, rather than a deed: *Co.Litt.* 309b.

[15] Littleton, *Tenures*, s.551.

[16] A leasehold reversion could not be transferred in this way because the Statute of Uses (1536) only executed a use (i.e. turned it into a legal conveyance) if the grantor was 'seised', and a leasehold tenant did not have seisin: (1580) Dyer 369 pl.50.

[17] *Co.Litt.* 309b. No attornment was necessary on a transfer to the Crown in any event: ibid.

[18] The Statute of Enrolments made a deed necessary with effect from 31st July 1536. There was a brief period beforehand, in which a legal estate could be transferred under the Statute of Uses (1536) by parol. Before that, a bargain and sale only took effect in equity.

[19] *Mallory's case* (1600) 5 Co.Rep 111b.

[20] Before 1529, a leasehold term could be destroyed by a collusive recovery, except where the tenant intervened in the action, in which event, enforcement would be postponed until the end of the term; see ch.4 heading 'Fixed terms'. By

equity could compel a tenant to attorn,[21] if there was no good reason for refusing to do so.[22] Eventually, in 1705, the need for an attornment on a transmission of a reversion was abolished generally.[23]

When a tenant attorned, the new landlord's title would relate back to the date of the transfer,[24] so that the new landlord would be treated as having become the landlord on that date, and not on the date of the later attornment.[25] Of course, the tenant might have continued to pay the rent to the old landlord in the meantime, in ignorance of the transfer. But that was not a reason to refuse to attorn, because there was an exception to the 'relation back' rule in those circumstances.[26] The new landlord only acquired the right to recover any rent falling due between the transfer and the attornment,[27] if the tenant had not already paid it to the old landlord. If the tenant had done so, that discharged the tenant's obligation, and the new landlord had to recover it from the old landlord instead, by bringing an action for money had and received. Similarly, in those cases, before 1705, where no attornment was necessary,[28] the tenant would, at common law, obtain a good discharge for rent which had fallen due, by paying it to the old landlord before receiving notice of the transfer.[29]

---

s.3 Recoveries Act 1529, tenants acquired a general right to falsify a recovery, and by s.2 of that Act, the recovery took effect as a transmission of the reversion instead. But an attornment was still necessary before the new owner could sue for the rent, or distrain, or bring any action on the covenants: *Co.Litt.* 320a, *Long* v. *Buckeridge* (1715) 1 Strange 106.

[21] *Philips* v. *Sandford* (1579) Cary 4, '18 Attornment' Tothill 14. The new landlord could not levy a distress before the attornment: Littleton, *Tenures*, s.579.

[22] *Philips* v. *Stanford* (1579) Cary 3. *Shute* v. *Mallory* (1607) Moore 805.

[23] s.9 Administration of Justice Act 1705. See now s.151 Law of Property Act 1925.

[24] *Co.Litt.* 310b.

[25] Where the reversion was transferred by a deed which had been delivered in escrow, the right related back to the date when the escrow condition was fulfilled, and not to the original delivery of the deed: *Perks*, ¶.10.

[26] *Long* v. *Hemming* (1590) 4 Leon 215, 1 Anders 256, Cro Eliz 209, *Birch* v. *Wright* (1786) 1 Term Rep 377.

[27] *Saris* v. *Strudhay* (1582/3) Tothill 13.

[28] See the previous paragraph.

[29] *Sir John Watts* v. *Ognall* (1607) Cro Jac 192. The transfer of a copyhold reversion, by entry on the manorial rolls, was sufficiently notorious that no further notice was required: *Black* v. *Mole* (1661) T.Raym 18. But enrolment of a bargain

That rule was expressly preserved as a statutory defence in 1705, when the requirement to attorn was abolished generally.[30]

For a landlord, however, an action in debt to recover rent[31] had two substantial[32] disadvantages, compared with an action to enforce a covenant.

The first, as William Noy, writing in the seventeenth century, explained, was:[33]

> If a lessee assign over his term the lessor may charge the lessee or assignee at his pleasure. But if the lessor accept the rent of the assignee, knowing of the assignment, he has determined his acceptance, and shall not have an action of debt against the lessee, for rent due after the assignment.

In *Wadham* v. *Marlow*[34] Lord Mansfield went further and said that any assent on the part of the lessor to the assignment would have the same effect.[35]

The second was that a successor to the original landlord did not

---

and sale under the Statute of Enrolments 1536 was not: *Mallory's case* (1600) 5 Co.Rep 111b, 113b.

[30] s.10 Administration of Justice Act 1705, *Moss* v. *Gallimore* (1779) 1 Douglas 279, 282. See now, s.151 Law of Property Act 1925.

[31] By s.14 Distress for Rent Act 1737 rent due under a lease not made by deed could be recovered by bringing the claim in assumpsit, for use and occupation, instead of in debt; the award being of an amount equivalent to the agreed rent, rather than of the rent itself. See ch.9 heading 'Assumpsit'. The action could be brought by an assignee of the reversion (*Rennie* v. *Robinson* (1824) 1 Bing 147) but only against someone who would have been liable, had the claim been made in debt.

[32] There were procedural disadvantages with the action too: see ch.9 heading 'Debt'.

[33] *Noy's Grounds and Maxims of the Law of England*, 9th edn. (Reprinted Oxford, Professional Books Ltd, 1985) 170. In the sixteenth century, it was still doubtful whether the original tenant could be liable in debt following an assignment at all: see Simpson, *History of the Common Law of Contract*, 85–86, *Sir John Port's Notebook* (1986) 102 SS 96, *Dalison's Reps* (1554) 124 SS 70 pl.29, *Hill* v. *Grange* (1556) Plowden 164, Dyer 107, *Anon* (1566) Dyer 247b, *Anon* (1584) 1 Brownlow 56, *Walker's Case* (1587) 3 Co.Rep 22a, *Marrow* v. *Turpin* (1599) Moore KB 600, Cro Eliz 715. In *Marsh* v. *Brace* (1614) Cro Jac 334 the law is stated, as in Noy, as depending on the landlord's acceptance of the assignee, but as late as 1667, it was suggested that giving notice of the assignment to the landlord was sufficient to discharge the original tenant in all cases: *Knight* v. *Buckley* (1667) T.Raym 162. See also Viner's *Abridgment* 'Estates' B.b.18 pl.11.

[34] (1784) 8 East 314n.

[35] 'Hence the caution with which some gentlemen give their receipts for rent, expressing it to be received of the tenant by the hands of the assignee or occupier': Preston, *Conveyancing*, vol. 2 193.

even have that choice. A claim for rent in debt made by a successor to the original landlord, could only be made against the person who was actually the tenant at the time the rent fell due, and only after he had attorned to that successor, where necessary.[36]

This accounts for the introduction of express[37] covenants to pay rent too,[38] for if the original tenant had covenanted to pay the rent throughout the term, it would not matter if the landlord or a successor (see the next section) later lost the right to bring an action in debt against the original tenant: the original tenant would still remain liable to pay on the covenant.[39] As Lord Kenyon explained, in *Auriol* v. *Mills*:[40]

> It is extremely clear, that a person who enters into an express covenant in a lease, continues liable on his covenant notwithstanding the lease be assigned over. The distinction between the actions of debt and covenant, which was taken in earlier times, is equally clear: if the lessee assign over the lease, and the lessor accept the assignee as his lessee, either tacitly or

---

[36] *Humble* v. *Glover* (1594) Cro Eliz 328, Holdsworth, *HEL* vol. 7 272–273. An order could be made in equity, forcing the former tenant to reveal the name of the assignee, so that the landlord would know who to sue: *Stauden* v. *Bullock* (1596) Tothill 9. For the cases where an attornment was necessary, see above.

[37] In the absence of any express covenant, a covenant would be implied as a matter of law from the use of the words 'paying' or 'yielding' in the reddendum, assuming that the tenant had executed the lease as a deed. But the implied covenant was only to pay the rent accruing due whilst the lease was vested in the tenant (see ch.5 heading 'To pay rent'). So a landlord relying on the implied covenant would be no better off than one bringing the action in debt: *Pitcher* v. *Tovey* (1692) 12 Mod. 71. In *The Compleat Clerk*, 3rd edn. (London, Place, 1671) 755 there is a precedent for a lease of a manor with a covenant that the rent shall only be recoverable by distress, and the tenant shall not otherwise be liable for the rent.

[38] There was an additional advantage with a covenant to pay rent, in that an action could be brought before any demand had been made: *Anonymous* (1626) Bryson's Exch Cas 24.

[39] *Noy's Grounds and Maxims of the Law of England*, 9th edn. (Reprinted Oxford, Professional Books Ltd, 1985) 170 fn.c. See also (1533/4) Brook's New Cases pl.74, *Bachelour* v. *Gage* (1630) Cro Car 188, Sir W Jones 223, *Norton* v. *Acklane* (1640) Cro Car 579, *Jenkins* v. *Hermitage* (1674) 1 Freeman 377, Platt, *Leases*, vol. 2 352–353.

[40] (1790) 4 Term Rep 94, 98. See also J. Fonblanque, *A Treatise on Equity*, 5th edn., vol. 1 (London, Clarke, 1820) 362 fn(a).

expressly, it appears by the authorities that the action of debt will not lie against the original lessee; but all those cases with one voice declare, that if there be an express covenant, the obligation on such covenant continues.

So, by including an express covenant to pay the rent, the landlord would have the choice, after an assignment of the term, of recovering the rent from the current tenant, by bringing an action in debt, or from the original tenant, by bringing an action on the covenant.[41]

That, however, still left a gap in the scheme. An intermediate assignee, who had already assigned the lease on to someone else, was liable to the landlord neither in debt, nor on the covenants given by the original tenant, for any obligation accruing due after the assignment.[42] In 1667 it was decided that this rule applied, even if the landlord knew nothing of this further[43] assignment.[44] So an assignee, holding an onerous lease, who wished to be rid of any of further liability to the landlord, would usually be advised to assign it over to a beggar or pauper, who would be paid a few shillings for agreeing to take it.[45]

The ingenious conveyancing solution to this problem, which

---

[41] See below heading 'Covenants'.

[42] *Overton* v. *Sydall* (1597) Cro Eliz 555, *Treakle* v. *Cook* (1683) 1 Vern 165, *Pitcher* v. *Tovey* (1692) 12 Mod. 71.

[43] On a first assignment by the original tenant, the original tenant would remain liable in debt until the landlord accepted the assignee, and in covenant throughout the term. So the rule only applied on a second or subsequent assignment, where the assigning party's only liability was as a result of privity of estate.

[44] *Keightly* v. *Buckley* (1667) 1 Lev 215, *Pitcher* v. *Tovey* (1692) 12 Mod. 71.

[45] *Richmond* v. *City of London* (1702) 1 Brown PC 516, *Valliant* v. *Dodemede* (1742) 2 Atk 546, *Rowley* v. *Adams* (1839) 4 Myl & Cr 534, Platt, *Covenants*, 194–195, 504, Platt, *Leases*, vol. 2 416–418, Coote, *Leases*, 324. In H. Bullow, ed. J. Fonblanque, *A Treatise on Equity*, 5th edn. vol. 1 (London, Clarke, 1820) 362 it was said: 'But where a man makes a lease, rendering a rent, if the lessee assigns to a beggar or insolvent person in equity the lessee shall be bound to pay the rent, which is common cause'. It became impossible to argue that there was any such exception after the decision in *Walters* v. *Northern Coal Mining Co* (1855) 5 De G M & G 629. But it might be that equity would still grant an injunction against assigning to an insolvent person, even absent any express covenant against assignment, if the landlord was offering to accept a surrender instead: H. Bullow, ed. J. Fonblanque, *A Treatise on Equity*, 5th edn. vol. 1 362.

dates from the early nineteenth century,[46] was to alter the alienation covenant in the lease, so as to require any incoming assignee to enter into a new, separate covenant with the landlord to pay the rent and perform the other obligations contained in the lease throughout the residue of the term. The landlord's arsenal thus became complete: the landlord could bring an action against the original tenant, on the covenant given in the lease; or against any intermediate assignee, on the covenant given when taking the assignment of the lease, usually in the licence to assign; and the ultimate assignee would be liable, both on that covenant, and also in debt, as the current tenant.

So well did this scheme work, at least for landlords, that the right to recover rent as a debt continued to run with the reversion at common law,[47] until the rent was statutorily annexed to it by s.10 Conveyancing Act 1881. That provision was substantially re-enacted in s.141 Law of Property Act 1925, but so as to carry any arrears of rent owing at the time of the transfer too.[48]

Even more remarkably, the burden of the obligation to pay rent, as a debt, continued to run with the term of the lease at common law until as late as 1st January 1996, when the Landlord and Tenant (Covenants) Act 1995 came into force.

That Act now provides a complete code for the running of the benefit and the burden of the obligation to pay rent. For the purposes of the Act, leases are generally 'old' or 'new', depending upon whether they were made before or after that date. For 'old' leases, the law remains much as it did before, except that there is now a requirement to serve a statutory form of notice within six months of the rent falling due, if the landlord wishes to recover it

---

[46] The practice of obtaining a fresh covenant from the incoming assignee was prompted by the extraordinary rule in *Dumpor's Case* (1603) 4 Co.Rep 119b, that a condition (and perhaps also a covenant) against assignment without consent could only ever be enforced once, on the first assignment, and would be spent thereafter (see ch.5 heading 'Alienation'). By requiring the incoming assignee to enter into a deed, the landlord obtained a fresh covenant which could be enforced on the next assignment. See Preston, *Conveyancing*, vol. 2 199, and the precedent at 519–520, Platt, *Leases*, vol. 2 275.

[47] *Yellowly* v. *Gower* (1855) 11 Exch 274.

[48] *Arlesford Trading* v. *Servansingh* [1971] 1 WLR 1080. Before then, the right to the arrears remained vested in the assignor: *Midgley* v. *Lovelace* (1693) Catch 290, Holt KB 74.

from anyone other than the current tenant or the current tenant's surety;[49] and someone who pays pursuant to that notice is entitled to demand and take a statutory concurrent (or 'overriding') lease.

For new leases, the old law has been entirely swept away. The purely contractual liability of an original tenant, and of any intermediate assignee who has given a contractual covenant, is now determined by a lawful assignment over; so that, afterwards, the leasehold estate continues to exist, but the contractual liability of the assigning party is discharged.[50] The assigning tenant can generally be made to guarantee the liability of the person to whom that assignment is made, under an 'authorised guarantee agreement', but on the next lawful assignment over, that guarantee is discharged too.

2. Covenants.

A covenant is generally a promise which is enforceable because it is made by deed.[51]

At first, there was no special rule about covenants contained in a lease. The same privity rules applied to them as applied to any other covenant. In short, the rule was that the covenant could only be enforced between the original parties.[52] The benefit of the promise could not be assigned to anyone else,[53] and nor could anyone other than the original party be made to perform it.

Those rules worked well enough, if all the parties wanted was a relatively short-term, personal arrangement; for instance, a landowner letting a field to a local farmer, for a year, or from year

---

[49] s.17.

[50] s.5.

[51] For the detailed rules, and the exceptions, see ch.5 heading 'Express, implied and usual'.

[52] Executors and administrators counted as original parties for this purpose: *Rushden's Case* (1532) Dyer 4b. Where freehold land descended to an heir, the heir received it charged with the performance of any covenants which the deceased had expressly made on behalf of his heir: see ch.8 heading 'Liability of the heir and personal representatives'.

[53] *Lampet's Case* (1612) 10 Co.Rep 46b, 48a, *Brett* v. *Cumberland* (1616) Popham 138, Cro Jac 399.

to year, in return for a share of the annual produce or a fixed sum.[54] But they were wholly unsatisfactory for long leases, which were first used in the thirteenth century, as a way of lawfully giving land to the church and other religious houses.[55]

Under this pressure, by 1529, if not earlier, the common law had created an exception to the privity rule, where the tenant had given a covenant, and subsequently assigned the lease. In *Thirkill* v. *Gore*[56] the lease, which contained a tenant's covenant to pay 'all charges as well against the King as against others, had been assigned twice. The court unanimously resolved that the landlord could enforce that covenant against the current tenant. Similarly, before 1535,[57] Roger Yorke had noted a decision that the burden of a tenant's repairing covenant ran with the term, even if the word 'assigns' was missing.[58]

Thus by the middle of the sixteenth century, there was little doubt that if the tenant assigned the term to someone else, who accepted the assignment,[59] the original landlord would be entitled to enforce the tenant's covenants against the assignee of the lease, and the assignee of the lease would be entitled to enforce the landlord's covenants against the original landlord.

What was not clear was whether there was a similar exception where, instead of the tenant assigning the term, the landlord transferred the reversion. Did the benefit of the tenant's covenants and the burden of the landlord's covenants run with the reversion, in the same way, so as to be enforceable by and against the new landlord? If the covenant was a covenant implied as a matter of law

---

[54] 'Terms of years were originally granted to mere farmers or husbandsmen, who every year rendered some equivalent in money, provisions, or other rent, to the lessors or landlords; but, in order to encourage them to manure and cultivate the ground, they had a permanent interest granted to them, not determinable at the will of the lord. And yet their possession was esteemed of so little consequence, that they were rather considered as the bailiffs or servants of the lord, who were to receive and account for the profits at a settled price, than as having any property of their own': *Bl.Comm*. Bk.II 141–142.

[55] See ch.4 heading 'Fixed terms'.

[56] (1529) Spelman, 93 SS 75.

[57] It was probably the case in 1533/4 reported in *Brook's New Cases* pl.74.

[58] (2003) 120 SS 201. See also *The Dean and Chapter of Windsor's Case* (1601) 5 Co.Rep 24a.

[59] *William* v. *Bosenquet* (1819) Brod & Bing 238.

from the use of a particular word,[60] then it was probably already the law that the burden ran,[61] but nobody had yet decided that the answer would be the same if the covenant was an express covenant,[62] and there were formidable difficulties in the way of such a decision. Not the least of these was the fact that the action of *quare ejecit* had been given to tenants in 1235, to enable them to recover possession against successors in title to the original landlord, precisely because a tenant could not sue a successor landlord in covenant, and so recover possession of the term back in that way.[63]

The absence of any such decision quickly became a serious political problem, as the monasteries were dissolved. At first by forceful persuasion, and then by persuasive force, Henry VIII acquired 'land late belonging to monasteries and other religious and ecclesiastical houses dissolved'.[64] But when he tried to raise money by selling it on,[65] he found that purchasers were wary of buying it, and not just because of squeamishness about its provenance.[66]

Much of it had been let, or sub-let, on advantageous terms, and whilst (for the reason explained above) there was no problem with enforcement of covenants when buying a lease, there was a problem with buying a reversion: nobody could be sure that a purchaser of a reversion would be able to enforce the tenant's covenants; for the common law was thought to be that 'no stranger to any covenant, action or condition shall take any advantage or benefit of the same'.[67]

Henry, however, was not the sort of man to allow the common

---

[60] A covenant implied as a matter of law is not the same as a covenant implied as a matter of construction: see ch.5 heading 'Express, implied and usual' and *Williams* v. *Burrell* (1845) 1 CB 402, 432.

[61] *Harper* v. *Burgh* (1677) 2 Lev 206, *Vyvyan* v. *Arthur* (1823) 1 Barn & Cr 410, *Wedd* v. *Porter* [1916] 2 KB 91, 101, Platt, *Covenants*, 532, Platt, *Leases*, vol. 2 382.

[62] Platt, *Covenants*, 531.

[63] Bracton, vol. 3 161 (f.220). See ch.9 heading 'Ejectment'.

[64] Recital, Grantees of Reversions Act 1540.

[65] The Crown was already entitled to 'all advantages whether of covenants, conditions or the like' as the original lessor had, by virtue of the Suppression of Religious Houses Act 1539: Platt, *Leases*, vol. 2 383.

[66] Fitzherbert CJ 'on his death-bed in 1538 solemnly swore his children never to accept a foot of monastic land': T. Plucknett, *The Place of the Legal Profession in the History of English Law* (1932) 48 LQR 328, 332.

[67] Recital, Grantees of Reversions Act 1540.

law to stand in his way, and the Grantees of Reversions Act 1540 was an elegant solution to his problem.[68] The first section dealt with the rights of a purchaser of a reversion upon a lease, whether for years or for life. It gave the purchaser, as the new landlord, power to enforce rights of 're-entry, waste, forfeiture and in respect of conditions, covenants and agreements' contained in the lease.[69]

The second section gave tenants reciprocal statutory rights to enforce the landlord's obligations against the new landlord. Very shortly after the Act was passed, it was decided in *Hill* v. *Grange*[70] that the Act applied generally, and not just where the reversion had come into the hands of the Crown,[71] subject to the requirement of an attornment, in those cases where it would still have been required, in order to bring a claim in debt for the rent;[72] and by 1598 it was clear that it applied where the reversion was leasehold too.[73]

In effect, the Act declared that the exception to the privity rule for covenants, which already applied when a tenant assigned a lease, would now apply too when the landlord transferred the reversion.[74] The legislation did not deal with the enforcement of

---

[68] See generally *Co.Litt.* 215a.

[69] *Brett* v. *Cumberland* (No.2) (1619) Cro Jac 521.

[70] (1556) Plowden 164, 173.

[71] Dalison's Reps, 'Monastic Lands' (1553) 124 SS 27.

[72] *Mallory's Case* (1600) 5 Co.Rep 111b. See the previous section for the cases where an attornment was required in order to bring an action for the rent in debt.

[73] *Matures* v. *Westwood* (1598) Cro Eliz 599, 617, Gouldsborough 175 pl.109. In *Glover* v. *Cope* (1691) 4 Mod. 80 it was held that the statute applied to a copyhold reversion too. At the beginning of the seventeenth century, it had not: *Apleton* v. *Baily* (1608) 1 Brownlow 102, *Beal* v. *Brasier* (1612) Cro Jac 305. The Act, however, only applied where the lease had been granted by the legal reversioner. If appropriate steps were taken, covenants in leases granted under a power could be made to run with the reversion (Platt, *Covenants*, 461–461); otherwise, those covenants remained covenants in gross, until they were brought within the statutory scheme by ss.10-11 Conveyancing Act 1881. The more difficult case was where a lease had been granted out of an equitable interest in the land (eg. where the land had been mortgaged, and the mortgagor granting the lease only had an equity of redemption: see ch.2 heading 'Mortgages of leases and as leases'). It needed a sleight of hand with the law of estoppel in the nineteenth century to solve that problem: see *Oxford History of the Laws of England*, vol. 12 129–130, and ch.7 heading 'Estoppel and denial of title'.

[74] There was a jurisdictional difference: if the lease had been made in England but was of property in Ireland or one of the colonies, then a claim by or against an

covenants on an assignment of the lease at all. That was not because Henry was uninterested,[75] but rather because it was already well established that the benefit and burden of covenants could run with the term of the lease, and so there was simply no need for legislative intervention.[76] Similarly, because it was assumed that the benefit and burden of implied covenants (being covenants implied as a matter of law from the relationship of landlord and tenant)[77] already ran with the reversion at common law, the Act only dealt with express covenants and agreements.[78]

Of course, it did not follow from the fact that covenants could now run with the reversion and the term, that the benefit and burden of each and every covenant made between a landlord and a tenant would run. A tenant, for instance, might covenant to marry the landlord's son or daughter, as part of the consideration for the grant of the lease. Nobody would have thought that this meant that an assignee of the term would be obliged to enter into a bigamous marriage with the landlord's son too, or that a successor to the original landlord would be able to foist his own daughter on the tenant.

The rules about the circumstances in which the burden of a tenant's covenant would run were restated and clarified in *Spencer's Case*,[79] which quickly acquired the status of one of the great cases in English land law. But, like many great cases, it did not decide anything new. The rules in *Spencer's Case* were entirely orthodox land law at the time,[80] as Coke himself pointed out,[81] in

---

assignee of the reversion could be tried in England, but a claim by or against an assignee of the term could only be tried where the property was situate: *Wey* v. *Rally* (1704) 6 Mod. 194, *Patterson* v. *Scott* (1727) 2 Strange 776.

[75] Some of the land acquired from the monasteries was leasehold, and even that which was not, was sometimes disposed of on leasehold terms: *Earl of Arundel* v. *Lord Gray* (1561) Dyer 200b.

[76] Hence, s.2 of the Act, which annexed the burden of landlord's covenants to the reversion, expressly contemplated that enforcement would be by 'tenants and assigns', and not simply 'tenants'.

[77] See ch.5 heading 'Express, implied and usual'.

[78] *Harper* v. *Burgh* (1677) 2 Lev 206, *Vyvyan* v. *Arthur* (1823) 1 Barn & Cr 410, *Wedd* v. *Porter* [1916] 2 KB 91, 101. Platt, *Covenants* 41, 532.

[79] (1583) 5 Co.Rep 16a.

[80] *Anon* (1534) *Reports from the Time of Hen.VIII*, vol. 2, 121 SS 413, (1533/4) Brook's New Cases pl.74.

[81] 'Observe reader your old books, for they are the fountains out of which these resolutions issue . . . ' (18a). But although Coke often stressed the unreliability of abridgments and the importance of reading the original books (*Sir Thomas Palmer's* Case (1601) 5 Co.Rep 24b, 25a: 'Take heed, reader of all abridgments,

this instance at least, accurately.[82] Like many of the cases which Coke reported, it has had a disproportionate influence on the subsequent development of the law, not because of the importance, originality or even correctness of the decision at the time, but rather because Coke chose to report it, in his own accessible and authoritative style, when nothing else was being reported in quite that way.[83]

In *Spencer's Case* the original tenant had covenanted to build a new wall on the demised property, and the question was whether the burden of that obligation ran with the term, so as to be enforceable against an assignee. The court divided covenants into three types.

First, there were covenants which related to the land demised, in the state in which it existed at the time of the demise. The burden of that sort of covenant ran automatically, whether the tenant had expressly made the covenant on behalf of 'assigns' or not.[84]

Secondly, there were covenants which related to the land demised, but which would require something new to be done to it in the future. The burden of that type of covenant would only run if the tenant had expressly made it on behalf of 'assigns', thereby

---

for the chief use of them is as tables to find the book of large. But I exhort every good student to read and rely only the books at large, as in another place I have advised'), it appears unlikely that he always took his own advice: see W. Bolland, *A Manual of Year Book Studies* (Cambridge, Cambridge University Press, 1925) 85. See also Platt, *Covenants* 14–16.

[82] 'As a rule of thumb it is as well to remember that sentences beginning "For it is an ancient maxim of the common law" followed by one of Coke's spurious Latin maxims, which he could manufacture to fit any occasion and prove an air of authentic antiquity, are apt to introduce a new departure. Sentences such as "And by these differences and reasons you will better understand your books", or "And so the doubts and diversities in the books well resolved" likewise indicate new law': S. Thorne, *Sir Edward Coke 1552–1952* (Selden Society Annual Lecture 1952) 7. 'Both Lord Mansfield and Lord Thurlow expressed the highest opinion of Littleton, and a very different opinion of Coke': C. Butler, *Reminiscences*, 3rd edn. (London, John Murray, 1822) 115.

[83] See T. Plucknett, *The Genesis of Coke's Reports* (1942) 27 Cornell Law Quarterly 190.

[84] This included: covenants to repair the demised property, to pay rent, to discharge charges, to permit the landlord access to the retained property, husbandry covenants, personal residence covenants, and restrictive covenants. See Coote, *Leases*, 310. So a covenant against ploughing up pasture was held to run in *Cookson* v. *Cock* (1606) Cro Jac 125.

making it clear that the parties intended it to be more than a personal covenant,[85] a rule which was eventually reversed by s.79 Law of Property Act 1925.[86] Thirdly there were covenants that did not relate to the demised land at all. These were purely personal covenants, and so were caught by the common law rule that they could only be enforced against the original covenantor, even if the parties had purported to bind the assignees of the original tenant.[87] One result of this third rule is that burden of a lease of chattels still cannot run even today.[88]

Similar principles applied to the running of the benefit of tenants' covenants.[89]

Once it was accepted that the benefit and burden of covenants could run between landlord and tenant, three additional questions inevitably arose.

The first was whether the original covenanting party remained liable to perform the covenant, or whether the substitution of the assignee could be pleaded as a discharge of that liability, as it could be in a claim in debt. We have already seen that Lord Kenyon observed in 1790 that, in the case of express covenants, the cases declared 'with one voice'[90] that the original covenantee remained

---

[85] This echoed an earlier dispute about whether, if rent was reserved to the 'lessor', without mentioning successors in title, the rent abated on the death of the original lessor: see ch.3 heading 'Rent reservation' and Platt, *Leases*, vol. 2 89–90.

[86] 'The second paragraph removes the difficulty disclosed by the first and second resolutions in *Spencer's Case*. The net result of the section is that it will no longer be necessary in any case to covenant expressly on behalf of assigns': Sir Benjamin Cherry, *The New Property Acts* (London, Solicitors Law Stationary Society, 1926) 131.

[87] In 1601 it was unclear whether a covenant to deliver up with vacant possession at the end of the term was personal or not: *Matures* v. *Westwood* (1598) Cro Eliz 599, Gouldsborough 175 pl.109. The doubt was about whether it was an obligation which accrued during, or after, the term. In *Congleton* v. *Pattison* (1808) 10 East 130 Bailey J said: 'All the cases show that the assignee is not bound unless the thing to be done is upon the land demised'. So in *Woodall* v. *Clifton* [1905] 2 Ch 257, it was held that an option to acquire the reversion does not run with the lease.

[88] *James* v. *Blunck* (1656) Hard 88.

[89] *Jourdain* v. *Wilson* (1820) 4 Barn & Ald 266.

[90] *Auriol* v. *Mills* (1790) 4 Term Rep 94, 98, *Hornby* v. *Houlditch* (1737) Andrews 40, *Brett* v. *Cumberland* (No.2) (1619) Cro Jac 521. See also (1533/4) Brook's New Cases pl.74, *Fisher* v. *Ameers* (1611) Brownlow 20 and *Barnard* v. *Goodscall* (1612) Cro Jac 309 all of which involved repairing covenants.

liable, notwithstanding the assignment.[91] But the opposite rule applied in the case of implied covenants (or, to use the old language, a 'covenant in law' rather than a 'covenant in fact').[92] The rationale appears to have been that, since the court could not imply any obligation on the part of the original tenant to continue paying rent after the landlord had accepted an assignee, the court could hardly imply a covenant by the tenant to do anything else either, in those circumstances. So implied covenants are only enforceable between the landlord and the tenant for the time being, at the time the covenant is breached.

The second was whether an assignee could held liable in damages for breaches which a predecessor had committed before the assignment.[93] The answer was that the assignee could not be liable.[94]

The third was whether an assignment of the reversion or the term would carry with it the right to sue for pre-assignment breaches, or whether the right to sue for those breaches of covenant remained vested in the assignor. The answer was that the assignee could not sue for past breaches[95] but could sue for continuing breaches, and, in such a case, could recover for the pre-assignment loss too, though the point was not settled until well into the twentieth century.[96]

The rules in *Spencer's Case* continued to apply to the running of the benefit and burden of covenants on an assignment of the

---

[91] It made no difference whether the original covenantee was a landlord or a tenant; per Cozens-Hardy LJ in *Stuart* v. *Joy* [1904] 1 KB 362, 367–368. Nor did it make any difference that the assignment was involuntary: *Hornby* v. *Houlditch* (1737) Andrews 40.

[92] *Bachelour* v. *Gage* (1630) Cro Car 188, Sir W. Jones, 223, *Anon* (1670) 1 Sid 447 pl.9.

[93] The doctrine of interesse termini was ignored for the purpose of ascertaining the date of the assignment; *Walker* v. *Reeves* (1781) 2 Douglas 461n.

[94] *Grescot* v. *Green* (1700) 1 Salk 199, *Churchwardens of St. Saviour's, Southwark* v. *Smith* (1762) 1 Wm.Black 351, cf. *Hyde* v. *Dean and Chapter of Windsor* (1596) Cro Eliz 457(ii), 552 where the assignee was held not liable, because the covenant, as a matter of construction, was limited to the lifetime of the original tenant.

[95] *Lewes* v. *Ridge* (1601) Cro Eliz 863, Platt, *Leases*, vol. 2 387.

[96] *Mascal's case* (1587) 1 Leon 62, *London & County* v. *Wilfred Sportsman* [1971] Ch 764.

lease until 1st January 1996, when a statutory code was introduced by the Landlord and Tenant (Covenants) Act 1995 for 'new' leases granted after that date.

The provisions of the Grantees of Reversions Act 1540, annexing the benefit and burden of landlords' covenants to the reversion, were supplemented by ss.10 and 11 Conveyancing Act 1881, so as to bring leases granted under a power within the scheme, and were substantially re-enacted by ss.141-142 Law of Property Act 1925. But, for 'new' leases, the 1995 Act now provides a complete statutory code for those covenants too, under which the burden of covenants can run even on an equitable assignment. Yet, the ancient distinction between 'debt' and 'covenant' has not been entirely lost, for the 1995 Act continues to distinguish between actions to recover 'fixed charges' and other actions.

3. Contractual promises.

The action of covenant, unlike the action of debt, could generally[97] only be brought on a deed. Of course, many leases were made by deed. But some were not. It has always been possible to make informal short leases relatively easily (sometimes, inadvertently), and a long lease could be made by signed writing under the Statute of Frauds (1677). It was not until 1845 that a deed became necessary in all cases in order to grant a term of longer than three years.[98]

In the absence of a deed, an obligation to pay rent could be enforced in debt, but a non-rental promise could only be enforced[99] at common law by the action of assumpsit.[100]

The basic rule in assumpsit was the same as the original rule for covenants; the non-rental promises contained in the lease could only be enforced by and against the original landlord and the original tenant. The benefit and burden of those promises ran

---

[97] For the exceptions, see ch.5 heading 'Express, implied and usual'.

[98] s.3 Real Property Act 1845. See ch.1 heading 'Formalities'.

[99] The action of waste provided a means for indirect enforcement of alteration and maintenance obligations: see ch.9 heading 'Waste'.

[100] See ch.9 heading 'Assumpsit'.

neither with the term nor with the reversion.[101]

In practice, this caused few problems. A written or part performed agreement for a long lease could be enforced, in equity, by an order for specific performance,[102] forcing the other party to execute the lease as a deed, and afterwards there would be the necessary covenant. Informal short leases, on the other hand, rarely contained 'stipulations of the nature of covenants'.[103]

The main concern of the landlord under a short, informal lease was the rent, and on a transfer of the reversion the new landlord could bring an action for the rent in debt, or, after 24th June 1738,[104] in assumpsit instead.[105]

But, in the nineteenth century, the courts developed an exception to the basic rule.[106] If the successor paid or accepted rent, the position changed; for that established 'a conventional law' between the parties by novation,[107] 'equivalent to that of . . . leases under seal',[108] and assumpsit would lie accordingly. In practical terms, that was essentially a back-door attornment, and so the position for informal leases appears to have been that non-rental rights and obligations would run only after an attornment, notwithstanding the general abolition of the need for an attornment in 1705.[109]

---

[101] *Standen* v. *Christmas* (1847) 10 QB 135, *Elliot* v. *Johnson* (1866) LR 2 QB 127.

[102] See ch.1 heading 'Formalities'.

[103] W.A. Holdsworth, *The Useful Library: The Law of Landlord and Tenant* (London, Routledge, 1863) 24.

[104] By s.14 Distress for Rent Act 1737 rent due under a lease not made by deed could be recovered by bringing the claim in assumpsit, for use and occupation, instead of in debt; the award being of an amount equivalent to the agreed rent, rather than of the rent itself: *Rennie* v. *Robinson* (1823) 1 Bing 147.

[105] See ch.9 heading 'Assumpsit'.

[106] The popular practical advice given 1863 was: 'A tenant from year to year may, like a lessee, assign his interest. But he must recollect that he will be liable for the rent; and also for any waste which the person whom he thus substitutes as tenant may commit. Unless he makes a profit rent by sub-letting he had better, if possible, get the landlord to discharge him from his tenancy, and to accept the new tenant in his place': W.A. Holdsworth, *The Useful Library: The Law of Landlord and Tenant* (London, Routledge, 1863) 119.

[107] *Buckworth* v. *Simpson* (1835) 1 C M & R 834, *Assignments of Leases not under Seal* (1877) 21 SJ 256.

[108] Per Willes J in *Cornish* v. *Stubbs* (1870) LR 5 CP 334, 339.

[109] s.9 Administration of Justice Act 1705.

Almost as soon as the exception was created, however, it was made largely redundant, for the Conveyancing Act 1881 brought all written leases within the Grantees of Reversions Act 1540,[110] and when the legislation was re-framed in 1925, oral leases were brought within the statutory scheme for reversion transfers too.[111] The 'conventional law' principle continued to apply on an assignment of the term of lease not under seal until 1996. But now, for 'new' leases under the Landlord and Tenant (Covenants) Act 1995, the only difference between the rules for enforcement of a non-rental obligation contained in a lease made by deed, and in one made otherwise, is the limitation period.[112]

4. Conditions.

The word 'condition' here, is used in its proper land law sense of a 'condition subsequent' (namely, a stipulation for the early determination of an estate on the occurrence of a forbidden event) rather than in its contractual sense of a promissory condition. The usual condition subsequent found in a lease is the landlord's right of re-entry in the event of breach of the tenant's covenants or on the tenant's insolvency.

Littleton, writing in the fifteenth century, said:[113]

If a man letteth land to another for a term of life, rendering to the lessor and his heirs a certain rent, and for default of payment re-enter, and if afterwards the lessor granteth the reversion in the land to another in fee and the tenant for life attorn, if the rent be behind the grantee of the reversion may distrain for the rent, but he may not enter into the land and oust the tenant, as the lessor might do, or his heirs. But if the lessor be allowed to enter and oust the tenant, then he would be remitted to his former estate,

---

[110] *Weg Motors* v. *Hales* [1962] 1 Ch 49, 73–76 held that the word 'covenant' in s.142 was not limited to covenants under seal, but included all written contractual promises. The point had been left in doubt in *Wedd* v. *Porter* [1916] 2 KB 91 and *Barnes* v. *City of London Real Property Co* [1918] 2 Ch 18, 34.

[111] s.154 Law of Property Act 1925, 'other tenancy'.

[112] The limitation period is 12 years if the promise is made by deed: s.8 Limitation Act 1980. Otherwise, it is six years: s.5 Limitation Act 1980.

[113] s.347.

which he should not do since he has parted with it. Therefore, the entry is taken away for ever'.

In other words, in Littleton's time, a voluntary transfer of the reversion destroyed the landlord's right to re-enter: the original landlord could not enter, being no longer the landlord, and the new landlord could not enter, because the condition only ran for the benefit of heirs taking by descent on the death of the landlord,[114] and not purchasers.[115] Even if the rent had been reserved to 'the lessor, his heirs and assigns' the result would have been the same, because of the rule that seisin was the basis of title, and that, in order to recover seisin, a disseisee had to allege that he or an ancestor of his had been disseised.[116] The grantor, to whom the right of re-entry had been reserved, would not have been an 'ancestor' of a grantee seeking to exercise the right. Coke made a different point, at the beginning of the seventeenth century, when he said that no rights of entry or re-entry could be granted over, for they were personal and non-assignable, and the reason for this was to prevent maintenance.[117]

The rule only applied to a true condition subsequent giving the landlord a right of entry. It did not apply to a 'limitation' on the length on the estate.[118] A lease could be limited so that the tenant was never granted anything more than the right to enjoy it until the happening of a particular event, upon the happening of which it would determine automatically[119]—for instance, a letting for five

---

[114] Christopher St.Germain, writing in 1518, said that an heir could only re-enter for non-payment of rent falling due in the ancestor's lifetime, if the ancestor had demanded it before his death: *Doctor and Student* 58.

[115] Statham's *Abridgment* (1447/8) 'Assigne' pl.3. It was said in *Ernley* v. *Garth*, (1490) YB 5 Hen.8 f.18 pl.12, that it would be repugnant to the grant of the reversion if the grantee could enlarge the grant by exercising the condition.

[116] S. Thorne, *Sir Edward Coke 1552–1952* (Selden Society Annual Lecture 1952).

[117] *Co.Litt.* 214b.

[118] *Chedington's case* (1598) 1 Co.Rep 153b, Holdsworth, *HEL* vol. 7 84.

[119] In *Fish* v. *Bellamy* (1605) Cro Jac 71 a proviso for re-entry on death was agreed to be a condition rather than a limitation. But in *Lady Baltinglass's Case* (1671) 1 Freeman 23, the words 'so long as he pays the rent' were held to create a limitation, and not a condition. In *Colthirst* v. *Bejushin* (1550) Plowden 20, Hinde J said (32a): 'for no words make a condition, unless such as restrain the thing given, as upon condition that he shall not do such an act, or the like; but these

years or until a debt was repaid, whichever was earlier[120]—rather than giving the landlord a right of premature determination,[121] and there was never any difficulty in a purchaser of a reversion enforcing limitations of that nature,[122] even though the difference was only a matter of form rather than substance.

For conditions which did depend on an entry, the law was changing, even before the Grantees of Reversions Act 1540 expressly changed it. It had already been accepted that conditions implied as a matter of law[123] might run with the reversion,[124] and in 1599 the court thought that it had always been the law that a condition for non-payment of rent in a parol lease ran with the reversion at common law.[125]

By s.1 Grantees of Reversions Act 1540, all conditions against 'rent waste and other forfeiture' were expressly annexed to the reversion.[126] In 1612, the Act was held not to apply to a copyhold reversion.[127] But by 1691, it did.[128]

An attornment was still necessary, however, before the condition could be exercised, in all those cases where an attornment was necessary in order to bring an action for rent or to enforce a covenant,[129] and the statute only passed the right to forfeit for a condition broken after the transfer of the reversion. It was not until 1912 that the new reversioner also automatically[130] acquired the right to forfeit for events which had occurred before the transfer.[131]

---

words limit the time when the remainder shall commence, and do not restrain the thing given, and therefore may not be called a condition, but rather a limitation'. See also Challis, *Real Property* 260–261 and *Co.Litt.* 214b, 234b.

[120] A condition against bankruptcy probably originally fell into this category too: *Doe d. Mitchinson* v. *Carter* (1798) 8 Term Rep 57, 300.

[121] *Bl.Comm.* Bk.II 155, Challis, *Real Property,* 261.

[122] *Brett* v. *Cumberland* (1616) 1 Rol Reps 359, 360. See also *Co.Litt.* 214b.

[123] For example, the implied right of re-entry against a tenant for life who purported to grant over a greater estate; *Co.Litt.* 215a. See ch.7 heading 'Forfeiture'.

[124] *Wedd* v. *Porter* [1916] 2 KB 91, 101.

[125] *Davy* v. *Matthew* (1599) Cro Eliz 649.

[126] It did not apply to every condition. The words 'other forfeiture' were construed *eiusdem generis* with 'rent' and 'waste'.

[127] *Beal* v. *Brasier* (1612) Cro Jac 305.

[128] *Glover* v. *Cope* (1691) 4 Mod. 80.

[129] *Mallory's case* (1600) 5 Co.Rep 111b. See the heading 'Rent and attornment' ante.

[130] A right of entry was made assignable by s.6 Real Property Act 1845. See now s.1(2)(e) Law of Property Act 1925.

[131] s.2 Conveyancing Act 1911.

That change in the law made a certain amount of sense at the time, for the right to sue for arrears of rent passed automatically too,[132] unless expressly assigned back. But now that the rule for 'new' leases under the Landlord and Tenant (Covenants) Act 1995 is that those rights do not pass automatically, it is anomalous that the right to forfeit for them still does.[133]

5. Severance of parcels.

There are two ways in which an estate in land might be severed. It might be severed in time, by granting a shorter estate out of it, leaving a reversion in the grantor. Or it might be severed in space, by separating it into two or more physical parcels, held by different owners. This section of this chapter deals with physical severance of the parcels in space. The next two sections after that deal with severance in time.

By the beginning of the seventeenth century, it was already clear that rent would be apportionable, at common law, if the reversion was severed in space, as the result of some rule of law, rather than by the landlord's own voluntary act.[134] Soon afterwards, it was clear that the same rule would apply on a voluntary severance,[135] notwithstanding earlier doubts.[136] The logic was that, even on a voluntary severance of the reversion, the tenant would not be prejudiced beyond inconvenience, since the total amount of rent which the tenant would be obliged to pay would remain the

---

[132] *Re King, Robinson* v. *Gray* [1963] Ch 459. That said, when the change was made in 1912, the law was thought to be that arrears of rent did not pass on a conveyance of the reversion, unless expressly assigned: *Lewis* v. *Ridge* (1601) Cro Eliz 863, *Midgleys* v. *Lovelace* (1693) 12 Mod. 45, *Canham* v. *Rust* (1818) 8 Taunt 227.

[133] s.4.

[134] *Anon* (1613) 1 Rol Abr 237 pl.5, Platt, *Leases*, vol. 2 131. Where the letting was of land and chattels (eg. a flock of sheep) the whole rent went with the land, and there could be no apportionment on a grant over of the reversion: *Read* v. *Lawsne* (1562) Dyer 212b, Dalison's Reps (1554) 124 SS 70 pl.31.

[135] *Co.Litt.* 148a, *Ardes* v. *Watkins* (1599) Cro Eliz 637, 651, *Swansea* v. *Thomas* (1882) 10 QB 48, Platt, *Leases*, vol. 2 133, cf. (1587) Gouldsborough 44 pl.24.

[136] In 1553 Sergeant Bennoes suggested that a voluntary severance of a rent would destroy it, in the same way as it would destroy a right of re-entry: *Co.Litt.* 148a.

same.[137]

But there was no reason for allowing a tenant,[138] who had agreed to pay the whole rent, to reduce the extent of that obligation, by the tenant's own voluntary act. Consequently, no apportionment of rent was possible on a voluntary[139] severance of the parcels in the term. The tenant of each part continued to be liable to pay the whole rent,[140] and the landlord could distrain on each part for the whole.[141]

At the beginning of the nineteenth century, it was settled that the same principles applied to covenants. In 1813, in *Palmer* v. *Edwards*,[142] it was held that an assignee of part of the term could bring an action on the covenants contained in the lease against the landlord. That was confirmed in 1818, in *Twynam* v. *Pickard*,[143] which decided that an action in covenant could be brought both by and against an assignee of part of the property. Thereafter, the courts applied the same principle to covenants running with the reversion and the term as already applied to rent; namely, that the whole burden of an obligation attached to a voluntarily severed estate could be enforced against each part, but the owner of a severed part could only enforce a proportionate part of the benefit of the covenant or promise. So, in *Swansea* v. *Thomas*,[144] it was held that an assignee of part of the reversion could recover an apportioned part of the rent due under a covenant to pay rent. There was a special rule however if the covenant, by its nature, only

---

[137] If the two landlords agreed the apportionment between themselves, that would not bind the tenant. The tenant was entitled to insist on an apportionment by value, to be determined by the court: Platt, *Leases*, vol. 2 146. See now s.9 Landlord and Tenant (Covenants) Act 1995.

[138] On voluntary severance of 'lands holden in fee simple', any services owed to a superior lord were apportionable by the Statute of Quia Emptores 1290, Coke, *2nd Inst.* 502–504. There was no corresponding provision for a tenant for life or for years.

[139] On an involuntary severance, there could not be an apportionment in favour of a direct covenantee, but there could be in favour of someone liable as the current tenant only by reason of privity of estate: *Stevenson* v. *Lambard* (1801) 2 East 575.

[140] *Broom* v. *Hore* (1598) Cro Eliz 633. 'The act of the lessee shall not divide the action of the lessors': *Ipswich* v. *Martin* (1616) Cro Jac 411.

[141] *Rushden's Case* (1532) Dyer 4b, Dalison's Reps (1554) 124 SS 70 pl.30, *Broom* v. *Hore* (1598) Cro Eliz 633, *Whitham* v. *Bullock* [1939] 2 KB 81.

[142] (1813) 1 Douglas 187.

[143] (1818) 2 Barn & Ald 105.

[144] (1882) 10 QB 48.

applied to a particular part of the property. If so, no action on that covenant could be brought by or against a successor in title to the other part.[145]

None of that applied to conditions. The provisions of the Grantees of Reversions Act 1540, which allowed conditions to run with the reversion, did not apply if the landlord severed the parcels which comprised the reversion upon the lease.[146] The rule at common law remained that if a landlord[147] voluntarily[148] severed the parcels which comprised the reversion upon the lease, that destroyed the condition.[149] It was not until the enactment of s.3 Law of Property (Amendment) Act 1859 that the rule was reversed, in part, so as to allow a transferee of part to take advantage of the condition. That was extended to preserve the condition in favour of the transferor's retained part too, by s.12 Conveyancing Act 1881. But, whether the condition was exercised by the owner of the transferred part or of the retained part, it destroyed the whole lease, until 1926, when, by s.140(2) Law of Property Act 1925, it became possible to exercise the condition against the demised land within the severed part alone, subject to the tenant's right to elect to treat it as applying to the whole. Now, for 'new' leases, by s.4 Landlord and Tenant (Covenants) Act 1995, the benefit of a condition is annexed to 'the whole, and to each and every part of the reversion', and passes on an assignment of 'the whole or any part' of the

---

[145] In *Congham* v. *King* (1632) Cro Car 221 it was held that the burden of covenant to repair property that included a house was divisible, and followed the house. For leases granted since 1st January 1996, if the owner of the retained part and the owner of the severed part agree the apportionment of any covenant, it is possible to apply to the court to make that binding on the person who has the benefit of the covenant: ss.9–10 Landlord and Tenant (Covenants) Act 1995.

[146] *Co.Litt.* 215a, *Sir Richard Lee & Arnold's Case* (circa 1585–1588) 4 Leon 27, *Knight's Case* (1588) 5 Co.Rep 54b, 3 Salk 48. This included severing the parcels by accepting a surrender of part of the property comprised in the lease: *Rawlyns' Case* (1587) 4 Co.Rep 52a–b.

[147] There was an exception where the landlord was the Crown: *Knight's Case* (1588) 5 Co.Rep 54b.

[148] Where the severance was by operation of law, the condition was severed by operation of law too: *Piggott* v. *Middlesex County Council* [1909] 1 Ch 134.

[149] *Winter's Case* (1572) Dyer 308b, *Liddy* v. *Kennedy* (1871) LR 5 HL 134, 143. In Ireland, the rule was reversed by s.12 Landlord and Tenant Law Amendment Act (Ireland) 1860.

reversion in the demised premises. The tenant retains the right to elect to a treat any exercise of the right as applying to the whole lease.

6. Underletting.

The term of a lease is severed in time by granting an underlease for a shorter term[150] out of it. There being no privity of contract or estate between a landlord and an undertenant,[151] it was never suggested that a landlord might be able to bring an action in debt against an undertenant in order to recover the head-rent. In 1779, after some disagreement, the Court of King's Bench decided, in *Holford* v. *Hatch*,[152] that the burden of a covenant to pay the head-rent did not run so as to be enforceable against an undertenant either. Lord Mansfield said:

> For some time, we had great doubts, we have bestowed a great deal of consideration on the subject, and looked carefully into the books, and it is clearly settled; (and it is agreeable to the text of Littleton) that the action cannot be maintained unless against an assignee of the whole term.

It had already been decided, in 1682, that there was no equitable obligation on an undertenant to pay the headrent, except perhaps where the headtenant had become insolvent.[153] The existence of any such exception was denied in 1855,[154] at the same time as the consequences of insolvency were becoming increasingly regulated by statute.[155]

It remained the case that a landlord could not bring an action on

---

[150] For what counts as a shorter term, see ch.2 heading 'Underletting'.

[151] *Anon* (1490) YB 5 Hen.7 f.18 pl.12, *Rushden's Case* (1532) Dyer 4b, Simpson, *History of the Common Law of Contract*, 85. But see now s.6 Law of Distress (Amendment) Act 1908 and ch.3 heading 'Distress and replevin'.

[152] (1779) 1 Douglas 183.

[153] *Goddard* v. *Keate* (1682) 1 Vern 87, *Clavering* v. *Westley* (1735) 3 Peere Wms 402, H. Bullow, ed. J. Fonblanque, *A Treatise on Equity*, 5th edn. vol. 1 (London, Clarke, 1820) 358, Platt, *Covenants*, 295.

[154] *Walters* v. *Northern Coal Mining Co* (1855) 5 De G M & G 629.

[155] See ch.8 heading 'Bankruptcy and personal insolvency' and 'Corporate winding up and dissolution'.

any of the promises contained in the lease against a sub-tenant down to the middle of the nineteenth century, when as a result of the decision in *Tulk* v. *Moxhay*,[156] negative stipulations about the use of the demised premises in written leases became enforceable, in equity, against sub-tenants. There was the usual exception for a bona fide purchaser of a legal estate without notice, and a sub-tenant at a rent was a purchaser of a legal estate.[157] So restrictions in the headlease could not be enforced against a sub-tenant, unless the sub-tenant had actual or constructive notice of the restriction at the time the sub-lease was granted.[158] But otherwise the absence of privity of estate was no objection to the enforcement of the restriction, for it could be enforced against even a mere occupier.[159]

If the restriction is contained in a lease which was granted after 1925, and the lease remains outside the registered system,[160] then its enforceability against a sub-tenant still depends on the pure doctrine of notice,[161] because restrictive covenants between landlord and tenant are not registrable under the Land Charges Act 1972.[162] In the case of a registrable lease, registration takes the place of notice. A sub-tenant takes subject to all restrictive covenants contained in a registered lease.

In practice, however, landlords have only ever attempted to enforce covenants directly against sub-tenants where the terms of the headlease are onerous. Where there has been any value in the headlease, landlords have elected to forfeit instead; for it has always been the law that the exercise of a condition subsequent determines all derivative estates. So when a lease is forfeited for breach of a covenant or condition contained in the lease, all sub-leases fall with it automatically, and the landlord's 'former estate' is restored.[163]

---

[156] (1838) 2 Ph 774.
[157] Eq.Ca.Abr. vol. 1 353.
[158] *South of England Dairies Ltd* v. *Baker* [1906] 2 Ch 631, 638.
[159] *Mander* v. *Falcke* [1891] 2 Ch 555.
[160] See ch.1 heading 'Registration'.
[161] As modified by s.199 Law of Property Act 1925.
[162] s.2(5).
[163] Littleton, *Tenures*, ss.325-326. There are various statutory exceptions to this: e.g. s.137 Rent Act 1977, s.18 Housing Act 1988.

7. Concurrent letting.

The reversion upon a lease is severed in time by granting a concurrent lease out of the reversion.[164] There was never any doubt that the grant of a concurrent lease, in so far as a concurrent lease could be created at all,[165] would take effect as an assignment of the reversion upon the prior lease, and consequently the concurrent tenant would become entitled to the rent reserved by that prior lease, subject to an attornment, where necessary.[166]

Although the Grantees of Reversions Act 1540 did not apply on a severance of the reversioner's parcels, it did apply on a severance of the reversioner's estate. Consequently, after 1540 a concurrent tenant could enforce the tenant's covenants contained in a prior occupational lease.[167] Before 1792 it had already been decided, in *Leonard's Case*,[168] that conditions ran on the grant of a concurrent lease, though mere contractual promises contained in parol leases remained outside the statutory scheme until the late nineteenth century.[169]

The position now, however, is more complicated. The Landlord and Tenant (Covenants) Act 1995 was an unhappy compromise between a government, under political pressure to abrogate original tenant liability, and a powerful property industry, desperate to preserve the status quo, so far as possible. The unfortunate result was that the provisions dealing with concurrent leases were not properly thought out. The grant of a concurrent lease after 1995 is no longer treated as an assignment of the reversion upon the prior lease.[170] Instead, the concurrent landlord and the concurrent tenant (as immediate reversioner) together have the benefit and burden of

---

[164] A reversionary lease does not become a concurrent lease until its term has commenced, and then only if it is still subject to a prior occupational lease.
[165] See ch.2 heading 'Concurrent Leases'.
[166] See the heading 'Rent and attornment' ante.
[167] *Co.Litt.* 215a, *Attoe* v. *Hemmings* (1792) 2 Bulstrode 281.
[168] A common pleas case referred to by Coke CJ in *Attoe* v. *Hemmings* but not reported. This is probably a different case from the *Lernard's case* in 1582/3, which the editor of Dyer searched for in vain: Platt, *Leases*, vol. 2 253.
[169] See the heading 'Contractual promises' ante.
[170] s.28(5), s.3.

the covenants and conditions contained in the occupational lease.[171]

8. Tenant and former tenant.

There was never any doubt that rent could be reserved to the outgoing tenant, on an assignment of a lease for life, since a lease for life was a freehold estate, and rent could be reserved, either as a rent seck or as a rent charge, on a conveyance of a freehold estate. It was a rent charge if a power to levy distress was reserved expressly, and otherwise a rent seck.[172] After 1731, when it became possible to distrain for rents seck,[173] there was no longer any practical difference between a rent seck and a rent charge, although it was not possible to bring an action in debt for either before the lease ended until 1710,[174] for the obligation to pay rent was treated as a single whole obligation, rather than an obligation to pay by separate instalments.

The rule was different for periodic sums reserved on an assignment of a leasehold estate. Each instalment could be recovered from the assignee as soon as it became due in debt,[175] or in covenant if the assignee had executed the assignment as a deed. But these sums were not truly rent, since a rent cannot be reserved out of an assignment of a leasehold estate.[176] They were simply personal debts of the assignee.[177] The outgoing tenant could not levy distress for them[178] even after 1731, except by reserving a

---

[171] s.15(2). Even then, it only makes sense if 'reversioner' in s.15(1) means the concurrent landlord.

[172] See ch.3 heading 'Rent reservation'.

[173] s.5 Landlord and Tenant Act 1730.

[174] s.4 Landlord and Tenant Act 1709, Holdsworth, *HEL* vol. 7 263.

[175] *Wilston* v. *Pilkney* (1673) 1 Vent 242, 3 Keb 131, *Cartwright* v. *Pinkney* (1675) 1 Vent 272, *Loyd* v. *Langford* (1677) 2 Mod. 174.

[176] *Brediman* v. *Bromley* (1606) Cro Jac 142, *Langford* v. *Selmes* (1857) 3 K & J 220. See ch.3 heading 'Rent reservation'.

[177] The obiter dictum in *Newcomb* v. *Harvey* ((1690) Carthew 161, 162) that, on a further assignment of the lease, the new tenant would become liable to pay these sums, was plainly wrong.

[178] Brook's Abridgment, 'Dette' pl.39: 'If a man hath a term for years, and grants all his estate of the term, rendering rent, he cannot distrain'. See also *Lewis* v. *Baker* [1905] 1 Ch 46.

special power to do so,[179] which would not be binding on future assignees.

The obligation to make the payments could, however, be secured by annexing a power of re-entry to the assignment, for there was never any doubt that a right of re-entry could be annexed to an assignment, giving the assignor the right to forfeit the assignment,[180] although, since 1926, it has only been possible to annex such a right in equity.[181]

Anyone taking an assignment of a lease of unregistered land faces a particular problem: there is no means of finding out whether the landlord had title to grant the lease in the first place. As Lord Eldon observed in *Browning* v. *Wright*:[182]

> With regard to many estates in this town, held under the Duke of Bedford and the Duke of Portland, it would be next to impossible to show any thing but the lease itself; the vendors could not produce the muniments of their estates which are deposited in the family chests of those noblemen. It sometimes happens, therefore, that parties require covenants in assignments of this kind of property which are not required in conveyances of freeholds; such as an absolute covenant that the vendor holds a valid and indefeasible lease.

An early example of this is *Gainsford* v. *Griffith*.[183] But it was more usual, from the eighteenth century onwards, for the assigning tenant simply to covenant that the lease was still extant and vested in the tenant, and that the rent had been paid and all the covenants had been performed,[184] so that the risk that the landlord never had title to grant the lease would pass to the assignee. These standard covenants for title given by an assigning tenant were reduced to statutory form in 1881,[185] which annexed the benefit of those covenants to the term, so that future tenants could enforce them

---

[179] Platt, *Leases*, vol. 2 83.
[180] Littleton, *Tenures*, s.325, *Co.Litt.* 202b, *Southwall* v. *Huddleston* (1524) Port's Notebook 102 SS 90, *Doe d. Freeman* v. *Bateman* (1818) 2 Barn & Ald 168.
[181] *Shiloh Spinners* v. *Harding* [1973] AC 691.
[182] (1799) 2 Bos & Pul 13, 23.
[183] (1667) 1 Wms Saund 58.
[184] Stewart, *Practice of Conveyancing*, 93. Under an open contract, the purchaser could require the vendor to prove the title: Platt, *Leases* vol. 1 618.
[185] s.7(B) Conveyancing Act 1881.

against the original covenantor.[186] The standard covenants for title on an assignment of a lease are now found in ss.2 and 4 Law of Property (Miscellaneous) Provisions Act 1994.

In return, it was usual to require the assignee to give an indemnity for the future payment of the rent and performance of the covenants.[187] This was so even before it became common to include an express covenant to pay the rent in the lease.[188] Furthermore, the incoming tenant would be obliged to give an indemnity under an open contract even if the assignor was not giving any covenant for title.[189] As late as 1833, it was not the invariable practice for the terms of the indemnity to extend beyond the period during which the lease was vested in the assignee,[190] but by 1925 an indemnity for the remainder of the term of the lease had become a standard implied covenant.[191] Those indemnity covenants are not, however, generally implied into an assignment of a lease granted after 1995.[192]

No indemnity covenant was given by the assignee in *Burnett* v. *Lynch*.[193] Nonetheless, it was held that the assignee owed an implied duty to the assignor to perform all the covenants in the lease, after the assignment.[194] In *Hancock* v. *Caffyn*[195] Tindal CJ described this as an 'implied duty on an assignee to perform all the

---

[186] s.7(6).

[187] W. West, *Simboleograph* (London, Stationers Co., 1610) pt.1 s.453, *The Compleat Clerk*, 3rd edn. (London, Place, 1671) 67, 95, *Mayor* v. *Steward* (1769) 4 Burr 2439. See generally Platt, *Covenants*, 177–182, Platt, *Leases*, vol. 2 428.

[188] See ch.5 heading 'To pay rent'.

[189] *Staines* v. *Morris* (1812) 1 Ves & B 8. An oral agreement to provide an indemnity could be enforced in equity, even after execution of the assignment: *Pember* v. *Mathers* (1779) 1 Brown CC 52.

[190] *Wolveridge* v. *Stewart* (1833) 2 Cr & Mees 644, 659. The only indemnity covenant in Stewart, *Practice of Conveyancing* (1827) was a full indemnity covenant, 95. See also Platt, *Covenants* 77–78.

[191] s.77(1)(C) Law of Property Act 1925. s.24 Land Registration Act 1925 for registered leases.

[192] s.14 Landlord and Tenant (Covenants) Act 1995. Normally, an indemnity covenant is not needed because a lawful assignment discharges the liability of the outgoing tenant, but an indemnity might still be required on an unlawful assignment.

[193] (1826) 5 Barn & Cr 589.

[194] See also *In Re Healing Research Trustee* [1992] 2 EGLR 231.

[195] (1832) 8 Bing 358, 1 Moo & S 521.

covenants of the lease under which he holds',[196] and the analysis of this as an independent duty, owed by the person holding the lease for the time being, was supported by two subsequent decisions of the Exchequer Chamber: in *Wolveridge* v. *Stewart*[197] the original tenant's claim against the next assignee failed, because the lease had already been assigned on to someone else; whereas in *Moule* v. *Garrett*[198] the original tenant's claim against the ultimate assignee holding the lease succeeded, notwithstanding that there had been various intermediate assignments.

Later cases, however, have treated this not so much as an implied duty which comes from holding property, but rather as a species of subrogation. A former tenant, who is forced to pay the landlord's claim, is entitled to be subrogated to the landlord's rights against all subsequent assignees and sureties.[199]

Neither analysis is without its difficulties. Subrogation can explain why a sub-tenant who pays the head-rent in order to prevent a forfeiture or distress is entitled to be reimbursed by the head tenant,[200] but it cannot explain why a sub-tenant of part, who does so, has a right of contribution against the other sub-tenants.[201] Subrogation can also produce capricious results. For example, an original tenant under an old lease might, or might not, be subrogated to the landlord's rights against intermediate tenants, who have given the landlord a direct covenant in the usual terms,[202] depending upon whether the landlord has chosen to serve the necessary statutory notice on them in time.[203] But if the duty is one that is owed simply as a result of holding property, then that does not give the original tenant a route by which to recover against the ultimate tenant's surety, which justice plainly requires.

---

[196] cf. per Parke B in *Humble* v. *Langston* (1841) 7 M&W 517, 530: the original tenant is 'liable in the nature of a surety as between himself and the assignee'.
[197] 3 Moo & Sc 561.
[198] (1872) LR 7 Ex 101.
[199] *In Re Downer* [1974] 1 WLR 1460, *Becton Dickinson* v. *Zwebner* [1989] 1 QB 208. See also *Exall* v. *Partridge* (1799) 8 Term Rep 308, where a stranger, who was compelled to pay the rent in order to recover his distrained goods, recovered over against the original tenants, who remained liable to the landlord for the rent in covenant, and not merely against the ultimate assignee.
[200] *Ahearne* v. *M'Swinney* (1874) IR 8 CL 568.
[201] *Webber* v. *Smith* (1689) 2 Vern 103.
[202] See above heading 'Covenants'.
[203] s.17 Landlord and Tenant (Covenants) Act 1995.

In short, neither analysis is entirely satisfactory, and the only solution lies in some broader restitutionary theory.[204]

---

[204] *Moses* v. *Macfarlan* (1760) 2 Burr 1005.

CHAPTER 7
Termination

1. Expiry

2. Surrender and merger

3. Enlargement

4. Forfeiture

5. Relief from forfeiture

6. Estoppel and denial of title

7. Repudiation and frustration

8. Fixtures

9. Emblements

10. Compensation on quitting

This chapter is about the end of the lease.

It is about the various ways and means of ending it, and the consequences which follow when it has been brought to an end.[1]

---

[1] Statutory security of tenure is dealt with in ch.4.

1. Expiry.

A lease expires when it ends by effluxion of time.

A lease for life, before 1926,[2] was a freehold estate which determined automatically on the death of the individual upon whose life it depended. This was an exception to the rule that the law could take no account of fractions of a day. The lease ended at the very moment of death, rather than at midnight at the end of that day.[3]

In medieval England's agricultural economy, there was rarely any doubt about whether and when a property owner had died. But the increasing dispersal of the population, following the expansion of international trade and the colonisation of the New World in the sixteenth century, made those rare cases increasingly common. A statutory presumption of death, after an absence of seven years, was introduced by the Cestui Que Vie Act 1666,[4] and in 1707 it became possible to obtain an order, requiring someone positively to prove that the relevant individual was still alive, by personal attendance before the Chancellor, or by affidavit and examination abroad.[5]

Tenants for life under family settlements were often granted special powers to make sub-leases which would be binding on the reversioner,[6] and a reversioner could make an otherwise invalid sub-lease binding by deed of confirmation.[7] But absent any such power or confirmation, or if the power was not exercised properly, any sub-lease granted by a tenant for life would determine automatically on the death of the tenant for life,[8] at exactly the same moment.[9]

---

[2] s.149 Law of Property Act 1925.

[3] *Roe* v. *Hersey* (1771) 3 Wils 274. The tenant's executor (or the tenant, in the case of a lease pur autre vie) was allowed a reasonable time for removing any chattels: *Stodden* v. *Harvey* (1608) Cro Jac 204.

[4] ss.1-2. Coote, *Leases*, 30. For Ireland, 7 Wm.3 c.8 (Ir) (1695).

[5] ss.1-4 Cestui Que Vie Act 1707. In 1582/3 an order was made in Chancery forcing someone who claimed to be a tenant, to set down upon his oath, whether his lease was expired or not: '12 Answers', Tothill, 7 pl.1.

[6] See ch.1 heading 'Capacity' sub-heading 'tenants for life'.

[7] Littleton, *Tenures*, s.516, s.66 Law of Property Act 1925.

[8] (1532/3) Brook's New Cases pl.54 (generally), *Smith* v. *Widlake* (1877) 3 CPD 10.

[9] An agricultural sub-tenant, caught by this trap, could claim emblements; that is, a right to enter the land and reap any annual crop notwithstanding the termination of

There was a similar problem where a fee tail owner granted a lease, and died without barring the entail. If the lease was not granted in accordance with the power contained in the Enabling Act 1540,[10] then it would be voidable by the issue in tail, or (if the entail became extinct) void against the fee simple owner to whom the land would revert.

Since 1926, however, a lease for life at a rent or granted for a premium has automatically taken effect as a lease for a term of 90 years, subject to a right for the landlord to determine it on one month's notice, to expire on a quarter day after the relevant death.[11]

It was always the law that a tenancy for a fixed term of years expired automatically, without the need for any intervention of the parties, when that term came to an end. Hence there was never any need to serve a notice to quit to cause a fixed term to expire at common law.[12] The statutory exceptions where the tenant has security of tenure are discussed in chapter 4.

By contrast, a notice to quit is needed in order to cause a periodic tenancy to expire. The rules about the length of the notice required, who could give it, and on whom it could be served, all have their origins in the late eighteenth century, when the concept of a periodic tenancy was first recognised.[13]

---

the sub-tenancy: see below heading 'Emblements'. But as agricultural techniques became more sophisticated in the nineteenth century this proved increasingly unsatisfactory, and so s.1 Landlord and Tenant Act 1851 provided that a sub-tenancy at a rack rent would instead continue to the end of the year. That was changed to expiry at the end of a twelve month notice to quit, for agricultural land, by s.14 Agriculture Act 1920. See ch.4 heading 'Agricultural security'.

[10] See ch.1 heading 'Capacity' sub-heading 'tenant in tail'.

[11] s.149(6) Law of Property Act 1925.

[12] *Messenger* v. *Armstrong* (1785) 1 Term Rep 53, *Right d. Flower* v. *Darby* (1786) 1 Term Rep 159, Cole, *Ejectment* (London, Sweet, 1857) 36.

[13] By way of exception, in *Taylor* v. *Seed* (1696) Comberbach 383, Skin 649, the court upheld a special custom in London that six months' notice would be given to terminate a tenancy at a rent of 40s pa. or more and that three months' notice would be given to terminate tenancies at lower rents. The assertion in *Throgmorton d. Wandby* v. *Whelpdale* (1769) Buller NP 96, that the requirement to give a half year's notice to quit was as old as Henry VIII's time, is incorrect as a matter of law, although it might well have reflected the practice, for by s.18 Distress for Rent Act 1737 a penalty of double rent was imposed, on tenants who held over, after having given 'notice of his, her or their intention to quit the premises by him, her or them holden, at a time mentioned in the such notice'. Adams, *Action in Ejectment,* 4th American edn. (New York, Banks Gould & Co,

The starting point was a dictum of Wilmot J in 1765, that reasonable notice was needed to terminate a tenancy from year to year, which could vary according to the custom of different counties.[14] By 1769, he had been elevated to Chief Justice of the King's Bench, and was able to carry the whole court with him, when he resolved that what was actually required in the case of an annual tenancy was half a year's notice.[15] Subsequent decisions made it clear that the notice must expire on the the anniversary of the tenancy,[16] whatever the nature of the land,[17] except where there was some special local custom as to the expiry date.[18] That was changed to 12 months notice, in the case of annual lettings of agricultural land, by s.33 Agricultural Holdings Act 1883.[19] For shorter periodic tenancies, however, well into the Victorian period it was thought that the length of the notice required varied according to local custom,[20] and whilst notice equivalent to the length of the period of the tenancy was generally sufficient,[21] even as late as 1911 it was not entirely clear that this had become a fixed rule.[22] It was only confirmed as fixed rule by the decision in *Precious* v.

1854) 146 notes: 'It is singular that we do not find in the old authorities any decisions relative to notices to quit, although the practice of giving them has been long established'.

[14] *Timmins* v. *Rowlinson* (1765) 3 Bur 1603, 1609. Blackstone, writing in 1766, caught the change, and tacked onto a passage about emblements the comment that 'reasonable notice' was now required to terminate a periodic tenancy: *Bl.Comm.* Bk.II 147. *Gulliver d. Tasker* v. *Burr* (1766) 1 Wm. Black 596 decided that reasonable notice was needed even where the tenant had died during the term. See also *Doe d. Dagget* v. *Snowden* (1778) 2 Wm.Black 1224 and cf. *MacKay* v. *Mackreth* (1785) 4 Doug 213.

[15] *Parker d. Walker* v. *Constable* (1769) 3 Wils KB 25, *Barlow* v. *Teal* (1885) 15 QBD 501. See ch.4 heading 'Agricultural security'.

[16] *Roe d. Brown* v. *Wilkinson* (1774) cited in *Co.Litt.* 270b.fn (1), *Wilkinson* v. *Calvert* (1878) 3 CPD 360, 365.

[17] *Right d. Flower* v. *Darby* (1786) 1 Term Rep 159.

[18] *Roe d. Henderson* v. *Charnock* (1790) Peake 6.

[19] For agricultural holdings governed by the Agricultural Holdings Act 1986, that remains the general rule: s.25. For farm business tenancies governed by the Agricultural Tenancies Act 1995 there is an additional rule. The notice must not be given more than 24 months before its expiry date: s.6.

[20] W.A. Holdsworth, *The Useful Library: The Law of Landlord and Tenant* (London, Ruttledge, 1863) 30.

[21] *Doe d. Parry* v. *Hazell* (1794) 1 Esp 94.

[22] J.Williams, *The Law of Ejectment*, 2nd edn. (London, Sweet & Maxwell, 1911) 39–40.

Reedie.[23]

A statutory requirement of a minimum of 28 days notice for residential tenancies was first introduced by s.16 Rent Act 1957.[24]

In 1805 Lord Ellenborough decided that a notice to quit received by one joint tenant, would take effect as if it had been received by them all,[25] and that seems to have settled the point.[26] The question of whether a single joint tenant could give a notice to quit, which would take effect as if it had been given by the others too, remained open for much longer. It was assumed, in 1820, that all of them would have to join in giving the notice,[27] but ten years later it was said that, since the tenancy was a springing interest[28] which could only continue for so long as each joint tenant agreed, a notice to quit given by one of them alone would be sufficient,[29] and this view ultimately prevailed.[30] Those rules, of course, did not apply before 1926, where the letting was by tenants in common, or by one or more joint tenants of their undivided shares; for in those cases, there were separate lettings by each of them of their own interests, which could be determined independently of each other.[31]

A notice to quit has proprietary effect from the moment when it is served. It conclusively fixes the end date of the tenancy as a piece of property, and nothing which the parties do afterwards can

---

[23] [1924] 2 KB 149.

[24] See now s.5 Protection from Eviction Act 1977.

[25] *Doe d. Macartney* v. *Crick* (1805) 5 Esp. 196. Espinasse's reports, especially the later ones, are notoriously unreliable, and the ratio explained in the marginal note of this case is, in fact, the exact opposite of that to be deduced from Lord Ellenborough's judgment. Had the brothers in that case been tenants in common, the notice to quit would have been bad. But Espinasse was himself counsel for the brothers, so it is likely that the report contains a fairly accurate summary of what Lord Ellenborough actually said, notwithstanding the error in the marginal note. It had already been decided, in *Tooker's Case* (1600) 2 Co.Rep 66b, that an attornment by one joint tenant bound the other.

[26] The objection that the notice had only been given to one of the tenants was abandoned in *Doe d. Bradford* v. *Watkins* (1806) 7 East.551.

[27] *Goodtitle d. King* v. *Woodward* (1820) 3 Barn & Ald 689.

[28] See ch.4 heading 'Periodic'.

[29] *Doe d. Aslin* v. *Summersett* (1830) 1 Barn & Ad 135, 140.

[30] *Hammersmith & Fulham LBC* v. *Monk* [1992] AC 478.

[31] Ch.1 Heading 'Capacity', sub-heading 'joint tenants and tenants in common'.

change that. The same applies on the exercise of an unconditional[32] break option. The parties cannot unwrite history, and change the termination date of the tenancy whilst the notice is running. So the notice takes effect, notwithstanding any transfer of the reversion or the term in the meantime,[33] and serving a second notice cannot act as a waiver of the first.[34] The only way in which a valid notice to quit can be 'waived' is if the parties expressly or impliedly agree to create a new tenancy.[35] So if, after a notice to quit expires, a tenant without any security of tenure holds over, and continues paying rent, then the parties must have impliedly created a new tenancy; which will be a tenancy at will, if the parties are negotiating the grant of a new tenancy, or a new periodic tenancy, if they are not.[36]

2. Surrender and merger.

Coke defined a surrender as:[37]

> Surrender properly is a yielding up of an estate for life or years to him that has an immediate estate in reversion or remainder, wherein the estate for life or years may drown by mutual agreement between them.

Technically, a lease has a 'reversion' if the grantor retained the immediate reversion upon the lease at the time of grant, and a 'remainder' if he or she conveyed that reversion away to a third party contemporaneously with the grant.[38] In the law of landlord

---

[32] If the break option is conditional, then the recipient can impugn it, and preserve the lease, by proving that the condition has not been satisfied.

[33] *Birch* v. *Wright* (1786) 1 Term Rep 378.

[34] *Doe d. Williams* v. *Humphreys* (1802) 2 East 237.

[35] *Freeman* v. *Evans* [1922] 1 Ch 36, 42.

[36] *Digby* v. *Atkinson* (1815) 4 Camp 275.

[37] *Co.Litt.* 337b.

[38] *Pollock & Maitland* vol. 2 21, F. Bacon, *The Use of the Law* (London, Moore, 1630) 60, Challis, *Real Property* 77–79. 'The distinction between a remainder and a reversion is, that a reversion returns to him or the heirs of him that originally granted it, whereas a remainder is vested in someone to whom it was granted by a previous owner': B. Adkin, *Copyhold and Other Land Tenures* (London, Estates Gazette, 1907) 22. Similarly, *Williams on Real Property,* 23rd edn. (London,

and tenant, there is no practical difference.[39] A 'remainder' upon a lease is simply a reversion that happens to have been vested in a third party at the same time as the lease was granted.

A surrender can only be made to the immediate reversioner at the time of the surrender. It was decided in 1593 that the length of the immediate reversioner's estate was not a relevant consideration for this purpose. Even if the reversion was for a shorter term than the surrendered lease, a surrender to that reversioner would be effective,[40] except in the case of a lease for life.[41]

A surrender can either be effected by an express agreement or it can be inherent in the nature of the transaction. The first type is called an express surrender, and the second is called a surrender by operation of law.[42]

At common law, an express surrender of a lease of a corporeal hereditament could be made without any formality at all; for anything which could be created without a deed, could be surrendered without a deed.[43] So even a lease for life, which was a freehold estate, could be surrendered orally,[44] although an entry

---

Sweet & Maxwell, 1920) 361: 'If the tenant in fee simple should grant a lease for a term of years, or for life, he does not dispose of all his interest, for in each case the grantee has a less estate than himself. Accordingly, on the expiration of the term of years or on the decease of the tenant for life, the remaining interest of the tenant in fee will revert to himself or his heirs, and during the continuance of the smaller estate which he has so granted, called the particular estate, the interest of the tenant in fee is called his reversion. If, at the same time with the grant of the particular estate, he should also dispose of this remaining estate, or reversion, or any part thereof, to some other person, it then changes its name, and it is termed not a reversion but a remainder'.

[39] It can make a difference to statutory prescription: *Symons* v. *Leaker* (1885) 15 QBD 629.

[40] *Hughes* v. *Robotham* (1593) Cro Eliz 302. The point was that the current reversioner was treated as having power to accept the surrender on behalf of everyone who was interested in the reversion; *Challoner* v. *Davies* (1698) 1 Ld.Raym 400, 402, cf. *Willis and Whitewood's Case* (1589) 1 Leon 322, where the process is described as a determination by operation of law, on the grounds that a longer estate cannot drown in, nor therefore be surrendered in, a shorter one.

[41] A lease for life, being a freehold estate, could not be surrendered to a reversioner for years; *Perks.* ¶.589.

[42] Holdsworth, *HEL* vol. 7 293–296.

[43] *Co.Litt.* 204a. But if the tenant authorised another to surrender on his behalf, that authority had to be by deed: *Sleigh* v. *Bateman* (1596) Cro Eliz 487.

[44] *Co.Litt.* 338a.

was necessary in order to complete the surrender.[45] But leases of incorporeal hereditaments could only ever be created by deed,[46] and consequently, even at common law, a deed was necessary in order to effect an express surrender of a lease of an incorporeal hereditament. A reversionary lease, by contrast, can only be surrendered by operation of law, since the identity of the person to whom an express surrender should be made cannot be known until the lease commences.[47]

The Statute of Frauds (1677) introduced the requirement of a deed or signed writing for express surrenders of leases of corporeal property.[48] After 1845, a deed was necessary in order to effect an express surrender of all leases, excepting only parol leases granted for a term of three years or less, which could still be surrendered by signed writing.[49] The exception was removed in 1925.[50]

No formality is necessary for a surrender by operation of law. As early as 1459 it was held that a surrender by operation of law occurred whenever a tenant accepted a new lease of the same land,[51] and that applied even if the new lease was for a shorter term than the former lease,[52] or was made by a limited owner without power to bind the fee.[53] Similarly, taking a reversionary lease, to commence at some time during the term of an existing lease, effected an immediate surrender of the existing lease.[54] The surrender would be presumed in those circumstances, because the tenant could not agree to be its own landlord at any point during the

---

[45] *Peto* v. *Pemberton* (1628) Cro Car 101.

[46] See ch.1 heading 'Formalities'.

[47] (1482) YB 22 Ed.4 f.37 pl.10, *Anon* (1551) Bendloe 24 pl.95, *Co.Litt.* 338a, *Doe d. Rawlings* v. *Walker* (1826) 5 Barn & Cr 111. In *Wilson* v. *Sewell* (1762) 1 Wm.Black 617, 626 Yate J expressed the view that the same principle applied to a concurrent lease, but that cannot be right, for a concurrent lease has an immediate reversion.

[48] s.3. In *Roe d. Berkeley* v. *Archbishop of York* (1805) 6 East 86 it was held that this provision could not be avoided by obliterating the lease.

[49] s.3 Real Property Act 1845.

[50] s.52 Law of Property Act 1925.

[51] (1459) YB 37 Hen.6 f.17 pl.5, *Tompson and Trafford's Case* (1590) 2 Leon 188.

[52] 'Implied surrender of a greater estate' (1553) Dalison's Reps, 124 SS 30, Platt, *Leases*, vol. 2 507.

[53] *Willet & Wilkinson's Case* (1589) 4 Leon 7.

[54] *Ive's Case* (1597) 5 Co.Rep 11a, *Hutchins* v. *Martin* (1598) Cro Eliz 605.

term of the new lease.[55]

In 1559 it was held that even if the effect of a surrender would be to accelerate a reversionary lease vested in a third party, so that the new lease could only take effect as a concurrent lease, nonetheless a surrender by operation of law would be implied.[56] Since 1730, however, a tenant has at least been able to surrender an existing lease, and take a new lease, without altering the status of any sub-leases.[57]

By the beginning of the nineteenth century, there were a wide range of circumstances in which the court would presume a surrender by operation of law, in spite of or even contrary to the actual intentions of the parties.[58]

In *Thomas* v. *Cook*[59] the court of King's Bench held that there was a surrender by operation of law where a landlord, with the concurrence of the tenant, demanded and accepted the sub-rent directly from the sub-tenant.[60] Similarly, a surrender can be implied in some cases where the tenant has abandoned the premises and the landlord relets them.[61] What is required, in each case, is a consensual change of possession, so that the former tenant is no longer in possession of the lease.[62] This is an application of the wider principle that a surrender by operation of law occurs

---

[55] The intention would only be presumed if the new lease was valid. If it was defective, no surrender would take place: *Davison d. Bromley* v. *Stanley* (1768) 4 Burr 2210, *Roe d. Berkeley* v. *Archbishop of York* (1805) 6 East 86. But that exception for defective new leases only applies to a surrender by operation of law (*Doe d. Bishop of Rochester* v. *Bridges* (1831) 1 Barn & Ad 847), and the new lease probably has to be void, rather than merely voidable for it to apply; Platt, *Leases*, vol. 2 509, cf. *Mellow* v. *May* (1602) Cro Eliz 874. If a lease was granted to a husband and wife jointly, a surrender by operation of law would occur if the reversion was conveyed to the husband by feoffment (a conveyance completed by livery of seisin) though not otherwise: *Downing* v. *Seymour* (1602) Cro Eliz 911.

[56] *Wroteley* v. *Adams* (1559) Plowden 187.

[57] s.6 Landlord and Tenant Act 1730, now s.150 Law of Property Act 1925.

[58] *Lyon* v. *Reed* (1844) 13 M&W 285, 305–306 .

[59] (1818) 2 Barn & Ald 119. See also *Wallis* v. *Hands* [1893] 2 Ch 75, 82.

[60] Regular payment of rent by a third party, on its own, was not enough: *Copeland* v. *Watts* (1815) 1 Stark 95.

[61] *Wallis* v. *Atcheson* (1826) 11 Moore 379, cf. *Relvok Properties* v. *Dixon* (1972) 25 P&CR 1.

[62] *Wallis* v. *Hands* [1893] 2 Ch 75, 82.

whenever an act is done 'by or to the owner of a particular estate, the validity of which he is estopped from disputing, and which could not have been done if the particular estate had continued to exist'.[63]

Where the underlying commercial purpose of a lease has come to an end, the court can imply a surrender too.[64] So where a term was granted to trustees, to secure payment of an annuity, the court would presume a surrender by operation of law after the death of the annuitant,[65] on the basis that the commercial purpose of the term had been fully satisfied.[66] But there could be no surrender by operation of law where a new lease was granted to a third party, and the current tenant failed to give up possession.[67] Nor could there be a surrender by operation of law where there was a genuine possibility that the parties intended the disposition to work in some other way, if that was possible as a matter of law.[68]

It was already well established, before 1677, that where the common law required a deed for an express surrender,[69] and an attempt at an express surrender failed for that reason, it could be saved as a surrender by operation of law, if it had been acted upon.[70] After the Statute of Frauds (1677) introduced formal requirements for surrenders of all other leases, the same principle was applied to them too. Consequently, if, after an invalid parol surrender, the landlord accepted the keys back, that would effect a

---

[63] *Lyon* v. *Reed* (1844) 13 M&W 285, Per Parke B 306.

[64] *Doe d. Putland* v. *Hilder* (1819) 2 Barn & Ald 782, cf. *Relvok Properties* v. *Dixon* (1972) 25 P&CR 1.

[65] *Doe d. Burdett* v. *Wright* (1819) 2 Barn & Ald 710.

[66] For the law on these 'satisfied terms', see ch.2 heading 'Mortgages as leases and of leases'.

[67] *Wallis* v. *Hands* [1893] 2 Ch 75.

[68] Until the contrary was decided in *Leek and Moorlands BS* v. *Clark* [1952] 2 QB 788, it was thought that one joint reversioner could accept a surrender of a lease on behalf of all: Challis, *Real Property*, 88. Yet where a term was conveyed to a joint reversioner, no surrender by operation of law could be inferred, because the parties might have intended the conveyance to take effect as an assignment of the term to that one alone, rather than as a surrender to all of them: Challis, *Real Property*, 86.

[69] For example, where the surrender was made by a corporation, or the Crown, or the lease to be surrendered was of an incorporeal hereditament.

[70] *Case of Churchwardens of St Saviours, Southwark* (1613) 10 Co.Rep 66b, 67b, *Woodward* v. *Aston* (1676) 1 Vent 296.

surrender by operation of law.[71]

It has always been the law that a surrender must be made so as to take effect immediately. It cannot be made so as to take place on a future date,[72] though a deed of surrender can, of course, be executed in escrow, so as to be delivered when the condition is satisfied, at some time in the future. A surrender necessarily releases an original tenant, and anyone else liable on the tenant covenant, from all future liabilities under the lease, even if the landlord purports to reserve its rights against them, for a destruction of the estate necessarily discharges any dependent contractual liability.[73]

A merger is really a special type of surrender by operation of law.[74] The idea was that, just as an easement is extinguished if the dominant and servient tenement come into common ownership, so too, if an estate and a reversion came into common ownership, then the estate would be annihilated automatically in the reversion.[75]

The analogy with a surrender by operation of law meant that, because a lease could be surrendered to the immediate reversioner, even if the reversion was for a shorter term than the lease, or if the reversioner had granted a reversionary lease which had not yet commenced,[76] a merger would occur in those circumstances too.[77]

In equity, however, the two estates could be kept alive,

---

[71] *Natchbolt* v. *Porter* (1689) 2 Vern 112, *Whitehead* v. *Clifford* (1814) 5 Taunt 511.

[72] *Doe d. Murrell* v. *Millward* (1838) 3 M&W 328.

[73] *Clements* v. *Richardson* (1888) 22 LR Ir 535.

[74] *Shep.Touch.* 299, s.185 Law of Property Act 1925.

[75] Preston, *Conveyancing*, vol. 3 9. Consequently, a lease for a term of years (a chattel interest) would always merge in and be extinguished by a lease for life (a freehold interest) even if the lease for years was for longer than anyone could possibly live, for a freehold interest was, in law, a greater interest than any term of years: *Co.Litt.* 46a. As late as the beginning of the seventeenth century there was doubt about whether a term of years could merge in another term of years; Platt, *Leases*, vol. 2 515, *Hughes* v. *Robotham* (1593) Cro Eliz 302.

[76] *Anon* (1555) Dyer 112a.

[77] In *Salmon* v. *Swann* (1621) Cro Jac 619, a reversionary lease was granted first, then a lease for a term of 21 years. The court held that, when the reversionary lease was assigned back to the landlord, it merged with the landlord's interest, notwithstanding that it might otherwise have commenced within 21 years, at a time when the tenant of the 21 year lease would have been the immediate reversioner.

originally in order to preserve trusts[78] or to prevent fraud, and perhaps also to protect infants, and ultimately for the benefit of the parties to the transaction themselves, based on their presumed intentions.[79]

The common law continued to ignore the separate beneficial ownership of the estate and reversion,[80] but automatic merger at common law was abolished on 1st November 1875.[81] Since then, there has been no merger where there would have been none in equity. So mergers no longer take place automatically but rather depend on the expressed or presumed intention of the parties.

So far as third parties are concerned, Coke explained the position as follows:[82]

> But having regard to strangers, who were not parties or privies thereto, lest by a voluntary surrender they may receive prejudice touching any right or interest they had before the surrender, the estate surrendered has in consideration of law a continuance.

In *Saint* v. *Pilley*[83] the court went so far as to hold that where the tenant's fixtures had been sold beforehand, the purchaser's right to remove them survived the surrender.

On the same principle, it has always been the law that an underlease survives a surrender or merger of the headlease.[84]

But since there was no privity of estate between the head-

---

[78] Where a term was granted to secure payment of portions under a family settlement, once the portions were paid, the term was said to 'attend the inheritance' (ie be held on the same trusts as the fee). In equity, it merged with the fee, and so a court of equity would prevent the person in whom it was vested in law from setting it up as defence to a possession action by the heir, unless that person was a bona fide purchaser of the term without notice of the trusts: Ashburner, *Equity* 72. See also ch.2 heading 'Mortgages as leases and of leases'.

[79] Challis, *Real Property* 95–97.

[80] Preston, *Conveyancing*, vol. 3 285.

[81] s.25(4) Judicature Act 1873. Now, s.185 Law of Property Act 1925.

[82] *Co.Litt.* 338b.

[83] (1875) LR 10 Ex 137.

[84] Although *Mellor* v. *Watkins* (1874) LR 9 QB 400 is usually cited for the proposition that a surrender of a head lease has no effect on a sub-lease, that was conceded to be established law, 403. In *Smalley* v. *Hardinge* (1881) 7 QBD 524, 525 Lush LJ pointed out that s.6 Landlord and Tenant Act 1730 had been enacted on the assumption that a sub-lease survived a surrender.

landlord and the sub-tenant before the intermediate leasehold interest was extinguished by the merger or surrender, the unfortunate consequence was that, although the sub-lease continued as an estate in the land, the rents,[85] covenants and conditions in the underlease became unenforceable. There was no reversioner who could enforce them, because the immediate reversion upon the underlease had been extinguished.

That problem was solved, in part, by s.6 Landlord and Tenant Act 1730,[86] which preserved the immediate reversion, on a surrender and re-grant of the headlease, and annexed it to the new headlease.[87] Where there was no re-grant, the problem remained unresolved until the enactment of s.9 Real Property Act 1845,[88] which preserved the reversion, and annexed it to the next vested estate following the surrender.

3. Enlargement.

There are two types of enlargement.

The first occurs when a landlord 'releases' a reversion to the tenant. At common law, a lease for life,[89] or years, or even at will,[90] may be enlarged by a release, which is no more than a grant of the reversion to the tenant, rather than to a stranger.

Even before[91] the Statute of Enrolments 1536,[92] enlargement by

---

[85] Plowden, *Quaeries*, 1 pl.15 (75 ER 858).

[86] Now s.150 Law of Property Act 1925. In Ireland, see s.8 Landlord and Tenant Law Amendment Act (Ireland) 1860.

[87] There was no power beforehand to compel the undertenant to surrender and take a replacement underlease: *Colchester* v. *Arnet* (1700) 2 Vern 383.

[88] There had been a botched attempt to do the same thing in the previous year: see s.12 Transfer of Property Act 1844. See now s.139 Law of Property Act 1925.

[89] *Co.Litt.* 273b.

[90] Littleton, *Tenures*, s.460. A release cannot be made to a tenant at sufferance, for there is no privity of estate between a landlord and a tenant at sufferance: Challis, *Real Property*, 409.

[91] *Foster* v. *Holdiche* (1494) Caryll's Reps 115 SS 272, Kaye, *Medieval English Conveyances*, 333–334, J.Kaye, *A Note on the Statute of Enrolments* (1988) 104 LQR 617, 623.

[92] Coke, *2nd Inst.* 671–676.

release was sometimes employed as a means of conveying a fee simple or a life tenancy.[93] This involved three stages: first, granting a short[94] actual lease for years to the purchaser; secondly, the purchaser entering under that lease;[95] and finally, the vendor releasing the freehold to the tenant by deed. The advantage of conveying a freehold in this way was that vendor did not need to attend at the land, nor to appoint an attorney to do so, to go through the ceremony of delivering seisin to the purchaser, as was required for a conveyance by feoffment and livery of seisin.[96] But it was the Statute of Enrolments 1536[97] which made this form of conveyance popular.

The statute required every conveyance of a freehold made by a bargain and sale after 31st July 1536 to be registered within six months, otherwise it would be void for the purpose of conveying a legal estate.[98] The purpose of the Act is usually said to have been to ensure that the Crown could not be deprived of customary revenues by secret conveyancing,[99] but land owners were fond of secret conveyancing, for precisely that reason. A lease and release was ideal for secret conveyancing, because neither instrument would be registrable.[100] The preliminary short lease would not be registrable, because it was not a freehold interest,[101] and the release would not

---

[93] Littleton, *Tenures*, s.532.

[94] There are precedents for leases for a term of six months or one year, to be granted for that purpose, in O. Bridgman, *Conveyances*, 3rd edn. (London, Atkins, 1699) 108, 279. The usual term afterwards was one year.

[95] The tenant had to enter because a release could not be made to someone who had a mere interesse termini: see ch.1 heading 'Entry and interesse termini'.

[96] See ch.1 heading 'Formalities'.

[97] Coke, *2nd Inst.* 671–676.

[98] So where a freehold reversion was transferred to a third party by bargain and sale, the reversioner had to plead the enrolment within six months, in a claim to recover rent from the tenant: *King* v. *Somerland* (1646) Aleyn 19. There was an exception for land in cities, boroughs and corporate towns, which kept their own records; *Chibborne's Case* (1564) Dyer 229a, *Darby* v. *Bois* (1608) 1 Brownlow 141.

[99] It may be that the purpose of requiring enrolment was simply to distinguish between an indenture which was intended to take effect as an executory contract and one where the intention was that it should take effect as the conveyance; see J.Kaye, *A Note on the Statute of Enrolments* (1988) 104 LQR 617.

[100] Halsbury's Laws, *Real Property*, vol. 39(2), 4th edn., ¶.238.

[101] Challis, *Real Property* 421. 'Clandestine bargains and sales of chattel interests, or leases for years, were thought not worth regulating, as such interests were

be registrable, because it would take effect as a conveyance of the freehold at common law, and not as a bargain and sale executed by the Statute of Uses (1536).[102] So a freehold interest could be conveyed by two secret deeds, made on the same or succeeding days.[103]

The problem with making this work was that the purchaser needed to make an entry, in order to complete the short lease, before taking the release; for otherwise the purchaser would only have an interesse termini, and the release would be ineffective.[104] That was a particular problem where the land was already let to someone else or was in one of the colonies.[105] By ancient tradition, Sjt. Sir Francis Moore[106] is credited with having worked out the solution to this problem, when he was trying to arrange a secret conveyance for Lord Norris, who had reasons to conceal what he wanted to do from his own relatives, rather than from the Crown. Sjt. Moore realised that an entry would not be necessary, if the preliminary lease was granted to the 'use' of the purchaser by bargain and sale, because the Statute of Uses (1536) would convert that to an actual lease, if it was granted out of a freehold,[107] without any need for an entry.[108]

---

precarious till about six years before; which also occasioned them to be overlooked in framing the Statute of Uses: and therefore such bargains and sales are not directed to be enrolled. But how impossible is it to foresee, and provide against all the consequences of innovations!': *Bl.Comm.* Bk.II 338–339.

[102] In practice, both transactions took place at the same time, and the real consideration was paid on delivery of the two deeds. Challis, *Real Property,* 420. The lease would be granted for a rent of a few shillings or a peppercorn (if it were rent free, then it would not be a 'bargain and sale'), but the true consideration for the transaction would appear in the release: Stewart, *Practice of Conveyancing* 107–108.

[103] Preston, *Conveyancing,* vol. 2 241, B.Adkin, *Copyhold and Other Land Tenures* (London, Estates Gazette, 1907) 39.

[104] Littleton, *Tenures,* s.459. See ch.1 heading 'Entry and interesse termini'.

[105] See ch.2 heading 'Concurrent leases'.

[106] *Barker v. Keat* (1677) 2 Mod. 249, J. Lilly, *The Practical Register,* 2nd edn. (London, Ward & Wickstead, 1735) 436, *Bl.Comm.* Bk.II 399, Preston, *Conveyancing,* vol. 2 219–220, Holdsworth, *HEL* vol. 7 361.

[107] *Challoner v. Davies* (1698) 1 Ld.Raym 400, 402.

[108] *Lutwich v. Mitton* (1620) Cro Jac 604, *Iseham v. Morrice* (1628) Cro Car 109, 110. Noy did not believe that it worked (W. Noy, *Dialogue & Treatise,* 9th edn. (Reprinted, Abingdon, Professional Books Ltd, 1985) 289–290 fn.(a)) and some corporations could not take advantage of the Statute of Uses (1536), because they

Later, it became the practice for the purchaser to engraft family settlements onto the release,[109] so that the release would be to the purchaser, on the trusts declared in that release.[110] Between 15th May 1841[111] and 7th August 1874,[112] the lease and release could be contained in the same deed, and that has also been possible since the abolition of the doctrine of interesse termini in 1926, although there has been no good reason for using this form of conveyance since 1st October 1845, when it became possible to convey land by a single simple deed.

The alternative means of enlarging a term is statutory.

Statutory enlargement is a partial solution to a particular problem, which occurred where long leases had been granted, reserving a ground rent, without any provision for review. When the value of money fell, due to inflation, it ceased to be worth the landlord's while to collect the rent, and, eventually, the lease would be lost or forgotten, and the tenant's successors would assume that they held in fee simple. But the landlord did not always forget, and the tenant would sometimes have a nasty surprise at the end of the term.[113]

This was less of a problem before the middle of the nineteenth century, because it was thought that the landlord's right to recover possession at the end of the term could be barred by a tortious feoffment:[114] in other words, if the tenant had conveyed the land

---

did not have power to stand seised to a use: *Co.Litt.* 272a.fn(1). So they could not acquire (nor, probably, dispose of) land by lease and release, without an entry in between; Preston, *Conveyancing*, vol. 2 253.

[109] *Co.Litt.* 272a.fn(1).

[110] 'By a release in fee, the estate of a particular tenant is enlarged, and, if his estate is only a chattel interest, his mere possession is turned into an actual seisin; and uses capable of being executed by the statute may be declared upon the seisin so acquired': Challis, *Real Property*, 409.

[111] 4 & 5 Vic. c.21 (1841), s.1.

[112] s.1 Statute Law Revision Act 1874.

[113] This example is given under 'Canterbury' in *Blount's Tenures of Land and Customs of Manors*, 5th edn., ed. W. Hazlitt (reprinted, Epsom, Barsby, 1999): 'In 1887 the Corporation claimed a private residence in the city, which had been held on a 300 year lease, granted about 1598, at a peppercorn rent of eightpence a year. This rent had never been paid within memory. The municipal authorities only then became aware of their right, and were advised that non-payment of the nominal rent was no bar'.

[114] Holdsworth, *HEL* vol. 7 382–383.

openly[115] as if it were a freehold estate, by a feoffment completed by livery of seisin, or by a fine or recovery, and if the landlord had failed to take steps to recover it within twenty years,[116] then the landlord would be barred.[117]

Those forms of conveyance, however, were made impossible by s.2 Fines and Recoveries Act 1833 and s.4 Real Property Act 1845. The legislative response, in s.65 Conveyancing Act 1881, was to give tenants of terms granted for 300 years or more, at no more than a nominal rent, the right to enlarge the term to a fee simple by deed, where at least 200 years of the term remained. That right is now found in s.153 Law of Property Act 1925, but it is still not clear whether this is a statutory form of subinfeudation, or a statutory conveyance, or an extinguishment of the former landlord's fee simple.[118]

4. Forfeiture.

A forfeiture occurs when a lease determines prematurely because the tenant has breached a condition contained in it.[119]

A premature determination for any other reason is not a forfeiture. So, for instance, the exercise of a landlord's option to determine for other reasons, or for no reason at all, is not a forfeiture. Nor is the automatic cessation which occurs because of some 'limitation' on the estate. Of course, it can sometimes be difficult to distinguish a 'condition' from a 'limitation'. Ultimately, the difference between saying that a grant will only last until the happening of a contingent event (a limitation) and saying that the happening of that event is a breach which will end the grant (a

---

[115] *Weller* v. *Stone* (1885) 54 LJ Ch 497.

[116] ss.1-2 Real Property Limitation Act 1833.

[117] By s.12 Distress for Rent Act 1737 tenants were required to give notice to their landlords if a stranger brought ejectment against them (to prevent collusive recoveries).

[118] Challis, *Real Property* 333–335.

[119] No condition for re-entry can be reserved except to the feoffor, or to the donor, or the lessor, or their heirs: Littleton, *Tenures*, s.347.

condition), is entirely a matter of form.[120] The difference is not that a 'limitation' determines the estate automatically, for a 'condition' (except in the case of a lease for life)[121] can provide for automatic determination too.

Indeed, originally, a condition[122] that the lease would become 'void' if the tenant breached any of the covenants meant exactly that.[123] The first move away from that was in *Sir John Masham* v. *Goodere*,[124] where it was said that an actual demand for the rent was necessary, before the lease could become void for non-payment, though the law was still thought to be otherwise if the clause said 'the term shall cease'.[125] But Lord Ellenborough, in 1817, construed the word 'void' as meaning 'voidable by the landlord', on the ground that tenants would otherwise be able to get out of their leases whenever they wished, simply by choosing to commit a breach of covenant.[126]

In 1825, Richard Preston still thought that the question

---

[120] See ch.6 heading 'Conditions'.

[121] A lease for life was a freehold estate, and the rule for freehold estates was that they could not become void for breach of a condition without a re-entry: *Pennant's Case* (1596) 3 Co.Rep 64a, *Manning's Case* (1609) 8 Co.Rep 95b, *Co. Litt.* 214b, 218a. They could, however, end automatically as the result of a limitation: *Co.Litt.* 214b, Preston, *Conveyancing*, vol. 2 196.

[122] Littleton said that the words 'provided always' create a condition: Littleton *Tenures*, s.329. So, sometimes a 'proviso' to a covenant will be interpreted as carrying with it an implied 'condition' for re-entry; see *Lord Cromwell's Case* (1601) 2 Co.Rep 69b, Gouldsborough 116, pl.14 71b-72b, *Earl of Pembrooke* v. *Barkley* (1601) Gouldsbrough 130 pl.27, *Geery* v. *Reason* (1628) Cro Car 128, cf. *Anon* (1571) 3 Leon 16. On other occasions, a proviso will be construed as a covenant: *Samways* v. *Eldsly* (1676) 2 Mod. 73.

[123] *Browning* v. *Beston* (1553) Plowden 135, *Sir Moil Finch's Case* (1590/1) 2 Leon 134, *Pennant's Case* (1596) 3 Co.Rep 64a, *Anon*, 3 Salk 4, Chambers, *Leases*, 186, *Co.Litt.* 214b, Holdsworth, *HEL* vol. 7 292–293.

[124] (1677) 1 Freeman 243.

[125] J. Lilly, *The Practical Register,* 2nd edn. (London, Ward & Wickstead, 1735) vol. 2 192–193.

[126] *Rede* v. *Farr* (1817) 6 M & S 265. The same observation had been made in *Lady Baltinglass's Case* (1671) 1 Freeman 23. In *Hanson* v. *Norcliffe* (1621) Hob 331 the landlord sued for rent, and the tenant responded that the lease had said that it would become 'void' if he failed to pay the rent. The court held that the lease would only become void if the landlord made a demand for the rent, and the defence failed because the tenant had not pleaded any such demand.

depended on the language of the particular proviso in each case,[127] but Lord Ellenborough's reasoning prevailed, with the result 'void' has always since been held to mean 'voidable at the election of the landlord'.[128]

Avoiding one problem, however, often creates another, and because forfeiture now always depends on the landlord making an election between forfeiture and affirmation, it follows that the landlord can also always waive the right to forfeit, by making an election to affirm the lease instead. The essential principles for that were established at the end of the sixteenth century.[129] In 1576 it was held that, where a landlord had a right to forfeit for late payment of rent, acceptance of that late payment did not waive the right to forfeit, since the payment became due before the right to forfeit for its lateness accrued.[130] If, however, the landlord accepted rent accruing due at the same time as[131] or after the right to forfeit had arisen, or levied a distress,[132] or otherwise did anything else which depended on the continued existence of the lease afterwards; then it was held, by two decisions in 1596, that this would amount to an implied representation that the landlord had chosen to dispense with the condition, and affirm the lease,[133] provided that the landlord had been aware of the event giving rise to the right to forfeit at that time.[134] That, however, would only be a waiver of the right to forfeit for that particular breach, not a general licence to

---

[127] Preston, *Conveyancing*, vol. 2 195–196.

[128] Coote, *Leases* 378–379, *Doe d. Bryan* v. *Bancks* (1821) 4 Barn & Ald 401, *Doe d. Nash* v. *Birch* (1836) 1 M&W 402, *Magdalene Hospital* v. *Knotts* (1879) 4 App.Cas. 324, 332–333, *Alghussein* v. *Eton College* [1988] 1 WLR 587. See also *Oxford History of the Laws of England*, vol. 12 125–126.

[129] Platt, *Leases*, vol. 2 468–472.

[130] *Greene's Case* (1576) 1 Leon 262, *Harvie* v. *Oswel* (1597) Cro Eliz 572.

[131] *Harvie* v. *Oswel* (1597) Cro Eliz 572.

[132] *Co.Litt.* 211b. The point was that a landlord could only distrain whilst the lease was still extant (s.7 Landlord and Tenant 1709, which empowers a landlord to distrain up to six months after expiry, does not apply after a forfeiture). So distraining, even for old arrears, is an election to treat the lease as extant at the time when the distress is levied. There is an exception if the lease does not dispense with the need for a formal demand, and the landlord is relying on the right to forfeit in s.210 Common Law Procedure Act 1852.

[133] *Marsh* v. *Curtis* (1596) Cro Eliz 525, 1 Brownlow 78, Platt, *Covenants* 428.

[134] *Pennant's Case* (1596) 3 Co.Rep 64a.

commit the breach in the future,[135] which meant that if the breach was re-committed or continued afterwards, the landlord would acquire a fresh right to forfeit for it again.[136]

There is, in theory, nothing to prevent someone drafting a forfeiture clause which dispenses with the need to make an entry in order to forfeit the lease, and which provides that the forfeiture will happen when the landlord communicates the decision to do so to the tenant.[137] Indeed, where a forfeiture clause provides that a lease for years will become 'void' in the event of breach, the lease can be forfeited in this way without an entry.[138]

But precisely because of the problems identified by Lord Ellenborough[139] associated with the use of the word 'void', the universal practice since the middle of the nineteenth century has been to provide that the landlord may exercise a right of forfeiture by re-entry on the premises, or on part of the premises in the name of the whole, rather than to say that the lease shall be void.[140]

So where the forfeiture clause is in the modern usual form, simply making an election in favour of forfeiture does not, in itself, end the lease. Writing to the tenant saying: 'I hereby elect to forfeit your lease' is not enough to forfeit it, because that does not amount to an entry. But it does amount to an election to forfeit, which prevents the landlord affirming the lease subsequently. Having chosen to forfeit, the tenant could force the landlord to do so. But it is the landlord's entry[141] which ends the lease.

What counts as an entry? Any act done by the landlord, at a time when the right to re-enter has accrued, which would otherwise be actionable by the tenant as a physical trespass on the land, is

---

[135] *Doe d. Boscawen* v. *Bliss* (1813) 4 Taunton 735. See now s.148 Law of Property Act 1925.

[136] *Doe d. Ambler* v. *Woodbridge* (1829) 9 Barn & Cr 376.

[137] 'Some make the estate, whereunto they are annexed, voidable by entry or claim, and some make the estate void ipso facto, without entry or claim': *Co.Litt.* 201a–b, 214b, 215a, D'Anvers, *Abridgment*, vol. 3 167.

[138] D'Anvers, *Abridgment*, vol. 3 167, J. Lilly, *The Practical Register,* 2nd edn. (London, Ward & Wickstead, 1735) vol. 2 194, *Moore* v. *Ullcoats Mining Company* [1908] 1 Ch 575, 588.

[139] Supra.

[140] Stewart, *Practice of Conveyancing* 336.

[141] J. Williams, *The Law of Ejectment*, 2nd edn. (London, Sweet & Maxwell, 1911) 10–13.

treated as an actual physical re-entry. The landlord is not allowed to say that the intention was to commit an unlawful trespass instead.[142]

But service of forfeiture proceedings also counts as an entry too. The reason why is because, until the middle of the seventeenth century, in order to bring an action in ejectment to recover the land, it was necessary first to make a physical entry on the land; and that would be the entry which would forfeit the lease.[143] During the Protectorate, however, it became possible to bring the action relying on a fictional entry, and soon afterwards the courts accepted that the fictional entry in the action could also be treated as an entry which forfeited a lease too.[144] When the fictions were all swept away in 1852,[145] the rule that service of the proceedings was a notional entry which forfeited the lease was preserved.[146] For the same reason, where the claim for forfeiture is made by counterclaim against the tenant, rather than by original action, then the lease determines on service of the counterclaim.[147]

If the landlord instead re-lets the property to a new occupational tenant, the election and entry are made when the new tenant physically enters, or when proceedings are served against the former tenant seeking to recover possession, for the same reasons.[148]

---

[142] *Pollard* v. *Jekyl* (1553) Plowden 89, 92, *Doe d. Hanley* v. *Wood* (1819) 2 Barn & Ald 724.

[143] See ch.9 heading 'Ejectment'.

[144] *Langhorne* v. *Merry* (1664) 1 Sid 223, *Wither* v. *Gibson* (1673) 3 Keb 218, *Anon* (1673) 1 Vent 248, *Abbot* v. *Sorrel* (1674) 3 Keb 282, *Little* v. *Heaton* (1702) 1 Salk 259, *Goodtitle* v. *Cator* (1780) 2 Douglas 477, 484. See also s.2 Landlord and Tenant Act 1730. Curiously, the fictional entry was not sufficient to terminate a tenancy at will: *Right d. Lewis* v. *Beard* (1811) 13 East 210.

[145] See ch.9 heading 'Ejectment'.

[146] *Dendy* v. *Evans* [1910] 1 KB 263, 268, *Canas Property Co* v. *KL Television Services* [1970] 2 QB 433, [1970] 2 All ER 795.

[147] The right to make a counterclaim was first created by rules made under the Judicature Act 1873. For limitation purposes, the counterclaim relates back to the date of issue of the originating process, unless the court severs it (*Ernst & Young* v. *Butte Mining (No.2)* [1997] 1 WLR 1485) but the rules applicable to limitation have nothing to do with the question of when the entry and election are made. For that purpose, it is a pure cross-claim.

[148] *Canas Property Co* v. *KL Television Services* [1970] 2 QB 433, [1970] 2 All ER 795.

It is important to know when the entry is made, because the tenant's estate in and right to possess the lease determines at the moment when the entry is made; and the landlord's reversion, free of the lease, is accelerated with effect from then. Subject only to the possibility of relief,[149] the landlord becomes entitled to possess the estate free from the burden of the lease with effect from that exact moment. When the court makes an order for possession in a forfeiture claim, it is deciding that the lease ended when the entry took place, and not later. Consequently, if the tenant remains in possession in the meantime, the landlord's claim for mesne profits runs from the date of the entry.[150]

The Statute of Gloucester (1278)[151] gave landlords an automatic implied right of forfeiture (and treble damages) if the tenant committed an act of waste, even if no right of forfeiture had been reserved in the lease.[152] It was in force until 1879,[153] although it was generally supposed to have been a bare husk after 1834.[154] Similarly, the Statutes of Mortmain gave the Crown and mesne lords an automatic right of forfeiture, if a lease was granted or assigned in mortmain between 1279 and 1960.[155]

At common law, there were also various implied rights to forfeit leases of offices.[156] More generally, a landlord had an automatic implied right of forfeiture on a tortious alienation by the tenant; that is if the tenant purported to convey a greater estate than the tenant possessed, by feoffment and livery of seisin, or by levying a fine, or by colluding in a recovery, all of which would dispossess the landlord of the reversion.[157] The modern equivalent

---

[149] See the next heading.

[150] See ch.9 heading 'Mesne profits'.

[151] Coke, *2nd Inst.* 299–306.

[152] Forfeiture under the Statute of Gloucester destroyed derivative interests, unlike forfeiture for a tortious alienation in fee (see the next paragraph): *Co.Litt.* 233b.

[153] s.59 Civil Procedure Acts Repeal Act 1879.

[154] The point was that, in order to enforce the right to treble damages and forfeiture, it was necessary to bring the action of waste, rather than an action on the case in waste (see ch.9 heading 'Waste'), and the action of waste was abolished on 1st January 1834 by s.36 Real Property Limitation Act 1833.

[155] See ch.8 heading 'Mortmain'.

[156] Littleton, *Tenures*, ss.378–379.

[157] *Co.Litt.* 215a, 233b, Platt, *Leases*, vol. 2 492–493, D'Anvers, *Abridgment*, vol. 3 220. See below, heading 'Estoppel and denial of title'.

would be the tenant who attempted to have itself registered as proprietor of the landlord's estate at the Land Registry. The final implied right was where the tenant denied, as a matter of record,[158] that the landlord was the landlord;[159] or, in the case of a periodic tenant, even if the denial was not made as a matter of record.[160]

By the fourteenth century, it was clear that a landlord needed to make a formal demand, before forfeiting for non-payment of rent.[161] A formal demand is made by attending at the most worthy and notorious part of the property,[162] at sunset[163] on the last day before a forfeiture can be effected,[164] and demanding the exact amount of money due.[165] If the lease provides that the demand has to be made at a special place on the land, the demand has to be made there, and not on the land generally.[166]

A decision in 1526, that it was not necessary to make a formal demand if the lease required the rent to be paid at a particular place and day,[167] was overruled in 1596,[168] which confined that privilege

---

[158] Viner's *Abridgment* 'Estates' F.b.

[159] (1412) YB 13 Hen.4 f.13a pl.5.

[160] *Doe d. Bennett* v. *Long* (1841) 9 Car & P 773 ('You are not my landlord'). Adams, *Action in Ejectment*, 4th American edn. (New York, Banks Gould & Co, 1854) 156–157. The reasoning was a throwback to time when periodic tenancies were nothing more than tenancies at will: a periodic tenant who had denied the tenancy, had no right to insist on a regular notice to quit: Platt, *Leases*, vol. 2 496.

[161] (1366) YB 40 Ed.3 Lib. Ass. f.241 pl.11, *Co.Litt.* 202a.

[162] *Co.Litt.* 153a, 201b, *Sweton* v. *Cushe* (1603) Yelv 36, *Smith* v. *Doe* (*lessee of Earl Jersey*) (1819) 7 Price Exc Rep 281, 325, 500.

[163] Rent did not technically become due on any day before sunset: see ch.3 heading 'Payment'.

[164] *Hill* v. *Grange* (1556) Plowden 164, 172, Dalison's Reps (2007) 124 SS 106.

[165] *Fabian* v. *Winston* (*or Windsor*) (1589) Cro Eliz 209, 1 Leon 395. A formal demand has to be made 'at the setting of the sun at the last instant of that day' at the 'most open place upon the land' where the rent ought to be paid, being 'where the greatest and most going is', and the person making the demand 'ought to stand still and not walk up and down': *Knap* v. *Pier Iewelch* (1607) 1 Brownlow 138. 'If the lessor after his demand in the morning departeth off the land, and before the last instant returneth, and stays upon the land till sun-setting, there is a continuance of a demand, without any further demand': Per Caitlin J in *Wood and Chivers Case* (1572) 4 Leon 179, 180.

[166] *Ventris* v. *Farmer* (1607) 1 Brownlow 96.

[167] Reports from the time of Hen.8 vol. 1 (2003) 120 SS 57 pl.42, (1491) YB 6 Hen.7 f.3 pl.6, *Kidwelley* v. *Brand* (1551) Dyer 68a.

to forfeitures by the Crown.[169] In other cases, all it did was change the location at which the formal demand had to be made.[170] But as early as 1551 it was clear that there was no need to make a formal demand if the lease expressly dispensed with it,[171] nor, after 1730, was it necessary to make a formal demand where the rent was at least six months in arrears, there were insufficient distrainable goods present on the premises to satisfy the arrears,[172] and the landlord was forfeiting by court process.[173]

The universal practice now is to dispense with a formal demand in the re-entry clause, by using the words 'whether formally demanded or not', but even as late as 1825, this was not always the case.[174]

At that time Richard Preston's advice was that a tenant should resist a forfeiture clause that allowed re-entry for non-rental breaches, because of the absence of any jurisdiction to relieve against forfeiture for those beaches[175] and the fact that the landlord did not need to take any formal step before exercising the right. In practice, rights of re-entry for non-rental breaches were frequently included in leases by the middle of the eighteenth century,[176]

---

[168] *Boroughe's Case* (1596) 4 Co.Rep 72b.

[169] See also *Anon* (1583) 1 Leon 12. Successors to the Crown do need to make a formal demand: *Burrough* v. *Taylor* (1596) Cro Eliz 462.

[170] (1541) 'Note' Dyer 51b. There was, perhaps, no need to make a formal demand if the place specified was the landlord's own home: *Rede* v. *Farr* (1817) 6 M & S 265, Platt, *Leases*, vol. 2 335.

[171] *Newdigate's Case* (1551) Dyer 68b, *Dormer's Case* (1593) 5 Co.Rep 40a–b.

[172] *Doe d. Forster* v. *Wandlass* (1797) 7 Term Rep 177.

[173] s.2 Landlord and Tenant Act 1730. Platt, *Leases*, vol. 2 340. Now s.210 Common Law Procedure Act 1852.

[174] Instead of dispensing with need for a formal demand, the advice of Richard Preston was that the re-entry clause should allow a formal demand to be made at any time, and not simply on the last day: Preston, *Conveyancing*, vol. 2 190–191. Platt, however, was more of a landlord's man—see, e.g., his advice that a tenant's break clause should be made conditional on absolute compliance by the tenant with the covenants contained in the lease: Platt, *Leases*, vol. 2 76 — and he said that these words should in all cases be rejected, and instead the words should be 'although no legal or formal demand of the rent be made': Platt, *Leases*, vol. 2 342.

[175] See the next heading 'Relief from forfeiture'.

[176] 'Tis best to make this or like covenant part of the proviso for making the lease void': E. Wood, *Conveyancing*, vol. 3 (London, Stratham & Woodfall, 1793) 86, Stewart, *Practice of Conveyancing*, 336. Before the eighteenth century, forfeiture clauses were sometimes very tenant-friendly. In the medieval period, the right to forfeit for non-payment of rent was normally conditional upon there being no

though that practice was deprecated by James LJ in *Hodgkinson* v. *Crowe*,[177] who, in the course of refusing to imply such a provision into a lease as one of the 'usual' covenants and conditions, said:[178]

> I am bound to say, having had some experience in these cases, that I do not consider it a proper and reasonable thing to introduce, but to my mind it is a most odious stipulation, it is offensive, and it is oppressive beyond measure; and it never, in my opinion, has been submitted to by lessees except upon a general notion that lessors are men of honour and liberality, and will not incur the odium which they would incur in the eyes of their neighbours if they endeavoured to enforce their strict rights by insisting on a forfeiture of a valuable estate in which, perhaps, the whole of the lessee's fortune may have been embarked, because he has through inadvertence committed a breach of covenant which may not have done a shillingworth of damage.

The need to serve a preliminary notice, giving the tenant the opportunity to remedy (if possible) a non-rental breach and to pay compensation for any damage, in order to prevent a forfeiture, which is now found in s.146 Law of Property Act 1925, was introduced by the Conveyancing Act 1881.[179] The Leasehold Property (Repairs) Act 1938 made it harder to forfeit a house, with a rateable value of £100 or less, for disrepair where more than five years of the term remained, by permitting the tenant to serve a counter-notice, which would make it necessary for the landlord to obtain consent from the court, on one of a number of grounds,

---

sufficient distress on the land (Kaye, *Medieval English Conveyances*, 265) and in *Grygg* v. *Moyes* (1600) Cro Eliz 764 the clause required the rent to be in arrears for a year, and for there to have been no distrainable goods on the premises for the whole of that year. West's *Simboleograph* (London, Stationers Co., 1610) pt.1 treated re-entry clauses for non-payment of rent (s.451) and generally (s.442) as optional extras. There is a precedent in *The Compleat Clerk* (London, Place, 1671) for a lease of a brew house where the right to re-enter for non-payment of rent is conditional upon the rent being 56 days in arrears.

[177] (1875) LR 10 Ch App 622.

[178] 626–627. On the meaning of 'usual' covenants, see ch.5 heading 'Express, implied and usual'. A right of re-entry for non-rental breaches had become usual by 1971: *Chester* v. *Buckingham Travel* [1981] 1 WLR 86.

[179] The landlord's right to recover the costs of the notice as a debt was introduced by s.2 Conveyancing Act 1892.

before forfeiting.[180] In 1954, that was altered so as to cover all properties (other than agricultural holdings) where three years or more remained unexpired of an original term of at least seven years.[181] The purpose of the Act was to stop speculators buying up small properties in an indifferent state of repair, at a very low price, and then obtaining vacant possession by serving a long schedule of dilapidations on the tenant, requiring the tenant to do works out of all proportion to the value of the property.[182]

   Tenants who acquired statutory security of tenure during the twentieth century,[183] also generally acquired protection against forfeiture. So, from 1914 onwards, if a landlord forfeited a Rent Act protected tenancy, and the tenant was occupying the property as a residence at the time, the court could not make an order for possession unless the landlord could also prove a statutory ground too.[184] When public sector residential tenancies became 'secure' in 1980, they also became unforfeitable,[185] and the same scheme was applied to 'assured' tenancies granted under the Housing Act 1988,[186] which replaced Rent Act protection. Agricultural holdings, under the 1948 and 1986 Acts, were, in practice, unforfeitable,[187] and the same probably[188] also applies now to farm business tenancies under the Agricultural Tenancies Act 1995. But ordinary business tenancies are an exception. Nothing in the Landlord and Tenant Act 1954 affects a landlord's right of forfeiture.[189] Nor, surprisingly, was there any significant[190] legislative intervention

---

[180] s.1.

[181] s.51 Landlord and Tenant Act 1954.

[182] *National Real Estate and Finance Co* v. *Hassan* [1939] 2 KB 61, 78, *Sidnel* v. *Wilson* [1966] 2 QB 67, 76.

[183] See ch.4 headings 'Agricultural, Business and Residential security'.

[184] s.1(3) Rent and Mortgage Interest Restrictions Act 1915, *Bolnore Properties* v. *Cobb* [1996] EGCS 42.

[185] s.82(1) Housing Act 1985.

[186] s.45(4) Housing Act 1988.

[187] *Parry* v. *Million Pigs* (1981) 260 E.G. 281.

[188] The reason for the doubt is the definition of 'termination' in s.38(1) Agricultural Tenancies Act 1995.

[189] *William Skelton* v. *Harrison & Pinder* [1975] QB 361.

[190] s.16 Landlord and Tenant Act 1954 contained anti-avoidance provisions, designed to ensure that landlords could not prevent a statutory tenancy arising on

specifically to prevent the forfeiture of long leases of residential property, before the enactment of s.81 Housing Act 1996, which prevented forfeiture for disputed service charge arrears; and real protection for those leases was not acquired until 2005, when ss.167-168 Commonhold and Leasehold Reform Act 2002 were brought into force.[191]

5. Relief from forfeiture.

In theory, common law courts had no inherent jurisdiction to grant relief against forfeiture, whether for non-payment of rent or otherwise. If the landlord could prove that the right to forfeit had accrued and had been duly exercised, that was supposed to be the end of the matter, so far as those courts were concerned. The landlord had proved its right to possession, and so was entitled to judgment.

The intellectual justification for this was that a claim for relief was an equitable claim, and so fell exclusively within the jurisdiction of the Chancellor and courts of equity.[192] Only the Chancellor, and his courts, had inherent jurisdiction to mitigate the harshness of the common law, by granting tenants relief from forfeiture. This was done by granting an injunction against the landlord, which either forbade the landlord from prosecuting the common law possession claim to judgment[193] or, if the landlord had already obtained a common law possession order, compelled the landlord to grant the tenant a new lease on the same terms as before.[194] It was not until as late as 1895 that it was decided that there was also an inherent equitable jurisdiction to relieve against a peaceable re-entry too.[195]

---

the expiry of a long lease of residential premises, by forfeiting the fag-end contractual term.

[191] These sections prohibit forfeitures for small amounts of ground rent and for disputed breaches generally.

[192] See ch.9 heading 'Equitable relief '.

[193] *Dendy* v. *Evans* [1910] 1 KB 263, 266, Ashburner, *Equity* 360.

[194] J. Lilly, *The Practical Register,* 2nd edn. (London, Ward & Wickstead, 1735) vol. 1 678. Relief out of court by agreement between the parties restores the original lease: *Wilson* v. *Burne* (1888) 24 LR Ir 14, 35.

[195] *Howard* v. *Fanshawe* [1895] 2 Ch 581.

In practice, however, common law courts could and did grant a measure of relief, in claims involving non-payment of rent, by making procedural rules which made it impossible for the landlord to prosecute its common law claim to judgment.[196] From 1696 it was the practice of the common law courts to stay any claim to forfeit a lease for non-payment of rent indefinitely if the tenant paid the arrears and costs into court before execution of the judgment,[197] thereby saving the tenant the expense of making a routine application for relief in a court of equity.[198] The power to do that, up to the date of trial, but no later,[199] was confirmed by s.4 Landlord and Tenant Act 1730.[200]

Courts of equity never had any inherent jurisdiction to grant relief against a forfeiture by the Crown, nor a successor in title to the Crown. Accordingly, the first statutory intervention was the Crown Lands Act 1623 (which is still in force) which provided for automatic relief if the arrears of rent were paid before any proceedings were issued, or any commission was appointed on a petition of right,[201] but not otherwise.

Against other landlords there was inherent jurisdiction to grant relief in equity for breach of a condition.[202] Relief against forfeiture

---

[196] *Archer* v. *Snapp* (1738) Andrews 341, 2 Strange 1107.

[197] Rules of Court (1696) 2 Salk 597, *Goodtitle* v. *Holdfast* (1731) 2 Strange 900.

[198] The power could only be exercised in cases where a court of equity could grant relief: *Doe d. Mayhew* v. *Asby* (1839) 10 A&E 71.

[199] *Roe d. West* v. *Davis* (1806) 7 East 363.

[200] Now, s.212 Common Law Procedure Act 1852. The equivalent in the County Court was s.52 County Courts (Amendment) Act 1856, and it is now found in s.138(2) County Courts Act 1984. Under the 1856 Act, the County Court only had jurisdiction to deal with forfeitures for non-payment of rent. By s.59 County Courts Act 1888, it acquired general power to deal with claims in ejectment, where the land was not worth more than £50. That was increased to £100 by the County Courts Act 1903, and the value limit was increased by s.48 County Courts Act 1959 to any case where the rateable value was not more than £100. The jurisdiction is now unlimited: s.21 County Courts Act 1984.

[201] See ch.9 heading 'Crown Proceedings'.

[202] There is no jurisdiction to grant relief against a limitation rather than a condition. 'And though a court of equity may relieve to prevent the divesting of an estate; yet it cannot relieve to give an estate that never vested': H. Bullow ed. J. Fonblanque, *A Treatise on Equity,* 5th edn., vol. 1 (London, Clarke, 1820) 400. For the difference between a condition and a limitation, see ch.6 heading 'Conditions'.

was originally only granted in the case of accident or great hardship, but by the seventeenth century it was given as a matter of course where the forfeiture was for non-payment of rent, though the application still had to be made, at the latest, within a reasonable time of the common law judgment.[203] That was fixed, where the rent was at least six months in arrears, at six months from the date of execution, by s.2 Landlord and Tenant Act 1730.[204] The same Act required tenants to pay the arrears into court, when they applied for relief, and limited the compensation payable to tenants for being kept out of possession to whatever the landlord had actually made from the property in the meantime.[205]

The settled practice, at the beginning of the eighteenth century, was not to relieve against wilful breaches,[206] nor against breaches where the measure of damage was unclear,[207] nor against breaches of disposition[208] or user covenants,[209] nor against forfeitures by operation of law.[210] Most applications were for relief against forfeitures for non-payment of rent, although relief was sometimes granted for other breaches too.[211] But in 1811 Lord Eldon decided, in *Hill* v. *Barclay*,[212] that there was no inherent jurisdiction to grant relief against forfeiture for non-rental breaches, except in wholly exceptional circumstances.[213]

This narrow interpretation of the limits of the inherent power

---

[203] A year and a half was not a reasonable time in *Bromwich* v. *Smith* (1675) 1 Nottingham's Chancery Cases, 73 SS 266.

[204] Re-enacted in s.210 Common Law Procedure Act 1852.

[205] s.3 Landlord and Tenant Act 1730. Re-enacted as s.211 Common Law Procedure Act 1852.

[206] *Descarlett* v. *Dennett* (1722) 9 Mod. 22.

[207] *Wafer* v. *Mocato* (1724) 9 Mod. 112.

[208] *Peachy* v. *Duke of Somerset* (1721) 1 Strange 447.

[209] *Macher* v. *Foundling Hospital* (1813) 1 Ves & B 188.

[210] *Peachy* v. *Duke of Somerset* (1724) 1 Strange 447.

[211] *Hack* v. *Leonard* (1724) 9 Mod. 90 (minor disrepair), *Sanders* v. *Pope* (1806) 12 Ves Jun 283 (failure to lay out money).

[212] (1811) 18 Ves Jun 56. See also *Peachy* v. *Duke of Somerset* (1721) 1 Strange 447, 453.

[213] In *Rolfe* v. *Harris* (1811) 2 Price 210 it was said that relief could be granted in the case of 'inevitable accident' for non-rental breaches, but *Bracebridge* v. *Buckley* (1816) 2 Price 200 settled the question that relief could only be granted for rental breaches. See also *Reynolds* v. *Pitt* (1812) 19 Ves Jun 134.

produced a succession of statutes during the nineteenth century, giving both common law courts and courts of equity ever widening statutory powers to grant relief.

First came Lord St Leonards' Act,[214] which empowered courts of equity to relieve, once only, against forfeiture for failure to insure, if the insurable event had not yet happened.[215]

That was followed by the Common Law Procedure Act 1860, ss.1 and 2 of which gave common law courts the same powers to relieve against forfeiture for non-payment of rent and for failure to insure as courts of equity already possessed.[216]

That power became redundant in 1875, as a result of the Judicature Acts 1873 and 1875, which created one High Court, each division of which had all the common law and equitable powers possessed by the others.[217]

Finally, the Conveyancing Act 1881 gave the new High Court a general power to grant relief against forfeiture for non-rental breaches too,[218] except where the forfeiture was for breach of a disposition covenant or of a mining lease.[219] That general power was extended in 1925, and now only some covenants in mining leases[220] and some forfeitures on bankruptcy or taking in execution[221] remain irrelievable.

---

[214] s.4 Law of Property Amendment Act 1859.

[215] C. Bunyon, *The Law of Fire Insurance* (London, Layton, 1867) 132–133, *Oxford History of the Laws of England*, vol. 12 125. Before the Act, the courts would struggle to say that there had been no breach, in order to prevent a forfeiture: see *Pitt* v. *Laming* (1814) 4 Camp 73 and *Doe d. Pittman* v. *Sutton* (1841) 9 Car & P 706. In *White* v. *Warner* (1817) 2 Meriv 459 the landlord succeeded in forfeiting a lease for a technical breach of the insurance covenant, notwithstanding that the tenant had spent £3,000 on the building. In *Hodgkinson* v. *Crowe* (1875) LR 10 Ch App 622, 627 James LJ recalled a case, in which he had been counsel, where 'extensive copperworks were forfeited by reason of a breach of covenant in not keeping up a fence which had become perfectly useless, and the not keeping up of which did not do one shillingworth of damage to anybody'. See also *Green* v. *Bridges* (1830) 4 Sim 96.

[216] ss.1–2 Common Law Procedure Act 1860 were repealed by s.7 Conveyancing Act 1881.

[217] Now s.38(1) Senior Courts Act 1981. See ch.9 heading 'Equitable relief'.

[218] s.14(2).

[219] s.14(6).

[220] s.146(8)(ii) Law of Property Act 1925.

[221] s.146(8)(iii)–(iv) ibid.

Where a head-lease was forfeited, the inherent jurisdiction of the Chancellor and courts of equity beneath him to grant relief against that forfeiture could be exercised on an application made by a sub-tenant too. But there was no inherent jurisdiction to grant relief to the sub-tenant in its own right.[222] The application by the sub-tenant had to be to restore[223] the headlease,[224] which would incidentally restore the sub-lease below it.[225] When courts acquired statutory powers to grant relief during the nineteenth century, sub-tenants were permitted to take advantage of those provisions in the same way, by applying to restore the forfeited head-lease;[226] and in 1845 it was also decided that a sub-tenant could obtain an automatic stay of any proceedings to forfeit the headlease for non-payment of rent, by paying the arrears and the costs into court, taking advantage of s.4 Landlord and Tenant 1730.[227]

Sub-tenants first[228] acquired the ability to obtain relief in their own right under s.4 Conveyancing Act 1892, which empowered the court to vest a new lease in the sub-tenant directly, without restoring the headlease.[229]

---

[222] *Burt* v. *Gray* [1891] 2 QB 98, *Nind* v. *Nineteenth Century BS* [1894] 2 QB 226.

[223] If the head-landlord voluntarily granted the head-tenant a new lease, equity could compel the head-tenant to grant a new sub-lease: *Anon* Cary 18.

[224] For that purpose, it was generally necessary to join the head-tenant to the application, since the head-tenant might want to argue that the forfeiture should stand; *Hare* v. *Elms* [1893] 1 QB 604, *Abbey National* v. *Maybeech* [1985] Ch 190. Relief could not be granted on any better terms than the head-tenant could have obtained; *Webber* v. *Smith* (1689) 2 Vern 103.

[225] In *Doe d. Whitfield* v. *Roe* (1811) 3 Taunt 402, relief was granted directly to a mortgagee, but the mortgage had not been granted by way of mortgage term (which would have put the mortgagee in the position of an undertenant). It was granted by way of assignment with a proviso for reconveyance, so the mortgagee was the tenant. Similarly, in *Bromwich* v. *Smith* (1675) 1 Nottingham's Chancery Cases 73 SS 266, where relief was refused to a mortgagee on the facts, the mortgage was by assignment. s.2 Landlord and Tenant Act 1730 (now s.210 Common Law Procedure Act 1852) contained a proviso saving the rights of mortgagees who were not in possession, but that was probably confined to cases where the mortgage was by assignment too, because it referred to the 'first lessee or lessees' in contradistinction to the mortgagee.

[226] *Escalus Properties* v. *Robinson* [1996] QB 231, [1995] 2 EGLR 23.

[227] *Doe d. Wyatt* v. *Byron* (1845) 1 CB 623.

[228] *Burt* v. *Gray* [1891] 2 QB 98, *Nind* v. *Nineteenth Century BS* [1894] 2 QB 226.

[229] Now, s.146(4) Law of Property Act 1925.

That right granted to sub-tenants was entirely general, and so extended to breaches for which no relief could be given to the head-tenant. The extended right was inadvertently lost in 1926, but restored in 1929.[230] Until 1992, it was thought that the power did not apply if the landlord had re-entered peaceably,[231] but in *Billson* v. *Residential Apartments*[232] the House of Lords held that, properly interpreted, it could be invoked even after a peaceable re-entry.

6. Estoppel and denial of title.

Estoppel as to, and denial of, title are really opposite sides of the same coin. The landlord, by making the grant, is estopped, as against the tenant, from saying that it lacked power to do so.[233] The tenant, by accepting the grant, is likewise estopped, as against the landlord, from saying that the landlord lacked power to make it.[234] Originally, that mutual estoppel only applied if the grant was made by deed[235] but by the end of the eighteenth century it was being applied to parol tenancies too.[236] By the nineteenth century, it was performing the useful function of making leases that, for technical reasons, were equitable only, enforceable as legal leases in

---

[230] Law of Property (Amendment) Act 1929.

[231] *Rogers* v. *Rice* (1884) 12 QBD 165.

[232] [1992] 1 AC 494.

[233] There is no estoppel if the absence of title appears on the face of the lease: *Pargeter* v. *Harris* (1845) 7 QB 708, cf. *Bruton* v. *London and Quadrant Housing Trust* [2000] AC 406.

[234] Coote, *Leases*, 24, *First National Bank* v. *Thomson* [1996] 1 Ch 231.

[235] (1546/7) Brook's New Cases pl.319, Littleton, *Tenures*, s.58: '. . . it is a good plea for the lessee to say, that the lessor had nothing in the tenements at the time of the lease, except the lease be made by deed indented, in which case such plea lieth not for the lessee to plead'. See also *Monroe* v. *Lord Kerry* (1710) 1 Brown PC 67. The party relying on the estoppel had to take the point, otherwise the other party could obtain judgment relying on the plea of lack of title: *Trevivan* v. *Lawrence* (1704) 1 Salk 276.

[236] Holdsworth, *HEL* vol. 7 245–246, *Cooke* v. *Loxley* (1792) 5 Term Rep 4. See *Veale* v. *Warner* (1669) 1 Wms Saund 323, 326.fn(f). Coke thought that acceptance of rent was enough to create an estoppel: *Co.Litt.* 352a. In *Chettle* v. *Pound* (1701) 1 Ld.Raym 746, Holt CJ ruled that the estoppel on a written agreement applied if the landlord had previously been in possession of the demised property but not otherwise.

common law courts: both parties were estopped from denying that the landlord had power to make a legal lease.[237]

The estoppel ceases to bind the tenant if a third party with title paramount evicts,[238] or threatens to evict, the tenant. It is wrongly broken by a tenant who otherwise denies that the original landlord had power to make the grant. So if the tenant of a corporeal hereditament purported to convey the reversion by livery of seisin or by levying a fine[239] or suffering a recovery, or, in any proceedings,[240] either denies the existence of the tenancy,[241] or claims to own the landlord's interest, or asserts that the landlord's interest is vested in someone else,[242] the landlord could and can elect to treat that as a determination of the lease.[243] That right is part of an ancient feudal principle of fealty between a lord and the lord's tenants. Break the bond of fealty, and there is an implied condition that lord is entitled to forfeit the property which the tenant holds of that lord.[244] But purporting to grant an underlease for years for a term longer than the lease did not break the bond because, it could not prejudice the landlord,[245] and the same applied to a purported conveyance of the landlord's interest by bargain and sale or a covenant to stand seised.[246] These were 'innocent' conveyances.

As a result of the estoppel, in *Cook* v. *Loxley*[247] it was held that

---

[237] *Oxford History of the Laws of England*, vol. 12 129–130.

[238] (1506) YB 21 Hen.7 f.26 pl.3.

[239] *Whaley* v. *Tankred* (1672) T.Raym 219, *Doe d. Gray* v. *Stanion* (1836) 1 M&W 695.

[240] Or perhaps in the case of a periodic tenancy, if not made in proceedings; see ante heading 'Forfeiture' fn.160.

[241] *Doe d. Calvert* v. *Frowd* (1828) 4 Bing 557, *Doe d. Graves* v. *Wells* (1839) 10 A&E 427.

[242] D'Anvers, *Abridgment*, vol. 3 165, Bac Abr Lease T.

[243] Lightwood, *Possession of Land* (London, Stevens, 1894) 237.

[244] 'Nothing can be more evident than that Littleton was intensely puzzled when he wrote that part of s.132 which refers to terms of years. He knew that a term of years was no estate at all, but a mere contract, at the common law, yet he found termors allowed to do fealty': H. Challis, *Are Leaseholds tenements?* (1890) 6 LQR 69.

[245] *Eastcourt* v. *Weekes* (1698) 1 Salk 186.

[246] Holdsworth, *HEL* vol. 7 357.

[247] (1792) 5 Term Rep 4.

a tenant could not allege that his landlord's title was void. Lord Ellenborough said of that case, in *Hodson* v. *Sharpe*:[248]

> . . . the Court agreed that it was a universal rule, that a tenant should not be permitted to set up any objection to the title of his landlord under whom he held; that this was not a mere technical rule, but one founded in public convenience and policy.

In *Palmer* v. *Ekins*[249] it was held that the estoppel bound assignees, and in *Phipps* v. *Sculthorpe*[250] it was held that the estoppel meant that an informal assignee of a lease, who had attorned to the landlord, could not plead that the lease was still vested in the original tenant, as a defence to claim for rent.

A side effect of the estoppel as to title is that, if the landlord subsequently acquires the necessary title, the estoppel is 'fed', and there is no need for the landlord to make a new grant.[251] But there was an exception before 1926 where the landlord was a tenant for life: acquiring a freehold reversion would not feed the estoppel so as to make any existing sub-tenancy endure longer than the former tenancy for life.[252]

7. Repudiation and frustration.

The question here is whether, and to what extent, the rules for termination of executory contracts, developed in the action of assumpsit in the nineteenth century, apply to an executed contract, such as a lease.[253] The same issue arises both for fault based

---

[248] (1808) 10 East 350, 352–353.

[249] (1728) 2 Strange 817.

[250] (1817) 1 Barn & Ald 50. Where the tenant acknowledges someone as an assignee of the reversion, the tenant is not estopped from alleging that the reversion is, in fact, vested in someone else: *Gregory* v. *Doidge* (1826) 3 Bing 474.

[251] *Smith* v. *Stapleton* (1573) 2 Plowden 426, *Weale* v. *Lower* (1672) Pollex 54, 68. But this could not retrospectively turn an assignment into an underlease: *Langford* v. *Selmes* (1857) 3 K & J 220.

[252] *Rothwell's Case* (1628) Hetl 91.

[253] This is purely a common law question. It has nothing to do with rescission *ab initio* in equity. There has always been a separate equitable jurisdiction to allow rescission of an executed lease, for reasons other than failure to perform a promise

termination, relying on the other party's repudiatory breach of the contract, and non-fault based termination, where some external frustrating event prevents performance.[254]

Since the earliest times, leases have contained express conditions in favour of landlords, allowing them to terminate the lease if the tenant commits a breach of covenant.[255] Usually, it takes the form of a general right of re-entry, though sometimes it takes the form of a proviso to a tenant's covenant.[256]

Express conditions in favour of tenants, entitling them to terminate the lease if the landlord commits a breach of covenant, have been rarer, but do occasionally occur,[257] and there has never been any conceptual difficulty in either party terminating a lease under an express power to do so.

Absent any express right to terminate, the rules on fault based termination were well worked-out in the action of covenant before the nineteenth century. The question of whether the failure of one party to perform a covenant excused the other party from further performance of its own covenants depended on whether the

---

contained in it, in the same way as any other conveyance or instrument can be avoided: e.g., for mistake (*Cooper* v. *Phibbs* (1867) LR 2 HL 149) or fraudulent misrepresentation (*Killick* v. *Roberts* [1991] 2 EGLR 10), but not, before the rule was reversed by s.1 Misrepresentation Act 1967, for innocent misrepresentation (*Angel* v. *Jay* [1911] 1 KB 666).

[254] There are other aspects of the same problem. For instance, if a tenant wrongfully repudiates the lease, is the landlord obliged to mitigate its loss, by accepting the repudiation as determining the lease and bringing an action for damages, or can the landlord insist on performance for the remainder of the term? The courts have recently re-affirmed the traditional rule that the landlord can insist on performance; *Reichman* v. *Beveridge* [2006] EWCA Civ 1659. In cases of exceptional hardship, however, the rule may be different; *Smith* v. *Morris* (1788) 2 Brown CC 311.

[255] See the heading 'Forfeiture' above.

[256] *Co.Litt.* 203b, *Whitchcot* v. *Fox* (1616) Cro Jac 398.

[257] Tenants are frequently granted options to terminate ('break rights') which are unconnected with any breach of covenant by the landlord: see ch.2 heading 'Options and break rights'. The only right to terminate for a landlord's breach which is encountered with any frequency in practice, is a right to terminate if the landlord fails, within a particular time, to lay out insurance monies reinstating the premises after destruction by an insured risk.

covenants were 'dependent', 'concurrent', or 'mutual'.[258] Whilst covenants in executory contracts (such as an agreement to grant a lease)[259] might be dependent or concurrent, the rule for covenants in executed contracts, such as the lease itself, was that the covenants were almost invariably mutual,[260] and therefore that termination for breach was not possible.

So, for instance, in *Boone* v. *Eyre*[261] the vendor sold an estate in Dominica with a stock of slaves, in return for payment of £500 and an annuity of £160. In breach of his covenant for title, it turned out that the vendor did not own all the slaves. But Lord Mansfield held that did not excuse payment of the annuity—it only sounded in damages—because the covenants of an executed contract which go to only part of the consideration are treated as being mutual.

As a result, it was clear law at the beginning of the nineteenth century that, absent any express right to terminate, a breach of covenant by one party to a lease did not excuse performance by the other: the landlord was obliged to continue performing the landlord's covenants, and the tenant was obliged to continue paying the rent[262] and performing the tenant's covenants, irrespective of any breach by the other.

If actions to enforce executed leases had always been brought in covenant, and if actions to enforce executory agreements to grant leases had always been brought in assumpsit, there would not have been any scope for subsequent confusion. But the question of which action was appropriate did not depend upon whether the contract was executory or executed. It depended on whether there was a deed or not.[263] So the common law cause of action for

---

[258] Platt, *Covenants*, 70 *et seq*, S. Siegel, *Is the Modern Lease a Contract or a Conveyance? A Historical Inquiry* (1975) 52 Journal of Urban Law 649, Lord Millet, *Repudiation of Leases*, Blundell Lecture 26.6.2000.

[259] *Curriton and Gadbary's Case* (1584) 1 Leon 275, *Baynes* v. *Lloyd* [1895] 1 QB 820, 822–823.

[260] There is a separate rule that where one party makes it impossible for the other to perform its covenant or satisfy a condition precedent, the covenant or condition precedent is treated as having been performed or satisfied: *Sir Anthony Main's Case* (1596) 5 Co.Rep 20b, *McKay* v. *Dick* (1881) 6 App.Cas. 251.

[261] (1777) 2 Wm.Black 1312.fn(t), *Campbell* v. *Jones* (1796) 6 Term Rep 570, 573.

[262] R. Brooke's *Grande Abridgment* (London, Tottel, 1568) 'Debt' pl.18 and pl.72.

[263] See ch.9 heading 'Covenant' and 'Assumpsit'.

enforcing short parol leases, or leases made by signed writing before 1845,[264] was assumpsit, notwithstanding that the lease was an executed contract. Similarly, if an agreement to grant a lease was made by deed, the common law cause of action to enforce it was covenant, notwithstanding that it remained executory. So, once it became possible to bring a claim in assumpsit for rent on an informal lease in 1738,[265] there was always a risk that the rules for the termination of executory contracts in assumpsit would bleed over and corrupt the rules for covenants in executed conveyances, and exactly that happened.[266]

The nineteenth century scheme for fault based termination of executory contracts in assumpsit was a two-fold categorisation of contractual promises as either contractual conditions or contractual warranties. A contractual condition was a promise which carried with it an implied right for the other party to terminate the contract if the promise was not performed. A contractual warranty was a promise where the only common law remedy for non-performance would be damages. In the twentieth century, it was found necessary to alter this simple scheme, by introducing a third class of promise: the 'innominate' or 'intermediate' term, where the right to terminate would depend on the seriousness of the breach.[267]

The doctrine of frustration, was similarly a nineteenth century development of the law of assumpsit, regulating the non-fault termination of executory contracts. Its origins lie in Lord Blackburn's decision in *Taylor* v. *Caldwell*,[268] which involved a licence to use a music hall, which burned down without the fault of either party, before the concert.

The first attempt to apply assumpsit rules on termination in order to defend claims involving executed leases occurred in three cases between 1825 and 1831, in each of which the landlord's claim for rent was brought in assumpsit, rather than in debt or

---

[264] See ch.1 heading 'Formalities'.

[265] See ch.9 heading 'Assumpsit'.

[266] cf. G. Treitel, *Frustration and Force Majeure* (London, Sweet & Maxwell, 1994) ch.11 esp.11–003.

[267] *Hongkong Fir Shipping* v. *Kawasaki Kisen* [1962] QB 26.

[268] (1863) 3 B & S 826, *Oxford History of the Laws of England*, vol. 12 513–516.

covenant.[269] In *Edwards* v. *Etherington*,[270] in *Salisbury* v. *Marshal*[271] and in *Collins* v. *Barrow*[272] tenants who had taken short leases of unfurnished houses were allowed to defend claims for rent on the basis that they had terminated the lease for the landlord's failure to provide a habitable house. In 1843, those decisions were applied by the Exchequer of Pleas, in *Smith* v. *Marrable*,[273] to a short furnished letting of a fashionable, but bug-ridden, house in Brighton. In that case, Parke B (with the concurrence of Alderson B and Gurney B) said:[274]

> These authorities appear to me fully to warrant the position that if the demised premises are encumbered with a nuisance of so serious a nature that no person can reasonably be expected to live in them, the tenant is at liberty to throw them up. This is not the case of a contract on the part of the landlord that the premises were free from this nuisance; it rather rests in an implied condition in law that he undertakes to let them in a habitable state.

The fourth member of the court, Lord Abinger, was more cautious. He expressly confined the principle to lettings of furnished houses.

The test of whether those rules applied generally to all lettings came later in the same year, in *Sutton* v. *Temple*.[275] In that case, a tenant of a field argued that he was entitled to abandon the tenancy because the land was contaminated with poisonous paint, and his cattle had died as a result. The Exchequer of Pleas held that this was no defence. Baron Parke retracted his previous dictum, and said that the implied right to terminate only applied to furnished lettings of residential accommodation. Lord Abinger agreed, and Gurney B said that he would have been willing to overrule *Smith* v. *Marrable,* if necessary.

Any remaining doubts that orthodoxy had been restored were

---

[269] For the reasons why these claims were brought in assumpsit, rather than debt or covenant, see ch.9, heading 'Assumpsit'.

[270] (1825) Ry & M 268.

[271] (1829) 4 Car & P 65.

[272] (1831) 1 Mood & Rob 112.

[273] (1843) 11 M&W 5.

[274] Ibid 9.

[275] (1843) 12 M&W 52.

resolved by *Hart* v. *Windsor*[276] which was an action in debt for rent due on an unfurnished letting. Parke B gave the judgment of the court, and he said:[277]

> ... to constitute a valid defence on the ground of the breach of this contract, the law must give also a right to abandon the lease upon breach of it; that is, to make a defence, the law must imply, not merely a contract, but a condition that the lease should be void if the house was unfit for occupation. The cases cited from Brooke's Abridgment 'Debt' 18 and 72 are decisive, that [even] where the lessor is bound by the custom of London, or by covenant, to repair, and does not, the tenant cannot quit.

The whole court agreed that the law had been wrongly stated in first three cases.[278] No general right to terminate for the landlord's breach could be implied into a letting of land or buildings alone.[279] The rule to the contrary in *Smith* v. *Marrable* survived only as an exception for furnished lettings.[280]

So it was settled that the rules for executory contracts were to be applied to furnished lettings, but no further,[281] and there matters rested, in this jurisdiction, until the controversy was stirred up again (remarkably, for what was just a County Court decision) by the judgment of Stephen Sedley QC[282] in *Hussian* v. *Mehlman*.[283] The judge put the issue in beguilingly simple terms:

> Although a contract of letting, whether for a term of years certain or for a periodic 'springing' term, differs from other contracts in creating an estate in land, it is nevertheless a contract: see *United Scientific Holdings Ltd* v. *Burnley Borough Council* [1978] AC 904, at pp 929E, 935B, 944B, 947B-C, 956F-H, 962A and 963H-

---

[276] (1844) 12 M& W 68.

[277] Ibid 85. The case on the custom of London is (1449) YB 27 Hen.6 f.10a pl.6.

[278] Ibid 88.

[279] *Wilson* v. *Finch Hatton* (1877) 2 ExD. 336 is to the same effect.

[280] *Oxford History of the Laws of England*, vol. 12 116–117.

[281] For the statutory implication of terms as to repair, see ch.5 heading 'Repair'.

[282] Afterwards, Sedley LJ.

[283] [1992] 2 EGLR 87. The actual decision might be supportable on the grounds that the tenancy as a furnished tenancy. The report does not reveal whether it was furnished or unfurnished.

964B, approving *C H Bailey Ltd* v. *Memorial Enterprises Ltd* [1974] 1 WLR 728; and, most recently, *Hammersmith and Fulham London Borough Council* v. *Monk* [1992] AC 478 at pp 1147C, G, and 1156C, G-H. Since, in the ordinary way, any contract may be brought to an end by one party's repudiatory conduct, the question to be answered is whether a contract of letting is an exception to the rule.

That analysis has been adopted, without argument, by the High Court[284] and the Court of Appeal[285] since.[286] But it is entirely new. The traditional rule is that if the lease is made by deed, then the true question is whether the covenants are dependent, concurrent or mutual, and if they are mutual, there cannot be any right to terminate; and even in cases where the lease is not made by deed *Sutton* v. *Temple*[287] and *Hart* v. *Windsor*[288] clearly establish that (statute apart)[289] the right to terminate can only be implied if the tenancy is a mixed letting of land and furniture. Otherwise, the landlord's promises have the force of warranties only.

The further question of whether the law of frustration of executory contracts applies to executed leases is more of an academic than a practical problem.

Long before there was any contractual doctrine of frustration which applied to executory contracts, it was accepted that complete annihilation of the physical land itself would discharge a lease. So, for instance, during the Protectorate, Rolle CJ thought that where land is wholly inundated by the sea, any lease of that land would determine,[290] though the position would be different if it were

---

[284] *Nynehead Developments* v. *Fibreboard Containers* [1999] 1 EGLR 7.

[285] *Chartered Trust* v. *Davies* [1997] 2 EGLR 83.

[286] In the first of those cases, it is hard to see how there was a breach of covenant at all, far less a repudiatory breach, and the decision in the second is inconsistent with *Morrison* v. *Chadwick* (1849) 7 CB 266.

[287] (1843) 12 M&W 52.

[288] (1844) 12 M&W 68.

[289] See ch.5 heading 'Repair'.

[290] 'Apportionment, Act of God', 1 Rol Ab 236 pl.2, Gilbert, *Rents* 186–187, Platt, *Leases*, vol. 2 130–131. In *Cricklewood Property Investment Trust* v. *Leighton's Investment Trust* [1945] AC 221, 229 Viscount Simon LC was willing to countenance that a lease might end 'if, for example, some vast convulsion of nature swallowed up the property altogether, or buried it in the depths of the sea'. Similarly, per Lord Porter, 242: 'The land in some form is there'. In *Carter* v.

inundated by freshwater, where there might still be a useful exclusive right to fish.

The reasoning was that leasehold tenure (like any other form of tenure) depended on there being some land which could be held. It followed that anything less than complete annihilation of the land would not be sufficient.[291] Accordingly, it was held in *Paradine* v. *Jane*[292] that occupation of the premises by hostile troops during the Civil War did not excuse the obligation to pay rent,[293] and similarly, in *Commissioners of Crown Lands* v. *Page*,[294] nor did emergency government requisition. The rule that nothing less than complete destruction of the land itself (and not merely any building on it) would discharge the lease, was the reason why it was necessary to give tenants of buildings destroyed in air raids during the Second World War a statutory right to disclaim their leases.[295]

The House of Lords was split on the question of whether the pure contractual law of frustration applied to leases in *Cricklewood* v. *Leighton*.[296] Lords Simon LC and Wright thought that it did. Lords Russell and Goddard thought that it could only apply if the physical land itself ceased to exist. Eventually, by a four to one majority, the House of Lords held that the pure contractual doctrine did apply to leases, in *National Carriers* v. *Panalpina*.[297] But they

---

Cummins ((1665) cited in *Harrison* v. *Lord North* (1667) 1 Ch.Cas 83) it was held that a tenant of a wharf remained liable for rent even after it had been carried away by an extraordinary flood.

[291] There can be no apportionment if land is only partly destroyed: *Richard Le Taverner's Case* (1543) Dyer 56a.

[292] (1647) Aleyn 26, *Oxford History of the Law of England*, vol. 12 509.

[293] It is possible that relief could have been obtained in equity; *Harrison* v. *Lord North* (1667) 1 Ch.Cas 83, Eq.Ca.Abr. vol. 1 365. In Scotland, by contrast, a lease of a fishery was held to be discharged by government use of the land as a bombing range: *Tay Salmon Fisheries* v. *Speedy*, 1929 SC 593.

[294] [1960] 2 QB 274.

[295] The Landlord and Tenant (War Damage) Acts 1939 and 1941. The problem was not entirely new. There is a precedent for a repairing covenant excluding damage done by 'foreign enemies' in W. West, *Simboleograph* (London, Stationers Co., 1610) pt.1 s.442.

[296] [1945] AC 221.

[297] [1981] AC 675. Dissenting on the point of whether a lease could end by frustration, Lord Russell said (709): 'I would reserve consideration of cases of physical destruction of flying leaseholds; and of the total disappearance of the site comprised in the lease into the sea so that it no longer existed in the form of a piece of terra firma and could not be the subject of re-entry or forfeiture. In that

pointed out that the nature of a lease was such that it would be difficult to think of any circumstances where a lease could be frustrated, short of the actual physical annihilation of the land, and there has been no case since in this jurisdiction in which it has been held that a lease has determined by frustration.

8. Fixtures.

A chattel becomes a fixture when someone attaches it to the land, or to a structure which forms part of the land.

The origin of the basic rule, that fixtures are irremovable, lies not in the law of landlord and tenant, but rather in the law of domestic inheritance. The issue was whether the fixtures in a house passed to the testator's executor, who could dispose of them as personalty, or descended with the land to the heir. The early policy of the law was to protect the heir, so far as possible, from any damage to the inheritance. So the executor was not allowed to disfigure the property by removing anything attached to it. Nor was a relict claiming a tenancy for life, imposed as a matter of law, by dower or curtesy. The same rule applied whether the testator had been a fee simple owner or merely a tenant for life.

That principle was already well established by 1267, when it first became possible to bring an action in waste against a tenant under a lease granted voluntarily,[298] and so it was applied to those tenants too.[299] Anything which the tenant attached to the property during the term became a part of the fee and a gift to the

---

last case it would not need the intervention of any court to say that the term of years could not outlast the disappearance of its subject matter: the site would no longer have a freehold lessor, and the obligation to pay rent, which issues out of the land, could not survive its substitution by the waves of the North Sea'. In 1557 Staunford J distinguished between a covenant to do something which had always been impossible, and a covenant to do something which became impossible subsequently. Impossibility discharged the covenant in the second case, but not in the first: *Anon* (1557) J. Baker and S. Milsom, *Sources of English Legal History*, 2nd edn. 285. See also Holdsworth, *HEL* vol. 7 274 fn.1, *Co.Litt.* 206a-b, and *Anon* (1366) 40 Ed.3 f.5 pl.11 where it was said that a covenant to maintain trees would be discharged if they were subsequently uprooted by a storm. For impossible conditions see *Bl.Comm.* Bk.II 156.

[298] See ch.9 heading 'Waste'.

[299] *Co.Litt.* 53a.

inheritance.[300]

But lettings for years were much more likely to be of business premises than of domestic mansion houses, and the policy considerations here were different. Commerce was to be encouraged as increasing the wealth of the kingdom, and there was pressure for an exception to be made accordingly. So, whilst in 1368[301] the right of a tenant for years to remove an oven was doubted,[302] and the case was adjourned, the right to remove trade fixtures attached to the floor, but not the walls,[303] was established by 1506, and that was extended to trade fixtures generally in 1703.[304] The analogy with rules of inheritance, however, meant that the exception only applied during the term. If the tenant failed to remove the fixtures before the end of the term, then they became gift to the landlord.[305]

In *Penton* v. *Robart*[306] Lord Kenyon held that a varnish house erected on a brick foundation was a removable fixture, but the court refused to extend this to agricultural buildings in *Elwes* v. *Maw*,[307] and confined it to buildings erected for the purpose of a trade. Parliament intervened in 1851,[308] giving agricultural tenants the

---

[300] (1324) YB 17 Ed.2 f.518 pl.17, (1494) YB 10 Hen.7 f.2 pl.3, *Herlakenden's Case* (1589) 4 Co.Rep 62a.

[301] YB 42 Ed.3 f.6 pl.19. In 1365 the custom of London was that a tenant for life or for years could not remove anything fixed with nails of iron or wood, nor any kind of mortar, nor plants rooted in the ground: J. Arnold, *The Customs of London* (London, Rivington, 1811) 138.

[302] Between an heir and an executor, it was clear law that an executor could not remove an oven: (1506) YB 21 Hen.7 f.26-7 pl.4.

[303] *Bodon* v. *Vampage* (1504) YB 20 Hen.7 f.13 pl.24, (1506) YB 21 Hen.7 f.26 pl.4, Caryll's Reps 116 SS 540.

[304] *Poole's Case* (1703) 1 Salk 368.

[305] *Bodon* v. *Vampage* (1504) YB 20 Hen.7 f.13 pl.24, (1506) 21 Hen.7 f.26 pl.4, Caryll's Reps 116 SS 540. There is no right to remove fixtures during an agreed stay of execution after the term; *Fitzherbert* v. *Shaw* (1789) 1 H.Black 258. But if the lease is renewed, the right to remove the fixtures is renewed too: *New Zealand Govt. Property Corpn.* v. *H.M.& S.* [1982] QB 1145, cf. *Thresher* v. *East London Waterworks* (1824) 2 Barn & Cr 608.

[306] (1801) 2 East 88, 4 Esp 33.

[307] (1802) 3 East 38. See also S. Grady, *The Law of Fixtures*, 2nd edn. (London, Wildy & Son, 1866) 74–96.

[308] s.3 Landlord and Tenant Act 1851, 14 & 15 Vic c.25. *Oxford History of the Laws of England*, vol. 12 118.

right to remove buildings, engines and machinery erected with the written consent of the landlord after 24th July 1851, and on 1st January 1884 any agricultural buildings or fixtures erected by the tenant became removable within a reasonable time after the expiration of the term.[309] That was extended to market gardens in 1895,[310] and to existing fixtures which the tenant had purchased in 1900,[311] subject, in all cases, to the landlord's right to purchase them at fair value instead. That basic scheme was continued by the Agricultural Holdings Acts of 1948[312] and 1986.[313] For farm business tenancies, regulated by the Agricultural Tenancies Act 1995, however, the rule is different. Buildings and fixtures erected by the tenant are removable by the tenant during the term, and during any period in which the tenant remains a tenant thereafter, but not otherwise.[314]

The protection afforded to the heir of domestic estates was gradually eroded in the eighteenth century, by the development of an exception which allowed an executor to remove ornamental and domestic fixtures,[315] although the exception remained in doubt until 1902,[316] and did not extend in favour of the executors of a fee simple owner.[317]

The rule that fixtures were irremovable never applied to chattels supported only by their own weight, which consequently remained chattels. Sometimes the court was willing to stretch the point. A decision in 1694 that a barn resting on wooden blocks was removable by the tenant[318] was subsequently justified on that basis,[319] and in 1818 it was even applied so as to allow a tenant to

----

[309] s.34 Agricultural Holdings Act 1883, s.21 Agricultural Holdings Act 1908. That became two months under s.58 Agricultural Holdings Act 1948.
[310] s.3(1) Market Gardeners Compensation Act 1895.
[311] s.4 Agricultural Holdings Act 1900.
[312] s.13.
[313] s.10.
[314] s.8 Agricultural Tenancies Act 1995.
[315] *Beck* v. *Rebow* (1706) 1 Peere Wms 94, *Ex parte Quincey* (1750) 1 Atk 477, *Harvey* v. *Harvey* (1740) 2 Strange 1141.
[316] *Leigh* v. *Taylor* [1902] AC 157.
[317] *Dudley* v. *Warde* (1751) Amb 113, *Elwes* v. *Maw* (1802) 3 East 38, 51.
[318] *Culling* v. *Tuffnal* (1694) Buller NP 34.
[319] *Elwes* v. *Maw* (1802) 3 East 38, 55.

dismantle an industrial crane.[320]

9. Emblements.

Emblements are crops which are sown and reaped annually.

Before the invention of the periodic tenancy in the eighteenth century,[321] most lettings of agricultural land to yeoman farmers were technically tenancies at will. In theory, that meant that the landlord could terminate the tenancy before the harvest. If the landlord did so after the tenant had sown a crop,[322] then as Littleton explained:[323]

> If the lessee soweth the land, and the lessor, after it is sowne and before the corne is ripe, put him out, yet the lessee shall have the corne, and shall have free entry and egresse and regresse to cut and carry away the corne, because he knew not at what time the lessor would enter upon him'.

The right was not confined to tenancies at will. It applied whenever a lease of agricultural land determined unexpectedly, without any fault of the tenant.[324] So if a tenant for life died, the emblements went to the tenant's executor,[325] and they could even be claimed by a tenant on an eviction by title paramount.[326] If necessary, an injunction would be granted to protect the right, even under a parol lease.[327]

But the right did not apply if a tenancy expired by effluxion of

---

[320] *Davis v. Jones* (1818) 2 Barn & Ald 165.

[321] See ch.4 heading 'Periodic'.

[322] The tenant had no remedy for the cost of ploughing and manuring the land if the landlord terminated the tenancy before the crop was sown: (1410) YB 11 Hen.4 f.90 pl.46. Nor could a claim be made if he sowed the land after the tenancy at will had come to an end: Statham's *Abridgment*, 'Entre Congeable' (1443) pl.18. But see the next section for later customary compensation on quitting.

[323] Littleton, *Tenures*, s.68.

[324] *Oland v. Burdwick* (1596) Cro Eliz 461, *Bl.Comm.* 122 *et seq.*

[325] Com Dig 'Biens' (g).

[326] *Sir Henry Knivet's Case* (1596) 5 Co.Rep 85a.

[327] *Harrison v. Chomeley* (1560/1) Cary 51.

time in the normal way[328] nor as a result of any voluntary act of the tenant. So the right was lost if the tenant ended a tenancy at will,[329] or committed a breach of covenant resulting in a forfeiture.[330] Similarly, where a lease was made determinable on the tenant's marriage, and the tenant married, then the emblements belonged to the landlord.[331]

The Landlord and Tenant Act 1851 introduced as special rule where a sub-tenancy at a rack rent determined on the death of the head tenant, and the sub-tenant would otherwise be able to claim emblements. It abolished the right to emblements and continued the sub-tenancy to the end of the year instead.[332] After 1920, in the case of an agricultural holding, the continuation was until the expiry of a 12 month notice to quit.[333]

10. Compensation on quitting.

Agricultural land: At common law, a tenant of agricultural land was entitled to compensation on quitting, in accordance with the 'custom of the country', unless that was specifically excluded by the tenancy agreement. This 'tenant-right' varied from county to county, and from time to time. At the beginning of the twentieth century, the tenant was entitled:[334]

---

[328] In some counties, by the 'custom of the country' (see the next section) there was an implied term that the tenant retained a right to emblements, after the expiry of the tenancy. By the nineteenth century, the custom was generally that the tenant would be compensated in money for the value of the 'going away crops' instead. Compensation based on the custom of the country was abolished on 1st March 1948: s.64 Agricultural Holdings Act 1948.

[329] *Parslow* v. *Cripps* (1711) 1 Comyn 204.

[330] *Davis* v. *Eyton* (1830) 7 Bing 154, 4 Moore & Payne 820.

[331] *Oland's Case* (1602) 5 Co.Rep 116a, Gouldsborough 189 pl.136 (copyhold terminated by the marriage of the female tenant).

[332] s.1. In *Haines* v. *Welch* (1868) LR 4 CP 91 it was held that this provision applied to a cottage with about an acre of land, only part of which was sown with corn and potatoes.

[333] s.14 Agriculture Act 1920, s.4 Agricultural Holdings Act 1948.

[334] T. Jackson, *The Agricultural Holdings Act 1908* (London, Sweet & Maxwell, 1912) 3.

. . . to be paid, in most counties, for the seed and labour in the last year and the preparation of the land in anticipation of a future crop, which the outgoer could not reap. In some districts allowances were made for artificial manures and the consumption of cakes and purchased feeding stuffs, whilst in eighteen English Counties and certain parts of South Wales allowances were made for improvements of a more permanent character, such as drainage, fencing, laying down pasture and buildings. Lincolnshire, Leicester, Yorkshire and Glamorgan, in particular, were counties where customs were somewhat definite, and fairly liberal allowances were made to the tenant for outlay on improvements.

The first attempt to regulate compensation by statute was in 1875,[335] but it was entirely impractical; first, because the compensation was based on the cost of the improvement rather than its value at the end of the term; and secondly, because the Act was entirely permissive, with the result that 'landlords were in such a hurry to contract out of the Act that before it had been in operation for three months it was a dead letter'.[336] A more successful attempt was made by a series of enactments between 1883 and 1900, known collectively as the Agricultural Holdings (England) Acts 1883 to 1900,[337] which were consolidated, with some amendments, into the Agricultural Holdings Act 1908.

Under these Acts, improvements to agricultural or pastoral land and market gardens were divided into three types.[338] Major improvements, such as reclaiming waste land or planting orchards, were only compensatable at the end of the term if carried out with the prior consent of the landlord, which could be given or withheld on any terms, in the case of pastoral or agricultural land,[339] but were compensatable without consent in the case of a market garden. Improvements to drainage were compensatable, if prior

---

[335] Agricultural Holdings Act 1875.

[336] T. Jackson, *The Agricultural Holdings Act 1908*, 2.

[337] The Acts were: The Agricultural Holdings (England) Act 1883, The Tenants' Compensation Act 1890, The Market Gardeners' Compensation Act 1895, and the Agricultural Holdings Act 1900.

[338] sch. 1 1900 Act.

[339] s.3 1883 Act.

notice had been given to the landlord, and if the landlord had not chosen to do the work itself, and increase the rent accordingly.[340] Minor improvements (such applying manure) were compensatable whether notice had been given or not, but the parties could make a separate agreement for 'fair and reasonable compensation' in respect of any improvement if they wished.[341] The amount of the compensation which the outgoing tenant was entitled to under the Acts was the unexhausted value of the improvement to an incoming tenant. But (except in the case of a tenant for life) adding manure to the holding was the only minor improvement for which compensation would be payable if it was carried out in the last year of the term.[342]

Disputes were settled by arbitration.[343] In 1890, the scheme was amended, so as to make it binding on a mortgagee.[344] Allotments and cottage gardens were dealt with in a similar way from 1887,[345] but the range of compensatable improvements was much smaller.

During the First World War, agricultural tenants were entitled to additional compensation for disturbance,[346] and tenants adopting special systems of farming acquired a right to additional compensation under the Agriculture Act 1920. All the existing Acts were consolidated into the Agricultural Holdings Act 1923, which contained a list of twenty-nine compensatable improvements, with compensation based on the value of the improvement to an incoming tenant. Or, if the tenant preferred, the tenant could make a claim based on custom or agreement, or otherwise in lieu of the compensation payable under the Act.[347]

The Agricultural Holdings Act 1948, which was re-enacted with amendments in 1986, introduced a different scheme for improvements made after 1st March 1948. The list of types of

---

[340] s.4 1883 Act.

[341] s.5 1883 Act.

[342] That did not prevent compensation being paid for those improvements under the custom of the country.

[343] s.2 1900 Act.

[344] s.2 1890 Act.

[345] The Allotments and Cottage Gardens Compensation for Crops Act 1887.

[346] Agricultural Holdings Act 1914.

[347] s.1(3) Agricultural Holdings Act 1923.

compensatable improvement grew to thirty five,[348] which were divided into the long term, medium term and short term improvements. Claims for compensation for disturbance for works done in the last year based on custom were abolished,[349] and instead those works were treated as short term improvements.[350] The compensation payable for short term improvements[351] was the value to an incoming tenant, calculated according to various tables.[352] Medium term improvements were only compensatable if either the landlord or the Minister of Agricultural had given consent to the improvement,[353] and long term improvements were only compensatable if carried out with the landlord's consent.[354] In both cases the amount of compensation was the amount of the increase in the value of the holding attributable to the improvement, taking account of its location and the needs of skilled farmers.[355]

In 1908 an agricultural tenant acquired an additional right to compensation for disturbance where a landlord unreasonably served notice to quit or refused to renew the tenancy,[356] which was continued, after agricultural tenants acquired security of tenure in 1948, for cases where the tenant actually left as result of a landlord's notice to quit or counternotice.[357]

Farm business tenants holding under the Agricultural Tenancies Act 1995 are entitled to compensation on quitting for physical improvements to the demised premises, and for the benefit of any planning permission obtained which remains unimplemented, provided that the landlord's written consent to the

---

[348] sch. 3–4 Agricultural Holdings Act 1948.

[349] s.64 Agricultural Holdings Act 1948.

[350] pt.II sch. 4 Agricultural Holdings Act 1948.

[351] Mole drainage (an earth-walled drain made by driving a cylinder through the sub-soil) was only compensatable if the landlord had been given notice of the intention to do the work: s.52 Agricultural Holdings Act 1948.

[352] Agriculture (Calculation of Value for Compensation) Regulations 1948, SI 1948 No.185.

[353] s.50.

[354] s.49.

[355] s.48.

[356] s.11 1908 Act.

[357] s.34 Agricultural Holdings Act 1948.

improvement or application was obtained first.[358] If the landlord refuses consent to a physical improvement, the tenant is entitled to refer that to arbitration. The amount of compensation is based on the increase in the value of the land.[359]

Business Tenants: Business tenants had no right to compensation on quitting, until the enactment of the Landlord and Tenant Act 1927,[360] which came into force on 25th March 1928.[361] The provisions of the 1927 Act dealing with compensation for improvements carried out by a business tenant, where the landlord is not willing to grant the tenant a new tenancy on reasonable terms, are still in force.[362] But it is rare for any claim to be made, because tenants do not generally comply with the statutory pre-condition that, three months before carrying out the work, plans and specifications must be served on the landlord, in order to give the landlord an opportunity to object or carry out the works itself.[363]

The 1927 Act also provided that if the landlord did not offer the tenant a new tenancy on reasonable terms, the tenant was, on quitting, entitled to compensation for 'adherent goodwill',[364] to the extent that the landlord would gain from it. If that sum was insufficient to compensate the tenant for the loss of its personal goodwill,[365] then the court could compel the landlord to grant the tenant one renewal tenancy instead, except where the landlord wished to redevelop or where the landlord, or the landlord's son or daughter, wished to occupy the property, or where that would be inconsistent with good estate management.

---

[358] ss.17-19.

[359] ss.20-21.

[360] For the provisions of that Act dealing with covenants against alteration, alienation and improvements, see ch.5.

[361] s.26.

[362] ss.1-3 Landlord and Tenant Act 1927.

[363] s.3.

[364] The classification of goodwill is zoological (*Whiteman Smith Motor Co* v. *Chaplin* [1934] 2 KB 35): the 'dog', who stays faithful to the person and not the location; the 'cat', who stays faithful to the location and not the person; the 'rabbit', who comes because it is close and for no other reason; and the 'rat', who is casual and is attracted to neither person nor location. Only the 'cat' goodwill was adherent to the tenant's business for the purpose of the Act; ibid.

[365] I.e. lost dogs.

The provisions of the 1927 Act dealing with goodwill were repealed with effect from 1st October 1954.[366] Since then, the compensation provisions have been in s.37 Landlord and Tenant Act 1954, which provides for the landlord to pay the tenant compensation on quitting, where the landlord successfully opposes or prevents renewal on a non-fault ground only.[367] The compensation is based on a multiple of the rateable value of the property, and there is a larger multiple where the business has been established at the premises for 14 years or more, though the right to compensation can be excluded contractually in a tenancy for a term of less than five years.[368]

Residential tenants: Residential tenants have never had any general[369] right to compensation for improvements or disturbance at the end of their tenancies.

---

[366] s.45 Landlord and Tenant Act 1954.

[367] s.37.

[368] s.38(3).

[369] Where an assured tenant is required to vacate on the grounds that suitable alternative accommodation is available, or on the grounds that the landlord wishes to redevelop, removal expenses are payable: s.11 Housing Act 1988.

CHAPTER 8
Death, Insolvency and Dissolution

---

1. Devolution on death

2. Liability of the heir and personal representatives

3. Bankruptcy and personal insolvency

4. Corporate winding up and dissolution

5. Mortmain

This chapter is about the ways in which the landlord and tenant relationship is changed, consequent upon a change in the status of one of the parties.

The changes are normally involuntary: death, insolvency, and dissolution. The rules for voluntary transfers are dealt with in chapter 6.

1. Devolution on death.

A fee simple: When a sole[1] fee simple owner of land dies, the land now vests automatically in his or her personal representatives. So where the reversion upon a lease is a fee simple, the personal representatives of the dead owner become the landlord.[2] But before

---

[1] For the devolution in the case of joint tenancies, see ch. 1 heading 'Capacity' sub-heading 'joint tenants and tenants in common'.

[2] A proving executor's title relates back to the date of the death. An administrator's title only takes effect from the date of the appointment: the land vests in the Public Trustee in the meantime. See below sub-heading 'leasehold land'.

1898,[3] the rule was completely different. If the fee simple owner died having made a will, which made a valid disposition of the land,[4] then the land vested automatically and immediately in the legatee under the will.[5] Otherwise, it descended automatically and immediately to the dead owner's heir at law,[6] or, if there was no heir, escheated to the lord. It never vested in the owner's personal representatives, as such, whether they were executors or administrators. So, if the reversion upon a lease was a fee simple, and the landlord died, the legatee, heir or superior lord would become the new landlord immediately.[7]

In the fourteenth century, it was suggested that the new landlord would be entitled to any rent arrears owing at the date of

---

[3] s.1 Land Transfer Act 1897.

[4] At common law, most freehold estates could not be devised by will, though there were some customary exceptions, most importantly, in London: these were 'burgage tenements devisable': *Bl.Comm.* Bk.II 84. Before 1536 it was possible to avoid this problem, by declaring a lifetime trust of the land, to take effect on death (Holdsworth, *HEL* vol. 7 363–364). That was prohibited by the Statute of Uses (1536), so practitioners experimented with schemes which involved incumbering the land with long leases, which could be devised instead (J. Baker and S. Milsom, *Sources of English Legal History*, 2nd edn. 135–137). The policy of prohibiting wills of freehold land was reversed by the Statute of Wills 1540 which made all of the testator's socage land, and two thirds of any land held under military tenure, devisable from 20th July 1540. The Tenures Abolition Act 1660 turned all freehold land into socage land, except frankalmoign, which was not devisable in any event, since it was held by the church.

[5] A legacy of freehold land which lapsed, because the legatee pre-deceased the testator, would not pass into residue: O.W. Holmes, *The Common Law* 268.

[6] The heir was the oldest descendant of the deceased, following the male line, and taking the issue of deceased elder sons in preference to living younger sons. If that descendant was male, he was the sole heir; if female, she would take equally with any sisters as coparceners (see ch.1 heading 'Capacity' sub-heading 'coparceners'). If there were no descendants at all, then the heir would be a collateral relative descended from a common ancestor of the deceased: for the rules in detail see, Holdsworth, *HEL* vol. 3 171–185, Simpson, *History of Land Law* 55–58, Challis *Real Property* 237–250. But there were various customary exceptions to this rule of primogeniture, most notably in Kent, where land passed to all surviving male children equally (gavelkind) and in some Borough-English towns, where it passed to the youngest son instead. See Challis, *Real Property* 14–17. The identity of the heir was fixed by law, and depended on who was living at the date of the death, for *solus deus heredum facere potest, non homo*: only god can make an heir, not man.

[7] For the consequences where the landlord died on a rent day, see ch.3 heading 'Payment'.

death too,[8] but a statute in 1540 confirmed that the arrears would go to the personal representatives instead,[9] except on the death of a married woman, in which event the right to distrain for the arrears, and sue for them in debt, passed to her widower.[10]

A fee tail: A fee tail could not be devised by will. Land held in fee tail would descend automatically to the next individual entitled, and the course of its descent could not be changed by will.[11] So where the reversion on a lease consisted of a fee tail, on the death of the landlord, the reversion passed automatically to the next entitled descendant, or, should the line have become extinct, to the successor of the original grantor.[12] But a fee tail could be barred, turning it into a fee simple, from the fifteenth century onwards, by a collusive recovery; and from 1834 by a simple disentailing deed;[13] and from 1926, by will, when a fee tail became an equitable estate subsisting behind a Settled Land Act strict settlement in any event.[14] Where it was barred, the land devolved in the same way as a fee simple.

A lease of life: A lease for life was a freehold estate until 1926,[15] which would expire automatically, at the very moment when the person, on whose life it depended, died.[16] If that person was also the current tenant of the lease, then it would end automatically on the

---

[8] Statham's *Abridgment*, 'Debt' (1348) pl.33 per Thorpe J. Paston J said, in 1431, that the heir could distrain for the arrears but would not be able to bring an action in debt: (1431) YB 9 Hen.6 f.16 pl.7.

[9] s.1 Cestui Que Vie Act 1540. There was always, however, some doubt as to whether that extended to arrears of rent owed by a leasehold tenant: see E. Vaughan Williams, *The Law of Executors and Administrators*, vol. 2 (London, Saunders and Benning, 1832) 605–607. Eventually, it was decided that it did not (Coote, *Leases* 439–440), and so power to collect the arrears was eventually granted by s.37 Civil Procedure Act 1833.

[10] s.3 Cestui Que Vie Act 1540.

[11] See ch.1 heading 'Capacity' sub-heading 'fee tail owners'.

[12] On the question of whether the tenancy would be binding against the successor, see ch.1 heading 'Capacity' sub-heading 'tenant for life'.

[13] s.15 Fines and Recoveries Act 1833.

[14] s.176 Law of Property Act 1925, *Otter v. Church Adams Tatham & Co* [1953] Ch 280.

[15] See ch.4 heading 'For life'.

[16] The consequences for undertenants are explained in ch.4.

tenant's death, and those entitled to the fee[17] in reversion or remainder would take the property free of the tenancy for life.

If, however, the current tenant died, and the lease was for the life of someone else—a lease pur autre vie[18]—who was still alive, then the lease for life would continue, but without a tenant. Yet the common law abhorred a vacancy in a freehold. So if the lease pur autre vie had been granted expressly to the tenant and the tenant's heirs, the lease devolved[19] upon the heir as 'special occupant'.[20] If, however, the lease had simply been granted to the 'tenant', the first person who entered or remained on the land after the tenant's death became entitled to the lease as 'general occupant'.[21]

That was changed by s.12 Statute of Frauds (1677), which effected two reforms. First, it allowed a legatee instead of the heir at law to take as special occupant, by making tenancies pur autre vie devisable. Secondly, it abolished general occupancy by vesting the tenancy in the executors[22] or administrators[23] of the tenant, if there was no special occupant.[24] Afterwards, an estate pur autre vie granted to the tenant and his personal representatives, would be

---

[17] The reversioner could not be a leasehold tenant for years, by reason of the rule that a lease for life could not be carved out of a lease for years: see ch.4 heading 'For life'.

[18] The life had to be in being at the time the lease was granted: *Doe d. Pemberton* v. *Edwards* (1836) 1 M&W 553.

[19] Strictly, it did not 'descend' upon the tenant's heir or legatee. What was inherited was a right of entry: Challis, *Real Property*, 358.

[20] Simpson, *History of Land Law*, 86. It was doubtful whether a personal representative could, at common law, be a special occupant, even if the grant was made to the tenant and the tenant's executors and administrators, since a freehold estate could not devolve upon personal representatives: Challis, *Real Property*, 359–361.

[21] *Co.Litt.* 41b, F. Bacon, *The Use of the Law* (London, Moore, 1630) 53. So in *Skelliton* v. *Hay* (1619) Cro Jac 554 a sub-tenant at will became the general occupant on the death of the tenant pur autre vie, 'for he being in possession, the law casts the freehold on him unless he waives it'.

[22] In *Oldham* v. *Pickering* (1696) 2 Salk 464, it was held that an executor could not be forced to account to the estate for the benefit of the tenancy, since it vested in the executor for the purpose of paying the testator's debts, and otherwise personally as the occupant. That rule was reversed in 1741 by 14 Geo.2 c.20, s.9.

[23] Richard Preston mischievously suggested that, on an intestacy, a stranger might still take as general occupant between the death and the grant of letters of administration, since an administrator's title (unlike that of an executor) does not relate back to the death: Preston, *Conveyancing*, vol. 1 44.

[24] See now s.6 Wills Act 1837.

treated as part of the tenant's personal estate.[25]

Originally, there was also a problem for leasehold tenants where the reversion upon a lease was land held in military tenure, the reversioner died, and the reversioner's heir was an infant. The term in the lease would be suspended, during the heir's infancy, so that the lord could enjoy the land free of the lease in exercise of his right of wardship.[26] But the courts reversed the priorities in the sixteenth century, so that the land would pass to the lord subject to the lease instead.[27] There was a similar problem with a widow's right to dower out of her husband's freehold land, which lasted much longer. If the lease was made before the marriage, then all the widow was entitled to was one third of the reversion.[28] But if it was made during the marriage, her right to dower took priority to the tenancy, the tenancy was suspended during her widowhood,[29] and the term had to be lengthened in compensation.[30]

Dower was eventually abolished by the Dower Act 1833, which replaced it with a widow's claim against her late husband's estate held at the date of his death.[31]

Copyhold land: Copyhold land passed directly to the legatee too, but for a different reason. In strict legal theory, at any rate, a copyhold tenement was held as a tenant at will of the lord of the manor. By the Elizabethan period, practises and customs within manors had hardened into rights, enforceable in equity.[32] These customs generally included heritability, though the practice varied from manor to manor: in some, a heriot of the deceased copyholder's best beast might be payable; in another, a monetary

---

[25] *Duke of Devon* v. *Atkins* (1726) 2 Peere Wms 381.

[26] Bracton, vol. 2 100 (f.30).

[27] See ch.4 heading 'Fixed terms'.

[28] *Co.Litt.* 32a, 208a.fn(1), J. Park, *The Law of Dower* (London, Clarke, 1819) 299–301.

[29] So leases sometimes contained a landlord's covenant that the landlord would provide his widow with full dower out of other land, or that if the widow recovered dower out of the demised property, the landlord's executors would grant a substitute lease out of other land: Kaye, *Medieval English Conveyances* 260–261.

[30] Bracton, vol. 3 397 (f.312), *Co.Litt.* 46a, *Shep.Touch.* 275.

[31] Holdsworth, *HEL* vol. 3 189–197.

[32] See ch.1 heading 'Capacity' sub-heading 'copyholders'.

fine; and in others, nothing at all. But, in all of them, the underlying structure was the same, and was dictated by the old common law theory that the copyholder was a tenant at will. Since a tenancy at will determines automatically on the death of either party, the transmission on the death of the copyholder was by surrender to the lord 'to the use of' (i.e. on trusts of) the will or the intestacy. The preliminary surrender became unnecessary in 1815[33] and copyhold land became an asset available to pay the testator's debts in 1833.[34]

Leasehold land: A leasehold term of years[35] has always vested in the tenant's personal representatives on death, as part of the testator's personal estate.[36]

Although the rule might have been in doubt, at the time it was propounded by Littleton in the fifteenth century, it was clearly settled by 1518.[37] This was so even if the lease was granted to the tenant as a corporation sole.[38]

If the personal representative was an executor, who proved the tenant's will, then the executor's title to the lease related back to the death of the tenant.[39] On an intestacy, between 1285[40] and 1858,

---

[33] s.1 Copyhold Act 1815.

[34] 3 & 4 Wm.4 c.104.

[35] The same applied to an option to take or renew a lease: *Chapman* v. *Dalton* (1565) Plowden 284.

[36] Littleton, *Tenures*, s.740. A lease for a term of years, unlike a freehold estate, could not be transmitted by words of limitation (eg to 'x' for life, remainder to 'y') except in the case of the Crown: Chambers, *Leases*, 2, Halsbury's Laws, *Real Property* vol. 39(2), 4th edn., ¶.104.

[37] *Doctor and Student* 66, Kaye, *Medieval English Conveyances* 258–259, Halsbury's Laws, *Real Property* vol. 39(2), 4th edn., ¶.103.

[38] *Co.Litt*. 46b. Leases granted to the Chamberlain of the City of London were an exception at common law (*Byrd* v. *Wilford* (1596) Cro Eliz 464, Coote, *Leases* 7, cf. Chambers, *Leases*, 2) and the general rule was reversed by s.3(5) Administration of Estates Act 1925.

[39] An executor was allowed to sue in ejectment for a wrongful ouster of the testator, notwithstanding the common law rule that actions in tort abated on the death of the perpetrator or the victim, by an equitable construction of the statute of 4.Ed.3 c.7, which allowed executors to sue in trespass for goods taken from the testator: (1406) YB 7 Hen.4 f.6b pl.1, J. Ames, *Lectures on Legal History* (Cambridge Mass, Harvard University Press, 1913) 233, G. Gilbert, *Law and Practice of Ejectment*, 2nd edn. (London, Nutt & Gosling, 1741) 69–70. The common law rule was reversed (except for defamation) by s.1 Law Reform (Miscellaneous Provisions) Act 1934.

the lease vested initially in the Bishop. After 1858, the initial vesting was in the Probate Judge.[41] The administrator acquired title only on appointment later, under the authority of the Bishop or Probate Courts.

Since it was personal estate, a leasehold tenancy could be devised by will, at common law, even if the term was for as long as a thousand years. For this reason, before freehold estates became fully devisable, leases for long terms of years were often created for estate planning purposes.[42] When periodic tenancies came to be recognised as valid at the end of the eighteenth century, it was natural that those should be treated in the same way as longer leases. In *Doe d. Shore* v. *Porter*[43] Lord Kenyon said:[44]

> The tenancy from year to year succeeded to the old tenancy at will, which was attended with many inconveniences. And in order to obviate them, the Courts very early raised an implied contract for a year, and added that the tenant could not be removed at the end of the year without receiving six months previous notice. And all the inconveniences which arise between the original parties themselves, and against which the wisdom of the law has endeavoured to provide by raising the implied contract exist equally in the case of their personal representatives.

There was one thing that an individual could do with a leasehold term by will, which could not be done by way of a lifetime disposition of it,[45] and that was to create successive interests in it.[46] A lifetime assignment of a leasehold interest to 'A' for life, with a remainder over to 'B', would take effect as an outright assignment to 'A'. The reasoning was that a life interest

---

[40] Statute of Westminster II (1285), Coke, *2nd Inst*, 397–398.

[41] s.19 Court of Probate Act 1858, s.9 Administration of Estates Act 1925. Since 1994, it has vested in the Public Trustee: s.14(1) Law of Property (Miscellaneous Provisions) Act 1994.

[42] See ch.4 heading 'Fixed terms'. cf Lord Mansfield's dictum in *Mackay* v. *Mackreth* (1785) 4 Doug 213, that the tenancy would go the executors if they were named in the grant, but otherwise would determine on the tenant's death.

[43] (1789) 3 Term Rep 13.

[44] Ibid 17.

[45] Holdsworth, *HEL* vol. 7 129.

[46] *Throgmorton* v. *Tracey* (1555) Plowden 145, 155.

was a higher estate than any estate for years,[47] even one of a thousand years, so a gift for life was necessarily a gift for the whole term.[48] A lifetime gift of a chattel for any lesser period of time was a gift forever too.[49] Originally, exactly the same rule was applied to a devise of leasehold land. But the law changed to allow these executory devises between 1568 and 1612,[50] with the result that although a life interest still could not be created in a leasehold term during the tenant's lifetime, except in equity by way of trust, it could be created by will. Since 1926, however, successive terms created by will operate in equity only.[51]

There was also a curious exception to the rule that the length of a leasehold term must be 'certain', where the testator granted his personal representatives a term by will to pay his debts from the income of the lease. In that case the term was valid against the heir or legatee, notwithstanding the absence of any certainty about how long the term would last.[52]

At common law, one of two joint executors could assign a term vested in them as such[53] and a lease granted by one executor was binding on all.[54] After 1926, they all had to join in any assignment or grant.[55]

2. Liability of the heir and personal representatives.

Where freehold land descended to an heir, the heir was not under any obligation to pay the debts of the deceased. That was the duty of the personal representatives, and they were obliged to

---

[47] *Welcden* v. *Elkington* (1578) Plowden 516, 520. Hence a term of years would always merge in a lease for life: see ch.7 heading 'Surrender and merger'.

[48] J. Gray, *The Rule against Perpetuities*, 3rd edn. (Boston, Little Brown, 1915) ¶.808.

[49] J. Gray, *The Rule against Perpetuities*, 3rd edn. ¶.822, J. Baker and S. Milsom, *Sources of English Legal History*, 2nd edn. 265, 206.

[50] *Lampet's Case* (1612) 10 Co.Rep 46b, Holdsworth, *HEL* vol. 7 131–132.

[51] s.1 Settled Land Act 1925, *Re Bird* [1927] 1 Ch 210, 216.

[52] *Sir Andrew Corbet's Case* (1599) 4 Co.Rep 81b, *Blamford* v. *Blamford* (1615) 3 Bulstrode 98, 100, D'Anvers, *Abridgment*, vol. 3 233.

[53] *Anon* (1536) Dyer 23b.

[54] *Doe d. Hayes* v. *Sturges* (1816) 7 Taunt 217.

[55] s.2(2), s.3(1)(i) Administration of Estates Act 1925.

satisfy those debts out of the deceased's personal estate alone. If the deceased's personal estate proved insufficient for the purpose, the heir might make up the difference as a matter of honour, but he was under no legal obligation to do so.

There was one common law exception to this. Where freehold land descended to an heir, it was automatically charged with the performance of any covenant which the ancestor had expressly made on behalf of his heir,[56] whether the covenant related to that land or not.[57] There was nothing to stop the heir disposing of the land free from that charge, but the heir's personal obligation to perform the covenant, up to the value of the land, remained. Freehold land held in trust for the heir and estates pur autre vie which descended to the heir as special occupant[58] were made subject to the same obligations by ss.10 and 12 Statute of Frauds (1677), and legatees of freehold land, including estates pur autre vie,[59] were put in the same position as an heir by the Fraudulent Devises Act 1691.[60] Between 1881 and 1897 the testator's freehold land was charged with performance of all covenants, whether purportedly made on behalf of the heir or not,[61] and it became available to meet a deficiency of the personal estate for other debts generally in 1833.[62] In practice, well drawn wills often incumbered the testator's freehold land with a lease granted to the executors for the purpose of paying the testator's debts,[63] and has already been noted,[64] those leases were exempt from the rule that the length of a leasehold term must be certain.

---

[56] *Kaynes* v. *Berevylle* (1277) YB 5 Ed.1 pl.1, 111 SS 82, (1536) Dyer, Note, 14a.

[57] Platt, *Covenants*, 63, 448–449, *Bl.Comm.* Bk.II 243–244. So landlords usually insisted that the tenant's covenants contained in a lease were made by the tenant expressly on behalf of 'heirs' as well as personal representatives, so that if the tenant's heir inherited any freehold land, it would be charged with performance of the covenants in the lease: Platt, *Leases*, vol. 2 165.

[58] See the previous section.

[59] *Westfaling* v. *Westfaling* (1746) 3 Atk 460.

[60] Repealed and re-enacted in the Debts Recovery Act 1830. See *Re Atkinson* [1908] 2 Ch 307.

[61] s.59 Conveyancing Act 1881.

[62] 3 & 4 Wm.4 c.104.

[63] See e.g. *Sir Andrew Corbet's Case* (1599) 4 Co.Rep 81b.

[64] See the previous section.

Where a lease vests in a personal representative, there are two quite separate ways in which he or she can be made liable to pay the rent and perform covenants.[65]

The first is called the 'representative' liability. A personal representative owes a duty to all the creditors of the estate, including any landlord, to get the assets in, and pay the testator's debts out of those assets,[66] before making any distribution out to a legatee. The debts which must be paid in this way include any arrears of rent or other sums due under the lease at the date of death,[67] as well as sums accruing due during the period of administration, whilst the lease remains vested in the personal representative.

If sued by the landlord in this representative capacity, the representative can defend the claim by pleading *plene administravit*, meaning that the assets collected proved insufficient to pay all the debts in full, and that each creditor has been a paid a due proportion. Someone sued as a personal representative, whether for rent or not,[68] is able to do this because a money claim made against someone in that capacity can only be brought on the

---

[65] Claims in simple contract under a parol lease were provable too: see *Norwood* v. *Read* (1558) Plowden 180.

[66] Before 1870, debts due under covenants had to be paid in priority to ordinary contract debts. Ordinary contract debts were put in the same footing as covenants by Hinde Palmer's Act 1869. Before that Act, even rent under a parol lease had the same priority as a debt due under a covenant; *Phillips* v. *Lee* (1679) 1 Freeman 262. In *Re Hastings* (1877) 6 CP 610 it was held that the Act had abolished that special priority too.

[67] That included damages for breach of a covenant committed before the testator died: *Anon* (1536) Dyer 14a. But it did not include damages for any tort committed by the testator. The rule for torts (until it was reversed by specifically for waste by s.26(5) Administration of Estates Act 1925, and then generally for torts other than defamation by s.1 Law Reform (Miscellaneous Provisions) Act 1934) was that the cause of action died with the testator. This included any liability the testator had to pay mesne profits, although not for use and occupation: *Monypenny* v. *Bristow* (1830) 2 Rus & Mylne 117, 124. For the difference, see ch.9 heading 'Mesne Profits'. In equity, a personal representative could be made to pay a sum equivalent to mesne profits, if the claimant had been prevented by an injunction from proceeding against the testator during his or her lifetime, on the principle *actus curiæ neminem gravibit*: an act of the court shall prejudice no one. Ashburner, *Equity* 3–4.

[68] *Boulton* v. *Canon* (1673) 1 Freeman 336, *Jenkins* v. *Hermitage* (1674) 1 Freeman 377.

basis that the representative is wrongly 'detaining' money, and not on the basis that the representative 'owes' the money too.[69] But if the lease is income producing, then the income must be applied first towards the rent, rather than the general body of creditors, and the defence as to the rest will *plene administravit praeter*.

There was a problem, however, with contingent liabilities. Once the representative had disposed of the lease—either by selling it in the course of administration or assenting it out to a legatee— there was always the possibility that the ultimate tenant might become insolvent, and that the landlord might try to enforce the covenants in the lease against the representative again; for representatives stand in the shoes of the testator, and if the testator would have remained liable on the covenants after an assignment, the testator's estate remained liable too.[70] In theory, that meant that the representatives could not safely distribute even a solvent estate without first setting aside a fund against that eventuality, or insuring against it,[71] or going to the expense of distributing under the protection of an administration order.[72] Parliament intervened, in 1859, by limiting the representatives' duty to make provision for contingent liabilities under a lease to 'any fixed or ascertainable sum which the tenant agreed to lay out on the property', and otherwise allowing the representatives to distribute,[73] excusing them from further representative liability.

The second way in which a personal representative can be made liable on the lease is called the 'personal' liability of the representative. The rule is that if a personal representative enters into possession of the property, then he or she becomes personally liable as an assignee of the term, even though possession has only

---

[69] In an ordinary claim to recover a debt, the allegation was 'debet and detinet': he owes and he detains. Against a representative, sued as such, it could only be 'detinet'; Platt, *Leases*, vol. 2 368.

[70] *Wilson* v. *Wigg* (1808) 10 East 313. It was possible that the executors might be liable in debt too, if the landlord had not accepted the assignee: *Overton* v. *Sydall* (1597) Cro Eliz 555, Gouldsborough 120 pl.6.

[71] *Nector* v. *Gennet* (1595) Cro Eliz 466, *Wildridge* v. *M'Kane* (1828) 1 Molloy Cas Ch 122, 125, *Fletcher* v. *Stevenson* (1844) 3 Hare 360.

[72] *Buckley* v. *Nesbitt* (1880) 5 LR Ir 199.

[73] ss.27-28 Law of Property Amendment Act 1859, s.8 Law of Property Amendment Act 1860, s.26 Trustee Act 1925.

been taken for the benefit of the deceased's estate.[74]

If sued personally, a representative cannot plead *plene administravit*,[75] is liable on implied covenants in the same way as on express covenants,[76] and must pay in full, irrespective of whether there are sufficient assets in the estate to meet that liability or not.[77]

The harshness of this rule has resulted in two curious exceptions. First, in order to mitigate the rental liability, the representative is allowed to plead that the open market rental value of the land is less than the passing rent, in which event the representative's personal liability for the rent is limited to the rental value.[78] Secondly, although there is no 'value' limitation on a representative's liability for the other covenants, such as the covenant to repair,[79] the liability can be capped by offering to surrender the lease, and if the landlord refuses, the representative is excused from liability on any non-rental covenant accruing due for performance afterwards.[80]

3. Bankruptcy and personal insolvency.

Individual bankruptcy was originally a criminal matter.[81]

---

[74] *Caly* v. *Joslin* (1647) Aleyn 34, *Re Owers* [1941] 1 Ch 389.

[75] *Paule* v. *Moodie* (1619) 2 Rol Reps 131.

[76] *Newton* v. *Osborn* (1653) Style 387.

[77] *Buckley* v. *Pirk* (1710) 1 Salk 316.

[78] *Buckley* v. *Pirk* (1710) 1 Salk 316, *Hopwood* v. *Whaley* (1848) 6 CB 743, *In Re Bowes, Earl of Strathmore* v. *Vane* (1887) 37 Ch.D 128. In *Mawle* v. *Cacyffr* (1619) Cro Jac 549 it was said that, if this was pleaded specially, then the representative's liability would be discharged, and in *Remnant* v. *Bembridge* (1818) 8 Taunt 191 the court went even further and held that an executor was chargeable only with the rent actually received, but that was disapproved in *Hopwood* v. *Whaley* (1848) 6 CB 743 and in *Whithead* v. *Palmer* [1908] 1 KB 151, 157.

[79] *Tremeere* v. *Morison* (1834) 1 Bing NC 89, *Hornidge* v. *Wilson* (1840) 11 A&E 645, 655.

[80] *Reid* v. *Lord Tenterden* (1833) 4 Tyrw 111. But see Platt, *Covenants* 201–202 and *Holtzapffel* v. *Baker* (1811) 18 Ves Jun 115.

[81] Bankruptcy Act 1543.

Non-criminal bankruptcy (or something close to it) became possible, for merchants engaged in trade,[82] under an Elizabethan statute,[83] which empowered the Chancellor to appoint bankruptcy commissioners to seize the property of a bankrupt trader, and then distribute it for the benefit of the trader's creditors.[84] In 1604, the scheme was changed,[85] and reinforced in 1732,[86] so that the commissioners would vest the bankrupt's property by deed in assignees appointed by the creditors, who would distribute it instead. A court of bankruptcy was established to control the process in 1831,[87] which maintained a panel of thirty official assignees, one of whom would be chosen initially to get in all the property of the bankrupt, and then (after the creditors had appointed their own assignees) to join with them in administering the bankrupt trader's estate. The vesting in the assignees under the 1831 Act was automatic.[88] A bankrupt who co-operated in the process could obtain a discharge[89] in respect of all the provable debts,[90] with the consent of the creditors[91] or by petition to the court of chancery.[92]

Where the bankrupt trader's property included a lease, the lease did not vest unconditionally in the assignees appointed under the commission, either when the commissioners assigned it to them

---

[82] *Bl.Comm.* Bk.II 473–474. For the gradual extension of this category, see *Oxford History of the Laws of England*, vol. 12 781.

[83] s.1 Bankruptcy Act 1570.

[84] This was based on the model for criminal bankruptcy contained in the Bankruptcy Act 1543. It provided that a three member commission drawn from Privy Councillors and the Chief Justices of King's Bench and Common Pleas, could examine the bankrupt on oath about his assets and direct a sale and rateable distribution. There was no discharge, and the bankrupt remained personally liable for unsatisfied debts.

[85] s.13 Bankruptcy Act 1604.

[86] s.30 Bankruptcy Act 1732, *Roe d. Hunter* v. *Galliers* (1787) 2 Term Rep. 133.

[87] Bankruptcy Act 1831.

[88] ss.25–26.

[89] s.19 Bankruptcy Act 1705, 4 Anne c.17 s.19, 7 Anne c.25.

[90] Unliquidated claims for tort damages were not provable, but the claim against the bankrupt survived any discharge. The same applied to contingent debts: *Mayor* v. *Steward* (1769) 4 Burr 2439.

[91] 5 Anne c.22.

[92] 14 Geo.3 c.77, s.59, 16 Geo.3 c.38, s.69.

before the 1831 Act, or afterwards, when it vested in them automatically.[93] The vesting was suspended,[94] so that, if the lease was onerous, they could reject it as *damnosa haereditas*. But the assignees had to make their election promptly, and if they took possession of the property, that would be treated as an election to accept it.[95]

If the assignees elected to accept the lease, they would become liable to the landlord for the rent and on the covenants contained in the lease, as if the bankrupt had assigned it to them personally on the date on which the tenant had committed the act of bankruptcy[96] which had caused him to be made bankrupt, and for so long thereafter as the lease remained vested in them.[97]

Their acceptance discharged the bankrupt from any further liability under the lease in debt,[98] but not on any express covenant in the case of a lease made by deed[99] nor in simple contract otherwise.[100] In 1809 the law was changed,[101] so that acceptance by the assignees discharged the bankrupt from further liability in covenant or contract too, and the landlord was given power to put the assignees to their election whether to accept the lease or not.[102]

If, instead, the assignees elected to reject the lease, it would remain vested in the bankrupt tenant, and the bankrupt tenant

---

[93] *Thompson* v. *Bradbury* (1834) 3 Dowl P. Pra. 147, 1 Bing NC 326.

[94] Platt, *Covenants*, 511–512. In Ireland, the effect of the Bankruptcy (Ireland) Act 1857 was that the lease remained vested in the bankrupt tenant until an assignee in bankruptcy elected to take it: *Hanway* v. *Taylor* (1873) IR 8 CL 254.

[95] *Hanson* v. *Stevenson* (1818) 1 Barn & Ald 303. Platt, *Covenants* 507–510.

[96] Fleeing abroad or locking yourself up in your house, for the purpose of avoiding your creditors, were the original acts of bankruptcy (Bankruptcy Act 1543). The list gradually increased. Composition agreements often produced a greater return for the creditors than formal bankruptcy, and these were encouraged by Acts which protected the debtor from bankruptcy (e.g. Debtor's Arrangement Act 1844).

[97] The assignees acquired the property by operation of law and so were only liable by privity of estate. Consequently, they did not need an indemnity covenant when they sold on: Platt, *Covenants*, 181.

[98] *Wadham* v. *Marlow* (1784) 8 East 314n.

[99] *Auriol* v. *Mills* (1790) 4 Term Rep 94.

[100] *Boot* v. *Wilson* (1807) 8 East 311.

[101] s.19 Bankruptcy Act 1809.

[102] It did not prevent a former tenant suing on an indemnity, and the amount of the indemnity being uncertain, it survived the bankruptcy: *Taylor* v. *Young* (1820) 3 Barn & Ald 521.

would remain liable for the rent and for the future performance of the covenants.[103] In 1825 the law was changed so that a bankrupt tenant who delivered the lease up to the landlord within 14 days of being notified that the assignees had rejected it, would be treated as having been discharged from all liability under the lease accruing due since the commission.[104]

Until 1861, non-criminal bankruptcy was a privilege that was only available to individuals engaged in trade. A trader, venturing his capital, might fail as the result of bad-luck or misfortune, but, for anyone else, incurring debts without having the ability to repay them was a form of fraud. So non-traders could be sent to rot in prison, until they did pay; or until the prisons became so full that it became necessary, periodically, to enact temporary legislation allowing them to be released if they disclosed all their assets. In 1812 permanent legislation made it possible for an imprisoned debtor to petition for his release,[105] but the debtor had to deliver an assignment of all of his property to a provisional assignee at the same time as lodging his petition.[106] The provisional assignee would subsequently assign the property on to assignees appointed by the creditors,[107] whose title would relate back to the original petition, as if they had been appointed originally.

Under this scheme for the relief of insolvent individuals, the creditors' assignees were allowed a reasonable time to decide whether to accept the lease or not, and if they accepted it, that discharged the insolvent tenant from all further liability on the lease.[108] The landlord could apply to the court requiring them to

---

[103] *Copeland* v. *Stephens* (1818) 1 Barn & Ald 593.

[104] s.75 Bankruptcy Act 1825. If the bankrupt was an assignee, the original tenant would remain liable on a covenant to pay the rent, even after the lease had been delivered up: *Manning* v. *Flight* (1832) 3 Barn & Ad 211.

[105] 52 Geo.3 c.165 s.12. The drafting was badly botched, and it was necessary to amend it several times soon afterwards: 53 Geo.3 c.6, 54 Geo.3 c.23, 7 Geo.4 c.57. This was also briefly possible during the Protectorate: H. Scobell, *Acts and Ordinances 1640–1646* (London, Hills & Field, 1658) 23. Under 5 & 6 Vic. c.116 it became possible, by this means, to obtain protection from being imprisoned in the first place.

[106] The assignment became automatic under s.37 Insolvent Debtors Relief Act 1838.

[107] This too became automatic under s.45 Insolvent Debtors Relief Act 1838.

[108] s.50 Insolvent Debtors Relief Act 1838.

elect between accepting the lease and delivering the property up to the landlord.[109] But if they otherwise declined to accept it, then the insolvent tenant remained liable on the covenants,[110] and there was no equivalent of the procedure in bankruptcy for relieving the insolvent tenant of that liability. Since the insolvent debtor himself initiated the procedure, the transfer to the assignees was a voluntary disposition for the purpose of alienation covenants.[111]

In 1861, the general bankruptcy scheme was extended to insolvent individuals who were not engaged in any trade,[112] and the role of the official assignee was changed, so that instead of acting with the creditors' assignees, the official assignee would instead be discharged on their appointment. The title of the creditors' assignees also ceased to relate back to the act of bankruptcy, and instead related back only to the date of the bankruptcy order.

The official assignee was replaced by the registrar of the bankruptcy court in the Bankruptcy Act 1869, which also replaced the creditors assignees with a trustee supervised by a committee of creditors.[113] By s.23 of that Act, the trustee acquired a statutory power to disclaim the lease after having accepted it. The power could only be exercised with the permission of the court,[114] and if it was exercised, the lease would be deemed to have been surrendered on the date when the bankruptcy order had been made. Whether this deemed surrender also discharged third parties liable on the tenant covenant was controversial,[115] until the House of Lords decided in *Hill* v. *East and West India Dock Co*[116] that it did not.

An 'official receiver' was substituted for the registrar of the court as the initial trustee by the Bankruptcy Act 1883,[117] which

---

[109] Ibid.

[110] Platt, *Leases*, vol. 2 354.

[111] Platt, *Leases*, vol. 2 255. For the inter-relationship between insolvency and disposition covenants, see ch.5 hearing 'Alienation'.

[112] s.69 Bankruptcy Act 1861.

[113] s.14.

[114] r.28 Bankruptcy Rules 1871.

[115] *Smalley* v. *Hardinge* (1881) 7 QBD 524, *Ex parte Walton, In Re Levy* (1881) 17 Ch.D 746.

[116] (1884) 9 App.Cas. 448. Lord Bramwell dissented, observing (460): 'I should say undoubtedly that the weight of authority is so against me that I must somehow be wrong, though I cannot see it'.

[117] s.66 Bankruptcy Act 1883.

was 'an enactment of a very different and much more explicit kind upon this part of bankruptcy law'.[118] The power of disclaimer in s.55 of that Act was in substantially the same terms as the power which is now found in ss.315-317 Insolvency Act 1986.[119] The disclaimer discharges the bankrupt, but does not affect the rights or liabilities of third parties, except in so far as necessary to discharge the bankrupt.[120] In *Stacey* v. *Hill*[121] the Court of Appeal held that, because a tenant's guarantor would otherwise have right of indemnity over against a bankrupt tenant, a disclaimer necessarily relieved the guarantor from liability too.[122] The House of Lords eventually decided that was wrong,[123] and that the effect of the disclaimer was to release the guarantor's right of indemnity against the disclaiming tenant, and not the guarantee. In the intervening period, however, it had become the practice to avoid the problem, by requiring the guarantor to grant the landlord a 'put' option, empowering the landlord to require the guarantor to take a substitute lease, within three months of any disclaimer. Those options are still often found in guarantees, and are specifically permitted as a term of an authorised guarantee agreement for leases made after 1995, although the commercial reason for including them no longer exists.

Where a trustee in bankruptcy exercises the power to disclaim, then the property is deemed never to have vested in the trustee in bankruptcy at all.[124] The result is that the trustee is retrospectively released from the personal liability which otherwise attaches by virtue of the statutory vesting of that property in him or her. The trustee does, however, remain liable to administer the bankrupt's estate as if that property had continued to exist down to the date of disclaimer, and as if liabilities had continued to accrue under it down to that date. Furthermore, anyone suffering loss consequent

---

[118] *In Re Cock, ex parte Shilson* (1887) 20 QBD 343, per Cave J 346.

[119] It has been exercisable without the need to obtain permission from the court since 1986.

[120] s.55(2) Bankruptcy Act 1883.

[121] [1901] 1 KB 660.

[122] See also *Murphy* v. *Sawyer-Hoare* [1993] 2 EGLR 61, *Allied Dunbar* v. *Fowle* [1994] 1 EGLR.

[123] *Hindcastle* v. *Barbara Attenborough Associates* [1997] AC 70.

[124] s.315(3) Insolvency Act 1986.

upon the disclaimer may prove for it in the bankruptcy as an unsecured creditor.

So, if the property is a lease, the effect of the disclaimer is that the trustee is retrospectively discharged from personal liability to pay the rent and to perform the other covenants in the lease. But the landlord may prove in the bankruptcy for any unpaid rent or damages for breach of covenant up to the date of the disclaimer,[125] and may also prove for any future loss caused by the disclaimer,[126] credit being given for the likelihood of reletting.[127]

Furthermore, if, in the meantime, the trustee has entered into possession of the lease, the trustee must treat the unpaid rent for that period as an expense of the bankruptcy, rather than simply as an unsecured debt, so that it must be paid in full before anything is paid to the general body of unsecured creditors.[128]

A disclaimer has no effect on the property rights of third parties. As between a landlord and anyone else claiming an interest in the property, the disclaimed lease is treated as if it were still extant.[129] So the disclaimed lease can be forfeited, for the purpose of destroying an underlease, and the undertenant of a disclaimed lease can claim relief from forfeiture, either under the inherent jurisdiction or under the statutory jurisdiction of the court.[130]

The court first acquired power to make an order, vesting the disclaimed lease in someone else having an interest in the lease, in 1869.[131] That power was preserved in s.55(6) of the 1883 Act, and is now found in ss.320-321 Insolvency Act 1986. Sub-tenants and persons liable to perform the tenant's covenants in the lease are entitled to a vesting order in priority to the landlord; and if they decline to take one, they are barred from claiming any interest in the property. The landlord is only entitled to a vesting order if no sub-tenant and no person liable to perform the tenant's covenants

---

[125] s.178(4) Insolvency Act 1986.

[126] s.178(6) Insolvency Act 1986.

[127] *Re Park Air Services* [2000] 2 AC 172.

[128] *Goldacre* v. *Nortel* [2010] Ch 455.

[129] *Re A E Realisations* [1988] 1 WLR 200, *Hindcastle* v. *Barbara Attenborough Associates* [1997] AC 70.

[130] *Barclays Bank* v. *Prudential Assurance* [1998] BCC 928.

[131] s.23(1) Bankruptcy Act 1869.

wants one.[132]

In *Drake* v. *Mayor of Exeter*[133] the court refused to enforce an option to renew, where the term had been assigned by a commissioner in bankruptcy, presumably on the grounds that the assignee could not be in a better position to claim specific performance than the original tenant, and specific performance would not have been ordered in favour of the original tenant, because he was bankrupt. That was reversed by Sir Samuel Romilly's Act 1809,[134] so that specific performance will now be ordered in favour of a trustee in bankruptcy, provided that the trustee is personally willing to enter into the covenants contained in the lease.[135]

4. Corporate winding up and dissolution.

The corporation most commonly encountered today is a company limited by shares incorporated under the Companies Act 2006. But that is a relatively recent form of incorporation. The first Act to allow the incorporation of companies with separate legal personality generally was the Joint Stock Companies Act 1844, and limited liability for members did not come in until the Limited Liability Act 1855. Before then, corporations were occasionally created by private Act of Parliament, but more often by royal charter, and many existed by virtue of prescription alone.

Corporations which exist by charter or prescription only may be dissolved by surrender to the Crown, forfeiture or by the action formerly known as scire facias,[136] but which is now simply an action by the Crown for its dissolution. The Joint Stock Companies Winding-Up Act 1844 provided for insolvent companies to be wound up by the court, and then dissolved, following the model for

---

[132] Per Cave J. in *In re Cock ex parte Shilson* (1887) 20 QBD 343, 349. For the order of priority, as between sub-tenants, and as between persons liable to perform the tenant's covenants, see *Re AE Realisations* [1988] 1 WLR 200, 211.

[133] (1664) N Ch Rep 102. 1 Ch.Cas 71.

[134] s.19. Platt, *Leases*, vol. 1 630.

[135] *Powell* v. *Lloyd* (1827) 1 Yo and Jerv 427, 2 Yo and Jerv 372, 378–379.

[136] The action was abolished by para.1(3) sch. 1 Crown Proceedings Act 1947.

dealing with the affairs of bankrupt individuals, with the difference that the company's property would not pass to its liquidator in the way that a bankrupt's property would vest in his trustee. Instead, the right to manage the company passed from its directors to its liquidator, for the purpose of winding it up, disposing of its assets and procuring its dissolution. Substantially the same scheme for winding up companies is now found in the Insolvency Act 1986. It was extended to chartered trading companies in 1862.[137]

Where a company is in the course of being wound up, the liquidator may disclaim property belonging to it,[138] including leaseholds,[139] on behalf of the company, whether the winding up is compulsory or voluntary. Since the property of a company does not vest in its liquidator, the liquidator never acquires any personal liability in respect of it, and so the disclaimer makes no difference to the liquidator's personal position. Otherwise, the effect of the disclaimer, so far as it concerns the administration of the company's property in the liquidation, is the same as the effect on a bankrupt's estate of a disclaimer by a trustee in bankruptcy.

In *Hastings Corporation* v. *Letton*[140] it was held that a leasehold estate determined automatically if the lease was still vested in a corporation when it was dissolved, since there could not be a lease without a tenant. But in *Re Sir Thomas Spencer Wells, Swinburne-Hanham* v. *Howard*[141] the Court of Appeal pointed out that a leasehold estate was a chattel interest, and the rule for chattels held by a corporation on dissolution is that they pass the Crown as *bona vacantia*; and there has not been any doubt that is the rule since.[142]

Sir Edward Coke believed that every conveyance of freehold land to a corporation was subject to an implied right of reverter on failure of the corporation,[143] and Lord Hardwicke agreed with him in *Attorney General* v. *Gower*.[144] As a result, Lord Brougham, in

---

[137] s.199 Companies Act 1862, *Re The Bristol Athenaeum* (1889) 43 Ch.D 236.

[138] s.178(2) Insolvency Act 1986.

[139] s.179 Insolvency Act 1986.

[140] [1908] 1 KB 378.

[141] [1933] Ch 29.

[142] For companies, see s.1012 Companies Act 2006.

[143] *Co.Litt.* 13b.

[144] (1740) 9 Mod. 224, 226.

1834, was clearly of the view that freehold land could not pass to the Crown by *bona vacantia*, and therefore it must escheat, to the mesne lord if there was one, and otherwise to the Crown.[145] But Coke's dictum was subsequently held to be incorrect.[146] Freehold land vested in a company registered under the Companies Act 2006 is now deemed to pass the Crown as *bona vacantia* on the dissolution of that company,[147] but the position for other corporations remains unclear. In either event, however, it passes subject to any subsisting lease.

Where property is still vested in a company on its dissolution, and vests in the Crown as *bona vacantia*,[148] the Crown may disclaim it subsequently,[149] with the result that it is deemed never to have vested in the Crown,[150] and company's interest in the property is terminated, without affecting the rights and liabilities of third parties.[151] In the case of leasehold land there is power to make a vesting order in favour of any undertenant or mortgagee instead,[152] and it is possible that, in the case of freehold land, the effect of a disclaimer is to cause it to 'boomerang' back to the Crown (in the absence of any mesne lord) by way of escheat.

5. Mortmain.

Mortmain was the conveyance of freehold land into the 'dead hand' of a corporation. That offended feudal principles because it deprived superior lords of the opportunity to make money by exercising customary rights each time the freeholder died. The

---

[145] *Henchman v. AG* (1834) 3 My & K 485, 492, Holdsworth, *HEL* vol. 3 67–73.
[146] *Re Wells, Swinburne-Hanham v. Howard* [1933] 1 Ch 29, *Re Strathblaine* [1948] Ch 228, G. Gray, *The Rule Against Perpetuities*, 3rd edn. (Boston, Little Brown, 1915) 48–51.
[147] s.1012 Companies Act 2006.
[148] Ibid.
[149] s.1013 Companies Act 2006. A crown disclaimer is not treated as disclaimer by a liquidator or trustee in bankruptcy for the purpose of surety covenant: *Re Yarmarine* [1992] BCLC 276.
[150] s.1014 Companies Act 2006.
[151] s.1015 Companies Act 2006.
[152] s.1017 Companies Act 2006.

corporation did not die. So, at common law, it was always necessary to obtain a licence from all superior lords, including the Crown, before conveying a freehold to a corporation.[153]

But most corporations, in the medieval period, were connected with the church, and the church 'ever had of their counsel the best learned men they could get'.[154] They developed a trick to avoid the rule: the donor would give the land to the church, but the church would immediately subinfeud it back to the donor. Only later would there be a collusive forfeiture of the re-grant,[155] leaving the church in possession of the land. When that was outlawed by Magna Carta[156] the church experimented with taking long leases for years instead,[157] the point being that a lease for a term of years was not a freehold. Indeed, at that time, it was barely more than a contract.

This avoidance technique was, itself, outlawed in 1279 by the Statute De Viris Religiosis[158] which provided:

> . . . if any person, religious or other, do presume either by craft or engine to offend against this statute, it shall be lawful for us and other chief lords of the fee immediate, to enter into the land so aliened, within a year from the time of the alienation, to hold it in fee as an inheritance.

So the Act did not apply directly to leasehold terms. It only made a lease forfeitable if, 'by reason the length of term granted or by reason of its other incidents could be regarded as an alienation in fee'.[159] In 1463 it was doubtful whether a lease of 100 years was

---

[153] The custom of London was that freemen could devise in mortmain: *Doctor and Student* 35, *Sir John Port's Notebook*, 102 SS 19, *Lancelot v. Allen* (1632) Cro Car 248, *Humphreys v. Knight* (1636) Cro Car 455.

[154] Coke, *2nd Inst.* 75.

[155] *Bl.Comm.* Bk.II 269.

[156] c.36, Coke, *2nd Inst.* 74–75, *Bl.Comm.* Bk.II 270. See also the Statutes of Westminster II (1285) c.32 and Quia Emptores 1290 c.3, Coke, *2nd Inst.* 504.

[157] *Bl.Comm.* Bk II 270.

[158] 7 Ed.1 stat.2 c.1. Evasion by conveyance on trust for the body corporate was prohibited in 1391 (15 Ric 2 c.5) and 1531 (23 Hen.8 c.10).

[159] *Attorney-General v. Parsons* [1956] AC 421 per Earl Jowitt 436.

caught by the prohibition[160] but by the sixteenth century it was settled that it was.[161] Thereafter, leases for less than 100 years were generally held not to be caught by the prohibition,[162] which is the origin of the practice of granting long leases for a term of 99 years, and no longer.

The Statute De Viris Religiosis was repealed by the Mortmain and Charitable Uses Act 1888, which loosened the restrictions on granting leases to charitable corporations. The prohibition on alienation in mortmain to companies registered under the Companies Acts was removed in 1948,[163] and at the same time, it became lawful to alienate in mortmain to a foreign company, if it had a branch registered within the jurisdiction.[164] But there was one last huzzah for the law of mortmain, before it was finally abolished. In *Morrelle* v. *Waterworth*[165] a lease was assigned a foreign company which did not have a branch registered within the jurisdiction. Although that would not have been an alienation in mortmain under the 1279 Act, the Court of Appeal held that, under the defective drafting of the Mortmain and Charitable Uses Act 1888, it was, and furthermore, that the effect of the disposition was automatically to vest all the liabilities of the tenant in the Crown. The House of Lords overruled that decision in *Attorney-General* v. *Parsons*,[166] and what was left of the law of mortmain was abolished by the Charities Act 1960.[167]

---

[160] (1463) YB 3 Ed.4 f.12, 13a pl.8, *Truro Corporation* v. *Rowe* [1901] 2 KB 870, 875, Holdsworth, *HEL* vol. 7 248.

[161] Roger Yorke's Notebook, 120 SS 133.

[162] *Viner's Abridgment*, 'Mortmain' 485, *A-G* v. *Parsons* [1956] AC 421, 453, Platt, *Leases*, vol. 1 541.

[163] s.14(1) Companies Act 1948.

[164] s.408 Companies Act 1948.

[165] [1954] 2 All ER 673. See also *Morelle Ltd* v. *Wakeling* [1955] 1 All ER 700.

[166] [1956] AC 421.

[167] s.38.

CHAPTER 9
Actions

This chapter is concerned with the different actions which could be brought between a landlord and a tenant.

Today, only limitation periods[1] are still fixed by reference to the nature of the cause of action. Otherwise, it is no longer

---

[1] Limitation Act 1980.

necessary even to specify the cause of action in the claim form: a short statement of the facts and the relief sought is all that is required, even if rather more is often provided. But, for common law claims before 1852,[2] it was necessary to pigeon-hole the facts within a particular cause of action. If the facts alleged and proved did not include all the ingredients of the cause of action specified in the writ, that would be procedurally fatal to the claim, even if those facts contained all the ingredients of a different cause of action.[3] Different writs had different advantages and disadvantages, and the law developed incrementally as lawyers pushed at the boundaries, in order to obtain some advantage for their clients.[4] Judges generally connived at this, if it meant more prestige or influence for their courts, or fees for them.[5]

So the substantive law was all concealed behind pleading points about the boundaries of each form of action, with a change in the boundary marking a change in the substantive law.[6] In the older cases, that means the debate is almost invariably about whether the facts have been properly pleaded, and whether they fit within the established limits of that cause of action; and the important cases are those where the courts allowed a boundary to be moved.

The development of the law of landlord and tenant has to be seen, and the cases have to be understood, in this context.

---

[2] s.3 Common Law Procedure Act 1852.

[3] In *Scott* v. *Sheppard* (1773) 2 Wm.Black 892, one of the leading cases on the law of personal injury, Blackstone J dissented on the grounds that the claim should have been brought in an action on the case rather than in trespass, because the injury had been inflicted indirectly.

[4] In *Reynolds* v. *Clark* (1725) 1 Strange 634, Raymond CJ said: 'We must keep up the boundaries of actions, otherwise we shall introduce utmost confusion'.

[5] C. Ogilvie, *The King's Government and the Common Law* (Oxford, Blackwell, 1958) 80.

[6] 'So great is the ascendancy of the law of actions in the infancy of the Courts of Justice, that substantive law has at first the look of being gradually secreted in the interstices of procedure; and the early lawyer can only see the law through the envelope of technical forms': H. Maine, *Early Law and Customs* (London, Murray, 1883) 389. 'Sometimes, indeed, one cannot help wondering whether the popular antithesis between substantive law and mere procedure is a very helpful guide to understanding a legal development': Simpson, *History of Land Law* 43.

1. Debt.

An action in debt is an action for a fixed sum. In the context of the law of landlord and tenant, that is usually, but not always,[7] a claim for rent.

Since the earliest times, a landlord has been able to bring an action in debt for the agreed rent due under a tenancy for a term of years[8] (including a tenancy for a period of less than a year)[9] or a tenancy at will,[10] even if the tenant has repudiated the relationship.[11] Until 1710, however, the landlord of a lease for life could not bring an action in debt whilst the lease was still extant.[12]

An action in debt could be brought, whether the lease was

---

[7] An action for 'double value' against a tenant who wilfully holds over after a written demand for possession, is an action which, by statute, must be brought in debt: s.1 Landlord and Tenant Act 1730.

[8] In the medieval period, the landlord might not have been able to bring an action in debt if the lease gave the landlord the alternative remedy of entering and holding the land until the debt was paid: (1350) Statham's *Abridgment*, 'Dette' 18. But Coke said that this case was 'false printed' and the true rule was that whilst no action for debt could be brought on a lease for life during the lifetime of the tenant, it could always be brought on a lease for years, unless a reserved right to enter, hold the land, and apply the profits towards the arrears of rent, had actually been exercised: *Co.Litt.* 203a.

[9] Blackstone said: 'If the lease be but for half a year, or a quarter, or any less time, this lessee is respected as a tenant for years, and is styled so in some legal proceedings; a year being the shortest term which the law in this case takes notice of': *Bl.Comm.* Bk.II 140. For the development of periodic tenancies, as tenancies for a 'term of years' see ch.4 heading 'Periodic'. See now the definition of 'term of years absolute' in s.205 Law of Property Act 1925.

[10] *Bellasis* v. *Burbrick* (1696) 1 Salk 209.

[11] In *Alexander and Dyer's Case* (1589) 2 Leon 99, the tenant had entered one day before the date permitted by the lease, and so claimed always to have been a trespasser. Clench J said: 'Be it a disseisin or not, or be it that the defendant entereth or not, he is to pay the rent'. Gawdy J said: 'The lessee is a disseisor, and continueth a disseisor, and yet debt lieth against him for the rent, by reason of the privity of contract'.

[12] s.4 Landlord and Tenant Act 1709, Gilbert, *Rents*, 93–94, Holdsworth, *HEL* vol. 7 263. The holder of a rent charge could bring a writ of annuity instead, and the holder of a rent seck, who had been seised of it, could bring an assize of rent, but neither remedy was available for a rent service: Gilbert, *Rents* 124–125. For the difference between a rent service and other rents, see ch.3 heading 'Rent reservation'.

made by deed or by less formal means,[13] and the main disadvantage of suing in debt—the risk that the defendant might defend the action by 'waging his law'[14]—never applied to claims for rent.[15] But anyone suing in debt who could not produce a deed[16] had to produce witnesses, to prove the amount of the debt,[17] the pleading rules were very strict, a claim against an assignee had to be brought in the county where the land was situate,[18] and the evidence had to show that the exact amount which had been claimed was due, otherwise the claim would fail.[19]

Originally, any claim which could be brought in debt, had to be brought using that form of action and no other.[20] So even in the case of lease made by deed, with an implied covenant to pay the rent,[21] the landlord could sue for it only in debt. But in 1505 Fineux

---

[13] *Prior of Bradstock's Case* (1371) YB 44 Ed.3 f.42 pl.46, Simpson, *History of the Common Law of Contract*, 171.

[14] In essence, that required the defendant to find a number of 'compurgators' or 'oath-helpers' (a euphemism for professional liars) who were willing to swear that the debt was not owed, and whose evidence would be conclusive on the point. At the common law courts in Westminster Hall, the porters were paid a fee to make the necessary oaths: J. Baker, *Introduction to English Legal History*, 3rd edn. (London, Butterworths, 1990) 87–88, Simpson, *History of the Common Law of Contract* 298. As late as 1824, someone attempted to recover a simple debt, by bringing an action in debt instead of assumpsit. Counsel for the defendant evidently had a sense of humour, because he applied to the court for directions, asking whether he needed to find six or eleven compurgators. Abbott CJ was not amused, and sniffily declined to say, so counsel threatened to bring eleven (which was, in fact, the right number), and the claimant gave up; *King* v. *Williams* (1824) 2 Barn & Cr 538. Parliament responded by abolishing wager of law by s.13 Civil Procedure Act 1833.

[15] *Prior of Bradstock's Case* (1371) YB 44 Ed.3 f.42 pl.46, (1422) YB 1 Hen.6 pl.3, 50 SS 12-14, (1481) YB 21 Ed.4 f.28b-30a pl.24, (1494) YB 10 Hen.7 f.4 pl.4, *Doctor and Student*, 28, Simpson, *History of the Common Law of Contract* 142–143 esp. fn.6 and 172.

[16] (1440) YB 18 Hen.6 f.17a pl.8, *Co.Litt.* 295a.

[17] O. W. Holmes, *The Common Law*, ed. M Howe (Boston, Little Brown & Co, 1963) 207.

[18] *Wey* v. *Rally* (1704) 6 Mod. 194, *Patterson* v. *Scott* (1727) 2 Strange 776.

[19] *Vaux* v. *Mainwaring* (1714) Fortescue 197. In *Thwaites* v. *Ashfield* (1696) 5 Mod. 212, the rule was relaxed, by allowing a landlord who had obtained a judgment for too much, to keep the rest.

[20] C. Fifoot, *History and Sources of the Common Law* (London, Stevens, 1949) 258–259.

[21] See ch.5 heading 'To pay rent'.

J suggested that the landlord of a lease made by deed could elect[22] to sue in covenant instead,[23] and that had become settled practice by 1600.[24]

That relaxation of the rule that the landlord must sue in debt did not help landlords of leases made by less formal means; for, by then, it was well established that (except in the cities of London and Bristol) an action in covenant could only be brought on the other party's deed.[25] In 1738, however, landlords of leases not made by deed were granted the right to sue in assumpsit for use and occupation in lieu of rent, instead of suing for that rent in debt,[26] and that seems to have prompted a relaxation of the pleading rules in debt, because by 1794 landlords were allowed to bring claims as 'debt for use and occupation', using entirely general pleadings, just like in assumpsit.[27]

In practice, of course, if the lease was still extant, a landlord would almost always try to recover the rent by levying a distress first.[28]

2. Covenant.

A covenant is a promise which is enforceable because it is made by deed.[29]

But it was not always so. There are cases in the early fourteenth century where tenants holding under oral leases were successfully sued in an action of covenant.[30] But, by 1346 it was clear beyond doubt that, except in the Cities of London and Bristol (where the

---

[22] *Bird* v. *Randall* (1762) 1 Wm.Black 373, 375.

[23] Simpson, *History of the Common Law of Contract* 18.

[24] *Sicklemore* v. *Simonds* (1600) Cro Eliz 789, C.Fifoot, *History and Sources of the Common Law* (London, Stevens, 1949) 259. Suing in covenant had the advantage that the action could be brought without making any demand: *Anon* (1626) Bryson's Exch Cas 24.

[25] See the heading 'Covenant' below.

[26] See below heading 'Assumpsit'.

[27] *Wilkins* v. *Wingate* (1794) 6 TR 62, Coote, *Leases*, 502–503.

[28] See ch.3 heading 'Distress and replevin'.

[29] See ch.5 heading 'Express, implied and usual'.

[30] *Picton* v. *St Quintin* (1304) YB 32 & 33 Ed.1 (RS) f.199 pl.55, D. Ibbetson, *A Historical Introduction to the Law of Obligations* (Oxford, Oxford University Press, 1999) 27.

old rules continued to apply as special customs)[31] an action in covenant could only be brought on an obligation contained in an instrument which the defendant had executed and delivered as a deed.[32] Consequently, if a landlord granted a lease by deed poll, the tenant would be able to sue the landlord in covenant relying on the landlord's deed, but the landlord would not be able to bring any action in covenant against the tenant.[33]

The action was 'invented chiefly for the enforcement of what we should call leases'.[34] The usual remedy in covenant was an award of damages against the party in breach. Originally, it was also possible to obtain specific relief too. So if a landlord evicted a tenant in breach of covenant, the court could order the landlord to give possession back to the tenant, in an action on the covenant.[35] But, in the fifteenth century, when more efficacious equitable remedies became available,[36] the common law courts abandoned their power to grant specific relief, and the remedy available in an action of covenant became limited to payment of a sum of money.

A landlord of a lease for life could not, until 1710,[37] bring an action in covenant for rent due under the lease while it was still extant.[38]

---

[31] *Sir John Port's Notebook*, (1986) 102 SS 10, S. Milsom, *A Natural History of the Common Law* (New York, Columbia University Press, 2003) 40, *Wade* v. *Bemboes* (1583) 1 Leon 2. The custom could not be relied on against executors (ibid). Fifoot noted a similar custom in Scarborough in 1435: C. Fifoot, *History and Sources of the Common Law* (London, Stevens, 1949) 294.

[32] *Anon* (1346) YB 20 Ed.3 vol.II (RS) 148, C. Fifoot, *History and Sources of the Common Law* 257–258.

[33] Platt, *Covenants* 55.

[34] *Pollock & Maitland* vol. 2 106, Maitland, *Equity* 341. In 1285 a litigant objected, unsuccessfully, to the action of covenant being used to enforce an agreement to exchange freehold land, on the grounds that the action was only ever intended as a means of enforcing leases: *Earliest English Law Reports*, 122 SS 294, cf. C. Fifoot, *History and Sources of the Common Law* 225.

[35] *Forest* v. *Villy* (1226) Bracton's Note Book pl.1739, Bellewe 115 'Couenaunt', *Pollock & Maitland* vol. 2 106, C. Fifoot, *History and Sources of the Common Law* 259.

[36] A party who disobeyed an order made by the Chancellor could be imprisoned immediately.

[37] s.4 Landlord and Tenant Act 1709.

[38] Coote, *Leases*, 490, Holdsworth, *HEL* vol. 7 263.

3. Assumpsit.

Assumpsit was an action founded upon a promise where the promise had not made by deed. In effect, it was the counterpart of 'covenant' for informal contracts. It was the action that was used to obtain monetary compensation for non-performance of contractual promises, and, in this form, dates from the middle of the sixteenth century.[39]

There were essentially two types.

Indebitatus assumpsit, also known as a general assumpsit, was the first. This was an action on the case to recover damages for the non-payment of a debt (otherwise known as an action in lieu of debt) based the debtor's fictional[40] later undertaking or 'assumption' of the obligation to pay the debt. Originally, it was limited to claims where, for one reason or another, the claimant could not bring an ordinary action in debt, but that rule was abandoned, for most debts, in 1602, by *Slade's Case*;[41] after which, instead of simply alleging the amount of the debt, the claimant also had to give some very general information about how the debt had arisen, but still much less than if the claim had been brought in debt itself,[42] and often pleading the same thing different ways using alternative ritualised formulæ.[43]

Medieval thinking about the nature of rent as part of the land,[44] however, meant that even after *Slade's Case*, indebitus assumpsit still could not be used to recover rent.[45] That, in practice, severely limited it usefulness between landlord and tenant because rent was the debt that was most likely to arise in that relationship.

The second type was special assumpsit.

---

[39] C. Fifoot, *History and Sources of the Common Law* 339.

[40] The fiction was introduced by the court of Queen's Bench, in the middle of the sixteenth century, in an attempt to wrest business from the court of Common Pleas, which continued to insist on the proof of an actual promise; *Anon* (1559) Dyer's Notebook, 110 SS 420, Simpson, *History of the Common Law of Contract* 292–295.

[41] (1602) 4 Co.Rep 92b, Simpson, *History of the Common Law of Contract* 295–7.

[42] J. Ames, *The History of Assumpsit. II. Implied assumpsit* (1888) 2 Harv. L. Rev. 53.

[43] C. Fifoot, *History and Sources of the Common Law* 369–370.

[44] See ch.3 heading 'Rent reservation'.

[45] *Bellinger* v. *Gardner* (1612) 1 Rol Reps 24, Coote, *Leases* 506.

In special assumpsit, instead of simply pleading a general debt, the claimant 'counted specially', giving full details of the transaction and the obligation breached.[46] As in indebitus assumpsit, the obligation might be an obligation to pay a sum of money.[47] But it could be any sort of obligation: an action for breach of promise of marriage was an action in special assumpsit.

One of the earliest forms of special assumpsit was an assumpsit where the count was for use and occupation At common law, it was quite possible to bring a special assumpsit based on an implied promise to pay for the occupation of land. So a tenant at will, who is allowed into occupation, without any express agreement to pay rent, is liable to pay at the open market rate, on the basis of an implied promise to do so.[48] The same applies if a person is allowed to remain in possession of land as a tenant at sufferance,[49] or if a rent review clause fails for uncertainty.[50]

No promise could be implied from someone whose occupation of land was unlawful. So a landlord could not bring the action after having made an election to treat the defendant as a trespasser.[51] But provided that the landlord had not already elected to treat the occupant as a trespasser, the landlord could waive the tort, and bring an action for compensation for use and occupation instead. This was important before 1833,[52] when claims in trespass died with the tortfeasor but contractual claims could still be proved against a personal representative.[53] It has been of less significance since, but it still matters on the quantum of damage. By waiving the tort, the contractual measure of loss can be recovered.

It was not, however, possible to bring a special assumpsit on an

---

[46] A 'special pleader' was usually employed to do this, for the process was full of traps. The trick was to plead the bare minimum allowed. Plead too little, and the count would be bad as a matter of form. Plead too much, and the claim would fail for 'variance', if the evidence did not exactly match the pleaded facts. Sometimes, but not always, the pleader who failed to establish a special assumpsit, could fall back on a count of general assumpsit: *Weaver* v. *Boroughs* (1725) 1 Strange 648.

[47] In special assumpsit, the action was brought on the pleaded agreement. In indebitus assumpsit, the agreement was merely given in evidence.

[48] *Churchward* v. *Ford* (1857) 2 H&N 446, 449, 450.

[49] *Bayley* v. *Bradley* (1845) 5 CB 396, 406.

[50] *Beer* v. *Bowden* [1976] 1 EGLR 83.

[51] *Birch* v. *Wright* (1786) 1 Term Rep 378, *Phillips* v. *Homfray* (1883) 24 ChD 439.

[52] s.2 Civil Procedure Act 1833.

[53] *Monypenny* v. *Bristow* (1830) 2 Rus & Mylne 117, 124.

express agreement to pay rent,[54] until that rule was reversed by statute with effect from 24th June 1738.[55] Afterwards a landlord of a lease, not made by deed, was able to bring a special assumpsit for breach of an express agreement to pay rent,[56] instead of suing for the rent in debt; and if the lease was in writing (albeit not by deed)[57] the landlord could rely on the reserved rent as evidence of the damage[58] suffered by reason of a breach of that promise.[59]

As has already been noted, a special assumpsit might, like indebitus assumpsit, be a claim for damages for breach of an obligation to pay money. But it could also be a claim for damages for breach of any other enforceable obligation, not being an obligation owed under a deed. An informal lease, for this purpose, was treated like any other contract, and after the seventeenth century, there was never any difficulty in bringing a special assumpsit on the non-rental promises (including implied promises) made between landlord and tenant in a lease made otherwise than by deed.[60]

The pleading rules for assumpsit were all swept away, after a

---

[54] *Symcock* v. *Payn* (1600) Cro Eliz 786, *Clerk* v. *Palady* (1601) Cro Eliz 859, *Bellinger* v. *Gardiner* (1612) 1 Rol Rep 24 pl.1, *Slack* v. *Bowfal* (1623) Cro Jac 668 (a note by George Croke 669), *Munday* v. *Bailey* (1647) Aleyn 29, Simpson, *History of the Common Law of Contract*, 300. There was an exception if the action was brought on an express collateral promise to make the payment, rather than on any promise contained in the agreement itself: *Trever* v. *Roberts* (1660) Hard 366, *Brookbank* v. *Taylor* (1624) Cro Jac 685, *Acton* v. *Symon* (1636) Cro Car 415.

[55] s.14 Distress for Rent Act 1737.

[56] Physical occupation of the demised property was not necessary. It was enough that the landlord had not retaken possession; see *Izon* v. *Gorton* (1839) 5 Bing NC 502 (premises destroyed by fire).

[57] Assumpsit did not lie if the lease was made by deed: *Dungey* v. *Angove* (1794) 2 Ves Jun 303, 306.

[58] Hence s.19 Limitation Act 1980, which provides for a six year limitation period for the recovery of arrears of rent, refers to an action to recover arrears of rent 'or damages in respect of arrears of rent'.

[59] In *Boot* v. *Wilson* (1807) 8 East 311, 318, Lord Ellenborough said: 'There is no distinction in this respect between an agreement and a covenant, which is an agreement under seal, except as to the form of the remedy upon it'.

[60] *Powley* v. *Walker* (1793) 5 Term Rep 373. Before the seventeenth century, an action to enforce a parol agreement for quiet enjoyment was enforceable and would have been brought by action on the case (ie assumpsit) or in deceit; *Co.Litt.* 101b, 365a, 384a.

disastrous earlier attempt at reform in 1834,[61] by the Common Law Procedure Act 1852, s.2 of which provided that it should 'not be necessary to mention any form or cause of action in any writ of summons', and s.49 of which provided that immaterial averments like 'promises in indebitatus counts and mutual promises to perform agreements' should be omitted.[62] But lawyers are conservative by nature, and pleaders particularly so. Even today claims to recover simple debts are often pleaded using short form particulars of claim,[63] which are directly descended from the general or 'common' counts used in a declaration of indebitus assumpsit.[64]

If a lease made by deed expires, and the tenant holds over under a new parol tenancy, then although all the terms of the old tenancy are imported into the new one,[65] they are not imported as covenants, for there is no new deed, and consequently any common law action to enforce them had to be an action in assumpsit.[66] Sometimes today leases try to avoid this problem by deeming 'the term' to include any period of non-statutory holding over, but the effect of that is to make the length of the term uncertain from the outset.[67]

---

[61] 'The purpose was beneficent; the results disastrous. Never were the reports so encumbered with technicality. Plaintiffs were constantly non-suited, after the most gratifying display of erudition, on the threshold of success. Baron Parke was driven to confess himself at a loss to interpret the language of his own rules': C. Fifoot, *History and Sources of the Common Law* 370.

[62] Schedule B to the 1852 Act had model forms of pleadings for various actions, the brevity of which would astonish modern litigators. Plea number 24 was a claim for terminal dilapidations, which barely ran into the seventh line. A 'criminal conversation' (pl.27) only needed ten words, before the tort was abolished in 1857 (20 & 21 Vic c.85, s.59).

[63] Eg., 'The defendant owes the claimant [amount] under the invoices attached for goods sold and delivered to the defendant'.

[64] 'In a general count the terms of the agreement are not specially set out, but the plaintiff alleges in a general way, that the defendant was indebted to him in a certain sum of money for goods sold and delivered (or other cause of action), and that being so indebted, he promised the plaintiff to pay the same upon request, but has not done so, to the plaintiff's damage of so much': W. Fox, *A Treatise on Simple Contracts* (London, Stevens and Norton, 1842) 98.

[65] *Digby* v. *Atkinson* (1815) 4 Camp 275, Coote, *Leases* 410–411.

[66] *Kimpton* v. *Eve* (1813) 2 Ves & B 349.

[67] See ch.4 heading 'Fixed terms'.

4. Ejectment (action for recovery of land).

There was a stark contrast, at the beginning of the thirteenth century, between the remedies available to an evicted tenant for life and an evicted tenant for years.

A tenant for life was seised of a freehold estate, even if a rent or other service was reserved. It was relatively easy for an evicted freeholder, such as a tenant for life,[68] to recover possession, by bringing the action of novel disseisin—as the name suggests, the complaint was simply one of recent dispossession[69]—litigating out the underlying merits, if necessary, by bringing one of the real actions later. A dispossessed tenant for years could do none of that, because a claim to be put into possession of a lease for a term of years was not a claim to recover seisin of a free tenement.[70]

---

[68] *Prude* v. *Abbot of Selby* (1285) 122 SS 313-315.

[69] Milsom argues convincingly that the writ was originally 'precisely tailored to [a] specific mischief', namely, the lord who forfeited an estate for failing to provide seigniorial services without due process in his own court: S. Milsom, *A Natural History of the Common Law*, 87–92, S. Milsom, *What was an Entry?* [2002] CLJ 561, cf. Simpson, *History of Land Law* 68–69.

[70] A lease for years was never a free tenement, even if it had been granted for 300 years, and so for a term longer than any life estate could possibly last: (1358) YB 32 Ed.3 Lib Ass f.105 pl.6. As early as the thirteenth century, Beresford JCP said that a widow could not claim dower of leasehold land because her late husband 'ne fu pas seisi' (*Anon* (1278–1289) 112 SS 360) and by the sixteenth century it was settled law that a tenant for years could never acquire seisin: Simpson, *History of Land Law* 36–37. Whether a tenant for years could be 'seised' before then, is unclear: see Littleton, *Tenures*, s.324, cf. s.567, F. Maitland, *Seisin of Chattels* (1885) LQR 324, F. Maitland, *The Mystery of Seisin* (1886) 2 LQR 481, K. McNeil, *Common Law Aboriginal Title* (Oxford, Clarendon Press, 1989) 8 fn.3, S. Milsom, *A Natural History of the Common Law*, 92. But perhaps the true explanation of the rule is that novel disseisin was originally a very narrow remedy (see the immediately preceding footnote), and that whilst judges were willing to extend it to help dispossessed freeholders, they felt no incentive to extend it further to help a dispossessed tenant for a term of years, at a time when short leases were commonly granted in connection with moneylending transactions, which were thought to be immoral; and that the tenant's lack of 'seisin' is a later rationalisation of this position. Thus Glanvill, writing in about 1180, noted (Glanvill, *Treatise on the Laws and Customs of England*, ed. and trans. G. Hall (Oxford, Clarendon, 1965) 126, 192–194): 'If the creditor loses seisin of his gage, whether by act of the debtor or of someone else, he shall not recover seisin of it with the aid of the court, not even by a recognition of novel disseisin. For if he has

In fact, there was only one circumstance in which an evicted tenant for years could recover possession at that time, and that was if the lease happened to be made by deed and the eviction was by the original landlord. In that event, the court could make an order restoring possession to the tenant in an action in covenant. Otherwise, the tenant's only remedy was in damages,[71] either against the landlord for breach of warranty, when evicted lawfully by a third party,[72] or against the evictor in trespass, for the loss suffered up to the time of the judgment, if the eviction was unlawful.[73]

The first step away from this was taken in about 1235[74], with the introduction by William Raleigh of the writ of *quare ejecit infra terminum*; a writ for recovery of the term. Bracton, writing in about 1250, explained that:[75]

> [termors] . . . when they were ejected before the expiration of their term, once sued by writ of covenant, but because that writ did not lie between any persons, only between him who had given the land to farm for a term and him who had accepted it, because the obligation of agreement could not bind others, and also because even between such persons the matter could hardly be determined without difficulty, by counsel of the court a remedy is provided to the termor against any who have ejected him by this writ - a writ for recovery of a term.

But the writ turned out to be of very limited use, for whilst it allowed the tenant[76] to recover possession from a successor to the

---

been disseised of his gage unjustly and without a judgment by someone other than the debtor, the debtor himself may have an assize of novel disseisin. If on the other hand he was disseised by the debtor himself, the court will not aid him to recover the gage from the debtor or to re-enter except through the debtor; for the creditor should have recourse to the principal plea to constrain the debtor to make satisfaction to him for his debt'.

[71] Andrew Horne, a thirteenth century London fishmonger, listed the inability to recover a term as a disseisin as one of his 'abuses' of the law in *The Mirror of Justice* (Washington, Byrne, 1903) 242.

[72] See ch.4 heading 'Title and quiet enjoyment'.

[73] *Brancaster v. Wallis* (1383) 6 YB Ric.2 pl.2 (Ames, 1996) 208.

[74] *Pollock & Maitland* vol. 2 107.

[75] Bracton, vol. 3 161 (f.220). See also Holdsworth, *HEL* vol. 3 214, S. Milsom, *Trespass from Hen.III to Ed.III* (1958) 74 LQR 195, 198–201.

[76] This included an assignee: Com. Dig. 'Quar.ej.' (A).

original landlord,[77] judicial conservatism[78] prevented it being used to recover possession from a stranger,[79] or even the original landlord.[80] Its use was already rare in the fifteenth century,[81] and by the eighteenth century, it was obsolete, having been subsumed in the general action of ejectment.[82]

The general action of ejectment (otherwise, '*ejectione firmæ*' or an action of 'trespass in ejectment') is the action which eventually became the general action for recovery of land.[83] It was the action by which a leasehold tenant could recover possession from anyone, except someone who has a better title to possession than the tenant.

There is a hint that it might have had a statutory origin.[84] In any event, in 1383 it was clear that it provided a remedy only in damages for past loss.[85]

By 1455 this was in doubt,[86] and in 1499 it was finally settled,

---

[77] Even then, it did not work if the original landlord colluded with the successor, and allowed the successor to make a recovery on the basis of a pretended title paramount. The tenant had no power to prevent this, because a leasehold tenant had no standing to intervene in the action. The Statute of Gloucester in 1278 (6 Ed.1 c.11, Coke, *2nd Inst.* 321–323) gave tenants of leases made by deed power to intervene in the action in order to ensure that execution of any collusive default judgment would be postponed until after the expiry of the lease, but it was not until the enactment of the Recoveries Act 1529 that the gaps were filled in other cases: see *Co.Litt.* 46a, Challis, *Real Property,* 64, *Oxford History of the Laws of England,* vol. 6 638.

[78] For an alternative view, see J.Adams, *Action in Ejectment,* 4th American edn. (New York, Banks Gould & Co, 1854) 7–8.

[79] Holdsworth, *HEL* vol. 2 214, cf. *Brancaster* v. *Wallis* (1383) 6 YB Ric.2 pl.2 (Ames, 1996) 208, and Introduction 175–176.

[80] *Pynchemore* v. *Brewyn* (1481) YB 21 Ed.4 f.10 pl.1, f.30 pl.25, J. Ames, *Lectures on Legal History* (Cambridge Mass, Harvard University Press, 1913) 222, cf. *Sir John Port's Notebook,* (1986) 102 SS 127.

[81] *Oxford History of the Laws of England,* vol. 6 635.

[82] *Bl.Comm.* Bk.III 206–207.

[83] See generally Holdsworth, *HEL* vol. 7 4–23, *Gledhill* v. *Hunter* (1880) 14 ChD 492, 498–500. In England, it was still 'commonly spoken of as an action in ejectment' in 1920 (per Eve J in *Marshall* v. *Charteris* [1920] 1 Ch 520, 523) and in Australia, it still is.

[84] (1383) 6 YB Ric.2 (Ames, 1996) Introduction, 175–176. See also S. Milsom, *Studies in the History of the Common Law* (London, Hambledon Press, 1985) 4–6.

[85] *Brancaster* v. *Wallis* (1383) 6 YB Ric.2 pl.2 (Ames, 1996) 208.

[86] Simpson, *History of Land Law,* 87, Port's Notebook 102 SS 127.

in accordance with dicta in 1481,[87] that a tenant could use it to recover possession of the term, even against a stranger.[88] When the court gave judgment, it ordered that possession be delivered up by a writ called *habere facias possessionem*. It may be that the impetus for the change was the increased willingness of the Chancellor to grant injunctions protecting leasehold tenants, drawing business away from the common law courts.[89]

Ironically, the tenant's remedy of ejectment became quicker, cheaper and more convenient than the landlord's writ of entry *ad terminum qui preteriit*, being the action by which a freeholder could recover possession from a tenant on expiry of the term.[90] It was also much faster and less technical than the assize of novel disseisin[91] or the other real actions, by which a freeholder could recover possession from a stranger.[92] So the action 'explodes into wide use' in the 1550s, no doubt as a result of disputes arising out of the dissolution of the monasteries.[93] By the end of the sixteenth century, 'all titles of land are for the greatest part tried in actions of ejectments',[94] even where the defendant claims to hold in ancient demesne[95] or where the claimant is nothing more than the tenant of a copyholder.[96]

---

[87] (1481) YB Ed.4 f.10 pl.1, (1481) YB 21 Ed.4 f.30 pl.25.

[88] J. Ames, *Lectures on Legal History* 222, Holdsworth, *HEL* vol. 3 214–217, *Oxford History of the Laws of England*, vol. 6 636, *Gernes* v. *Smyth* (1499) 94 SS 181.fn.(7).

[89] G. Gilbert, *Law and Practice of Ejectment*, 2nd edn. (London, Nutt & Gosling, 1741) 2–3, Reeves, ed. W. Finlason, *History of English Law* (London, Reeves and Turner, 1869) vol. 3 177, J. Baker, *Spelman's Reports*, Introduction 94 SS 181.

[90] Holdsworth, *HEL* vol. 3 12.

[91] Holdsworth, *HEL* vol. 3 8–10.

[92] Coke blamed the decline of the assize and real actions on 'unjust and superfluous delays' and 'feigned, dilatory and curious pleadings' (Preface 8 Co.Rep). It did not help that the action was conducted in a mixture of latin and law french: Lilly, *Assize*, 1719 (170 ER).

[93] *Oxford History of the Laws of England*, vol. 6 537.

[94] *Alden's Case* (1601) 5 Co.Rep 105a.

[95] Ibid.

[96] *Rumnay & Eves's Case* (1588) 1 Leon 100, C. Gray, *Copyhold, Equity and the Common Law* (Cambridge Mass, Harvard University Press, 1963) 65–66. By this means, copyhold titles could be tried in Royal courts. The court of Common Pleas was a little slower to accept this than King's Bench: see Reeves, ed. W. Finlason, *History of English Law* (London, Reeves and Turner, 1869) vol. 3 750, Simpson, *History of Land Law*, 154–155, and *Stephens* v. *Elliot* (1596) Cro Eliz 484.

The problem with that, of course, was that the action had to be brought by a leasehold tenant, and it was an action to be put in possession of a leasehold estate. So, at first, someone who was not a tenant for years, but who wanted to use the action in order to recover possession, had to physically enter on the land[97] and grant a genuine lease for years to a third party,[98] so that, if evicted, that third party could bring the action in ejectment, to be put back into possession of the new lease, relying on the landlord's title to grant it.[99] Eventually, however, the lease, entry and eviction all became

---

[97] An entry was necessary to complete the grant of the lease for two reasons. First, without an entry, the plaintiff would only have an 'interesse termini', which would not be sufficient to give the plaintiff standing to recover possession from a third party (see ch.1 heading 'Entry and interesse termini'). Secondly, the tort of maintenance was committed by someone who granted a lease when out of possession; see *Willis and Jermine's Case* (1589) 2 Leon 97, *Co.Litt.* 214a, J. Adams, *Action in Ejectment*, 4th American edn. (New York, Banks Gould & Co, 1854) 12, D'Anvers, *Abridgment*, vol. 3 165. By the Maintenance and Embracery Act 1540 (see also the Statute of Westminster II (1285) c.49) a landowner could only make a valid lease if he or she had already been in possession for one year. But that difficulty was brushed aside, in the case of leases made to try a title: see *Partridge* v. *Strange* (1553) Plowden 77, Holdsworth, *HEL* vol. 7 11.fn(1). The point was still in doubt in 1610. There is a precedent in W. West, *Simboleograph* (London, Stationers Co., 1610) pt.1 s.449 for: 'A lease for years whereupon ejectione firmæ may be brought, which must be delivered upon the lands leased, and commence at some day before the date thereof, which some think to be without the compass of the statute of buying titles'. Coke thought leases made to try a title were not within the statute, unless 'made to a great man or in any other way to sway' the cause: *Co.Litt.* 369a-b.

[98] *Newdigate's Case* (1551) Dyer 68b, *Nokes's Case* (1599) 4 Co.Rep 80b, *Greenly* v. *Passy* (1607) 1 Brownlow 131, *Oxford History of the Laws of England*, vol. 6 724.

[99] Since the claim was to be put into possession of the lease, the judgment could only be granted and enforced whilst the lease was extant. So, in *Puliston* v. *Warburton* (1697) 5 Mod. 332, the judgment was set aside, because the claimant mistakenly alleged a lease commencing on 10th April 1697, which was too late for an action tried in 1696. The opposite problem occurred in an *Anonymous* case in 1704 (6 Mod. 130). The lease had been granted for five years, which ought to have to have been long enough. But, after the claimant had obtained judgment, the defendant obtained an injunction staying its enforcement, pending resolution of his separate claim to have an equitable defence, and the Chancellor had not made any final decision about that claim before the lease expired. An application to extend the lease afterwards failed, on the grounds that this could only be done by consent. Holt CJ pointedly added that 'there wanted a clock-house over against the hall-gate'. Whether he was being rude about the Chancellor's delays, or referring to an

'an absolute fiction',[100] a development usually credited to Rolle CJ, during the Protectorate.[101] 'The action was commenced, without any writ,[102] by a declaration, every word of which was untrue:[103] it alleged a lease from the claimant to the nominal plaintiff (John Doe); an entry by him under and by virtue of that lease; and a subsequent ouster by the nominal defendant (Richard Roe):[104] at the

---

old anecdote about the use made of a fine paid by Sir Ralph Hengham for altering a court record, or both, is not entirely clear: see H. Roscoe, *Westminster Hall* (London, Knight, 1825) 226. Later, however, courts were willing to grant fictional extensions (*Oates* v. *Shepherd* (1748) 2 Strange 1272) though in *Doe d. Reynell* v. *Tuckett* ((1819) 2 Barn & Ald 773) the fictional extension was refused, because the claimant had not enforced the judgment for 20 years. It was no objection that the fictional lease was for a longer term than the claimant's own interest: *Doe d. Shore* v. *Porter* (1789) 3 Term Rep 13.

[100] Per Kenyon CJ in *Doe d. Shore* v. *Porter* (1789) 3 Term Rep 13, 18. This was described as the 'new way of practice' in J. Lilly, *The Practical Register,* 2nd edn. (London, Ward & Wickstead, 1735) vol. 1 675. In a claim by a landlord against a tenant, it remained the practice to grant an actual lease: W.Tidd, *Tidd's Practice,* 9th edn. (London, Butterworths, 1828) 1204. For the other cases where it remained necessary to grant an actual lease, see G. Gilbert, *Law and Practice of Ejectment,* 2nd edn. (London, Nutt & Gosling, 1741) 34–41, C. Runnington, *History Principles and Practice of Ejectment,* 2nd edn. (London, Butterworths, 1820) 171–175. At the start of the eighteenth century, there was a difference in practice between King's Bench and Common Pleas. Common pleas required the lease to be granted to a real person and an affidavit of the granting of the lease, the entry, and the ouster. None of this was necessary in King's Bench, after Rolle CJ (who was Chief Justice of the Upper Bench during the Protectorate) fictionalised the process: Simpson, *History of Land Law,* 139. But to obtain a default judgment in the Kings Bench Division (but not Common Pleas) it was necessary to verify the granting of the lease by affidavit: *Anon* (1704) 6 Mod. 309, Bull NP 96.

[101] G. Gilbert, *Law and Practice of Ejectment,* 2nd edn. (London, Nutt & Gosling, 1741) 5, C.Runnington, *History Principles and Practice of Ejectment,* 2nd edn. (London, Butterworths, 1820) 19, J. Adams, *Action in Ejectment,* 4th American edn. (New York, Banks Gould & Co, 1854) 17, *Fairclaim* v. *Shamtitle* (1792) 3 Burr 1292, 1297. But it may be that fictitious casual ejectors were being sued on real leases as early as 1635: see the book of entries called *Judgments in the Upper Bench* (London, Roycroft, 1655) 80.

[102] The original writ was a claim by the nominal tenant against the nominal ejector: *Bl.Comm.* Bk.III 273, App.vii.

[103] 'It is an ingenious fiction for the trial of titles to the possession of lands; and in form, it appears as a trick between two to dispossess a third, by a sham suit and judgment; an artifice which would be highly criminal unless the court converted it into a fair trial between the proper parties': Per Mansfield CJ in *Fairclaim* v. *Shamtitle* (1792) 3 Burr 1292, 1294.

[104] Sometimes, different names were used: eg *Goodtitle d. Read* v. *Badtitle* (1799) 1 Bos & Pul 384, *Thrustout* v. *Troublesome* (1738) 2 Strange 1099, *Fairclaim* v. *Shamtitle* (1792) 3 Burr 1292.

foot of such declaration was a notice addressed to the tenants in possession, warning them that unless they appeared and defended the action within a specified time, they would be turned out of possession'.[105]

In effect, the current possessor had to come into the action and defend it, for otherwise the claimant would obtain judgment in default.[106] But in order to come in and defend the action, the actual possessor had to admit the non-existent lease, and the entry and eviction of the notional new tenant.[107] By this elaborate means, it was possible for the action to proceed solely as a test of the title of the real claimant,[108] (i.e. the landlord of the notional tenant) against the title of the person who was in possession.[109]

---

[105] *Bl.Comm.* Bk.III App.viii, Cole, *Ejectment* (London, Sweet, 1857) 1. The declaration in ejectment was treated as a kind of writ: *R* v. *Unitt* (1723) Strange 567, J.Adams, *Action in Ejectment*, 4th American edn. (New York, Banks Gould & Co, 1854) 258.

[106] The claimant had to give the possessor a notice, purportedly written by the non-existent person in possession as 'his loving friend', which read as follows: 'I am informed that you are in possession of, or claim title to, the premises mentioned in this declaration of ejectment, or to some part thereof; and I, being sued in this action as casual ejector, and having no claim or title to the same, do advise you to appear on [date] at [address of court], by some attorney of that court, and then and there, by a rule to be made of the same court, to cause yourself to be made defendant in my stead; otherwise I shall suffer judgment to be entered against me, and you will be turned out of possession'. The person serving the notice had to explain what this actually meant: J. Day, *The Common Law Procedure Acts* (London, Sweet, 1868) 141. Even if the casual ejector was a real person, he or she could not simply admit the claim: *Hooper* v. *Dale* (1722) 1 Strange 530.

[107] After 1820, anyone wanting to come in and defend the action also had to admit that he or she had been in possession of the land claimed: *Regula Generalis* (1820) 4 Barn & Ald 196. If the actual possessor failed to make the necessary admissions, the claimant could sign judgment by default against the casual ejector, and the person in possession would be evicted when that judgment was enforced: W. Tidd, *Tidd's Practice*, 9th edn. (London, Butterworth, 1828) 1245–1246.

[108] *Bristow* v. *Cormican* (1878) 3 App.Cas. 641, 661, *Ocean Estates Ltd* v. *Pinder* [1969] 2 AC 19, 25–26, *Bl.Comm.* Bk.III 203, Simpson, *History of Land Law*, 138.

[109] There was a problem where the actual possessor was a tenant, who refused to defend the action. The landlord could not force the tenant to do so (*Goodright* v. *Hart* (1729) 2 Strange 830). It was solved by giving the landlord a statutory right to come in and defend the action in the landlord's own name (ss.12-13 Distress for Rent Act 1737, *Jones* v. *Edwards* (1745) 2 Strange 1241), which was unnecessary, because the landlord already had that right, as did anyone else who claimed a title

The tenant's action of *ejectione firmæ* thus became the general action of ejectment. But the judgment was always for recovery of a leasehold term, and this meant that the judgment was not technically binding between the real parties to it.[110] It was a judgment that the claimant's fictional tenant, Mr Doe, should recover possession against the person actually in possession. This meant that the same claim was often re-litigated between the same real parties, but with a different, fictional claimant in each action. William Woodfall, who at the beginning of the nineteenth century wrote what is still the leading practitioners' work on the law of Landlord and Tenant, said of this:[111]

> This in one respect may be deemed an advantage, because the parties are not concluded by one trial in case the real merits (from accident, partiality, want of evidence, which might be afterwards supplied, or the like) happened not to have been fairly tried between them; but in another respect, much mischief may result from it, as the spirit of litigation is thereby kept alive.

In *Earl of Bath* v. *Sherwin*[112] Mr Sherwin kept the mischievous spirit of litigation alive by making five successive claims, each of which he lost, until the House of Lords finally granted an injunction on a bill of peace to prevent him trying again,[113] thereby taking the first step towards recognising that the judgment should be binding between the real parties to the action, and not merely the notional ones.[114]

---

to the land: *Fairclaim* v. *Earl Gower* (1792) 3 Burr 1292, 1 Wm.Black 357. See generally Holdsworth, *HEL* vol. 7 14-15.

[110] Holdsworth, *HEL* vol. 7 16.

[111] *Law of Landlord and Tenant*, 514.

[112] (1709) 4 Bro PC 373, Prec Ch. 261, Toml 373, *Mitford on Pleadings*, 3rd edn. (London Clarke & Sons, 1814) 116. Mr Mitford became Lord Redesdale.

[113] See generally Holdsworth, *HEL* vol. 7 17, W. Holdsworth, *Historical Introduction to Land Law* (Oxford, Oxford University Press, 1927) 173. But, in the eighteenth century it was still not the practice to grant the injunction until after two or three actions (Eq. Cas. Abr. vol. 2 'Injunction' 522), and as late as the mid-nineteenth century, an injunction to prevent a further action was still exceptional: J. Adams, *Action in Ejectment*, 4th American edn. (New York, Banks Gould & Co, 1854) 421. See also C. Runnington, *History Principles and Practice of Ejectment*, 2nd edn. (London, Butterworths, 1820) 17.

[114] By 1720, common law courts were themselves refusing to permit a second claim to be brought to try the same title, unless the costs of defending the first action had been paid; *Leighton* v. *Leighton* (1720) 1 Strange 404, *Lord*

The real actions were abolished by Real Property Limitation Act 1833.[115]

Thereafter, the choice which freeholders had already made voluntarily to use ejectment to recover possession became compulsory. The fictions were finally all swept away by s.168 Common Law Procedure Act 1852, which directed: 'Instead of the present proceedings by ejectment a writ shall be issued, directed to the persons in possession by name, and to all persons entitled to defend the possession of the property, which property shall be described in the writ with reasonable certainty'. Now the action formerly known as ejectment is called an action for recovery of land.[116]

5. Trespass quare clausum fregit.

Trespass quare clausum fregit was, and is, the cause of action for damages for wrongful intrusion upon or occupation[117] of land. It is now called simply an action for trespass to land. In 1322 it was decided that a tenant for years could bring the action against strangers[118] and a tenant at will could do that too by 1440.[119] By

---

Coningsby's case (1723) 1 Strange 547, *Short* v. *King* (1726) 2 Strange 681, *Thrustout* v. *Troublesome* (1738) 2 Strange 1099, *Doe d. Hamilton* v. *Hatherley* (1741) 2 Strange 1152, *Kene d. Angel* v. *Angel* (1796) 6 Term Rep 740. That did not extend to the costs of any subsequent bill in equity, nor the costs of prosecuting the first action: *Doe d. Williams* v. *Winch* (1820) 3 Barn & Ald 602, *Roberts* v. *Cook* (1694) 4 Mod. 379. Cf. Lord Mansfield's judgment in *Aslin* v. *Parkin* (1758) 2 Burr 665, 668: 'That the lessor of the plaintiff and the tenant in possession are, substantially, and in truth, the parties and the only parties to the suit . . . The tenant is concluded by the judgment, and cannot controvert the title . . . This judgment, like all others, only concludes the parties, as to the subject matter of it'. For more modern applications of the principle, see *Mcabe* v. *Bank of Ireland* (1889) 14 AC 413 and *Thames Investments* v. *Benjamin* [1984] 1 WLR 1381. See also J. Adams, *Action in Ejectment*, 4th American edn. (New York, Banks Gould & Co, 1854) 425.

[115] s.36.

[116] *Secretary of State for the Environment* v. *Meier* [2009] 1 WLR 2780.

[117] See the next heading.

[118] *John of Star's Case* (1322) YB 15 Ed.2 f.458 pl.2.

[119] (1440) YB 18 Hen.6 f.1 pl.1. Copyholders were able to bring the action before this: Simpson, *History of Land Law*, 153.

1490 tenants could bring the action against their own landlords,[120] and it was the usual method of trying leasehold titles until the middle of the sixteenth century, even though the only remedy was damages,[121] after which it became clear that ejectment would serve the same purpose better.

But a tenant cannot bring an action in trespass against third parties before the tenant has made an entry under the lease.[122] This continues to be the law, notwithstanding the abolition of the doctrine of interesse termini in 1926,[123] for no entry was needed to complete a lease made under the Statute of Uses (1536), but the rule that the tenant needed to make an entry before suing third parties always applied to those leases too.[124] Similarly, a landlord cannot bring an action in trespass against strangers, until the landlord has made an entry against the tenant.[125]

6. Mesne profits.

A claim for mesne profits is a claim for damages in trespass.

As such, it is conceptually different from an action for compensation for use and occupation. A claim for compensation for use and occupation was an action in assumpsit based on an implied promise to pay, arising out of the consensual enjoyment of land.[126] So a tenant who holds over with the consent of the landlord is liable to pay compensation for use and occupation, based on the implied promise to pay given in return for that consent, whereas a tenant who holds over without any consent is liable to pay mesne profits for wrongfully keeping the landlord out.

Since the cause of action for mesne profits is *trespass quare clausum fregit*, and the complaint in trespass is of an application of

---

[120] *Anon* (1490) YB 5 Hen.7 f.10 pl.2, *Oxford History of the Laws of England*, vol. 6 636. A tenant at will, of course, could not bring an action in trespass against its own landlord, for an entry by the landlord would terminate the tenancy at will; see ch.4 heading 'At will'.

[121] *Oxford History of the Laws of England*, vol. 6 636.

[122] *Edge* v. *Strafford* (1831) 1 Compt & Jerv 391.

[123] See ch.1 heading 'Entry and interesse termini'.

[124] See *Lutwich* v. *Mitton* (1620) Cro Jac 604.

[125] *Trevillian* v. *Andrew* (1698) 5 Mod. 384.

[126] See the heading 'Assumpsit' above.

force,[127] it followed that where a landlord was complaining that a tenant had remained in occupation of land (rather than that someone had entered on the land)[128] without consent, the landlord's claim for mesne profits would not automatically run from the expiry of the lease.[129] It would run instead from the date when the landlord attempted to re-enter afterwards, and was kept out by the tenant.[130]

In equity, an occupier could be made to account for the benefit of any occupation in the meantime, if the entry was delayed as the result of a mistake,[131] or if the landlord was an infant,[132] but the common law did not find a way of bridging the gap for other cases until the middle of the eighteenth century, which was eventually done by exploiting one of the fictions in the action of ejectment. Since the action was technically a claim for possession by a new, fictional, tenant of the landlord, and since the defendant was obliged to admit the entry by the fictional new tenant, as a condition of being allowed to defend the claim,[133] all the landlord needed to do was to allege that the new lease had been granted immediately after the defendant's lease had expired. The defendant would have to admit that, in order to defend the ejectment claim, and that admission could be used later to prove the claim for mesne profits from the expiry of the lease. In that way, the claim for mesne profits could be made to relate back to the expiry of the defendant's lease.[134]

That still works today, even against a former tenant who never

---

[127] The writ complained about the use of force and arms—'vi et armis'.

[128] Sometimes, the initial entry would be treated as unlawful with retrospective effect under the doctrine of trespass *ab initio*: see *The Six Carpenters' Case* (1610) 8 Co.Rep 146a.

[129] *Scrope* v. *Hyk* (1511) 2 Caryll's Rep 116 SS 618, 619, *Trevillian* v. *Andrew* (1697) 5 Mod. 384.

[130] *Metcalfe* v. *Harvey* (1749) 1 Ves 249.

[131] *Bolton* v. *Deane* (1719) Prec Ch. 516.

[132] *Hicks* v. *Sallitt* (1854) 3 De G M & G 782, 814–815.

[133] See heading 'Ejectment'.

[134] Sir F.Buller, *The Law Relative to Trials at Nisi Prius*, 7th edn. (London, Pheney, 1817) 88, J. Adams, *Ejectment* (London, Reed, 1812) 339. Similarly, a mortgagee's right to mesne profits against a third party would relate back to the actual or notional (see above heading 'Ejectment') entry made against the mortgagor: Ashburner, *Equity* 269.

files a defence, for a defendant who does not file a defence is deemed to admit all the allegations in the claim.[135] But it does not work against a former tenant who holds over yet gives up possession before any proceedings for possession are issued. In such a case, it is still the position that no common law claim for mesne profits can be made for any period prior to the date when the landlord makes an actual entry against the former tenant. Whether a judge today, faced with that problem, would follow the old authorities, is open to doubt. The temptation might be to use restitutionary theory to imply a promise to pay for that period, allowing the landlord to bring the claim as compensation for use and occupation of land instead.

In practice, landlords would usually wait until they had recovered possession from a former tenant before bringing an action for mesne profits.[136] The point was that a claim for mesne profits was an entirely separate action to the possession claim,[137] and the court could only award mesne profits down to the date of judgment in the mesne profits action. So if the trial of the mesne profits claim took place before the landlord had enforced its possession order, the landlord would have to bring a second mesne profits claim later in any event. In most cases, it was cheaper and easier to wait until possession had been recovered, and then bring one mesne profits action afterwards.[138]

By the Recovery of Possession by Landlords Act 1820, however, a court hearing an action in ejectment was empowered to make an award of mesne profits, down to the date of judgment or some preceding day, in the same action. Originally, that power only applied to possession claims against tenants of expired written

---

[135] *Cribb* v. *Freyberger* [1919] WN 22, *Kok Hoong* v. *Leong Mines Ltd* [1964] AC 993.

[136] In the sixteenth century, before the action of ejectment was adapted so that it could be used by freeholders, a genuine leasehold tenant could recover mesne profits in the action: Holdsworth, *HEL* vol. 7 15. There is a precedent in the book of entries called *Judgments in the Upper Bench* (London, Roycroft, 1655) 80 for such a judgment in 1635, which appears to have been in favour of a real leasehold tenant, against a casual ejector and the real defendant.

[137] G. Gilbert, *Law and Practice of Ejectment*, 2nd edn. (London, Nutt & Gosling, 1741) 7–8.

[138] Someone who had been made a defendant in the possession action, could not deny the claimant's title in the mesne profits action. But anyone else could: *Jefferies* v. *Dyson* (1734) 2 Strange 960.

leases for a fixed term or from year to year, but that limitation was abolished by s.214 Common Law Procedure Act 1852,[139] which authorises the award of mesne profits in all possession claims. Under that section, the award can be made down to the date when possession is given up, even if that is after the date of the judgment,[140] obviating the need ever to bring a second action entirely.

7. Nuisance.

In a 'seminal article',[141] 'The Boundaries of Nuisance,' Professor Newark explained:[142]

> The roots of nuisance go deep into the history of the common law. Glanvill and Bracton knew of nuisance and they had no doubt what was signified by the term. *Disseisina, transgressio* and *noncumentum* covered the three ways in which a man might be interfered with in his rights over land. Wholly to deprive a man of the opportunity of exercising his rights over land was to disseise him, for which he might have recourse to the assize of novel disseisin. But to trouble a man in the exercise of his rights over land without going so far as to dispossess him was a trespass or a nuisance according to whether the act was done on or off the plaintiff's land . . .

The assize of nuisance, like all assizes, was only available to freeholders.[143]

So leasehold tenants could not bring the action. But the assize

---

[139] The same applied in the County Court under s.51 County Courts Act 1856. But the County Court only had jurisdiction where the value of the property was £50 pa. or less. That was increased to £100 by County Courts Act 1903. The jurisdiction is now unlimited: s.21 County Courts Act 1984.

[140] *Southport Tramways* v. *Gandy* [1897] 2 QB 66.

[141] Per Lord Goff in *Cambridge Water* v. *Eastern Counties Leather* [1994] 2 AC 264, 299.

[142] F. Newark, *The Boundaries of Nuisance* (1949) 65 LQR 480, 481.

[143] J. Ames, *Lectures on Legal History*, 231, C. Fifoot, *History and Sources of the Common Law*, 93 *et seq.*

was supplemented, at the end the thirteenth century,[144] by the action of nuisance on the case.

That was designed to be a complimentary action, to provide a remedy for those cases where the assize was not available,[145] including claims made by leasehold tenants.[146] At first freeholders could only use it for partial interferences with their rights,[147] but in 1601 freeholders were given the option of suing in nuisance on the case even where they could have brought the assize,[148] and thereafter, there was never any doubt that both freehold and leasehold tenants[149] could bring an action on the case in nuisance,[150] subject to the same restrictions as applied to an action in trespass.

The assize itself was abolished in 1833,[151] and the modern action in nuisance is an action for nuisance on the case.

8. Waste.

'Voluntary' waste is a positive act which does lasting damage to the demised[152] property: 'permissive' waste is neglect which has the same effect; for 'whatever does lasting damage to the freehold or inheritance is waste'.[153] But damaging the property in order to

---

[144] Statute of Westminster II (1285).

[145] *Rickhill* v. *Parsons of Bromaye* (1400) YB 2 Hen.4 f.11 pl.48, *Yevance* v. *Holcomb* (1566) Dyer 250b.

[146] (1469) YB 9 Ed.4 f.35b pl.10, *Anon* (1565/6) 3 Leon 13.

[147] (1523) YB 14 Hen.8 f.31 pl.8, J. Ames, *Lectures on Legal History* 232, C. Fifooot, *History and Sources of the Common Law* 94.

[148] *Cantrel* v. *Church* (1601) Cro Eliz 845.

[149] This included tenants of incorporeal hereditaments: *The Earl of Shrewsbury's Case* (1609) 9 Co.Rep 42a, 46b.

[150] *Ayre* v. *Pyncomb* (1649) Style 164.

[151] s.36 Real Property Limitation Act 1833.

[152] *Goodright d. Peters* v. *Vivian* (1807) 8 East 190.

[153] *Abbot of Stratford* v. *Pykeryn* (1498) Caryll's Reps, 115 SS 375, *Bl.Comm.* Bk.II 281. An action for 'dilapidations' was originally an action for a type of ecclesiastical waste. If the incumbent of a benefice did, or failed to do, anything that would have been waste between a landlord and tenant, then he could be punished in the Ecclesiastical court by censure, sequestration or deprivation of his living: *Bl.Comm.* Bk.III 91–92. The term 'dilapidations' is found in the long title of the Ecclesiastical Leases Act 1571. It is now normally used to describe breaches of a repairing covenant under a lease of commercial premises.

increase its value (for example, pulling down an old wall in order to erect a better, new one)[154] is 'meliorating' waste, and is not actionable.[155]

At common law, a landlord could not bring an action in waste against a tenant holding under an express grant.[156] The action could only be brought by a reversioner against those who held life estates created by act of law, such as a widow holding part of her late husband's land in dower, or a widower holding part of his late wife's lands in curtesy. In 1267 the Statute of Marlborough[157] extended the action against tenants generally,[158] and that was reinforced in 1278 by the Statute of Gloucester,[159] which imposed a penalty of automatic forfeiture and treble damages.[160]

The action of waste had fallen into desuetude by the end of the seventeenth century. The reason for that was simple enough. Procedurally, it was much more convenient to bring 'an action on the case in the nature of waste', which also had the advantage that it could be brought by leasehold reversioners too.[161] So the action

---

[154] But changing the character of the property is waste. Coke said (Co.Litt. 53a): 'If a tenant build a new house, it is waste, and if he suffers it to be wasted, it is new waste.' In Cole v. Forth (1672) 1 Mod. 94 pulling down a brewhouse to turn it into houses was held to be actionable, and damages of £120 were awarded.

[155] The fourth type of waste is 'equitable waste'. This is malicious damage by someone with a limited interest in the land, who is not otherwise liable for waste at common law, and is restrainable in equity. This simply does not arise between landlord and tenant, because landlords have never granted leases which specifically authorise the tenant to commit common law waste.

[156] Doctor and Student, 102, 106. But this may be an over-simplification. See Pollock & Maitland vol. 2 9.

[157] c.24.

[158] The statute actually used the word 'firmarii' (farmers). But Coke, 2nd Inst. 145, explained that firmarii 'do comprehend all such as hold by lease for life or lives or for years made by deed or without deed'. Blackstone said (Bl.Comm. Bk.II 318): 'a farmer, farmarius, was one who held his lands upon payment of a rent or feorme' See also Bl.Comm. Bk.II 283.

[159] 6 Ed.1 c.5.

[160] Coke, 2nd Inst. 299–306, Holdsworth, HEL vol. 3 121–123. The claimant could also obtain a writ of prohibition, which was equivalent to an injunction. An assignee of the reversion could bring the action too; Darell v. Wybarne (1561) Dyer 204a, 206b.

[161] Greene v. Cole (1670) 2 Wms Saund 252.fn(7). The action of waste could only be brought by the immediate freehold reversioner (Co.Litt. 218b.fn(2)) though the

of waste was formally abolished on 1st January 1834, and the Statute of Gloucester was formally repealed in 1879.[162] Thereafter, every action for waste was technically an action on the case in the nature of waste, rather than an action in waste itself.

Waste has always been a strict liability tort, like nuisance, rather than a claim for enforcement of a promise, like covenant or assumpsit.[163] This had five important consequences.

First, it was settled in 1531/2 that the action died with the perpetrator. The action could not be brought against his estate.[164] That rule was reversed for trespass in 1833,[165] for waste by s.26(5) Administration of Estates Act 1925, and then generally for torts other than defamation by s.1 Law Reform (Miscellaneous Provisions) Act 1934. Secondly, the benefit of the action cannot be assigned,[166] although it is possible to avoid that rule by assigning the fruits of the action and granting the right to sue in the name of the assignor instead.[167] Thirdly, a landlord can elect to sue in waste, even if the same ground is covered by an express covenant.[168]

---

ultimate reversioner (if there was an intermediate lease for life) could obtain equitable relief: *Anon* Cary 19.

[162] s.59 Civil Procedure Acts Repeal Act 1879. The Law Commission, in 2010, suggested that c.23 Statute of Marlborough 1267 was obsolete and ought to be repealed, on the mistaken premise that it criminalised bad farming: Statute Law Reform, Consultation Paper, SLR/310, 14–15. If acted upon, that will abolish the tort of waste.

[163] The Statute of Westminster II (1285) c.14 provided for the claim to be made by writ of summons. Before then, it was made by writ of prohibition. It could only be brought in respect of the demised property. So if the wasted property had been reserved to the landlord, the claim had to be made in trespass rather than waste: *Anon* (1536) Dyer 19a.

[164] *Doctor and Student*, 128, (1531/2) Brook's New Cases pl.42, Dalison's Reps (1554) 124 SS 46. If the victim died, however, then his heir could bring the action under the Statute of Waste (1292) 20 Ed.1 stat.2.

[165] s.2 Civil Procedure Act 1833.

[166] *Defries* v. *Milne* [1913] 1 Ch 98. It followed, on a transfer of the reversion, that the right to sue for waste committed before the transfer was lost. The transferor lost the right to sue by transferring the reversion, and the transferee could not sue because the right could not be assigned: *Perks*, ¶.95.

[167] *Glegg* v. *Bromley* [1912] 3 KB 474.

[168] *Kinlyside* v. *Thornton* (1776) 2 Wm.Black 1111. In *Jones* v. *Hill* (1817) 1 Moore CP 100) Gibbs CJ tried to confine this to claims for voluntary waste. But the authority of that case was undermined by *Yellowly* v. *Gower* (1855) 11 Ex 274, 293–294 (where only the inferior report at 7 Taunton 392 was referred to). Performance of a covenant is a defence to waste, even if the covenant could have been performed in another way: *Anon* (1561) Dyer 198b.

Fourthly, whilst the tenant is strictly liable for waste committed by third parties,[169] destruction by lightning or other act of god is a good defence.[170] Fifthly, third parties who encourage or assist the tenant to commit waste are liable too.[171]

It was a settled rule, from 1600 to 1805, that the word 'firmarii' in the Statute of Marlborough 1267 covered both tenants for life and tenants for years, and that they were liable for both voluntary waste and permissive waste.[172] Nor was there any doubt that the expression 'tenants for years' included any tenant who held for a term, no matter how short. As Blackstone explained:[173]

> If the lease be but for half a year, or a quarter, or any less time, this lessee is respected as a tenant for years, and is styled so in some legal proceedings; a year being the shortest term which the law in this case takes notice of.

A tenant at will, however, did not have a 'term' at all, and consequently could be sued neither for voluntary nor for permissive waste.[174] But it was established in 1600,[175] that since a tenancy at will continues only for so long as both parties wish it, and since the landlord could hardly want it to continue whilst the tenant was

---

[169] *Doctor and Student*, 112.

[170] *Doctor and Student*, 113, *Colthirst* v. *Bejushin* (1550) Plowden 20, 28, *Rook* v. *Worth* (1750) 1 Ves Sen 460, 462, Holdsworth, *HEL* vol. 3 122. Liability for other accidental, non-negligent, damage caused by fire was abrogated by the Fires Prevention (Metropolis) Act 1774. See ch.5 heading 'Repair'.

[171] *Mancetter Ltd* v. *Garmanson* [1986] 1 QB 1212. This, in practice, proves very useful as a means of ensuring that the administrators of a tenant take care when stripping out tenant's fixtures for sale, for although administrators have no personal liability on the company's contracts (including the lease) they are personally liable for torts.

[172] *Co.Litt.* 54b, *Bl.Comm.* Bk.II 281–282.

[173] *Bl.Comm.* Bk.II 140. Hence also the definition of 'term of years' in s.205(xxvii) Law of Property Act 1925 as including 'a term for less than a year, or for a year or years and a fraction of a year or from year to year'.

[174] (1374) Statham's *Abridgment*, 'Waste', 23, *Burgh* v. *Potkyn* (1522) 119 SS 125, 120 SS 82, YB 14 Hen.8 f.10 pl.6, *Countess of Shrewsbury* v. *Crompton* (1600) 5 Co.Rep 13b, Cro Eliz 777, 784, *Torriano* v. *Young* (1833) 6 Car & P 8. It followed that a copyholder could not be sued in waste, although a lessee of a copyholder could be: *Dalton* v. *Gill* (1576/7) Cary 63.

[175] *Countess of Shrewsbury* v. *Crompton* (1600) 5 Co.Rep 13b, Cro Eliz 777, 784.

doing lasting damage to the property,[176] a tenancy at will would end automatically if the tenant did anything equivalent to voluntary waste, with the result that the former landlord would be able recover for the damage in trespass instead.[177] Somewhat illogically, thirty years later, it was decided that if a tenant at sufferance did an act equivalent to voluntary waste, the landlord would have the choice of either suing in waste, or treating the tenant as a trespasser, and suing in trespass.[178]

Doubts began to be expressed about whether other tenants were liable for permissive waste in the nineteenth century. The root of the problem, as is so often the case, was a report of a decision at nisi prius;[179] in this case, the decision of Sir James Mansfield CJ in *Gibson* v. *Wells*[180] That was an action against a tenant at will for permissive waste. It should have been dismissed on the ground that a tenant at will could not be sued for either type of waste. Instead, according to the report, Sergeant Bayley told the court that a tenant at will could be sued for voluntary waste, and the judge responded by saying that he would not hold a tenant at will liable for permissive waste. So the claim was rightly dismissed, but that exchange was used in *Herne* v. *Bembow*[181] as support for the proposition that a tenant for a fixed term could not be liable for permissive waste either. The point was left in doubt by *Jones* v. *Hill*,[182] but in *Yellowly* v. *Gower*[183] the Court of Exchequer put the law back onto a correct course by holding that a 'tenant for years' was liable for permissive waste, and that is the law now.[184]

Yet, in an extraordinary twist, that decision of the Court of Exchequer has been taken as being authority for the proposition

---

[176] Ibid. See also *Co.Litt.* 55b.

[177] (1472) YB 12 Ed.4 f.8 pl.20, *Co.Litt.* 57a.

[178] *West* v. *Treude* (1630) Cro Car 187.

[179] The problem with nisi prius reports is that they are decisions made by single judges, who were under pressure to make instant decisions, working through a busy trial list, whilst on circuit and without access to a proper library. See R.Megarry, *Second Miscellany at Law* (London, Stevens, 1973) 131 cf. *Oxford History of the Laws of England*, vol. 12 116.

[180] (1805) 1 Bos & P (NR) 290.

[181] (1813) 4 Taunton 764.

[182] (1817) 1 B Mo 100.

[183] (1855) 11 Ex 274, 293–294.

[184] *Davies* v. *Davies* (1888) 30 Ch.D 499, 503, *Dayani* v. *Bromley LBC* [1999] 3 EGLR 144; per contra *Re Cartwright* (1889) 41 Ch 532.

that nobody other than 'tenants for years' can be liable for permissive waste,[185] with the result that the only tenants who are now liable for permissive waste are tenants for a fixed term of more than one year,[186] which had certainly not been the case previously.[187]

9. Equitable relief.

The actions listed above were all common law actions, meaning that they were actions which, before the Judicature Acts 1873 to 1894, were brought in courts which exercised common law jurisdiction: first, the court of Common Pleas, also called Common Bench,[188] which dealt with private disputes between common people; secondly, the court of King's or Queen's Bench (Upper Bench during the Protectorate) which dealt with claims in which the state had an interest; and thirdly the Exchequer of Pleas, which dealt with financial claims involving the state.[189] In fact, the jurisdictions substantially overlapped, as, by a series of fictions, the courts attempted to wrest profitable business from each other. A claim for money could, for instance, be brought in the Exchequer of Pleas, simply by pretending the defendant's failure to pay the claim was the delaying the payment of a debt which the claimant owed to the Crown. A claim for ejectment could be brought in all three courts.[190]

There were essentially two disadvantages to common law actions.

---

[185] So, in *In Re Cartwright, Avis* v. *Newman* (1889) 41 Ch.D 532, it was held that a tenant for life was not liable for permissive waste.

[186] *Keen* v. *Holland* [1954] 1 QB 15, 21, *Regis Property Co Ltd* v. *Dudley* [1959] AC 370, 407.

[187] In *Burgh* v. *Potkyn* (1522) 120 SS 82, 83, Pollard J and Brudenell CJ 'agreed that someone may make a lease for ten days, ten months, one month, a quarter of a year, or a quarter of a whole year; and in all such cases it seems clearly that, if a writ of waste is brought, the writ shall be worded 'which he holds for a term of years', and yet the plaintiff must make a special declaration of the actual facts'. See also Littleton, *Tenures*, s.67.

[188] *Bl.Comm.* Bk.III 37.

[189] The Court of Exchequer had a separate 'equity side', which exercised equitable jurisdiction, on bills brought before it, from the sixteenth century until 1841.

[190] Holdsworth, *HEL* vol. 7 8–9.

First, the range of remedies available in the common law courts was very limited. The only specific relief which the common law courts could grant, in an action between landlord and tenant, was the making of a possession order. Otherwise, the only thing that the courts could do was to order one party to pay a sum of money to the other.

Secondly, and more perhaps seriously, equitable rights could not be relied upon, either by way of claim or by way of defence, in common law courts.[191] Those courts administered the common law only, and gave judgment strictly according to common law rights. 'The courts of law, in the exercise of their jurisdiction, ignored not only the doctrines, but also the existence of the Court of Chancery'.[192]

So someone with an equitable right[193] or defence had to file a bill[194] in a court of equity to obtain an injunction,[195] either to prevent the other party from prosecuting or defending a common

---

[191] So, for instance, an equitable mortgagee could not bring an action in ejectment (a possession action): Ashburner, *Equity* 270, W. Tidd, *Tidd's Practice*, 9th edn. (London, Butterworth, 1828) 1193–1194.

[192] Ashburner, *Equity* 12.

[193] 'An equitable right is not equivalent to a legal right. Between the contracting parties an agreement for a lease may be as good as a lease, just so between the contracting parties an agreement for the sale of land may serve as well as a completed sale and conveyance. But introduce a third party and then you will see the difference': Maitland, *Equity* 161.

[194] Claims in equity were commenced by 'bill'. A writ was only used to compel the defendant to swear and file a sufficient 'answer' to the bill. Witnesses gave evidence by written 'depositions', taken by supposedly independent commissioners or examiners, in the absence of the parties, which were all made public on the same date. If there was a conflict of evidence on a vital issue, then, until the practice was stopped by the Chancery Regulation Act 1862 (Rolt's Act), there would have to be a trial of that issue in a common law court, so that the facts could be found by a jury: Ashburner, *Equity* 32. For the jurisdiction and procedure up to the seventeenth century, see C. Ogilvie, *The King's Government and the Common Law* (Oxford, Blackwell, 1958) 34–42, 88–97.

[195] Curiously, in the eighteenth century, the practice was only to grant an injunction against acts of damage or destruction to land if committed by a stranger. No injunction would be granted against someone claiming a better title than the person in possession: Ashburner, *Equity* 9. For the general practice on granting interim injunctions before the Judicature Acts 1873 to 1894, see Ashburner, *Equity* 7, 18.

law claim to judgment,[196] contrary to those principles, or to prevent or set-aside the enforcement of a common law judgment given contrary to equitable principles afterwards.[197]

As Maitland observed,[198] before the Acts there was a visible distinction between the common law and equity. You could have gone to Westminster Hall, and seen a common law court grant judgment in a common law action begun by writ. Then you could have crossed to south-west corner of the Hall,[199] and seen the Chancellor grant a decree in an equity suit begun by bill.[200] He could not actually overturn a common law judgment. He could only

---

[196] For early examples, see *Riche* v. *Foard* (1558/9) Cary 38 and *Knot* v. *Jackson* (1558/9) Cary 40. By the nineteenth century, if the defendant to a bill in equity failed to acknowledge service and file a complete answer to the claim in time, then the claimant was entitled to a 'common injunction' as a matter of course. A common injunction was an interlocutory order preventing the service of any common law proceedings and staying the execution of any common law judgment. But it did not prevent the prosecution to judgment of any common law proceedings which had already been served. If there was a good reason why the common law claim should not be decided until after the equitable rights of the parties had been determined—if, for example, the equitable claim was for discovery of documents relevant to the common law right—then an application could be made to extend the injunction to prevent the trial of any common law proceedings which had already been served. The defendant could apply to dissolve a common injunction after serving an answer, and no common injunction could issue if the defendant acknowledged service and filed an answer in time. In that event, the claimant had to apply for a special injunction, either to prevent the commencement or continuance of the common law proceedings or the execution of the common law judgment. See generally J. Adams, *Equity*, 2nd American edn. (Philadelphia, Johnson, 1852) 195.

[197] A good example is *Steed* v. *Cragh* (1722) 9 Mod. 43, where the defendant only had an equitable right to a lease. The response of Ellesmere LC, when challenged in 1616 about the legitimacy of this by James I, is at Cary 115–132.

[198] Maitland, *Equity* 150.

[199] In the eighteenth and early nineteenth centuries the Chancellor sat in the Old Hall of Lincoln's Inn out of term time, which is where the opening chapter of Bleak House is set.

[200] The relationship between common law judges and chancery was not always easy. In *Holderstaffe* v. *Saunders* (1703) 6 Mod. 16 a judgment in ejectment had been obtained by fraud. Holt CJ said that if the Chancellor were to grant an injunction to stop him investigating the fraud, 'this court would break it and protect any that were in contempt of it'. The court subsequently made an order restoring possession to the tenant: *Saunders* v. *Melhuish* (1703) 6 Mod. 73.

subvert it, by making personal orders[201] against the litigants.[202]

On occasion, strong-headed judges rebelled against this. In *Weakly d. Yea* v. *Bucknell*[203] Lord Mansfield allowed a tenant whose lease was only enforceable in equity to defend an action in ejectment, on the grounds that it was pointless to give judgment for the claimant only 'for the sake of giving the court of Chancery an opportunity to undo it again'.[204] But Lord Kenyon CJ restored orthodoxy two years later in *Doe* v. *Staple*,[205] and thereafter, only legislation could change matters.

That legislative change came, in stages, during the course of the nineteenth century.

The County Courts Act 1846 established the present County Court system, as a cheaper alternative to the courts of Queen's Bench and Common Pleas for small value claims.[206] From their inception, the County Courts had a combined, albeit limited, common law and equity jurisdiction. Since 1990, the common law jurisdiction of the County Courts has been unlimited, but the equity jurisdiction is generally still limited to claims involving property

---

[201] If a court of equity ordered a person to deliver up possession of land, from the seventeenth century onwards it could also grant a writ of assistance, directing the sheriff to put the claimant in possession of it: Ashburner, *Equity* 41. In *Hawkes* v. *Champion* (1558) Cary 36, for instance, where the plaintiff had entered during the course of the action, an interlocutory injunction was granted, restoring possession to the defendant. Similarly, an injunction was granted for that purpose in *Dow* v. *Perrot* (1559/60) Cary 45.

[202] So where land was conveyed by a fraudulent fine in a common law court, equity could not set aside the fine, but it could order a reconveyance. Similarly, it could order a judgment creditor to acknowledge that the judgment had been satisfied, even though nothing had been paid: *Colverwell* v. *Bongey* (1559/60) Cary 45, Ashburner, *Equity*, 13, 34. This could have peculiar results. A judgment creditor had a common law right to send the debtor to the Fleet prison if the debt was not paid. A court of equity could not release the debtor, even if the creditor had defied its order by refusing to deliver an acknowledgment of satisfaction of the debt. But it could imprison the creditor too, for contempt: *Baker* v. *Beumont* (1663) 1 Ch.Cas 32, 3 Ch R 13. See also *Courtney* v. *Glanvil* (1614) Cro Jac 343.

[203] (1776) Cowper 473.

[204] 474. See also Ashburner, *Equity* 15, Holdsworth, *HEL* vol. 7 19–20.

[205] (1788) 2 Term Rep 684.

[206] The County Courts before that were incident to the jurisdiction of the sheriff, and heard claims for debt and damages where the amount claimed did not exceed 40 shillings: *Bl.Comm.* Bk.III 35.

worth less than £30,000.[207]

There was also piecemeal reform where the claim was for relief from forfeiture. Common law courts were already required to stay proceedings for forfeiture for non-payment of rent, where all the arrears and the costs had been paid.[208] In 1860, they were given the same powers as courts of equity to relieve against forfeiture for non-payment of rent and for failure to insure,[209] leaving only exceptional cases of fraud, mistake or inevitable accident outwith their jurisdiction.[210]

Common law courts were given power to rule on equitable defences in 1854,[211] and at the same time, they were given a general power to grant injunctions.[212] The Chancery Amendment Act 1858, gave courts of equity power to award damages in addition to or in substitution for an injunction or specific performance,[213] and the Chancery Regulation Act 1862 obliged courts of equity, when dealing with claims to equitable relief after 1st November 1862, to determine every question of fact or law cognizable in a common law court,

---

[207] s.23 County Courts Act 1984. There are currently proposals to increase it to £350,000.

[208] s.4 Landlord and Tenant Act 1730. Re-enacted in s.212 Common Law Procedure Act 1852. The equivalent in the County Court was s.52 County Courts (Amendment) Act 1856, and it is now found in s.138(2) County Courts Act 1984. The County Court only had jurisdiction to deal with forfeitures for non-payment of rent under the 1856 Act. By s.59 County Courts Act 1888, it acquired general power to deal with claims in ejectment, where the land was not worth more than £50. That was increased to £100 by the County Courts Act 1903, and the value limit was increased by s.48 County Courts Act 1959 to any case where the rateable value was not more than £100.

[209] ss.1-2 Common Law Procedure Act 1860 were repealed by s.7 Conveyancing Act 1881, s.14(2) of which extended the power of 'the Court' to relieve against other non-rental breaches too. But that was after the Judicature Acts 1873 and 1875, and although s.69(1) of the 1881 Act assigned all matters under that Act to the Chancery Division, every division of the High Court was obliged to administer the law in the same way; and s.14 itself anticipated that the power might be exercised by the King's Bench Division on a counterclaim: *Cholmedley's School* v. *Sewell* [1893] 2 QB 254.

[210] At the time, even courts of equity had no power to relieve against other, non-rental, breaches; see ch.7 heading 'Relief from forfeiture'.

[211] s.83 Common Law Procedure Act 1854.

[212] s.79 Common Law Procedure Act 1854.

[213] See now s.51 Senior Courts Act 1981.

upon which the right depended.[214]

The big change, however, happened with the Judicature Acts 1873 and 1875. Those Acts created one court of original jurisdiction, the High Court, and although that court was divided into five different divisions, it did not matter in which division a judge sat. The judge was required to administer the whole of the common law and the whole of equity, and give a single judgment equivalent to the combined effect of the two judgments which would have been given in the two different courts beforehand.[215] As Maitland said:[216]

> Every judge in whatever division he may be sitting is bound to apply every rule whether of common law or equity that is applicable to the case before him. He cannot stop short and say that is a question of common law which I am incompetent to decide, or, that is merely an equitable right and I can take no notice of it.

Apart from some very minor changes, made expressly by the Acts,[217] the substantive law after the Acts were passed was exactly the same as it had been before. The Judicature Acts did not 'fuse' law and equity, except in an administrative sense. As Lindley LJ said in *Joseph* v. *Lyons*:[218]

> Reliance was placed upon the provisions of the Judicature Acts, and it was contended that the effect of them was to abolish the distinction between law and equity. Certainly, that is the not the effect of these statutes, otherwise they would abolish the distinction between a trustee and a cestui que trust.

---

[214] Until then, the practice was to send the disputed issue of fact to be tried in a common law court. In the eighteenth century, it was tried on the basis of pretended £5 bet on the outcome of that issue: *Bl.Comm.* Bk.II 452.

[215] *Mostyn* v. *The West Mostyn Coal and Iron Co.* (1876) 1 CPD 145, 150. Complaints about the separate administration of the common law and equity had been made since the sixteenth century: C. Ogilvie, *The King's Government and the Common Law* (Oxford, Blackwell, 1958) 120.

[216] Maitland, *Equity* 151. See also *The Nile Rhapsody* [1992] 2 Lloyds LR 399.

[217] s.25 Judicature Act 1873, s.10 Judicature Act 1875.

[218] (1884) 15 QBD 280. See also *Ind Coope* v. *Emmerson* (1887) 12 App.Cas. 300, 308 Per Lord Watson.

What changed was the procedure for enforcing equitable rights. Instead of having to bring two different claims in two different courts, in order to reach one eventual result, the same result could be reached instead by bringing one claim in one court, and it no longer mattered which one.[219]

The five divisions of the High Court were reduced to three in 1880, when the Exchequer Division and Common Pleas were merged with Queen's Bench.

10. Summary possession proceedings.

An action in ejectment (an action for recovery of land) has been the usual method of recovering possession of land since the sixteenth century. But, at various times, there have been alternative statutory routes to the recovery of possession.

A persistent problem for landlords has always been the tenant who simply abandons the premises owing rent. In most cases, the landlord has been able to terminate the tenancy by exercising a right of re-entry, and, in the case of deserted premises, that can be done by physical re-entry without the assistance of the court. But, absent a right of re-entry, the landlord has no power to forfeit for the arrears, and sometimes, even if there is a right of re-entry, the landlord will want the protection of a court order, either for itself or to clear the title. In order to solve this problem, from 1738[220] magistrates were given the power to order that the landlord be put into possession, and that the lease be treated as void, where premises were let at a rent of at least three-quarters of their annual value, and they had been deserted leaving half a year's rent in

---

[219] In *Britain* v. *Rossiter* ((1882) 11 QBD 123, 129) Brett LJ said: 'I think that the true construction of the Judicature Acts is that they confer no new rights; they only confirm rights which previously were to be found existing in the Courts either of Law or of Equity; if they did more, they would alter the rights of parties, whereas in truth they only change the procedure. Before the passing of the Judicature Acts no one could be charged on this contract either at law or in equity; and if the plaintiff could now enforce this contract, it would be an alteration of the law'. See also *British South Africa Company* v. *Companhia de Mocambique* [1893] AC 602, and *Hanak* v. *Green* [1958] 2 QB 9, per Morris LJ 24–25.

[220] s.16 Distress for Rent Act 1737.

arrears with no sufficient distress. As originally enacted, that only solved half the problem. It did not apply unless there was a right of re-entry. In 1817 the Act was amended, so as to make a right of re-entry unnecessary.[221] Those provisions are still in force.

The Small Tenements Recovery Act 1838[222] was the standard means for evicting the Victorian working classes from rented accommodation held under a periodic tenancy;[223] for where a tenancy had expired, and the letting had not been for longer than 7 years nor at a rent of more than £20 pa., the landlord could obtain a summary order for possession in the Magistrates Court, which would issue a warrant requiring the police to evict the former tenant between 21 and 31 days later.[224] The Act became useless for private landlords, because the rental limits were never increased, but it continued to be used by public authorities (in whose favour the rental limits were generally disapplied)[225] and by mortgagees, relying on attornment clauses,[226] until its repeal in 1972.[227]

11. Crown proceedings.

The Crown was always in a special position. Whether by reason of the constitutional rule that the sovereign could do no wrong, or by reason of the impossibility of suing the sovereign in his or her own courts,[228] none of the normal actions applied to claims by or against the Crown.[229]

So it was not possible to sue the Crown in debt or covenant, nor for any tort such as trespass, nuisance and waste, nor was it

---

[221] The Deserted Tenements Act 1817.

[222] s.1. See also, for lettings by the church, s.59 Pluralities Act 1838, which is still in force.

[223] *Oxford History of the Laws of England*, vol. 12 124.

[224] The same procedure could also be used to recover possession of, inter alia, allotments, land occupied by schoolmasters, and almshouses: see J.Williams, *The Law of Ejectment*, 2nd edn. (London, Sweet & Maxwell, 1911) 316.

[225] s.5 Defence Act 1859, s.12 Admiralty Lands and Works Act 1864, s.158(2) Housing Act 1957, s.6(1) New Towns Act 1946.

[226] *Ingram* v. *Inland Revenue* [1997] 4 All ER 395, 422.

[227] s.35(5), 52(1) Rent Act 1965, SI 1972 No.1161, art.2.

[228] (1467) YB 7 Ed.4 f.16 pl.11.

[229] *Bl.Comm.* Bk.I 236.

possible to recover land from the Crown by suing in ejectment.[230] Nor could any of the usual equitable remedies be granted against the Crown by a court of equity. The theory was that the common law judges and Chancellor were all deputies for the sovereign, performing justice in the sovereign's name, and so there was simply no possibility of any sort of mandatory order ever being made against the Crown.

That is not to say that a subject could never obtain redress against the Crown. Before the Crown Proceedings Act 1947, the equivalent of the actions for debt and covenant, where the debt was owed by the Crown, was a petition for a 'liberate', which was a special writ authorising officials of the Exchequer to pay the sum claimed out of the treasury.[231]There was (and still is) no means of redress for torts committed by the sovereign personally,[232] but the immunity did not extend to crown agents or servants, who committed torts on behalf of the Crown. So the practice was to sue them personally in the ordinary courts, in the expectation that the Crown would provide them with an indemnity for any damages.

The procedure for recovering land from the Crown differed, depending on whether the claimant's title appeared as a matter of record in the Exchequer or not. If it did, then the remedy was a monstrans de droit.[233] Otherwise, the remedy was a petition of right.[234] This was granted as a matter of grace, and did not involve alleging that the Crown had committed any tort or other wrongful act. The allegation was simply that the Crown was currently holding property which properly belonged to the petitioner.[235] Originally, the procedure on a petition of right was very long and tedious, because the Crown had first to give permission for the

---

[230] (1483) YB 1 Ed.5 f.8 pl.13, *Doctor and Student*, 30, W.Noy, *Dialogue & Treatise*, 9th edn. (Reprinted, Abingdon, Professional Books Ltd, 1985) 34, *Doe d. Leigh* v. *Roe* (1841) 8 M&W 579.

[231] In 1874 it was decided that a debt could be recovered on a petition of right too: *Thomas* v. *R* (1874) LR 10 QB 31.

[232] *Tobin* v. *R* (1864) 16 CB(NS) 310, *Feather* v. *R* (1865) 6 B & S 257.

[233] A chancery order of amoveas manum or 'ousterlemain' (ouster of the hand of the Crown); *Note* (1509) 2 Caryll's Reps 116 SS 674, *R* v. *Hornby* (1695) 5 Mod. 29, 58.

[234] *Bl.Comm.* Bk.III 256.

[235] *Feather* v. *R.* (1865) 6 B & S 257, 294–297.

petition to be issued, then a commission had to be taken to find the right, and then a full search had to be made of the Exchequer, to see whether it held anything relevant to the action. It was much quicker after the reforms made by the Petitions of Right Act 1860, but until late into the nineteenth century, when judges stopped applying the rule,[236] the only compensation which could be recovered for the detention of the land in the meantime, were those actual profits which had not yet been paid into the Exchequer.[237]

All the old forms of proceedings against the Crown were abolished on 1st January 1948,[238] when the Crown Proceedings Act 1947 came into force, which also abolished the Crown's immunity for actions in tort, though not the sovereign's personal immunity.[239] The action now, in each case, is the same action as might be brought between subjects, but it is brought by or against an authorised government department or the Attorney-General, as the representative of the Crown.[240] Yet some remnants of the old rules remain. The court still cannot make a mandatory order, whether by way of injunction, specific performance or for the recovery of land, against the Crown representative.[241] It can only declare what the claimant's rights are, on the assumption that the Crown will comply. Similarly, a money judgment cannot be enforced in the usual way.[242] Instead, a certificate is issued, on the assumption that the Crown will pay.[243]

Before 1948, the Crown also had various advantages in litigation against a subject. Claims by the Crown were brought by 'information' laid by the Attorney-General in the Exchequer of Pleas, rather than by ordinary writ.[244]

So money claims were brought by an 'information of debt' and claims relating to land were brought by an 'information of intrusion'.

When it came to the recovery of land, the Crown had additional

---

[236] *In Re Gosman* (1880) LR 15 Ch.D 67.
[237] W.Clode, *The Law and Practice of Petition of Right* (London, William Clowes, 1887) 83–86.
[238] s.1.
[239] s.2.
[240] s.17.
[241] s.21.
[242] s.25(4).
[243] s.25.
[244] *Bl.Comm.* Bk.III 261.

advantages as a result of the rule that a subject could never dispossess the Crown.[245] Even complete a physical ouster could only ever be treated as a trespass to the Crown's possession.[246] Consequently, there was never any need for the Crown to develop or make use of any action equivalent to the action of ejectment.[247] The Crown could simply bring an information of intrusion, against anyone who was wrongfully in occupation of crown lands;[248] and because the Crown could never be out of possession there was no need for the Crown to make an entry against a tenant holding over first.[249] Before 1623, there was also a procedural advantage, in that the burden of proof was on the subject to justify his or her occupation.[250] Finally, encroachment on crown land was, and remains, a nuisance (purpresture)[251] which is perhaps punishable by forfeiture of the subject's adjoining land, if it is held as tenant in chief of the Crown.[252]

---

[245] One result of this was that, before the Nullum Tempus Act 1623, a subject could never acquire title against the Crown by adverse possession; *The Grounds and Rudiments of Law and Equity*, 2nd edn. (London, Osborne, 1751) 236–238.

[246] *Elvis* v. *Archbishop of York* (1619) Hob 315, 322, *R* v. *Bishop of Winton and Champion* (1604) Cro Jac 53, *Emmerson* v. *Maddison* [1906] AC 569, 575. Even so, the Crown could not sue for trespass quare clausum fregit: *Bl.Comm.* Bk.III 257. The Crown proceeded by way of 'information of intrusion', until that form of act was abolished by the Crown Proceedings Act 1947. Now the Crown can sue in ejectment or trespass as it pleases: s.13 Crown Proceedings Act 1947.

[247] Cole cited *Doe d. King William IV* v. *Roberts* (1844) 13 M&W 520 as authority for the proposition that the Crown could sue in ejectment: Cole, *Ejectment* (London, Sweet, 1857) 91. But that was not a claim by the Crown at all. The claim was brought by a genuine tenant of the Crown, in his own right, and the issue, between private persons, was whether the Crown had title to grant the lease, under a purchase made by Edward III.

[248] *Attorney-General* v. *Andrew* (1655) Hard 23, Roll Abr vol. 2 'Intruder' 215.

[249] *Finches' Case* (1591) 2 Leon 134, 143-4, K.McNeil, *Common Law Aboriginal Title* (Oxford, Clarendon Press, 1989) 98 fn.87.

[250] *Emmerson* v. *Maddison* [1906] AC 569, 576.

[251] *Bl.Comm.* Bk.IV 167.

[252] *Co.Litt.* 277b, K. Reid with ors., *The Law of Property in Scotland* (LexisNexis UK, 1996) ¶.83, cf. Statute de Bigimis (1276) c.4.

INDEX

Dalton, Michael. *Officium Vicecomitum.* London: Printed for the Companie of Stationers, 1623. New introduction by Thomas Garden Barnes [1930-2010], University of California, Berkeley. 8-1/2" x 11" Hardcover 2009. ISBN 978-1-58477-957-5. $295.

Fitzherbert, Anthony. *La Graunde Abridgement Collecte par le Iudge Tresreverend Monsieur Anthony Fitzherber* **[And]** *Tabula. Cy Ensuit la Table pur Trover les Titles.* London: Richard Tottell, 1577. New introduction and tables by David J. Seipp, Boston University School of Law. 9" x 12" Hardcover 2009. ISBN 978-1-58477-876-9. $395.

Fortescue, Sir John. *The Works of John Fortescue.* London: Printed for Private Distribution, 1869. 10" x 14" Hardcover 2009. ISBN 978-1-58477-958-2. 2 vols. incl. 57 illus., 17 in color. $695.

Foss, Edward. *The Judges of England.* London: Longman, Brown, Green, and Longmans, 1848-1864. Hardcover 2003. ISBN 978-1-58477-304-7. 9 vols. $895.

Hawarde, John; W. Paley Baildon, Editor. *Les Reportes del Cases in Camera Stellata, 1593 to 1609 From the Original MS. of John Hawarde.* [London]: Privately printed [by Spottiswoode & Co.], 1894. New introduction by Thomas Garden Barnes [1930-2010], University of California, Berkeley. Hardcover 2008. ISBN 978-1-58477-900-1. $195.

Hudson, William. *A Treatise of the Court of Star Chamber As Taken from Collectanea Juridica.* London: E. and R. Brooke, 1792. New introduction by Thomas Garden Barnes [1930-2010], University of California, Berkeley. Hardcover 2008. ISBN 978-1-58477-894-3. $150.

Hughes, William. *The Grand Abridgment of the Law Continued.* London: Printed by J.S. for Henry Twyford, George Sawbridge, Thomas Dring, and John Place, 1660-1662. New introduction by David J. Seipp, Boston University School of Law. Hardcover 2011. ISBN 978-1-58477-937-7. 3 vols. $295.

Kames, Henry Home, Lord. *Principles of Equity.* Edinburgh: Printed for J. Bell, and W. Creech, 1778. New introduction by Dr. Andreas Rahmatian, University of Glasgow. Hardcover 2011. ISBN 978-1-61619-167-2. 2 vols. $150.

Mackenzie, Sir George. *The Laws and Customes of Scotland, in Matters Criminal.* Edinburgh: Printed by George Swintoun, 1678. New introduction by James Chalmers, University of Edinburgh School of Law, Fiona Leverick, University of Aberdeen and Christopher Gane, University of Aberdeen. Hardcover 2005. ISBN 978-1-58477-605-5. $150.

Malynes, Gerard. *Consuetudo, Vel, Lex Mercatoria.* London: Printed for T. Basset, R. Chiswell, T. Horne, and E. Smith, 1686. Hardcover 2009. ISBN 978-1-58477-871-4. 2 vols. $295.

Manu (Lawgiver). *Institutes of Hindu Law. Verbally translated from the original Sanscrit. With a Preface, By Sir William Jones.* Calcutta: Printed by the order of the Government. London: reprinted for J. Sewell, 1796. New introduction by Steve Sheppard, University of Arkansas School of Law. Hardcover 2007. ISBN 978-1-58477-731-1. $150.

Marriott, William. *A New Law Dictionary.* London: Printed for W. and J. Stratford, 1797-98. New introduction by Bryan A. Garner, President, LawProse, Inc. Hardcover 2011. ISBN 978-1-61619-043-9. 4 vols. $495.

Megarry, Sir Robert; Edited by Bryan A. Garner. *A New Miscellany at Law. Yet Another Diversion for Lawyers and Others.* Clark, New Jersey: The Lawbook Exchange, Ltd., co-publishers, 2005. ISBN 978-1-58477-631-4. Hardcover with dust jacket. $45.

Plucknett, Theodore F.T. *A Concise History of the Common Law. Fifth Edition.* Boston: Little, Brown and Company, 1956.
Hardcover 2001, 2010. ISBN 978-1-58477-137-1 $65.
Paperback 2010. ISBN 978-1-61619-124-5. $49.95

Pollock, Frederick, and Frederic William Maitland. *The History of English Law Before the Time of Edward I. Second Edition.* Cambridge: Cambridge University Press, 1898.
Hardcover 1996. ISBN 978-1-886363-22-9. 2 vols. $250.
Paperback 2008. ISBN 978-158477-718-2. 2 vols. $65.

Selden, John. *Opera Omnia.* London: Guil Bowyer [Vol. One]; S. Palmer [Vol. Two]; T. Wood [Vol. Three], 1726. New introduction by Steve Sheppard, University of Arkansas School of Law. 10" x 16" Hardcover [with] (1) searchable DVD for the entire set. 2006. ISBN 978-1-58477-670-3. 3 vols. in 6 books. $1,995.

Selden, John. *Tracts Written by John Selden of the Inner-Temple.* London: Printed for Thomas Basset at the George in Fleet-Street, and Richard Chiswell, 1683. New introduction by Steve Sheppard, University of Arkansas School of Law. 9" x 12" Hardcover 2006. ISBN 978-1-58477-408-2. $195.

[Statham, Nicholas]. Klingelsmith, Margaret Center, Translator. *Statham's Abridgment of the Law.* Boston: The Boston Book Company, 1915. New introduction and Table of Contents by David J. Seipp, Boston University. Hardcover 2007. ISBN 978-1-58477-696-3. 2 vols. $350.

Sullivan, Francis Stoughton. *Lectures on the Constitution and Laws of England.* London: Printed for Edward and Charles Dilly, 1776. New introduction by Sean Patrick Donlan, University of Limerick School of Law. Hardcover 2003. ISBN 978-1-58477-379-5. $150.

[Twiss, Sir Travers]. *The Black Book of the Admiralty.* London: Longman & Co., 1871. Hardcover 1998, 2011. ISBN 978-1-886363-39-7. 4 vols. $250.

Viner, Charles. *A General Abridgment of Law and Equity*Aldershot: Printed for the Author, 1742-1753. ISBN 978-1-58477-977-3. 23 vols. 9" x 14" Hardcover [with] one CD-ROM. 2010. $3,995.

[Vulgate Edition]. *The Year Books.* London: by George Sawbridge, [etc]., 1678, 1679-80. New Introductory Notes and Tables in Each Volume Naming all Justices and Serjeants, and Listing Calendar Years of Law Terms, by David J. Seipp, Boston University, with Carol F. Lee, District of Columbia Bar. 9" x 14" Hardcover 2007. ISBN 978-1-58477-781-6. 11 vols. $2,495.

Wood, Thomas. *An Institute of the Laws of England.* London: Printed by W. Strahan and M. Woodfall, 1772. 10" x 14" Hardcover 2006. ISBN 978-1-58477-588-1. $250.

Please check our website for additional information on these titles, and more titles on English legal history.

THE LAWBOOK EXCHANGE, LTD.
ANTIQUARIAN & SCHOLARLY LAW & LEGAL HISTORY • PUBLISHER
33 Terminal Avenue Clark, New Jersey 07066 • 800-422-6686 • 732-382-1800 •
Fax: 732-382-1887 • Email: law@lawbookexchange.com
www.lawbookexchange.com

CPSIA information can be obtained at www.ICGtesting.com
Printed in the USA
BVOW010333120312

284776BV00001B/2/P